Music in American Life

A list of volumes in the series appears at the end of this book.

Barrio Rhythm

Barrio Rhythm

Mexican American Music in Los Angeles

STEVEN LOZA

University of Illinois Press
Urbana and Chicago

Publication of this book was supported in part by grants from the UCLA Office of Academic Development, the Ahmanson Foundation, and the National Academy of Recording Arts & Sciences.

1 2 3 4 5 C P 5 4 3 2

This book is printed on acid-free paper.

Library of Congress Cataloging-in-Publication Data

Loza, Steven Joseph.
    Barrio rhythm : Mexican American music in Los Angeles / Steven
Loza.
        p.   cm. — (Music in American life)
    Includes bibliographical references, discography, and index.
    ISBN 0-252-01902-4 (alk. paper). — ISBN 0-252-06288-4 (pbk. : alk. paper).
    1. Mexican Americans—California—Los Angeles—Music—History and
criticism.   2. Popular music—Mexico—History and criticism.
    3. Popular music—United States—California—Los Angeles—History
and criticism.   I. Title.   II. Series.
ML3558.L69   1993
781.62′6872079494—dc20   91-35181
                                                              CIP
                                                              MN

A mis padres,
  Rubén y Carmen

    A mi profe,
      Robert Stevenson

      A un colega,
        Juan Gómez-Quiñones

          y a los músicos

The dialectic of struggle and survival, of time and persistence, and of the soul and expression is to me metaphysically expressed through the notion of *barrio rhythm*. Through the purity and idealism of music, an indigenous image and meaning of hope converge with the conflict of survival itself. And life emerges.

—STEVEN LOZA

Contents

Chapter 7

Illustrations follow pages 40, 128, and 184

Acknowledgments

Words are only metaphors, including the word *metaphor*. But I must still use words to thank those who have brought me here.

Several agencies provided me various grants enabling me to complete this project. I am grateful to all of them, but I especially wish to acknowledge the Institute of American Cultures at UCLA, which funded the videotaping of the interviews. Essential to the research, revisions, and editing of the manuscript were UCLA Academic Senate research grants received during the years 1987 to 1990, as was a research assistant stipend provided by the UCLA Latin American Center. I am also indebted to the UCLA School of the Arts for commissioning Willie Herrón to create the cover art.

I passionately thank the following individuals for reading either all or part of the manuscript. I am grateful for their sincere and energetic readings and extremely helpful suggestions:

Rudy Acuña
Eddie Cano
Nati Cano
Teresa Covarrubias
Eddie Davis
José Delgado
Miguel Delgado
Bobby Espinoza
Jimmy Espinoza
Adelina García de Heredia
Tony García
Juan Gómez-Quiñones
Lalo Guerrero
Rubén Guevara
Willie Herrón
Charlotte Heth
María Padilla de Quintero
Manuel Peña
Louie Pérez
Tito Puente

Irma Rangel
Paul Reale
David Reyes
Cruz Reynoso
Luis Rodríguez
Pete Rodríguez
Linda Ronstadt
Andy Russell
Rudy Salas
Zachery Salem
Poncho Sánchez
Chico Sesma
Daniel Sheehy
Philip Sonnichsen
Robert Stevenson
Chris Strachwitz
David Torres
Don Tosti
Johannes Wilbert

I extend my respect and gratitude to Manuel Peña and Daniel Sheehy, scholars and friends whom I deeply admire. I thank both of them for critiquing the original draft of the book.

To the corps of individuals who have contributed to the editing, research, and administrative aspects of the project, I express my utmost gratitude for their dedication, which I found consistent, cautious, and caring. To Colleen Trujillo, who edited the manuscript, I extend my warm thanks for her excellent sense of criticism and style. I also am grateful for the work of my research assistants at different periods during the writing. Lindsay Clare spent a long, hot summer working on tedious photo and text releases, data searches, and editing. Edith Johnson did a large amount of editing on the first and second drafts. Maria Williams, Luis Hernández, Brenda Romero-Hymer, Johanna Hofmann, Manuel Fernández, and Rodrigo Geovanny Jurado, all young and emerging scholars, assisted me at various points.

For their assistance in transcribing the interviews, I thank Carmen Miranda Loza, Sylvia Morales, and Alicia Rodríguez. Ken Culley was the copyist for most of the musical transcriptions. My thanks also to María Ortiz, who did much of the initial word processing for the project. Shannon Morris, Grace Wax, and Caroline Kent, of the word-processing services office of the UCLA School of the Arts, prepared the manuscript in its final form. I reserve a prayerful thought for Grace, who died on November 1, 1991. She blessed us all.

I want to especially thank the fifteen artists whose stories form the nine case studies presented in chapter 4. They were the heart of the research and are the heart and life of the book. To the video crew that taped the nine interviews, Ramón Menéndez and Bill Day, I also extend my heartfelt thanks.

In January 1990 Plaza de la Raza, a Los Angeles cultural art center, asked me to chair "Chicano Musicworks," a competitive festival for emerging Chicano/Mexicano composers. I jumped at the opportunity without hesitation. We assembled a panel of judges consisting of important musical figures, each of whom influenced the writing of this book in some way. Miguel Delgado, for example, a longtime friend, highly talented choreographer, and festival director, did much of the photo research for the book, the Plaza de la Raza having decided to mount a modest photographic exhibit during the festival. I thank both Miguel and the Plaza for their invaluable assistance and inspiration.

I would like to thank my many colleagues at UCLA, especially Jihad Racy, Charlotte Heth, James Porter, Paul Reale, Leo Estrada, David Kaplan, and Pebbles Wadsworth. To two very special department staff members, Betty Price and Jennifer Wallace, goes my deep love. I also thank

Shana Riddick and Tom Lee for their constant help in the office. To Deans Robert Gray, Bernard Kester, and Robert Blocker, and to Associate Dean William Hutchinson, I express my gratitude for their faith in my ideas. To Henry Cobos, professor of music at East Los Angeles College, I give thanks for constant encouragement and support. I also wish to thank Johannes Wilbert, who has constantly supported my conviction that an academic can have an imagination.

Ford Foundation support has enabled me to develop a course at UCLA on musical aesthetics in Los Angeles, in which Chicano/Latino musical networks and specific experiences obviously play a major role. I am deeply grateful to Raymond A. Paredes, Associate Vice Chancellor for Academic Development, for generously making funds available to support publication of *Barrio Rhythm* for use in this course.

For the inspiration they have always provided, I thank my aunt, Sister Mary Cordé, in addition to Tia Vera, Uncle Joe, my cousin Raul Miranda, and some close friends—Danilo Lozano, Raúl Pérez, José Dufrasne Gonzáles, David Torres, and Tony García, who "lit the match."

The UCLA Latin American Center has been especially helpful with various aspects of the project, and I extend my deepest gratitude to its present director, Norris Hundley, and the center's staff. I also express my appreciation to the UCLA Chicano Studies Research Center for its constant encouragement since I began the research and for its role in the administration of the Institute of American Cultures grant.

I pay tribute here to the memory of Charles Boilés, who gave me much encouragement at the beginning stages of the research on which this book is based.

I wish to thank Judith McCulloh, executive editor of the University of Illinois Press, and the excellent staff, especially manuscript editor Bruce Bethell, for the patience, precision, and passion they have demonstrated during the publication of this book.

Finally, to the members of my family—my brothers, Mitch, Bob, Jerry, and of course, my folks, Rubén and Carmen—may God bless them and all of us.

The following publishers and individuals have generously given permission to use material from copyrighted works.

"El Lavaplatos" and "Se acabó el WPA," transcribed and translated by Guillermo Hernández and Yolanda Zepeda from *Texas-Mexican Border Music*, Folklyric LP 9021/Arhoolie Records; "Corrido de Juan Reyna" and "Suicidio de Juan Reyna," transcribed and translated by Silviano Barba,

Pepi Plowman, and the staff of the Latin American Library, Oakland, Calif., from *Texas-Mexican Border Music,* Folklyric LP 9004/Arhoolie Records. Used by permission of Chris Strachwitz.

"C/S," words and music by Rubén Guevara, © 1983 Cerco Blanco Music (BMI).

"Let's Say Goodnight," words and music by David Hidalgo and Louis Pérez, © 1985 Davince Music and No K.O. Music (BMI); "One Time, One Night," words and music by David Hidalgo and Louis Pérez, © 1988 Davince Music and No K.O. Music (BMI); "Will the Wolf Survive," words and music by David Hidalgo and Louis Pérez, © 1985 Davince Music and No K.O. Music (BMI). Administered by Bug. All rights reserved. Used by permission.

"Canción Mexicana," by Lalo Guerrero, © 1964 by Promotora Hispano Americana de Música S.A. Administered by Peer International Corporation. International copyright secured. All rights reserved. Used by permission.

"Chucos Suaves" and "No Way José." Published by Barrio Libre Music. Used by permission of Lalo Guerrero.

"The Wolf." Used by permission of Teresa Covarrubias.

"Música de la Gente." Used by permission of Irma D. Rangel.

"El Lay," lyrics and music by Willie Herrón, © 1981 Irving Music, Inc. All rights reserved. International copyright secured.

"The View of the Sixth Street Bridge: The History of Chicano Rock," by Rubén Guevara. From *The First Rock and Roll Confidential Report,* edited by Dave Marsh and the editors of Rock and Roll Confidential. © 1985 by Duke and Duchess Ventures, Inc. Reprinted by permission of Pantheon Books, a division of Random House, Inc.

Introduction

Para bailar la bamba
Se necesita
una poca de gracia
y otra cosita

In 1984, some months before I interviewed the popular group Los Lobos for this project, I had taken them to Tijuana, Mexico, to perform for a lecture that I was presenting at an academic conference related to research on the United States and Mexico.

We traveled in my car and in César Rosas's van, but when we reached the border we were not permitted to enter Mexico. Los Lobos had brought their electric instruments, and Mexico had just enacted an injunction preventing U.S. musicians from performing in Tijuana. This, I was later told, was a response to the problems Mexican musicians were encountering with the same type of injunction against them in San Diego.

It all seemed a bit ironic. Here we were, Chicanos trying to demonstrate the "fusion process" of the Mexican and the U.S. experience through music, and temporary, intercultural restraining orders were impeding our novel enterprise. We were told to obtain an official letter from the conference coordinators in order to return the next evening. We did so and went back to Los Angeles.

Los Lobos spent the next day taping a special Public Broadcasting System television program that coincided with the group's first album release for Slash Records (the album would later win a Grammy Award). We left for Tijuana with little time to spare.

Just after passing Oceanside, less than a half hour from the border, César's van broke down; it was a major engine problem. We were stuck at a gas station, quite convinced that we would fail in our second effort to appear at the conference. But we came up with an idea. We had enough money to hire a taxi to San Diego. From there, we could cross the border by foot and get a Tijuana taxi to the conference hotel. We were scheduled to appear during a dinner for the conference participants and had about a half hour before our presentation was to begin. Needless to say, we were forced to leave all the electric instruments in the van with "Mouse," the group's roadie (equipment manager). Our official letter now seemed useless.

We arrived at the border, paid the taxi driver, and crossed the line with less than ten dollars among us. We decided to speak only Spanish so that the Mexican border officials would not suspect we were U.S. musicians illegally entering Mexico.

Carrying the group's folk instruments in their cases, we made it across. We jumped into a taxi and arrived at the hotel. I was sure we would be late, but fortunately, the dinner was also running late. We entered the dining room as the conference participants were gathering. I presented my lecture while the participants and Los Lobos dined. After that, the group performed, the people danced, and a good time was had by all . . . and we even got paid with a bonus.

Another bit of irony—this was Los Lobos' first "international" performance. Since then, their lives have changed drastically. After ten years of playing Mexican and other Latin American folk music in and around East Los Angeles, the group was embarking on an unprecedented entry into the American mainstream of pop music.

The musical life of the Mexican people in Los Angeles has always taken and continues to take many forms; these forms of change, tradition, and survival can be traced back centuries. In this study, although I have surveyed activity dating to the eighteenth century, I have chosen to focus on a span of forty-five years, the post–World War II era, for a number of reasons. First, the period marks the emergence of the Mexican American, or Chicano, as a dynamic actor on the American stage—north and south of the U.S.-Mexican border. Second, by examining this period, I have been able to study many active artists and carry out some ethnological evaluation. Third, and perhaps in a way most essential, I have been able to study my own musical culture. I began to play the trumpet at the age of twelve in an eastside archdiocese youth band directed by a gentleman named Tony García. He plays and teaches music to this day in that same East Side and in other locales throughout the world.

Thus, in this case, I am the native ethnographer. I suppose there are both advantages and disadvantages to this situation. For me it has been an advantage to be a sibling in my own family. I have, after all, actually performed with most of the people who have provided the ethnographic data for this study. I am therefore even more than a native—I am a member of a special group of musicians.

Fortunately, I have been able to supplement my own observations, experiences, and analysis with others' valuable accounts of the music of Mexican Americans. Manuel Peña, author of *The Texas-Mexican Conjunto: History of a Working-Class Music* (1985a), has noted the extensive research that has been conducted on the music of Mexican people in New Mexico and in Texas—for example, Arthur Campa's *Hispanic Culture in the Southwest* (1979), John D. Robb's *Hispanic Folk Music of New Mexico and the Southwest* (1980), and Américo Paredes's *A Texas-Mexican Cancionero: Folksongs of the Lower Border* (1976). Peña writes, "It thus happens that of the three most important areas inhabited by people of Spanish-Mexican descent for as long as three centuries, only California has remained relatively unexplored with respect to the music of this ethnic minority" (1989:64).

Two articles assessing the state of musicological scholarship in California are Michael Heisley's "Sources for the Study of Mexican Music in California" (1988) and Peña's "Notes Toward an Interpretive History of California-Mexican Music" (1989). Of paramount importance as an adjunct to this book are three recent articles by Robert Stevenson: "Los Angeles" (1986; in *The New Grove Dictionary of American Music*); "Local Music History Research in Los Angeles Area Libraries: Part 1" (1988; in *Inter-American Music Review*); and "Music in Southern California: A Tale of Two Cities" (1988; in *Inter-American Music Review*).

The first section of the book is structured chronologically. Chapter 1 briefly surveys the social and musical history of Mexican Los Angeles up to the year 1945. Activity after 1945 (the postwar to recent periods) is more comprehensively examined in the following two chapters. Chapter 2, which specifically focuses on sociopolitical history, segues to chapter 3, which covers the same period by chronicling musical events and their constantly evolving, contextual developments. The decision to divide the scope of the latter two chapters is largely a practical one based on the nature of the content and the diversity of sources, themes, and descriptions. Another reason for the division is the significant interrelation of social and artistic dynamics in the period of principal focus, the postwar era to recent times; these two elements constitute the essential polemic forces presented for further analysis in this book.

One methodological problem in the historical account comprising the first section of the book is its mammoth dimensions and comprehensive nature and the difficulty in integrating the diverse documented sources and oral data available. Add to this the absence of a previous formal study of such a multitude of musical styles, hybridizations, and cultural questions in terms of conflict and assimilation, and the task becomes monumental if not tempered and controlled. The next level of the study, therefore, is designed reflective. The second section of the book consists of a series of nine individual profiles based on case studies of Mexican Americans and their musical lives in Los Angeles. The data for these profiles, found in chapters 4 and 5, were extracted from ethnographic interviews conducted separately with the individual artists. Song and text examples accompany selected profiles to demonstrate the vast diversity in the musical styles of the artists. These artists and their commentaries are the heart of this book. My experience in conducting the interviews with them and thereby learning from them molded the structure and spirit of the study. To them I owe that spirit of vitality, energy, and love.

Chapter 6 is an ethnological analysis of the concepts of learning a musical culture, changing within that culture, and thereby developing new stylistic trends and practices of human expression. In assessing the notions of enculturation, intercultural conflict, and the formation of style, the analysis stresses three processes inherent in the evolution of musical expression among Mexican Americans in Los Angeles—maintenance, change, and adaptation. The ethnographic data analyzed are extracted largely from the case studies in chapters 4 and 5, selected as representative examples. The last chapter (chap. 7) examines in a more philosophical mode the emergence of an "eastside renaissance," new integration within the music industry, and hope for the future of a once marginal musical culture.

Part I
History

Chapter 1

Society and Music in Mexican Los Angeles

The barrio is not a ghetto, though there are ghettos in the barrio. It is a microcosm of a Chicano city, a place of dualities; a liberated zone and a prison; a place of love and warmth; and a place of hatred and violence, where most of La Raza live out their lives. So it is a place of weddings, *bautismos, tardeadas, bailes, velorios,* and patriotic "enchilada dinners." It is a place of poverty and self-reliance, of beloved *ancianos,* of *familias,* of *compadres.*

—LUIS VALDEZ

The history of the Mexican in Los Angeles can be traced to a group of northern Mexican pioneers who founded the pueblo in 1781. Spanish governor Felipe de Neve had sent an expedition to establish pueblos, missions, and presidios with the intention of securing Spain's claim to the remote hinterland. The original contingent of founders, recorded in documents as criollos, *indios, mestizos, and mulattoes,* included forty-four settlers and four soldiers. Already occupying the land, of course, was the indigenous population that had migrated into the area now referred to as southern California at least 20,000 years before (Griswold del Castillo 1979:1). "By 1770 they numbered about 5,000 and were divided into many tribes. They spoke various dialects of Shoshone, but are all referred to as 'gabrieleño' after the mission the Spanish established on their lands" (Griswold del Castillo 1979:2). The Gabrieleños lived in the area bordered by the Santa Susana Mountains to the north and Aliso Creek to the south. The Mojave Desert lay to the east, and San Clemente Island constituted the westward extension.

The name of Los Angeles was actually established before a formal charter was drawn. In 1769 *visitador* José Gálvez organized a series of expeditions to explore Alta California. On 2 August 1769 the Los Angeles River was named El Río de Nuestra Señora la Reina de Los Angeles de Porciún-

cula by Captain Gaspar de Portola. He was accompanied by Fray Junípero
Serra, the founder of the California missions. The official and popular name
of the pueblo became El Pueblo de la Reina de Los Angeles.[1]

Like the city's name, the recorded musical legacy of Los Angeles also
began before any city charter. Stevenson (1986:107) describes the early
development of religious music:

> The early history of religious music in Los Angeles is the history of
> the San Gabriel Mission, which was founded in 1771. The Beneme
> and Geniguechi Indians gathered there each day, and sang an *alabado*
> (praise song) at dusk and dawn and a *bendito* (grace) before each meal.
> In 1776 Pedro Font, a Franciscan from Mexico, visited the mission
> and led a mass that he accompanied on his psaltery; until 1834 the
> singing of the mass was always accompanied by instruments (such as
> flutes, violins, and trumpets) that local Indians had been taught to
> play by missionaries.

Active in the teaching of Western music to the Indian neophytes of
the California missions was the Franciscan Narciso Durán (1776–1846),
who developed a basic pedagogy to teach church music. In talking about
selected passages from Padre Durán's *Prólogo*, Swan (1952:87) wrote the
following in his *Music in the Southwest, 1825–1950:*

> He had determined to show his Indians how to read music. He had
> begun by teaching the instruments so that "by seeing the distances
> between notes on the instruments, due to the various finger posi-
> tions, the boys might gain some idea of the same intervals in singing,
> modulating their voices accordingly." He then instructed his neo-
> phyte musicians in "the scale of natural notes . . . and the scale of half
> notes . . . making them sing and play it at one and the same time." So
> that the problems of intervals in the different keys or tones would not
> trouble his choir, Father Durán transposed all of the compositions in
> his book to the "Fa natural, which is a note neither high nor low and
> very suited to the voices of boys." In music for more than two voices
> the staff consisted of six tied lines, in order that "the performers may
> see all the voices at a glance and sing with more uniformity." Each
> voice read his part from a staff dotted with notes colored red, black,
> yellow and white, and Father Durán deemed it advisable that instru-
> ments should always accompany the singing . . . not permitting [the
> boys] to go flat or sharp, as regularly happens without this precau-
> tion."

In the chronicle of the Jedediah Smith expedition of 1826, Harrison
Dale describes the small orchestra at the San Gabriel Mission as "a band

of musik that played for two hours, . . . consisting of two violins, one bass viol, a trumpet and a triangle. They made tolerable good music, the most in imitation of whites that I ever heard" (Dale 1941:208). Alfred Robinson, visiting the same mission in 1828, wrote that "the solemn music of the mass was well selected, and the Indian voices accorded harmoniously with the flutes and violins that accompanied them" (1891:45).

The mission choirs developed an extensive repertoire. They performed an abundance of the plain chant for several masses in addition to the chant of the Proper of the Mass for Sundays and feast days. They also sang several two- and four-part homophonic masses such as the Misa de Cataluña and the Misa Vizcaina, both very likely compositions of Father Durán. Also practiced as part of the mission choirs' repertoires were vespers and compline, as well as liturgical hymns (see Stevenson 1988b:54–57).

Independence from Spain

Mexican independence from Spain in 1821 inaugurated the Mexican period of the Southwest, an era characterized by instability and insurrections, both among Mexican citizens and U.S. immigrants. Among the Mexicans, "the twin traditions of internal conflict and legitimate revolt became part of the fabric of Californio political life" (Griswold del Castillo 1979:20). On at least three occasions during the twenty-five years after Mexican independence the *pobladores* rebelled against local government. The Californios also frustrated the Mexican central government's attempt to restrict foreign immigration from the United States. "This resulted more from refusal to carry out the laws than from disagreement with the purpose of the laws, which was to prevent another Texas episode" (Griswold del Castillo 1979:22; one of the precepts of the Texas Republic was evidently in disagreement with Mexican law and was cited as one of the reasons for secession from Mexico). As the immigrants prospered, many adopted the attitudes of manifest destiny. Griswold del Castillo cites one such immigrant, Lansford Hastings, who wrote the then highly influential *Emigrant's Guide*. Until the 1848 gold rush, Hastings's book attracted many foreigners to the wonders of California. It also aroused strong anti-Mexican sentiments among newly arrived Anglo-Americans.

In 1833, relatively soon after independence from Spain, the Mexican government secularized the mission lands. Much controversy persists about the merits or demerits of this action and its consequences. Many believe that the rapid disintegration of the mission communities led to more inequities for the Indians, whereas others claim that the mission system itself placed the acculturated California Indians in a dependent position, destined for the chaotic social experience of the hacienda (rancho) system.

Regardless of the aftermath of the mission system, the Franciscans felt thwarted. Writing to Pio Pico, the last Mexican governor of California, Durán described the demise of his efforts: "There are other runaways, such as Antero, Toribio, Juan de Dios, and I know not which others, whose absence I do not mind, except that they are musicians whom it cost me twelve years of labor to teach" (Cleland 1944:42–43).

Swan notes that in spite of the constant political uncertainty and change that culminated in the Mexican-American War, life flourished in California during what he calls its "golden age." "The rancheros and their large families lived carefree, Arcadian lives in the midst of an army of Indian retainers. . . . Cattle were plentiful, and their hides, the 'California bank notes,' could be used in trade for the few items not provided by the resources of the rancho" (1952:90). William Heath Davis recorded his impression that the people seemed to have a talent and a taste for music. "Many of the women played the guitar skillfully, and the young men the violin. In almost every family there were one or more musicians, and everywhere music was a familiar sound" (1929:61).

Throughout California, feast days, rodeos, weddings, funerals, and other special occasions were accented by music, and events were preceded or followed by a *fandango* or a *baile*. Judge Benjamin Hayes observed a Los Angeles funeral procession and recalled the experience in his *Pioneer Notes* (1929:122).

> I witnessed the funeral procession of an infant, attended by women and girls only, with flags flying and music playing in front, cheerful airs. . . . The bells meant to their hearers that there was another angel in Heaven. They ring this lively note of joy, rather than that of grief, when the young and innocent are withdrawn from the snares and dangers of this bad world. I like this custom of the native Californians, the merry peal of the bell, the beautiful trappings of the little cold form, the gay flags that flaunt in the breeze as the procession moves, and even the music of the guitar or violin that guides the step as they march to the grave.

Davis also witnessed fiestas that continued for several days. One was a wedding party where he estimated that "one hundred guests danced all night, slept for three hours after daylight, enjoyed a *merienda*, or picnic, in the forenoon, and then again began their dancing. This was the order for three days" (Swan 1952:91). When Pio Pico married María Ignacia Alvarado in 1834, the celebration in Los Angeles lasted eight days.

The musical forms themselves frequently consisted of the formal invitational *baile* or the informal *fandango* and were usually accompanied by harp, violin, and flute (Swan 1952:91). Dance genres included traditional Spanish forms in addition to the more recent styles of the *vals* (waltz) and *quadrillo* (quadrilles). The Church decried the popularization of the waltz, which had been considered indecent.

Especially popular was the *fandango*, which featured a *tecolero*, or master of ceremonies, who called out each woman for her turn. Swan (1952:92) notes that during the festivities, many *cascarones* (eggshells filled with confetti) were broken over the heads of celebrating participants. Improvised song-ballads were also featured at fiestas. In his memoirs, Edwin Bryant provided the following description: "During the progress of the dance the males and females improvise doggerel rhymes complimentary of the personal beauties and graces of those whom they admire . . . which are changed with the music of the instruments, and the whole company joins in the general chorus at the end of each verse" (1936:409).

It is interesting to note that the city council (*ayuntamiento*) deemed it necessary to regulate music performance by official pronouncement. Article nineteen of the pueblo's ordinances contained the following stipulation: "A license of $2.00 [pesos] shall be paid for all dances, for which permission shall be obtained from the judge of the city" (Guinn 1901:61). Another ordinance stipulated fines for infractions: "All individuals serenading promiscuously around the streets of the city at night without first having obtained permission from the Alcalde will be fined $1.50 for the first offense, $3.00 for the second offense, and for the third punished according to law" (Guinn 1901:6).

One of the more interesting aspects of life in California during the "golden age" was the assimilation of Mexican culture by immigrants from the United States. Many married into Mexican families, learned to speak Spanish fluently, and became active in the Mexican political hierarchy. Swan (1952:92) offers the following summation:

> The music of the Californios, together with their economic, social, and religious customs, continued to be influential in the southwest long after the arrival of the first Americans. To all interests these Yankees became just as much a part of the country as if they had been native born. Thus, the Americans who had homes in the pueblos must have participated in this very pleasant observance described by Don Antonio Coronel to his friend, Helen Hunt Jackson: "It was the custom of the town [Los Angeles] in all of the families of the early settlers, for the oldest member of the family—oftenest it was grandfather or grandmother—to rise every morning at the rising of the morning star and at once to strike up a hymn. At the first note every person in the house would rise, or sit up in bed and join in the song. From house to house, street to street, the singing spread; and the volume of musical sound swelled, until it was as if the whole town sang. (*Century Magazine* 1883:196)

U.S. Annexation

During the years following independence from Spain, the distance between Los Angeles and the capital in Mexico City was too great for Mexico to maintain firm political control. After the annexation of Texas, Mexico began to fear for its remote northern provinces, but the task at hand became insurmountable. Preparations were made for a possible conflict with the United States. After a period of alarm, reports of peace resulted in demobilization. Shortly afterward, the Angelino Pio Pico was installed as interim governor of California. He promptly moved the state capital from Monterey to Los Angeles and built a power base of officials within the pueblo. He also completed the secularization of the missions that had been mandated by the Mexican government in 1834 as a provision of separation of church and state, one of the essential goals after independence. With the secularization of the missions, California's most fertile land became private property, and 15,000 mission Indians could be exploited as laborers. Authorities believed that secularization would lure settlers from the interior of Mexico. Such migration never occurred, and a small group of ranchers monopolized the former mission lands. Identifiable class divisions began to develop between the Californios and newly arrived Mexican colonists, who were referred to as *cholos* and tended to work as manual laborers. The conflict between the two classes increased as California became more firmly incorporated into the U.S. market. By the 1840s, many landowners and merchants considered U.S. trade a more lucrative future than allegiance to Mexico's economy, which was still recuperating from the wars of independence.

The outbreak of war with the United States initially unified the opposing Californios, the *abejeños* (southern Californios) and the *norteños* (northern Californios). The leaders of the two regions, Pico and Castro, respectively, met and issued a joint proclamation calling on all loyal Mexican citizens to come to Mexico's defense. The Plan de Los Angeles, a formal document signed by several Mexican insurgents, set forth the reason for their action and called all loyal *mexicanos* to arms. The plan expressed the fears of the Mexican populace regarding the American invasion and conquest.

Swan (1952:94), noting the "native fondness for music" in Los Angeles, contends that the U.S. military utilized music as a buffer during army occupations of the Mexican pueblo.

> When in August, 1846, Commodore Stockton marched into Los Angeles at the head of his marines, he found that the California army under Governor Pico and General Castro had fled the city, leaving

behind them a bitter and discontented populace which was ready to revolt at the first opportunity. According to the story of W. D. Phelps, a Boston seaman who was attached to the expedition, the commodore acted on a suggestion that a band play in the plaza each day about sunset. Said Phelps: "At first, the children on the hill ventured down and peeped around the corners of the houses. A few lively tunes brought out the 'vivas' of the elder ones, and before closing for the day quite a circle of delighted natives surrounded the musicians. The following afternoon, the people from the ranchos at a distance, hearing of the wonderful performance, began to come in. I saw the old priest of the mission of San Gabriel sitting by the church door opposite the plaza. 'Ah,' said he, 'that music will do more service in the conquest of California than a thousand bayonets.'" (Phelps 1871:307–8)

Soldiers of the band of the New York Volunteers performed music in California pueblos and reportedly presented the first dramatic productions in the far west. These took place at Monterey, Santa Barbara, and Los Angeles in the summers of 1847 and 1848 and in early 1849 and 1850 (Swan 1952:95). In 1848 the company of volunteers stationed in Los Angeles performed in a theater structure built as part of the house of Don Antonio Coronel.

The actors built a drop curtain and a proscenium, and painted a few scenery pieces. Their audiences sat out under the stars, for the theater possessed no roof, although its cost of construction had approximated five thousand dollars. Until the regiment was disbanded in September, 1848, to seek their fortunes in the mines (of the gold rush in northern California), the inhabitants of Los Angeles were entertained with biweekly dramatic performances in English, interspersed with comic songs and dances. These productions alternated with presentations of Spanish and Mexican *comedias* offered by a company of native Californios. (Swan 1952:96)

With defeat in 1848 Mexico ceded the major portion of the Southwest to the United States. The Treaty of Guadalupe Hidalgo provided for the exchange of land in return for 15 million dollars and certain provisions to protect the rights of the Mexicans and their future offspring. Both the pact and its interpretations have been historically controversial and, from the Mexican viewpoint, have constituted a bitter issue for more than a century.

When the U.S. incorporated California, Mexicans were still firmly established in Los Angeles. Their political and economic status changed with the 1848 gold rush, which stimulated the migration of 100,000 Anglo-

Americans and the restructuring of the local Catholic church. Prior to the conquest, priests and prelates were Spaniards or Mexicans.

Mexican priests were replaced with Spanish, French, and Italian clergy to cater to the elites. In 1873, Bishop Taddeus Amat told his congregation that the Church was "the main support of society and order, which imperatively demands respect for legitimate authority and adjuration to legitimate laws." By 1876, the newer St. Viviana's Cathedral served Anglo-Americans, while the placita [the colloquial name for the church in front of the plaza in downtown Los Angeles] was attended by poor Mexicans. (Acuña 1984:5)

Ironically, defeat actually created unity among the Californios. After the cease-fire, the most volatile element of the pueblo returned to Mexico in disgust. This exodus included generals Flores, Castro, and Andrés Pico, along with a considerable portion of the army. The newly appointed governor, John Fremont, reinforced this unification by allowing the Angelinos to continue their local government and traditional fiestas. However, when California became a state in 1850, the old Mexican form of government with its dual *alcaldes* and electoral system was abolished. As Griswold del Castillo remarks, "the Mexican community began a painful process of changing its traditional way of life" (1979:29).

Mexican Transition, 1848–1900

In *An Illustrated History of Mexican Los Angeles, 1781–1985* (1986:96), Ríos-Bustamante and Castillo cite the transitional period after the Mexican-American War as one of accommodation and cultural maintenance.

On a more symbolic level, the years between 1848 and 1900 forced the Mexican community to relinquish important dreams. The town that they had founded and built was no longer theirs to control. Their plans for the future and their visions of all that the city might have been were rendered irrelevant by a political and cultural encroachment that they could not stop. If they had been formerly preoccupied with economic expansion and political in-fighting, they were now concerned with cultural solidarity and survival.

In the face of armed conflict with Anglo invaders and the threat of cultural extinction, Mexicans in Los Angeles persevered. Indeed, at the end of the nineteenth century, several experts were predicting

that, as an organized force in community life, the Mexican population would soon disappear. Like American Indians, Mexicans were
held to be a vanishing people. In this light, their ability to persist as
a distinct culture and to maintain an identity separate from their new
Anglo neighbors may be seen as their greatest victory of the postwar period. And just as the city's first fight for social continuity had
been waged by poor farmers and artisans, this new effort to maintain
cultural unity came from the community people themselves, from the
laboring class majority of the Mexican population.

By the 1850s, visiting musical attractions in Los Angeles included army
bands and minstrel groups from various parts of the United States. Mexican musical traditions continued in strong fashion. Ignacio Coronel had
opened a school north of Arcadia Street in 1844. He was assisted by his
daughter, Soledad, a harpist.

As late as the mid-1850s the harp remained the favorite instrument of
the local aristocracy. By this time musical performances were being
described in a newly established local newspaper. *La Estrellita de Los
Angeles,* a weekly, bilingual production, noted in 1852 that a "competent band" had played the overture to José Zorrilla's drama *Don
Juan Tenorio.* Musical events were given fuller treatment in two newspapers in Spanish, *El Clamor Público* (published from 1855 to 1859)
and *La Crónica* (from 1872). (Stevenson 1986:107)

El Clamor Público (3 July 1858) printed a program of Latin liturgical
and English secular music sung by a girls' Catholic school choir trained
by six Sisters of Charity, three of whom were from Spain. During the
same period, Blas Raho (1806–62), a Lazarite from southern Italy, arrived
in Los Angeles with an appointment as parish priest at Our Lady of the
Angels Church (this church, which eventually became known as La Placita,
was located across from Olvera Street). Raho, a trained musician, purchased a new organ and arranged for the organization of a choir for church
services (Stevenson 1986).

A rich Spanish/Mexican tradition that continued into the second half
of the nineteenth century throughout the U.S. Southwest was that of the
pastores and *pastorelas.* Based on the birth of Christ, these musical dramas
depicted the journey of the shepherds to the Nativity manger. *Pastorelas*
were often enacted at churches or private homes in conjunction with the
posada, a social, religious gathering where songs celebrating the Christmas
season were sung.

According to Bandini (1958:16–17) the last major nineteenth-century performance of the *pastores* in Los Angeles took place on Christmas eve 1861.

The place selected on this occasion was the site on which now stands the present Pico House, then a large courtyard pertaining to the Pico homestead. This was the residence of Don Pio Pico and his brother Don Andrés—the former the last Mexican Governor of California, and the latter the commander of the few rancheros, poorly armed and organized to resist the American occupation. These good gentlemen told the pastores to make the greatest display possible, as it would probably be the last time that the play would occur, for the people must soon choose between the North and the South. Though the storm was far to the east from us, still the distant but threatening muttering could now and then be plainly heard in our western land. Such being the promising outlook for the future, the pastores went to work with a will. First came countless carretas loaded down with willow branches and tule for stall and wall. Ready hands soon unloaded these and the work of decoration commenced; side-booths brightened with greenery, others with costly hangings, sprang into existence as if by magic; confusion reigned supreme; shrill cries, expostulations and silvery Spanish oaths filled the air. Caterers— *tamale* men and women; candy and fruit vendors—*enchilada* and *tortilla* women; proprietors of musical taverns—all struggled and even fought for choice locations exactly as the American hawkers do at our modern fairs. Above all the din could be heard the twangings of guitars, shriekings of violins and songs interspersed with blank verse. All these came from the booths already occupied by their more lucky or energetic proprietors. At last all the ambitious, one-day merchants seemed to have found a place, and some quiet is restored. Gaily dressed rancheros and more soberly attired townspeople walk around visiting, admiring and patronizing the different stands. If you wish to know the rank, wealth or social standing of each individual, watch the actions of any proprietor of a booth; see how deferential his smile to some, and with what humble but all-absorbing interest he listens to their conversation. But suddenly he straightens up, stands on tip-toe, looks shocked and offended, and whispers, but loud enough to be heard by his visitors. "Sh! sh!" What is the matter, you wonder. Why, he is only rebuking and silencing two *pelados* (impecunious ones) for daring to talk so loud near such presence.

Bandini adds that the more dramatic and more elaborately produced *pastorela* was also enacted during the 1860s. According to his account, the priests of the order of St. Vincent de Paul, who had arrived in Los

Angeles to found St. Vincent's College, contacted the highly influential Don Antonio Coronel to assist them in patronizing three performances of the *pastorela*. The plays were staged in the upstairs hall of the county courthouse. Bandini describes the preparations as follows (1958:18–19):

> Here all the *dramatis personae,* good, bad and indifferent, held forth, and this was the place selected for the Pastorela. I remember well what indescribable joy and exultation filled my boyish heart when my mother, at the earnest solicitation of Don Antonio Coronel, at last gave her consent to my taking the part of the Archangel Michael. The character of Satan was given to a magnificent fellow named Ramón V——.
>
> For months before Christmas we had rehearsals three times a week, at the residence of Señor Coronel, his sister, Doña Soledad, an artist with the harp, furnishing the music. Those rehearsals were a source of continual joy to us, and with such practice, and the inexhaustible patience of our instructor, by the time the eventual Christmas Eve came, everything—acting, costumes and scenery—was simply perfect. Before the play commenced, two orations, one in Spanish, and the other in English, had to be made before the curtain. Mr. Coronel's nephew spoke in Spanish and I in English. My speech was composed by some individual whose name, fortunately for him, I have forgotten. Fragments of that famous discourse have remained with me to the present time. For this tenacity of memory I can give but two reasons, namely, first—the numberless hours of hard work I spent learning it; secondly—my dear old mother, who, by the way, understood but very little English, would make me recite it to her numerous friends in detail.

Antonio Coronel was a civic leader during both the Mexican and United States eras; he served both as mayor of Los Angeles and as treasurer of the state of California. He was active in various cultural programs, such as the Los Angeles County Museum, and was a member of the Los Angeles Board of Education and part owner of *La Crónica*. He had adapted a manuscript of a *pastorela* in 1839, and it is speculated that performances of this same Christmas play were staged at various times and places during the tenure of the old Californios who lived during the midnineteenth century, including the occasion described by Bandini. Coronel's manuscript is stored in the archives of the Seaver Center for Western History Research at the Natural History Museum of Los Angeles County, along with sets of other religious and secular songs among Coronel's memoirs.

In November 1865, the Gerardo López del Castillo Spanish Company from Mexico City appeared at the Temple Theater, where it performed one act of Verdi's *Attila* between acts of *La trenza de sus cabellos* by Tomás Rodríguez Rubí. During the 1870s and 1880s, three major concert halls were constructed—the Merced Theater (1870), Turnverein Hall (1872), and Ozro W. Childs Grand Opera House (1884). In June and July of 1875 Teresa Carreño, an internationally renowned pianist originally from Venezuela, and her husband, violinist Emile Sauret, appeared at Turnverein Hall.

> Sauret also played duos with the guitarist Miguel S. Arévalo (b. Guadalajara, Mexico, 5 July 1843; d. Los Angeles, 29 June 1900). Arévalo had studied in Mexico [Guadalajara], taught for two years in San Francisco, and moved to Los Angeles in 1871, where he became music director of the newly formed Los Angeles Musical Association. For three decades he was a leading concert performer, composer, and teacher, as well as a founder of *La Crónica*. He helped the area's Mexican culture withstand the pressure of German and Anglo-American musical influences that resulted from waves of immigration in the 1880s. (Stevenson 1984:108)

Arévalo had become highly noted in Los Angeles, especially as a concert guitarist, and on his arrival from San Francisco was elected musical director of the Los Angeles Musical Association. He was rated in the *Daily Evening Express* of June 28 (2:4) as "probably the best that has come to Los Angeles." Among his noted compositions is his guitar solo (or duo) *La Súplica, danza habanera,* which is stylistically based on the Cuban *habanera* musical genre. The piece was first published in *Compositions and Arrangements for the Guitar,* compiled by Manuel Y. Ferrer, also a Mexican. In addition to compiling the latter data on Arévalo, Stevenson (1988a:26) cites a concert in honor of the guitarist/composer.

> Again on Friday evening, May 6, 1881, Turn-Verein Hall was the scene of a "Grand Testimonial Benefit." This event, in honor of the paramount Mexican-born musician in Los Angeles, "Prof. M. S. Arévalo," was managed by Madame Franzini Marra. After H. Wangeman's orchestra performed the overture to Rossini's *L'Italiana in Algeri* and selections from Donizetti's *La Favorita,* Arévalo and Eduardo Arzaga played a guitar duet arrangement of Septimus Winner's *Listen to the Mockingbird.* Next, Mrs. B. Lawrence sang Elena's siciliana (= bolero), *Mercé, dilette amiche,* from Act V of Verdi's *I vespri siciliani,* followed by Mme. Franzini Marra's singing of Jean-Baptiste Fauré's *Alleluia d'amour.* The advance program next announced Arévalo's playing of his own *Carnival of Venice* variations to end Part I. Part II was announced to include Act IV of *Il Trova-*

tore sung by Norma Ferner (Leonora) and other pupils of Madame Marra.

The Evening Express of Saturday, 7 May 1881 (3:5), carried a review headed "Sr. Arévalo's Concert." Stevenson (1988a:26) paraphrases the reviewer:

> Marra's singing of Fauré's *Alleluia d'amour* "fairly carried away the house." She and Rosalie Herdman ("a rich contralto") then sang what the reviewer called the first Los Angeles rendition of Jakob Blumenthal's *Venetian Boat Song*. . . . As an encore to the *Mockingbird* guitar duet, Arévalo and compatriot Arzaga played Luigi Arditi's *Il Bacio* waltzes arranged for two guitars. Both guitar duets "were given in a truly masterful manner." But (according to the reviewer) the crown of the evening was "Arévalo's playing of the very difficult 'Carnival of Venice,'" in which he displayed "wonderful" virtuosity.[2]

On 12 January 1882 a "complimentary concert" was given in honor of pianist Maria Pruneda, "one of two music teachers among the fourteen faculty members of the newly founded University of Southern California listed in its first catalogue, 1880–1881" (Stevenson 1988b:65). The *Los Angeles Times* announced the concert the same day: "The complimentary concert given to Miss Maria Pruneda occurs this evening at Turnverein Hall. Among the musical people of the city there is not one more worthy to receive, at the hands of this community, a rousing benefit. An excellent and very thorough musician, Miss Pruneda unites with this a lovable disposition and she has never yet failed to respond to the call of charity or refused her services to any worthy object."

Included in Pruneda's program for the evening was her interpretation of Liszt's *Rigoletto* paraphrase. Also performing at the concert were numerous musicians, including Miguel S. Arévalo (see Stevenson 1988b:60–61). The concert was also reviewed in the *Times* the following day: "Turnverein Hall was crowded last night to overflowing with the most fashionable audience that has met there for some time past, the occasion being a complimentary concert tendered to Miss Maria Pruneda. The programme was carried out as published in yesterday's Times in a most pleasing manner, every participant being encored two or three times. Miss Pruneda is really an excellent performer on the piano, and was received with loud applause."

Performing at the Grand Opera House in 1886 (January 22–23) was the Orquesta Típica from Mexico City, directed by Encarnación García, who played a ninety-nine-string *salterio*. Stevenson (1988b:62) cites a review of the ensemble published in the *Times:* "Encarnación García on his ninety-nine stringed instrument, resembling an old fashioned dulcimer, was especially melodious. The clarinet solo by Señor Adrián Galarza was rapturously encored and a repetition insisted on. Señor Carlos Certi's xylophone solo also made a great hit. The Mexican dance, 'El Jarabe Mexicano,' was immense and the audience demanded a repetition and stayed to see it."

In 1887 the *Times* advertised appearances by numerous U.S. opera companies and minstrels, in addition to Zerega's Royal Spanish Troubadours. A Hispano-Mexicano Opera Company performed *zarzuelas* (*El reloj de Lucerna* and *El sargento Frederico*) by Asenjo Barbieri and Joaquín Gaztambide at Armory Hall in May of 1888 (Stevenson 1986:109).

— Early Twentieth-Century Los Angeles

With the turn of the century, Mexican Los Angeles entered an era of widespread change with regard to issues such as revolution, immigration, discrimination, acculturation, and, ultimately, modes of expression. In his evaluation of the musical cycle of the Mexican in California, Peña recognizes this integral stage of musical activity.

> Consequently, due to the low density of its far-flung population, California-Mexican culture—the one lived by real people, not the "fantasy heritage" invented by Anglo romantics in the twentieth century (McWilliams, 1968)—succumbed rather easily to the onslaught of an American invasion that began with the Gold Rush and culminated in the 1870s with completion of the first railroads to Southern California. It was therefore left to the later immigrants from Mexico, those who arrived beginning in the early twentieth century, to revive Mexican culture and, with it, music in the Golden State. Thus, the music of California-Mexicans today traces its main outlines to the early twentieth century, when the first wave of Mexican immigrants transplanted a culture that served as the foundation for later musical developments in the Golden State. (1989:66)

Mexicans would witness considerable change in demographic, economic, and social patterns during the early twentieth century. The original humble pueblo changed dramatically, coming face to face with the dilemmas of the 1910 Mexican Revolution and World War I. Stratified demographic patterns began to take form.

> Coincidental with the infusion of new arrivals was the growing concentration of Mexican residents in a section adjacent to the original site of the pueblo's town plaza. Until the turn of the century, both Mexicans and Anglos recognized "Sonoratown," with its Mexican stores and social activities, as the heart of the Spanish-speaking com-

munity. Sonoratown remained the Mexican center of Los Angeles until the first World War, when new industrial forces and urbanization changed the face of the old Plaza community. (Romo 1983b:vii)

During the early twentieth century, between 1904 and 1912, writer/photographer Charles F. Lummis produced a collection of sound recordings of Mexican folksongs. They were originally recorded on 340 wax cylinders but have been rerecorded on magnetic tape and are catalogued and housed at the Southwest Museum in Los Angeles. These may be the first sound recordings of Mexican-American folksongs in California. Although most of the collection was not widely disseminated, Lummis did publish fourteen of the songs in 1923 (transcribed by Arthur Farwell) in *Spanish Songs of Old California.*

> Among the performers on these recordings was Rosendo Uruchurtu, a talented guitarist who sang in the Mexican *canción* tradition and accompanied others on the Lummis recordings. The [Southwest] museum's Braun Research Library also has lyrics and musical transcriptions of some of the songs, the latter prepared by composer Arthur Farwell, Lummis' collaborator on this project. There are also three handwritten notebooks of early California-Mexican song lyrics in the Lummis manuscript collection at the Southwest Museum. The oldest of these manuscripts dates from the late nineteenth century and is by José de la Rosa, a printer who came to California in 1833 and was an accomplished guitarist and composer (Baur 1973). The second notebook is from Manuela García and contains lyrics to most of the 150 songs which she recorded for Lummis in 1904. The notebooks in which Lummis jotted down his field notes and the lyrics to some of the Spanish-language songs which he recorded are also found in this collection. (Heisley 1988:57)

A great many, if not most, of the recordings reflect the Mexican *canción* that had developed by the early twentieth century. The technique of blind guitarist Rosendo Uruchurtu was quite proficient and attests to the high level of professional skill attributed to him. In many of the recorded *canciones* sung by Manuela García, Uruchurtu accompanies her on guitar. Among García's songs recorded by Lummis and inscribed by García in her notebook are "Memorias dolorosas," "La sinaloense," "Mientras tú duermes," "La pepa," "No me niegues," "La noche está serena," and "El desvalido."

Other songs recorded on the cylinders are "La barbaridad," "El marinero," "Despierta blanca paloma," "Cuando el hombre goza de la vida," "Las pulgas," "La pasión funesta," "Valse de Milán," "La indita," and "El

joven." In addition to García and Uruchurtu, others who recorded for
Lummis were Adalaida Kemp (of Ventura), sisters Luisa and Rosa Villa,
Francisco Amate, and Tulita Wilcox Miner, among others. Even Lummis
himself, who sang and played guitar, recorded a version of the song "Don
Simón."

Lummis is an important part of the musical history of early twentieth-
century Los Angeles. Of course, the Lummis cylinder collection, although
of paramount value, represents but a small part of the musical activity
among Mexicans at this time. Listening to the fascinating work of Lummis, I continually found myself wondering how far the range of musical
styles and techniques within the Mexican quarters in general might have
extended beyond the sound on these cylinders. Without the invaluable
cross-cultural enterprise of Lummis, however, my question might not have
even arisen. In a publication honoring the 1985 centennial of Lummis's
arrival in Los Angeles, Michael Heisley wrote:

> Charles F. Lummis was a pioneer in the recognition and recording
> of the folklore of Mexican Americans in New Mexico and Southern
> California. He was among the first Anglo observers willing to set
> aside prejudices against Mexican character and culture and, for the
> most part, sympathetically record the traditions of a people poorly
> understood by outsiders. Lummis' folklore data gathering and writ-
> ings, however, reflect the romanticization, journalistic style, and cru-
> sader's notion of historiography which marked his work in other
> fields. Lummis was not simply an antiquarian dedicated to recon-
> structing the past for its own sake through studies of folklore. Rather,
> he wanted to revive many of the seemingly outdated customs which
> he encountered in the Southwest and bring them into mainstream
> American life. Like Walt Whitman, who prophesied in 1883 that "to
> the composite American identity of the future, Spanish character will
> supply some of the most needed parts," Lummis saw in the culture
> of the Mexican peoples of the Southwest a leavening for the Puritan
> spirit. Mexican-American folklore evoked in Lummis' mind a sense of
> deeply rooted traditions which he associated with the Old World and
> the early Spanish pioneers in the Americas. Consequently, he viewed
> Mexicans residing in the United States as a people living in the past.
> (Heisley 1985:60)

Lummis's own words reflect his own insight even more vividly:

> Personally, I feel that we who today inherit California are under a filial
> obligation to save whatever we may of the incomparable romance
> which has made the name California a word to conjure with for

400 years. I feel that we cannot decently dodge a certain trusteeship to save the Old Missions from ruin and the Old Songs from oblivion. And I am convinced that from a purely selfish standpoint, our musical repertory is in crying need of enrichment—more by heartfelt musicians than by tailor-made ones, more from folksong than from pot-boilers. (1923:3)

In addition to possessing the Lummis materials, the Southwest Museum holds photographs taken by Lummis of Spanish violinist Marie Azpiroz and a few of her press notices and promotional materials. Born in Madrid in 1889, Azpiroz was apparently a virtuoso of the classical repertoire, including pieces by Beethoven, Mendelssohn, Vieuxtemps, Wieniawski, Sarasate, and Monasterio. After leaving Spain, she concertized extensively in Cuba, South America, Mexico, and throughout the United States, receiving positive reviews in New York, San Francisco, and Los Angeles, where she evidently settled, performing and teaching both privately and at the Fillmore School of Music. Her period in Mexico seems to have been especially successful; she was reported to have "had the honor of being the only European artist ever allowed to play in the theatre of the National Conservatory" (*New York World,* n.d.).[3] Although not a Mexican, she was quite possibly involved with the Mexican musical community in Los Angeles.

Growth, Industrialization, and the Early Radio and Recording Industries

Massive numbers of Mexicans arrived in Los Angeles during the early twentieth century. This movement coincided with the rapid growth of industrialization in the city. Although promoted as a worker's paradise during these formative years, Los Angeles failed to attract European immigrants and American blue-collar workers because of the "comparatively low wages and a reluctance among most of these workers to work in a city troubled by labor strife" (Romo 1983b:vii). Meanwhile, Mexicans began to adapt to industrialization and to create an ethnic community in one of the fastest growing cities in the United States. Throughout southern California, Mexicans filled a labor shortage caused by an absence of domestic and immigrant workers in the years before and after World War I. "By 1929, these newcomers from Mexico numbered over 100,000 and, through their labor in hundreds of occupations, played an essential role in the city's drive for domination of international trade in the Western Pacific region" (Romo 1983b:vii).

It was also during the early 1900s that large numbers of Mexicans arrived in Los Angeles fleeing from the bitter fighting and violent turmoil following the Mexican Revolution. With housing conditions already congested, their choice of residence was restricted to existing barrios; the Plaza district remained the most popular entry port. Job discrimination forced many Mexicans to work for extremely low wages that were often below subsistence level. World War I intensified the degree of discrimination toward Mexicans, who were accused of being pro-German: "Living conditions were stark throughout the decade. In 1914, although Mexicans comprised five percent of Los Angeles, 11.1 percent of deaths were Mexican. A 1919 survey showed that they lived in deplorable housing, with almost four out of every five families living in quarters without baths. Infant mortality was three times higher than among whites" (Acuña 1984:9).

Mexicans made their homes in the flat lowlands along the Los Angeles River amidst the old housing developments that had belonged to Europeans of an earlier generation. Financially discouraged from settling in the other sections of Los Angeles, they found the inexpensive housing on the East Side more compatible with their depressed standard of living. During the era of the interurban railroad and the beginning of the age of the automobile, "the barrio became a haven for a Mexican population which faced discrimination in housing, employment, and social activities in Anglo parts of the city" (Romo 1983b:8). Eastside Mexican residents began to organize socially and politically: they founded Spanish-language newspapers, established radio programs, and supported businesses and cultural programs that recognized and met their needs.

The prosperity resulting from the period of extraordinary industrial and demographic expansion in Los Angeles came to a halt with the Great Depression. The rate of Mexican immigration declined greatly during the 1930s, but the legacy of the three previous decades remained. By 1929 Los Angeles was the fifth largest city in the country, and the largest among western and southern states. In 1930 the population of the eastside barrio of Los Angeles was more than 90,000, larger than the capital cities of three of the largest states: Albany, New York; Sacramento, California; and Austin, Texas (Romo 1983b:3).

Growth of the Mexican community was accompanied by growth in the music of Mexicans in Los Angeles. Such growth, however, was affected not only by the transplantation of Mexican musical forms but also by the character and development of such settlement and by factors such as migration, immigration, and the radio and recording industries. Heisley (1988:58–59) assessed the musical activity among Mexicans in California from the period of the Mexican Revolution to the 1930s:

> Migration and immigration to California from Mexico have been constant features of the history of Spanish-speaking peoples in Cali-

fornia since the first settlements of *pueblos* such as San Jose and Los Angeles in the eighteenth century. It was the Mexican Revolution of 1910–1917 which, perhaps more than any other factor, intensified this movement of people across the border. Mexican immigrant songs and music in California from the Mexican Revolution through the Depression . . . have not received adequate attention from scholars. It was during this period that the Mexican *colonias* in rural areas and urban *barrios* developed and became centers in which Mexican immigrant and Mexican American lifestyles flourished and influenced one another. Notably, this process took place not in isolation but in interaction with other minorities and the dominant Anglo society. As a result of the establishing of these immigrant and ethnic neighborhoods (often in segregated areas of a community) two important trends emerged in Mexican music in California. First the already established *corrido* (ballad) tradition became an important vehicle for expressing the concerns of many immigrants who came to the area from Mexico. Frequently, *corridos* and other songs expressed the immigrant's sense of victimization and injustice which was born of experiences north of the border. Second, in urban *barrios*, a nascent Spanish-language radio and recording industry emerged. This latter development, which happened somewhat earlier in California than in other parts of the Southwest, provided both entertainment and an important bond for the Mexican community during this period. Through programs featuring local artists, the electronic media during the 1920s and 1930s expanded the audiences of numerous traditional forms of music. Recordings, home phonographs, and *sinfonolas* (jukeboxes) put these songs in the hands of large numbers of listeners and helped expand the careers of local singers and musicians of Mexican descent to areas outside of the state.

Exemplary of such experience was the musical activity among Mexicans in Los Angeles in the 1920s and 1930s. Spanish-language radio broadcasts began in the late 1920s. During the mid-1920s recording companies such as Victor, Brunswick, Decca, and Columbia "began to exploit for commercial gain the musical traditions of Mexicans in California and in the Southwest" (Peña 1989:67). Genres recorded and marketed included the *canción mexicana,* the *corrido,* boleros, and *huapangos.* Instrumentation was frequently based on ensembles such as the trio and the mariachi. The latter had evolved from its rural identity into a larger and more commercialized instrumental format in Mexico, incorporating, by the 1930s, violin, *vihuela,* guitar, and *guitarrón,* and later the trumpet.

Sociocultural expression marked the music of Mexicans in Los Angeles in a number of compositions and recordings during the 1920s and 1930s. Themes based on intercultural conflict, human conditions, and political actions characterize songs of the period such as "El lavaplatos," "Se acabó el WPA," "Consejos al maje," and the *corridos* dedicated to Juan Reyna.

The *corrido* "El lavaplatos" (The Dishwasher) was composed by Jesús Osorio, who recorded the song with Manuel "El Perro" Camacho on 19 May 1930, on the Victor label. It was recorded by Los Hermanos Banuelos on 1 July 1930 (on the Brunswick/Vocalion label) and by Chávez y Lugo on Columbia. Incorporating satire into the expression of an immigrant's illusion and disillusion with the dreams and myths of Hollywood, the song is a tragicomic sociocultural commentary. This *corrido* studies and expresses contemporary life. Moreover, Peña (1989:67) cites this particular *corrido* as a thematically significant one because of its reference to "political and economic issues that were at the heart of the Mexican's subordination in the capitalist Anglo order that reigned over the Southwest by this time."

"El lavaplatos"

Soñaba en mi juventud
ser una estrella de cine
Y un día de tantos me vine
a visitar Hollywood.

I dreamed in my youth
of being a movie star
And one of those days I came
to visit Hollywood.

Un día muy desesperado
por tanta revolución
Me pasé para este lado

sin pagar la inmigración.

One day very desperate
because of so much revolution
I came over to this side [of
    the border]
without paying the
    immigration.

Que vacilada,
que vacilada,
me pasé sin pagar nada.

What a fast one,
what a fast one,
I crossed without paying
    anything.

Al llegar a la estación
me tropecé con un cuate
Que me hizo la invitación
de trabajar en "el traque."

On arriving at the station
I ran into a friend
Who gave me an invitation
to work on the track.

Yo "el traque" me suponía,
que sería algún almacén

I supposed the track
would be some kind of a
    store.

Y era componer la vía
por donde camina el tren.

Ay, que mi cuate,
ay, que mi cuate,
como me llevó pa'l traque.

Cuando me enfadé del traque

me volvió a invitar aquél
A la pizca del tomate
y a desahijar betabel.

Y allí me gané indulgencias
caminando de rodillas
Como cuatro o cinco millas
me dieron de penitencia.

Ay que trabajo,
tan mal pagado,
por andar arrodillado.

Mi cuate, que no era mage,
el siguió dándole guerra

Y al completar su pasaje

se devolvió pa' su tierra.

Y yo hice cualquier bicoca
y me fuí pa' Sacramento
Cuando no tenía ni zoca
tuve que entrarle al cemento.

Ay, que tormento,
ay, que tormento,
es el mentado cemento.

Héchale piedra y arena
a la máquina batidora
Cincuenta centavos hora
hasta que el pito no suena.

En la carrucha mentada
se rajaron más de cuatro

And it was to repair the road
where the train ran.

Oh, my friend,
oh, my friend,
how he took me to the track.

When I became angry with the
    track
he invited me again
To the picking of tomatoes
and the gathering of beets.

And there I earned indulgence
walking on my knees
About four or five miles
they gave me as a penance.

Oh, what work,
and so poorly paid,
for going on one's knees.

My friend, who was no fool,
continued giving them a bad
    time
And on completing [enough]
    for his fare
he returned to his land.

And I earned but a trifle
and I left for Sacramento
When I had nothing
I had to work with cement.

Oh, what torment,
oh, what torment,
is that famous cement.

Toss some gravel and sand
in the cement mixer
Fifty cents an hour
until the whistle blows.

Four or more of us
strained at that famous
    pulley

Y yo pos' como aguantaba
mejor me fuí a lavar platos.

And I, how could I stand it
I was better off washing
    dishes.

Que arrepentido,
que arrepentido,
estoy de haberme venido.

How repentant,
how repentant,
I am for having come.

Es el trabajo decente
que lo hacen muchos chicanos
Aunque con l'agua caliente
se hinchan un poco las manos.

It is the decent work
done by many Chicanos
Although with the hot water
the hands swell a little.

Pa' no hacérselas cansadas
me enfadé de tanto plato

To make it short
I got tired of so many
    dishes

Y me alcancé la puntada
de trabajar en el teatro.

And the thought came to me
of working in the theater.

Ay qué bonito,
ay qué bonito,
circo, maroma, y teatrito.

Oh, how pretty,
oh, how pretty,
circus, somersaults and
    little shows.

Yo les pido su licencia
pa' darles estos consejos
A los jóvenes y viejos
que no tengan experiencia.

I ask your leave
to give this advice
To the young and old
who are inexperienced.

Aquél que no quiera creer

That one didn't want to
    believe

que lo que digo es verdad
Si se quiere convencer
que se venga para acá.

that what I say is true
If he wants to be convinced
let him come over here.

Y que se acuerde
de este corrido
es único que le pido.

That you remember
this ballad
is all that I ask.

Ya el estage va salir
ya empezamos a correr
Ojos que te vieron ir
¿cuando te verán volver?

The coach is about to leave
soon we will get going
Eyes that saw you leave
when will they see you
    return?

Adiós sueños de mi vida

Goodbye dreams of my life

adiós estrellas del cine	goodbye movie stars
Vuelvo a mi patria querida	I am going back to my beloved homeland
más pobre de lo que vine.	much poorer than when I came.
Nos despedimos,	We take our leave,
adiós paisanos,	goodbye my countrymen,
porque ahora si ya nos vamos.	because now we are leaving.[4]

Representative of the *canción mexicana* style were "Consejos al maje" (Advice to the Naive) and "Se acabó el WPA" (The WPA Has Ended). Composed by E. Nevárez and recorded by Los Madrugadores (Chicho y Chencho)[5] with Los Hermanos Eliceiri in 1934, "Consejos al maje" satirically and tactfully addresses the issue of consumerism in the United States, alluding to the commercial pretenses of clothing, two-story houses, radios, Ford automobiles, insurance, dyed hair, entertainment spots, womanizing, and general foolishness and the wasting of money.

Referring to the termination of the Work Projects Administration of President Franklin D. Roosevelt's New Deal program, "Se acabó el WPA" satirizes the project that provided food and financial supplement to communities throughout the United States. The song was composed by Alfredo Marín and recorded by Los Madrugadores (Chicho y Chencho) in 1937.

"Se acabó el WPA"

Se acabó el WPA:	The WPA has ended
yo lo siento por mi raza,	and I'm sorry for my people,
artistas, pintores,	artists, painters,
camellos y vagos,	workers and loafers,
se los llevó la desgracia.	they all have gone to the dogs.
Ya no habrá rentas pagadas	Now there won't be any rents paid
ni sacos de provisión	or sacks of food
de ésa que viene marcada,	the kind with the label
que dice: "Not to be sold."	saying: "Not to be sold."
Se acabó el WPA:	The WPA has ended
hay muchos que hasta	there are many who are even happy
se alegran,	about it,
a darle al trabajo,	let's get to work

ya no anden de vagos,
lo que es que ahora si
se friegan.

Ya tendremos piscadores,
también habrá lavaplatos;
se acabaron los gorrones:

"zapatero, a tus zapatos."

Se acabó el WPA:
los mandaron al infierno,

ya no habrá más casas
ni carros pagados
con los cheques del gobierno.

Unos disque se enfermaban
y no querían trabajar,
los demás se emborrachaban

por cuenta de la ciudad.

Se acabó el WPA:
les quitaron ya la ayuda
tendrán que ganarse
los nickles y dimes
para curarse la cruda.

don't loaf any more
'cause now you'll really get
    it.

Now we'll have pickers
there'll be dishwashers, too;
the free-loaders are
    finished:

"shoemaker, get to your
    business."

The WPA has ended
they've sent them all to
    hell,
there won't be no more houses
or cars that are paid
with checks from the
    government.

Some pretended to be sick
so they wouldn't have to work
the rest of them would get
    drunk
at the expense of the city.

The WPA has ended
the aid was taken away
now they'll have to earn
their nickels and dimes
to cure their hangovers.[6]

During the early 1930s, at least six *corridos* were written about Juan Reyna, who was accused of murdering a Los Angeles policeman on 11 May 1930.[7] Highly publicized, largely due to questions related to ethnic tensions and the nature of Reyna's arrest, the case was settled in November 1930. Reyna was convicted of manslaughter and assault with a deadly weapon and began a one-to-ten-year sentence at the California State Penitentiary at San Quentin. The jury had recommended clemency, and a vigorous campaign organized by the Mexican populace in Los Angeles assisted Reyna in paying his legal fees. In May 1931, five months prior to his parole release date, Reyna committed suicide while still in prison.

Two of the six *corridos* about Juan Reyna are reproduced here. Both were recorded in the general period of 1930–31.

"Corrido de Juan Reyna"

(Luis M. Banuelos)

Voy a cantar un corrido
aunque con bastante pena,
Es todo lo sucedido
al compatriota Juan Reyna.

I will sing a ballad
although it pains me much,
About all that happened
to my countryman Juan Reyna.

Dicen que el once de mayo

apenas obscurecía,
cuando en el carro de Reyna
chocó él de la policía.

They say that on the 11th of
    May
it was just getting dark,
when Reyna's car
collided with the car of the
    police.

Un fuerte llegón le dieron
enchuecando las defensas.
Luego dos chotas bajaron

diciendo a Reyna insolencias.

It was a head-on collision
the bumpers were dented.
Then two cops got out of the
    car
saying insolences to Reyna.

Querían bajarlo del coche

y allí empezó la alegata,

Y luego uno de las chotas
lo estiró de la corbata.

They wanted to get him out of
    the car,
and that's when the flap
    started,
And then one of the cops
pulled him out by his tie.

"Díganme quíen son ustedes?"
les dijo ya estando en
    tierra.
Le respondieron con golpes,
llamándolo "hijo de perra."

"Tell me, who are you?"
he asked them being on
    firm ground.
They answered him with blows,
calling him a "son of a
    bitch."

Como iban sin uniformes

y haciendo mil tonterías

Reyna no estaba seguro
de que fueran policías.

Querían subirlo por fuerza

Since they were without
    uniforms
and they were just fooling
    around,
Reyna was not sure
if they were policemen.

They wanted to put him by
    force

al carro en que lo llevaron.

Como Reyna se opusiera
entonces más lo golpearon.

Eran cuatro los gendarmes
que al mexicano estrujaron,
Y al subirlo al otro carro

con un negro lo esposaron.

Luego el detective Brindley
buscando cosa sencilla,

le dió una fuerte patada

sangrándole la espinilla.

Y como en esos momentos
el auto empezaba a andar
sobre el pobre mexicano,
Brindley se vino a sentar.

Entonces el mexicano
con valor y con destreza,
Le arrebató la pistola
y le clavó la cabeza.

Pero el detective Miller
y el negro lo sujetaron.
Disparándole otros tiros
mientras que lo desarmaron.

Patadas, palos, moquetes,
le dieron a granizar.

Por lo que tuvo Juan Reyna,

que ir a dar al hospital.

El cónsul de la colinda
y el vice-cónsul Quiñones
Hablaron luego por radio
mostrando sus opiniones.

inside the car that would
   take him.
Since Reyna opposed
they gave him more blows.

There were four policemen
who mistreated the Mexican,
And as they put him in the
   other car
he was handcuffed to a Negro.

Then detective Brindley
looking for a simple thing
   [to do]
Gave him [Juan Reyna] a
   bloody kick
which connected with his
   shin.

Since at about this time
the car began to run,
up against the Mexican,
Brindley came to take a seat.

Then the Mexican
with bravery and agility,
Snatched away the gun
and hit him on the head.

But the detective Miller
and the Negro caught him.
Other shots were fired
while trying to disarm him.

Kicks, blows, and more blows,
they gave him like a
   hailstorm.
And because of what Juan
   Reyna got,
he had to go to the hospital.

The consul from the area
and vice-consul Quiñones
Talked over the radio
expressing their opinions.

Explicaron bien el caso

y la colonia atendió,
Porque al insultar a Reyna,
a México se insultó.

Mandaron toda su ayuda
como buenos mexicanos,
Probando lo que nos duele,
el maltrato a los paisanos.

Muy pronto juntó dinero

el cónsul digno y argente,
Y a la defensa de Reyna
puso a un hombre competente.

Ya lo que el fiscal pedía
que ahorcaran al delincuente.
el defensor luego dijo,

"Abranse que ahí va la mía."

Tuvieron muchos testigos,
agentes de policías,
Y el defensor luego dijo,
"Abranse que ahí va la mía."

Algo dijo Mr. Rude,
con que al fiscal le dió tos,
Y dicen por ahí las gentes
que hubo un encuentro de voz.

Se le hicieron dos jurados
y con toda claridad,
Unos pedían su castigo
los otros su libertad.

Por fin fallaron las damas,
las del segundo jurado,
Por homicidio de culpa
Juan Reyna fué sentenciado,

The case was carefully
    explained
and the colony attended,
Because by insulting Reyna,
Mexico was insulted.

They sent all their help
like good fellow Mexicans,
Proving the hurt to us all,
the mistreatment of our
    countrymen.

Right away money was
    collected
by the worthy consul
And to defend Reyna
he picked a competent man.

The prosecutor was asking
to hang the delinquent.
And the defense attorney
    said,
"I'll prove that he is
    innocent."

They had many witnesses
who were police agents,
And the defense attorney said
"It is now my turn."

Mr. Rude[8] said something,
the prosecutor coughed,
And now the people are saying
that their voices were raised.

Two juries were picked
and with all clarity,
Some asked for his punishment
and others for his freedom.

At last the ladies decided,
the ones on the second jury,
For intentional homicide
Juan Reyna was sentenced.

De un año a diez,
el juez Hardy a Reyna
le sentenció,
Salvándolo de la horca,
que el Mr. Blalock los pidió.

One year to ten,
Judge Hardy sentenced Reyna,

Saving him from hanging,
which was what Mr. Blalock[9]
    wanted.

Adiós Juan Reyna, supiste
defender tu dignidad,
Y hasta tu vida expusiste
por tu nacionalidad.

Goodbye Juan Reyna, you knew
how to defend your dignity,
You even risked your life
because of your
    nationality.[10]

"Suicidio de Juan Reyna"
(F. Galindo)

Vuela, vuela palomita,
vuela, vuela sin cesar,
Vé y cuenta ya a mis paisanos
lo que acaba de pasar.

Fly, fly little dove,
fly, fly without ceasing,
Go and tell my countrymen
what has just happened.

Voy a cantarles señores
con el alma entristecida,
Esta tremenda tragedia
en San Quentín sucedida.

I will sing, gentlemen
with my saddened soul,
This tremendous tragedy
that happened in San Quentin.

Faltándole cinco meses
pa' salir en libertad,
El mexicano Juan Reyna
se acaba de suicidar.

Lacking only five months
to leave a free man,
The Mexican Juan Reyna
has just committed suicide.

A la una de la mañana
un celador descubrió
En la celda de Juan Reyna
algo grave acontecío.

At one in the morning
the jailer discovered
In Juan Reyna's cell
something grave had happened.

Era un cuadro doloroso
todo lo que estaba viendo,
Juanito en su propia sangre
se estaba allí debatiendo.

It was a painful scene
everything that was seen,
Juanito in his own blood
was fighting for his life.

Con arma pulso cortante
se trozó la jugular
Estando Reyna en la celda
pensando en su libertad.

With a pulsing blade
he sliced his jugular vein
While he was in his cell
thinking of his freedom.

Pa' el hospital lo llevaron
tratando de darle auxilio,
Pero a los pocos momentos
ya Reyna había fallecido.

Como a las once del día

un mensajero llegó
En la casa de Juan Reyna
un telegrama dejó.

Con lágrimas en los ojos,
la madre de él se enteró
Viendo que su hijo querido
una herida se injerió.

En el segundo mensaje
que el alcalde le mandó,
Se daba cuenta que su hijo
en el hospital falleció.

Con la rapidez del rayo
por la ciudad se esparció

El triste acontecimiento
que en San Quentín sucedió.

Toda la gente de Watts
andaba muy afligida,
Diciendo que ya Juan Reyna

se había quitado la vida.

Con su conducta intachable
se granjió la simpatía
De todos sus compañeros
en la penitenciaría.

Las puertas de la prisión
se abrieron un día temprano
Para sacar el cadáver
del querido mexicano.

They took him to the hospital
trying to give him some help,
But in a very short while
Reyna had passed away.

At about eleven o'clock in
the morning
a messenger arrived
At Juan Reyna's house
and left a telegram.

With tears in her eyes
his mother found out
That her beloved son
had self-inflicted a wound.

In the second message
that the mayor sent,
She found out that her son
had passed away in the
hospital.

With the speed of light
throughout the city spread
news
Of the sad happening
that took place at San
Quentin.

All the people of Watts
were very grieved,
They were saying that now
Juan Reyna
had committed suicide.

With his blameless conduct
he gained the sympathy
Of all his comrades
in the penitentiary.

The prison doors
opened up early one day
to take out the corpse
of one beloved Mexican.

"Ah, hijito de mi vida,"   "Oh, little son of my life,"
decía la mamá de Juan,   Juan's mother would say,
"Yo te esperaba con vida[11]   "I waited for you alive
y hoy tu cadáver me traen."   and today they bring me your
                                            corpse."

Esto es muy triste señores,   This is very sad, gentlemen,
hay que ponerse a pensar   we should start thinking
Que harán los hijos de Reyna   Of what will become of
                                            Reyna's children
en su terrible orfandad.   now that they have been
                                            orphaned so terribly.

Siempre que Juan escribía,   Everytime Juan wrote,
a su madre le encargaba   he would entrust his mother
De la instrucción de sus   With the instruction of
  hijos   his children
que no los fanatizara.   to not let them become
                                            superstitious.

Hoy las confederaciones   Now the confederations
piden investigación   ask for an investigation
Como se mató Juan Reyna   Of how Juan Reyna killed
                                            himself
adentro de la prisión.   inside the prison.

Vuela, vuela palomita,   Fly, fly little dove,
vuela, vuela sin cesar,   fly, fly without ceasing,
Ya contaste a mis paisanos   You already sang to my fellow
                                            countrymen
lo que acaba de pasar.   what just happened.

Ya me despido señores,   Now I take my leave,
                                            gentlemen,
y les pido una oración   and I ask you for a prayer,
Pa' el valiente mexicano   For that brave Mexican
que se mató en la prisión.   who killed himself in prison.

Another *corrido* with a sociocultural theme, this one incorporating the historical referent of Joaquín Murrieta, legendary in California history and lore, was "El Corrido de Joaquín Murrieta" (recorded by Los Hermanos Sánchez y Linares in Los Angeles in the fall of 1934). For Peña the recording of the *corrido* is "a chronological puzzle, in that the events it depicted had occurred more than 80 years before it was actually recorded" (1989:67).

It is quite possible that the *corrido* was composed in Mexico during a much earlier period. Peña compares "Joaquín Murrieta" to its Texas-Mexican counterpart, "Gregorio Cortez" and finds the former especially significant for its literal expression of intercultural conflict between the Anglo and the Mexican in the Southwest.

Among Mexican artists in Los Angeles during the early 1930s, the group Los Madrugadores had perhaps the greatest commercial impact. Originally a trio consisting of the brothers Víctor and Jesús Sánchez and early Spanish-language broadcaster Pedro J. González (whom the Sánchez brothers had met at the music store La Casa de Música de Mauricio Calderón), the group premiered on radio station KMPC in December 1929 (Sonnichsen 1977b:15). The name Los Madrugadores, which was conceived by González, means "early risers"; it referred to the very early morning hours during which the group's live program was broadcast. (Air time at that hour cost much less than did prime radio time later in the day and evening.)

Soon after the KMPC program premiered, vocalist Fernando Linares joined Los Madrugadores, and in 1931 the group moved its program to radio station KELW in Burbank, where it aired daily from 4:00 to 6:00 A.M. Another musician who performed with the group was Ismael Hernández. Other artists who appeared on the program included La Prieta Caldera, Las Hermanitas del Río, Las Hermanitas Durán, and Chicho y Chencho (Narciso Farfán and Cresencio Quevas) (Sonnichsen 1977b:16), in addition to Calixo Cuevas, Carmen Caudillo, and Manuel Torres.[12] Aside from applying to the recording group that included the Sánchez brothers, the name Los Madrugadores also applied to the entire ensemble of artists who performed live on the program.

Los Madrugadores (the recording group) was considered a distinctive and high-quality ensemble that catered to the Mexican public's musical taste, especially in the interpretation of *corridos* and the *canción mexicana*. Los Madrugadores made numerous recordings during the 1930s, when the group consisted of the Sánchez brothers and Linares. In an interview conducted by Philip Sonnichsen (1977b:18), Víctor Sánchez estimated that he and his brother, Jesús, recorded over 200 78 r.p.m. shellac disc releases for seven different labels—RCA Victor, Columbia, Vocalion, Decca, Blue Bird, Imperial, and Tri-color.

Pedro J. González, who left Los Madrugadores after two years, proceeded to live a life of tragedy and legend. A veteran of the 1910 Mexican Revolution, in which he served as a telegraph operator under General Francisco Villa, he relocated to the Los Angeles area and settled there during its industrial boom of the 1920s. He worked in San Pedro as a longshoreman and was later hired by Mauricio Calderón to write and narrate

Spanish-language radio ads. González eventually established his own radio ad agency, which operated during the 1920s and 1930s. His early morning KMPC program with Los Madrugadores attracted hundreds of thousands of Mexicans and Latin American listeners daily. González broadcast the musical show from the Teatro Hidalgo, located in the Mexican barrio of downtown Los Angeles, and became the city's most popular personality of Spanish-language radio. As a musician, he not only performed guitar and vocals with Los Madrugadores but also composed or recorded songs such as "Mañanitas tapatías," "Sonora querida," "¿Porqué te fuiste?" and "Corrido de Juan Reyna."

In "The Ballad of an Unsung Hero," a PBS (Public Broadcasting System) video documentary on the life of González that was produced by San Diego–based Cinewest Productions (and from which the data on him have been extracted here), González talks about the racial tension in Los Angeles at the time of his radio broadcasts. In his opinion, the authorities in Los Angeles perceived him as a threat because of his outspokenness during his radio broadcasts. He recalls in the documentary, for example, that city officials became concerned when large numbers of Mexicans arrived at a work site with picks and shovels after he had announced a work opportunity on the radio. Apparently, to some it appeared to be an uprising. González openly criticized instances of discrimination and frequently used his program to voice his opinions. In 1930 he composed and recorded "El Corrido de Juan Reyna" (cited previously) and most likely performed the song with Los Madrugadores or played the record during his broadcasts.

In Gonzalez's mind, he became not only a threat to the non-Mexican leadership but also its target. There were attempts to revoke his broadcasting license, and finally, in 1934, he was accused and convicted of rape. His accuser was a dancer whom he had previously fired; eight months after his fifty-year sentence began she admitted that she had been coerced to perjure herself. Nevertheless, González served six years of his sentence at San Quentin before being paroled, after which he was immediately deported to Mexico. Relocating in Tijuana, Mexico, he formed a new Los Madrugadores and worked for thirty years at radio station XERU. In 1971 he was permitted to return with his wife to the United States, where his five children still lived. In 1988 the film *Break of Dawn*, based on his experience in Los Angeles, was released.

Another important development in Los Angeles during the 1930s and 1940s was the rise of the vocal duet Las Hermanas Padilla. The sisters, Margarita and María, began their musical career singing at fundraising benefits for local churches during the 1930s. Their first formal recognition came when they won first prize in a talent contest held at a park in Pico Rivera, a suburb just east of Los Angeles. Soon afterward, they appeared on the

Los Angeles–based radio show of Ramón B. Arnaiz, where they started singing with Chicho y Chencho. Their first recording, "La barca de oro," was an instant success (Sonnichsen 1984).

Arnaiz's radio program continued until 1941. In addition to Las Hermanas Padilla, other artists featured on the program included the host's orchestra, Adelina García, Los Madrugadores, the Trio Los Porteños de Miguel Aceves Mejía, and Leopoldo González. In 1941 Arnaiz went to Mexico and the radio station replaced live entertainment with records. Other significant radio personalities who hosted programs of Mexican music in Los Angeles around this time or who would later emerge included Tony Saenz, Rodolfo Hoyos (who was also an operatic singer), Elena Salinas, Salvador Luis Hernández, Martín Becerra, and Teddy Fregozo (also a songwriter).

An individual of immense importance in the 1930s and 1940s was Manuel Acuña. After emigrating from Mexico in the early 1930s, he worked with the orchestra of Rafael Gama and eventually became one of the leading musical directors in the Mexican radio and record industries in Los Angeles. Recognized as an excellent arranger and composer, Acuña also worked extensively with Felipe Valdez Leal, with whom he co-composed many songs recorded on the Columbia label. He later worked in A&R (artists and repertoire) for Vocalion/Decca and Imperial Records. Acuña was largely responsible for the early career promotion of Las Hermanas Padilla and composed and arranged a number of songs for Adelina García and many other major vocalists of the period.

Adelina García arrived in Los Angeles in 1939. Born in Phoenix, Arizona, she lived in Juárez, in the state of Chihuahua, Mexico, from the age of three to thirteen, after which she returned to Phoenix in 1937. On her arrival in Los Angeles as a very young woman, she began to perform on live radio and to record on the Columbia label (she was fifteen years old at her first recording date). A stylist of the bolero form, which was popular throughout Latin America at the time, she made several highly successful recordings during the 1940s, among them "Desesperadamente," "Vereda tropical," "Mi tormento," "Perfidia," and "Frenesí." At different points in her career, García performed at Los Angeles venues such as the Mason, Maya, and Million Dollar theaters.

Interestingly, after achieving international acclaim for her Columbia recording in Los Angeles, García toured Brazil before touring Mexico. In the Brazilian tour she was featured with the highly popular Mexican composer Gonzalo Curiel, who also performed on piano and directed an accompanying orchestra. Finally, in 1944, she arrived in Mexico City, where she was warmly received by the public; she subsequently performed throughout Mexico. She worked with numerous composers and various artists including Curiel, Mario Ruiz Armengol, Juan García Esquivel, and José Alfredo Jiménez. In Mexico City she sang extensively on live radio, notably radio station XEW, and also began to record for RCA Victor. She recorded on the label for eight years, although not exclusively. In Brazil, she recorded on the Odeón label, a subsidiary of Capitol Records. García also toured extensively in Cuba, Argentina, and many other Latin American countries, where she was very popular, in addition to California and the southwestern United States. In Mexico she also appeared in singing roles in three motion pictures.

In 1955 García returned to Los Angeles and two years later married José Heredia, a professional musician (drummer/percussionist) active in Los Angeles. Performing only for a few special events in the ensuing years, she dedicated herself to her family, which included three sons, one of whom (Joey Heredia) became a highly recognized drummer in the 1980s.[13]

Repatriation, 1931–34

In numbers, character, and activity, the Los Angeles eastside barrio had become by the 1930s a city within a city, its people a microculture within a macroculture. Between 1925 and 1929, 238,527 Mexicans entered the United States. The number declined to 19,200 between 1930 and 1934 and dropped even further, to 8,737, between 1935 and 1939 (Acuña 1972:136). Prior to 1929, growers and other industrialists had cooperated with the departments of state, agriculture, and the interior to prevent the restriction of immigrants entering the United States.

According to official records, between 1931 and 1934 about 300,000 Mexicans, many of them U.S. citizens, were returned to Mexico. The figure may well have reached a half million (Acuña 1972:138). About one-third of the Mexicans counted in the 1930 census were repatriated; about 60 percent of those repatriated were born in the United States and thus were U.S. citizens. Although the Mexican government supported the repatriation and many American officials emphasized its "voluntary" nature, in contrast to deportation, most Mexicans considered the movement a derogation. Norman D. Humphrey, an authority on Mexican America in the 1930s, wrote:

> Even the families of naturalized citizens were urged to repatriate, and the rights of American-born children to citizenship in their native land were explicitly denied or not taken into account. The case workers themselves brought pressures to bear in the form of threats of deportation, stoppage of relief (wholly or in part, e.g., in matters of

rent, or by means of trampling on customary procedures). (Humphrey 1941:505)

Mexico cooperated with the program mainly because it had lost approximately one-eighth of its population to the United States, but it could not accommodate this massive repatriation of workers and their families. The chaos of the 1910 Revolution still ravaged Mexico economically. Repatriates thus became disillusioned with the program.

Apart from the problems of the repatriations during the 1930s, mass roundups, newspaper hysteria, and public violence were also commonplace. The U.S. Bureau of Immigration was involved in numerous labor conflicts; arrests and deportations of strike leaders took place while the nation's press continued anti-alien practices. Public policy toward the Mexican population did not change until the war effort of the 1940s improved the economy and created a labor shortage. "In 1941, the Mexican American population in California reached 35,443. In Los Angeles City, Mexicans officially approached 100,000. Boyle Heights was a port of entry for Mexican Americans, as it had been for the Jews, Armenians, and Japanese before them. Even City Terrace, once the area's Beverly Hills, felt the Mexican's presence. Mexican Americans and white senior citizens also lived in Bunker Hill and Chavez Ravine" (Acuña 1984:13).

Wartime

As World War II became a reality, the *Los Angeles Times* shifted its coverage of Mexican Americans from the "fiesta" and "old California culture" stories that glorified a mythical past to negative accounts of the subculture dramatized by the image of the "zoot suit." "The communities east of the Los Angeles River were the target of racist reports that made Los Angeles the symbol of the pachuco, the Mexican American gang member" (Acuña 1984:14). Newspaper coverage exaggerated the degree of gang activity; less than 3 percent of the 30,000 school-age Mexican Americans in Los Angeles actually belonged to gangs. Drug abuse was not a significant problem in 1943, for only twelve Mexican Americans were arrested on such charges (Acuña 1984:14). Stereotyping had become common practice among local journalists interested in stories of gang members and law breakers. "The excesses of the Los Angeles press have been well documented elsewhere, especially its extent in coverage of the Sleepy Lagoon case (1942) and the Zoot Suit Riots (1943)" (Acuña 1984:14), the latter marked by clashes between U.S. servicemen and Mexican-American civilians. Not reported to any great extent was the Mexican-American participation in the war effort or the large number of Mexican-American draftees and volunteers. Ironically, young Mexicans in Los Angeles had been subjected to repatriation only ten years earlier. By the end of the war Mexican-American soldiers had been awarded more medals of distinction per capita than any other group in the country.

As World War II came to a close, segregation patterns in Los Angeles were well established. The city experienced a population boom and a restructuring of residential patterns. Demand for land around the civic center intensified. Land east of the Los Angeles River became even more attractive to developers. Freeway construction displaced thousands of Mexican Americans while downtown investors initiated efforts to redevelop Bunker Hill and other sectors of the city. "During the post-war years, fewer Russian Jews remained in Boyle Heights and City Terrace and most white residents migrated to midtown and West Los Angeles. By 1950, the Heights was no longer the integrated community that it had been in the past. And it began to rival Belvedere-Maravilla as the community with the heaviest concentration of Mexicans" (Acuña 1984:15).

Some local cultural and educational institutions were initiated during the wartime period. La Casa del Mexicano, a community center that would sponsor numerous important cultural functions, was dedicated in May 1945. The dedication was organized by the Mexican Federation of Belvedere and the Mothers of the Spanish American Soldier. East Los Angeles City College also opened, at first operating on the grounds of Garfield High School. This community college (eventually named East Los Angeles College) ultimately became immensely important for the education of returning Mexican-American veterans, in addition to later generations of eastside students.

The war had played a significant role in forming the political consciousness of the Mexican-American community in Los Angeles. The establishment of institutions and organizational activity would eventually plant the seeds of artistic self-identity and self-determination, especially in the social networks of musical life. The war period had become a reference point for the Mexican American.

> By the end of the War, the tone of the siege was established. Even before the Mexican American population had settled east of the Los Angeles River, interests in the downtown core determined the eventual fate of that community. Development moved a sizable portion of the Mexican population from the Plaza areas to Boyle Heights and unincorporated East Los Angeles. Mexican Americans lacked the capital and political power to influence important decisions such as zoning and freeway construction. Moreover, by the 1920s, the net-

work of businessmen, bankers, real estate developers, and powers like the *Los Angeles Times* was firmly entrenched. This "tidewater" occupation of centers gave this group an advantage that pioneer capitalists have always enjoyed. The absence of a committed English language press left working-class Mexicans vulnerable to the schemes of the downtown ruling class. During this period, the press was either hostile to or ignored the interests of the people east of the river. (Acuña 1984:19)

In 1943 the bracero program became another important element of Mexican society in Los Angeles. Under this program, Mexican workers were permitted to enter the United States and work by legal agreement with Mexico. Not all braceros worked on farms; by 1945 more than 65,000 were working on railroads (Acuña 1972:146). Although labor shortages diminished after the war, the bracero program continued. Contract negotiations with the Mexican government deteriorated, however, and in 1948 the United States effectively opened the border in order to import a needed labor supply. Between 1947 and 1949 alone 142,000 undocumented workers were certified, whereas only 74,600 braceros were hired by contract from Mexico (Acuña 1972:147). The bracero program "proved nationalistically humiliating. . . . The Mexican government did not have the power to end racial and religious discrimination; Mexicans performed the most menial work; and even many of Mexico's skilled workers bribed officials for the privilege of becoming a temporary migrant" (García y Griego 1973:1949).

Notes

1. Although the original name of Los Angeles has been cited as both "El Pueblo de Nuestra Señora la Reina de Los Angeles de Porciúncula" and "El Pueblo de Nuestra Señora la Reina de Los Angeles," the point of controversy is clarified in Kelsey (1977), Treutlein (1977), and Ríos-Bustamante and Castillo (1986:36).
2. A portion of Arévalo's variations of Paganini's *Carnaval de Venise* is reproduced in Stevenson (1988a:28–33).
3. This press quote is extracted from a notice in the *New York World,* a copy of which is included in the photograph archive file of Marie Azpiroz at the Southwest Museum. The date has not been recorded.
4. Transcribed and translated by Guillermo Hernández and Yolanda Zepeda. See Hernández (n.d.). Folklyric LP 9021/Arhoolie Records. Although the year 1926 has been cited as the year that "El lavaplatos" was originally recorded, the

19 May 1930 date seems to be well substantiated according to the personal collections of Zak Salem and Chris Strachwitz (personal communication). Both individuals reported that the date is cited in Spottswood (1990). Salem's collection of recordings also confirmed Jesús Osorio as the composer of "El lavaplatos." In the Public Broadcasting System video *The Ballad of an Unsung Hero* (see bibliography), credit is erroneously given to Pedro J. González as the composer.

5. Chicho and Chencho were part of the Los Madrugadores radio program, which consisted of a cycle of musical artists. The group that recorded during the 1930s under the name Los Madrugadores usually included Víctor and Jesús Sánchez and Fernando Linares.

6. Transcribed and translated by Silviano Barba, Pepi Plowman, and the staff of the Latin American Library, Oakland, California. Folklyric LP 9004/Arhoolie Records. See Hernández (n.d.) and Strachwitz (discography).

7. According to Sonnichsen (n.d.), at least six corridos were written about Juan Reyna. He provides substantial historical data on two of them: "Corrido de Juan Reyna," composed by Luis M. Banuelos and recorded by Los Hermanos Banuelos on the Vocalion label (ca. 1930), by Roca & Amador on Columbia (ca. 1930), and by González (Pedro J.) and Hernández on Okeh (ca. 1931); and "Suicidio de Juan Reyna," composed by F. Galindo and recorded by Nacho y Justino on Vocalion (ca. 1931) (also recorded as "La muerte de Juan Reyna" by Los Cancioneros de Chihuahua on Columbia in 1931).

8. C. V. Rude was the defense attorney.

9. Eugene W. Blalock was the assistant district attorney.

10. Transcribed and translated by Silviano Barba, Pepi Plowman, and the staff of the Latin American Library, Oakland, California. Folklyric LP 9004/Arhoolie Records. See Hernandez (n.d.) and Strachwitz (discography).

11. See note 10.

12. The latter three names were provided by Zak Salem in personal correspondence.

13. Data on Adelina García were extracted from an interview conducted by the author in 1985.

Misión de San Gabriel Arcangel de los Temblores, by Ferdinand Deppe, 1831. Sketch depicts the Corpus Christi Processional that took place in June 1828. Photograph by Max Bruensteiner, 1955. Courtesy of the Franciscan Fathers, Santa Barbara Mission Library Archives.

Franciscan Father Narcisco Durán directing Indian neophyte musicians. Sketch by A. Harmer in *The Missions and Missionaries of California,* Zephyrin Engelhardt (San Francisco: James H. Barry Co., 1915), 453.

"La Súplica," an original piece composed by Miguel S. Arévalo in the Cuban *habanera* style. The Mexican-born composer/guitarist Arévalo lived and worked in Los Angeles for three decades after his move to the city in 1871.

"La Noche 'sta Serena." Published song sheet from the Lummis/Farwell collaboration *Spanish Songs of Old California*. This example was taken from a Lummis-produced recording of Manuela García, who provided thirteen of the

fourteen recorded songs transcribed for the collection. © 1923 (renewed) by
G. Schirmer, Inc.; international copyright secured. Used by permission.

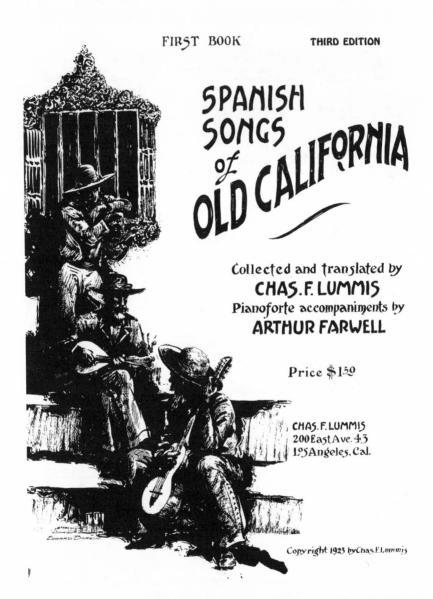

Spanish Songs of Old California. Front cover of the songbook published in 1923. The fourteen songs included in the collection were originally recorded on wax cylinders by Charles Lummis between 1904 and 1912. © 1923 (renewed) by G. Schirmer, Inc.; international copyright secured. Used by permission.

Chapter 2

Barrio Rhythm
Social Development since the Postwar Period

Both *rhythm* and *el barrio* are complexes of space, motion, and destination. As human expressions, they *arrive* somewhere; otherwise, they haven't fulfilled their purpose. In nature of their existence, however, they are infinite.

—STEVE LOZA

This chapter serves as a bridge to chapter 3, which specifically examines musical events of the same time period, from the postwar years to the present. The focus here is on sociopolitical developments rather than musical activity.

The Postwar Years

The post–World War II period was one of great expectations, especially among returning veterans who wanted to leave behind them the depression and ravages of war. Division of labor increased, and population growth led to the expansion of bureaucracies, big business, and other networks, all creating major structural changes in society and the community. "Once begun, this self-generating development made it increasingly difficult for groups with little power or resources to reach—much less influence—government" (Acuña 1984:22).

As the 1950s approached, changes in foreign relations and technology deeply affected international diplomacy and communication. The number of television sets in the country increased from 7 million in 1946 to 50 million in 1960. The beginning of the Cold War was reflected in the Truman Doctrine of 1947.

The Korean War began in 1950, and the McCarthy era followed. Like other citizens, Mexican Americans were subjected to loyalty oaths that questioned their patriotism. "Many progressives who were in a position to assist Mexican Americans in their quest for equality were purged out of government and trade unions" (Acuña 1984:23). In light of the socio-political changes under way, "many Chicanos were not prepared to return to their pre-war status of second class citizenship, and a growing emergence of ethnic consciousness took place" (Acuña 1984:24).

Mexican Americans in Los Angeles County were concentrated in the community of Belvedere-Maravilla until 1950, when Boyle Heights began to predominate. The local press—namely, the *Eastside Sun* and the *Belvedere Citizen*—discussed local concerns and interests such as land use, civil rights, efforts to enter mainstream politics, merchant concerns in relation to juvenile delinquency, and individual and organizational responses to McCarthyism. Cultural events received less attention in the press, but features on parades, organizational fiestas, dances, and events at the Casa del Mexicano did appear on an occasional basis.

In January 1948 the new campus of East Los Angeles College opened at its present location near Atlantic Boulevard and Floral Avenue, vacating its temporary facilities at Garfield High School. Simultaneously, thousands of people faced eviction in the East Los Angeles housing projects because of depressed economic conditions. Delinquency was a problem, and merchants complained about inadequate law enforcement. Gangs had begun not only to develop but also to proliferate as conflict among different barrios intensified.

The Korean War ended in 1952, and many Mexican-American GIs returned to the East Side, either alive or only as memories. The community expressed concern over the lack of public housing, the degree of drug abuse, and the extent of gang activity. With the postwar recession, some of the local press "announced the 'wetback' invasion, easily making scapegoats of undocumented workers" (Acuña 1984:40). Although the press continued to label the East Side as gang infested and violence ridden, some positive efforts to ease tensions took place. In conjunction with the First Street merchants, the sheriff's department initiated a basic car plan, intended to convert gangs into clubs. This program began the tradition of car clubs among eastside youth.

> In terms of government representation, the Mexican American was still far behind in the mainstream of U.S. politics in 1952. [Edward] Roybal was the sole Mexican American representative [member of the Los Angeles City Council]. He opposed the downtown powers and supported unpopular issues. Undoubtedly, his career suffered. Often, he alone defended civil liberties and the interests of the poor against the developers. His participation at the local level was crucial during these years. (Acuña 1984:43)

Although Mexican Americans did eventually start to achieve more po-litical representation, "they found themselves to be increasingly isolated from progressives in other parts of Los Angeles" (Acuña 1984:46). The plight of minorities in the United States had not yet become a major national issue, although the black population became active during the 1950s. The Mexican struggle for civil rights during this decade was not as dramatic as that of the blacks, for it was much more regional and many conflicts were not documented. Acuña states, however, that "it is a myth that nothing was happening in the Chicano communities east of the Los Angeles River in the 1950's" (1984:47).

In February 1956 the new campus of California State College, Los Angeles, was dedicated, located adjacent to the City Terrace and El Sereno sectors of the East Side. In May of the same year the college sponsored its first Institute of American Problems, which addressed the problems of Mexican Americans. Presentations to the institute were made both by Councilman Roybal and by Dr. Edward Lamas, president of the South-ern California Council of Mexican American Relations. In 1957 six UCLA students established the Council for Mexican American Education and founded a youth council panel, which raised scholarship funds for Mexican Americans who desired to enter the field of education.

Unemployment mounted in 1958 as manufacturers in Los Angeles and Orange counties terminated approximately 8,600 employees, especially in the auto, rubber, nonelectric machine, fabricated metal, and apparel indus-tries, all of which included heavy concentrations of Mexican Americans. The notion of incorporating the East Side gained momentum but never materialized. Had the movement been successful in 1959, East Los Angeles would have become the fifth largest city in the county.

The Chicano Movement

Motivated by hope for the future, self-determination, and the belief that they deserved to participate in the nation's institutions, Mexican Americans in the late 1950s began to recognize their political potential as a "sleep-ing giant." The black civil-rights struggle, the Cuban Revolution, and the battles against urban renewal projects politicized a great number of Chi-cano activists. The New Left emerged, mobilizing the activist population to form such groups as the National Committee for a Sane Nuclear Policy (SANE), the Student Nonviolent Coordinating Committee (SNCC), and the Students for a Democratic Society (SDS). Sit-ins and nonviolent pro-tests began to awaken a large segment of America.

Between 1950 and 1960 the Spanish-surname population doubled in Los Angeles County, increasing from 311,294 to 624,292. Approximately one-fourth of the Latino population lived in the East Side. The election of John F. Kennedy as president of the United States in 1960 had a significant impact on this community. The Kennedy campaign committee "was the first to nationally recognize the voting potential of Mexican Americans. It is also true that the Kennedy people, along with Chicano activists, helped to organize a regional network of 'Viva Kennedy clubs'" (Acuña 1984:84). Kennedy's charisma and his Roman Catholicism made him very attractive to a majority of the Mexican-American population. "The narrowness of the Kennedy victory only dramatized the importance and future potential of the Mexican American in the United States" (Acuña 1984:84).

Political progress in the community during the early 1960s did not come as rapidly as had been hoped. The 1960 California census illustrated the problems that lay ahead. Education statistics showed that Anglos completed a median 12.2 years of school, nonwhites 10.6, and Latinos 8.6. In Los Angeles County, only about 5 percent of Spanish-surname males were employed in professional or technical occupations; most worked in blue-collar or service categories.

The Chicano community's sense of a common political identity intensified during the early 1960s, in part because of the attention focused on blacks. More Chicanos became involved with the Mexican American Political Association (MAPA), "engaging themselves in political, rather than social and cultural solutions" (Acuña 1984:86). The Chicano movement's momentum politicized many of the sociocultural "solutions." Such political consciousness was especially apparent in visual art, literature, theater, and music.

In 1962 Councilman Roybal announced his candidacy for representative from the new 30th Congressional District; he won in a runoff election in November of that year. Roybal was the first Mexican-American representative from California in the U.S. House of Representatives. His vacated city council seat was not occupied by another Mexican American until the election of Richard Alatorre in 1986.

National events in 1963 had immense consequences in the Mexican-American community of Los Angeles. Unemployment was 12.1 percent among nonwhites but only 4.8 percent among whites. Civil-rights protest movements began across the country, especially among blacks who, together with whites, marched on Washington, D.C., alongside Martin Luther King, Jr., and became freedom riders in the South. "A new militancy emerged, with 'Black Pride' evolving towards the goal of 'Black Power'" (Acuña 1984:108).

President Kennedy was assassinated on 22 November 1963. Blacks and youths became more disillusioned, and student activists at the University of California–Berkeley began to receive national press coverage. "American students did not have a rich history of political activism, yet suddenly white middle-class college students appeared to be in revolt" (Acuña 1984:108). The escalation of the Vietnam War coincided with a rise in black militancy, and in August 1965 the Watts riots erupted. Located in south-central Los Angeles, Watts had been a Chicano barrio before it became a predominantly black ghetto. Fourteen thousand National Guardsmen and 1,600 police officers responded to the uprising. Entire blocks were burned and looted, and 4,000 persons were arrested. Of the thirty-four people killed during the riots, three were Mexican Americans.

Acuña notes that the effects of the Vietnam War and the Watts riots on Mexican Americans in Los Angeles have not been adequately documented. One reason, he surmises, is that the Los Angeles media began to focus on the black civil-rights movement and the Vietnam War. Presidents Kennedy and Johnson engaged east coast social planners with limited knowledge of Chicanos or other minorities; such planners thus "constructed irrelevant programs to fit familiar models" (Acuña 1984:110). Mexican-American scholars and activists found themselves in a stereotyped "War on Poverty" casting, molded by the black experience. Ironically, despite their common goals, competition between blacks and Chicanos for federal programs eventually ensued.

The unification of cultural identification and political goals was undeniably inspired and reinforced by the symbols of the black movement among Chicanos in the United States. César Chávez and the farmworkers movement represented the grass-roots extension of the Chicano movement. At the same time, a new immigration and naturalization act was passed; for the first time in U.S. history, a quota was placed on the number of Mexicans allowed to enter the country.

Education, especially at the secondary level, became another important issue among Mexican Americans during the late 1960s. In 1967 Julian Nava was elected to the Los Angeles Board of Education. A native of East Los Angeles and a graduate of Roosevelt High School and East Los Angeles Junior College, Nava earned his doctorate in history at Harvard University. He criticized the Los Angeles educational system and recommended an expansion of scholastic services. A school board ethnic survey revealed that the student population was 56 percent white, 20.8 percent black, and 19.2 percent Mexican/Latino. Although 138,210 Latino students were enrolled in Los Angeles schools, only 2.7 percent of the teachers (708) had Spanish surnames. For example, at Garfield High School, with a student body of 3,324, only six Latino teachers were employed. Nava's presence on the school board became an important form of representation for a community that was becoming more and more concerned about education.

Mexican-American youth had become actively involved in community affairs by 1968. With the escalation of the Vietnam War, funds for facilities such as teen posts were reduced, and concern for saving government programs increased in all sectors of Los Angeles. At the same time, autonomous youth groups emerged, including the Brown Berets, which represented a paramilitary style of political consciousness among young Chicano activists, and the United Mexican American Students (UMAS), an organization active on most Los Angeles college campuses. At California State College, Los Angeles, UMAS staged a major rally to oppose a tuition fee plan. At UCLA, UMAS sponsored a symposium on the educational inequity facing Mexican Americans that featured speakers Ralph Guzmán and Bert Corona. UMAS later became MEChA (Movimiento Estudiantil Chicano de Aztlán). As young people around the globe were protesting, the Mexican American also became aware of the need for greater political consciousness and awareness of national roots. *Aztlán,* the mythical Aztec homeland, became a symbol of self-determination throughout the Chicano Southwest. Marita Hernández makes the following comments in a *Los Angeles Times* series on southern California's Latino community:

> In the midst of the black civil rights movement and anti-war protest, a new generation of Mexican Americans took a hard look at their place in American society and grew angry at what they saw: the lowest per-capita income of any group in the country and one of the highest unemployment rates; half of their youngsters dropping out of high school and few making it to college; virtually no political representation, and young Chicanos dying in Vietnam at nearly twice the rate of others."
>
> Underlying it all, they discerned a lack of respect for their culture and little concern for their condition.
>
> The so-called silent minority had suffered in silence long enough. (Hernandez 1983:122)

A high secondary school dropout rate and underrepresentation in colleges and universities continued. The Chicano community criticized the school system, citing in particular the inadequate counseling system. Many students were advised to enroll in post–secondary school vocational programs instead of attending a university or pursuing a professional career. The community also questioned the content of curricula and the lack of courses on Mexican-American history and culture. Finally, in 1968, tension and controversy reached a climax with the "Eastside Blowouts." Students walked out of several eastside high schools, including Wilson, Roosevelt, Garfield, and Lincoln. Following the lead of Chicano students, blacks at Jefferson High School also staged walkouts. Congressman Roybal was the first politician to publicly support the students' objectives. During these local protests Martin Luther King, Jr., was assassinated, and the walkouts became a focus for national press attention. Thirteen students were indicted for conspiring to disturb the peace, and the case became a controversial issue in the community.

The Los Angeles Chicano movement reflected the general spirit of young people who rejected the term *Mexican American* in favor of *Chicano*, a word that symbolized defiance of the notions of cultural assimilation and represented an expression of pride, even though it was a derogatory word in many sectors, much like the word *black*, adopted by African Americans. In effect, Chicanos were evolving and creating their own sociopolitical ideology. Marita Hernández notes the sentiment of the time: "If the established institutions refused to open their doors to Chicanos, then Chicanos would build their own schools, publishing houses, political parties and facilities" (1983:122). Richard Cruz, a law student at Loyola University during the period of ferment and an East Los Angeles attorney today, also recalls that feeling of purpose: "We were young and naive and we really believed we were going to create a healthy, Chicano California, one big happy family. It was Aztlán, and we were really going to run with it" (Hernández 1983:122). Cruz estimated that during the late 1960s and early 1970s as many as 150,000 Mexican Americans participated in mass rallies and demonstrations in Los Angeles alone.

The Eastside Riots

Confrontations between eastside citizens and the police occurred more frequently as protest demonstrations continued and often involved shootings. A Chicano Moratorium took place on 29 August 1970. Approximately 20,000 antiwar demonstrators gathered in Belvedere Park. A theft of soft drinks at a liquor store near Laguna Park escalated into a confrontation between rally participants and the police, who fired tear gas canisters. One of the canisters was bulleted into the Silver Dollar Cafe, killing *Los Angeles Times* journalist and KMEX-TV news director Rubén Salazar. Two other persons were killed during the riot, and hundreds were arrested; property damage amounted to more than one million dollars. The local press condemned what was termed police aggression (Acuña 1984:203). In the spring of 1970 "the U.S. Civil Rights Commission issued a report, *Mexican Americans and the Administration of Justice in the Southwest.* The report documented the systematic abuse of Mexican Americans by law enforcement authorities and the lack of judicial justice for Chicanos. Another study, this one by the Equal Employment Opportunities Commission for the Colorado Civil Rights Commission, called the status of Chicanos a 'caste system'" (Acuña 1984:205).

A March for Justice moratorium was held in East Los Angeles on 31 January 1971. As the speeches ended, some participants went to the sheriff substation to protest police abuse. A riot ensued resulting in one death, fifty injuries, and eighty-eight arrests. Activists Rosalio Muñoz (student body president at UCLA) and David Sánchez (leader of the Brown Berets) turned their attention from antiwar demonstrations to La Marcha de la Reconquista, in which 500 Latinos marched from Calexico to Sacramento.

The Mexican-American population rose from 651,879 in 1960 to 1,228,594 in 1970, an increase of almost 90 percent. An ethnic survey of Los Angeles city schools showed that "minority" students were now the majority. Minority enrollment increased to 50.2 percent, of which 21.8 percent were Latino, 24.1 percent were black, and the remainder comprised other ethnic groups. It was projected that by the end of the 1970s the Chicano population would be double that of blacks and whites. The Office of Bilingual Education was established under the U.S. Office of Education, and by the late 1970s state and federal governments had invested 200 million dollars in bilingual education. The number of Chicano teachers also increased substantially. The Mexican American Business and Professional Men's Scholarship Association raised considerable funds and awarded substantial scholarship funds to Chicano students. Vikki Carr, the internationally celebrated singer, established her own scholarship program for Chicano college students, which continues to this day. Moreover, a spirit of cultural unity developed between Chicanos and other Latinos; many became members of the National Council of Spanish-Speaking Organizations.

Progress had been made since the postwar period. More Chicanos were entering government and the professions, although in proportion to the size of the Chicano population, the number was still low. In 1965 not one national Chicano organization existed; ten years later there were ten, advancing special interests such as affirmative action, bilingual education, and increased funding for various programs. Noteworthy among the defenders of the legal rights of Mexican Americans was the Mexican American Legal Defense and Education Fund (MALDEF). In 1970 the National Association for Chicano Studies was founded, dedicated to scholarship in an immensely rich human historical archive. Also prominent was the Association of Mexican American Educators.

These advances were soon undermined, however, by national events. "Most Chicano gains made in the 1960s eroded in the 70s" (Acuña 1984: 233). A recession and a changing labor market aggravated an already troubled economy. The only abundant jobs were those that paid wages below subsistence levels or those in agriculture. Educational progress had been made, but still only one-fourth of the eastside Chicano population had a high school diploma. In 1975 only about one-third of Latinos nationally had jobs in expanding industries. The high school dropout rate among Chicanos in Los Angeles was about 50 percent, nearly five times that of blacks.

Despite these organizational setbacks farmworker movements continued to be active in the Midwest, Texas, Arizona, and other southwestern states. "California remained the scene of the largest and most dramatic struggle, since its size and industrialized agriculture demanded a large response" (Acuña 1984:234). The Mexican/Chicano population of Los Angeles supported César Chávez in his defense of the rights of farmworkers and his organization's opposition to state measures considered detrimental to the effort to unionize farmworkers. Boycotts were common, especially against the grape and lettuce industries in general and such corporations as Gallo, Safeway, Coors, and Nestle in particular.

The Undocumented Worker

The Chicano movement greatly influenced national attitudes and policies toward undocumented workers. Chicano opposition to deportation of workers back to Mexico coupled with early research by Chicano scholars led to extensive study of the phenomenon, which was, in effect, a paradox. Chicanos were members of both the legal and illegal Mexican population. Eventually, they would either have to choose sides or perhaps play the role of mediator.

Much time and energy were invested in the question of illegal workers. Trade unionists no longer felt that the Mexican worker constituted a threat to their own jobs. A small number of Chicano organizations were "able to slow down repressive immigration legislation at the local, state, and national levels" (Acuña 1984:235). Finally, and perhaps most important, the issue created the necessary confrontation between the Chicano and Mexican national and international sectors in terms of support, communication, and interdependence. Chicano and Mexican scholars and activists therefore applied additional political pressure on the Mexican government to address the issue of the rights of Mexican citizens. This Chicano effort thus became an important element in the area of U.S.-Mexican relations; scholars and diplomats on both sides of the border began to assess the political and economic effects of international labor on immigration.

In 1970 Mexican president Luis Echeverría Alvarez toured the United States and conferred with Chicano leaders. He unexpectedly expressed his concern about the treatment of undocumented Mexican workers in the United States, setting a precedent that was followed by later Mexican presidents.

Unity among artistic organizations was encouraged by the emergence of two Latino actor/actress associations, Justicia and Nosotros. The two groups had similar goals but different tactics. Ray Andrade directed Justicia, and Ricardo Montalbán headed Nosotros, which was more moderate, although still political. Andrade intensely criticized the motion picture and television industries, spearheading protests against commercials considered offensive. Among these were the Frito Bandido series and those of the Elgin watch company, which pictured Emiliano Zapata, the Mexican revolutionary and agrarian reform leader, as having an urge to purchase one of the company's products. In contrast, Nosotros sought to establish a Latino network in the entertainment industry with the intention of becoming a permanent participant in the Hollywood mainstream. Specific Latino/ Chicano artistic projects were organized and supported. Increased industry work and opportunities for Latino entertainers, who were extremely underrepresented, became a prime objective.

The visual arts also became expressions of both cultural and political identity and alienation. The Eastside Mural Project was expanded in 1972, and the walls of Estrada Courts were among the first to be painted. Chicano art was exhibited at various festivals in Los Angeles and throughout the United States and Mexico. Professional muralists, such as the "Streetscapers of East Los Angeles," were commissioned. The Mechicano Art Center was established in 1971, and Plaza de la Raza at Lincoln Park received approval of its plans to construct new facilities dedicated to the arts of the Mexican/Chicano people of Los Angeles.

As the women's movement became a national issue, Chicanas began to question society's ignorance of their role in the Chicano movement. La Casa del Mexicano held a conference entitled "Is Society Meeting the Needs of the Chicana?" Workshops were conducted by Mariana Hernández of California State University, Los Angeles, and by Alicia Escalante, director of Católicos por La Raza. The Chicana Service Action Center, the Hispanic Women's Council, and La Comisión Femenil Mexicana Nacional were also established.

Acuña evaluates the early 1970s with the following commentary: "In the face of national recessions, conditions worsened and the level of activism declined east of the river. As was true in the 1950s, however, changes were under way that would affect future generations. Something was happening in East L.A. Even if activism had slowed down during this period of bad economy and resurfacing bigotry, it had not died" (1984:235).

The 1980s

In 1978 *New West* magazine published a special issue titled "The Decade of the Chicano: California's Emerging Third World Majority." In the lead article, Jonathan Kirsch referred to a statement that Mervin Dymally, then lieutenant governor, made to the Mexican American Political Association (MAPA): "If the present trends continued, the emerging ethnic group would constitute more than half the population of California by 1990, and California would become the country's first third world state" (Kirsch 1978:35).

Dymally's prediction has basically become fact in Los Angeles. Immigration laws have been a major political issue in the Chicano/Latino community since 1975. The political climate has also changed considerably since then. As affirmative action programs and community minority projects began to flourish and pay dividends, a backlash was also evident from sectors of the mainstream population. For example, in the highly publicized Bakke decision, the court upheld a medical school applicant's contention that federal quota systems in higher education constituted reverse discrimination. Claiming he was denied admission to the University of California–Davis medical school while minority candidates with lower entrance exam scores were admitted, James Bakke eventually appealed his rejection and was admitted to medical school.

Within the last decade, change has been reflected in the widening network and role diversification of Chicano politicians. Edward Roybal still sits in the U.S. House of Representatives. After serving in the state assembly, Art Torres was elected state senator representing Boyle Heights. Richard Alatorre was elected assemblyman for the Highland Park district and then to the Los Angeles City Council. Joining him later on the city council was Gloria Molina, who was eventually elected as a county supervisor. Other elected officials from Los Angeles County included Alex García, Esteban Torres, Matthew Martínez, Larry González, Lucille Roybal-Allard, Charles Calderón, and Richard Polanco.

The number of Chicano incumbents in city, state, and federal administrative posts also grew substantially. For much of Tom Bradley's tenure as mayor of Los Angeles, Grace Montañez Davis was the city's deputy mayor.

The implementation of bilingual education programs became more systematic throughout the school district, and Chicano studies is part of the curriculum at major universities and colleges. The number of Chicano/Chicana faculty at those institutions has increased, as have Chicano university enrollments, largely because of special admission and financial assistance programs. Progress has been slow, however, and these numbers still fall short of the percentage of Chicanos in the population at large.

Population remained the phenomenal conscience of comparative statistics and census results. Throughout the last decade, Los Angeles has remained the largest Mexican population center outside Mexico City. Additionally, 29 percent of Hispanics living in the United States live in California.

According to some optimistic business projections (in 1978) the Chicano Community in California boasted [a median] family income of more than $13,000, an annual spendable income of $7.7 billion, and a growing middle class of 400,000 households. A rising curve of Hispanic births and immigration, a renaissance of community development in the barrios, a new level of political sophistication among young Chicanos in law, government and education assures them of a decisive role in any political scenario over the next generation. (Kirsch 1978:35)

By 1988, the population of Los Angeles County was 8.4 million. Projections made by the Los Angeles County Department of Health Services in 1987 estimated that by 1990 over 3 million of this growing population would be Latino, the majority of Mexican extraction. California alone accommodates about one-third of all immigrants entering the United States. Fifty-five percent of those entering California settle in Los Angeles County. In 1986, Latin American and Asian immigrants each accounted for more than 40 percent of all immigrants entering the United States (U.S. Immigration and Naturalization Service *Annual Statistical Report* 1986).

At current trends, California will clearly be a minority state by the year 2020. In fact, equal proportions of majority whites and minorities are expected by the year 2005. *The much larger share of minorities will be of Latino origins.* Several factors of population growth and change are attributed to the race and ethnic shift in California.
    . . . In the 1980 census, 67 percent of Californians identified themselves as white; 19 percent of Spanish origin; 7 percent as black; 6 percent as Asian and Pacific Islander; and 1 percent as American Indian and Alaskan native. *By 2020, Latinos will number approximately 12 million in the state,* while whites will number 16 million; Asians and others will reach 5 million and blacks will number about 3.2 million. Whites will thus occupy 44 percent of the population while minorities will take 56 percent. *More than one-third of the state's inhabitants will be Latino. (Los Angeles County Latino Community Profile* 1988:4; emphasis in original)

One of the most rapidly expanding industries of the last decade has been the media entertainment business. Local Spanish-language television station KMEX started operations in 1963 under the direction of Daniel Villanueva. According to current estimates provided by the station, 818,000 different households view KMEX each week, with an average of 101,000 per quarter-hour. Currently, the station is an affiliate of the Miami-based Univision National Television Network. KVEA, another UHF station, first aired in 1985. Originally operated by New York–based Reliance Group Holdings, Inc., the station is currently owned by the Telemundo Group,

Inc., another national Spanish-language network also based in New York. Statistics provided by KVEA show close to 600,000 different household viewings per week among more than 1 million Hispanic television households in Los Angeles. National cable network Galavisión began operations in the United States in 1979. Another station, KWHY, operates in English on a daytime basis and in Spanish during evenings and weekend midmornings. Spanish broadcasts began in 1989, and estimates provided by the station indicate a 20 percent audience among approximately 1 million Hispanic television households. It was also estimated that 80 percent of the Hispanic television audience watches Spanish-language television.

In terms of Spanish-language radio, six principal stations currently operate in Los Angeles. KALI, launched in 1952, estimates that the station is listened to daily by about 60 percent of the Hispanics in Los Angeles. KWKW, which began operations in 1942, was programming exclusively in Spanish by 1962, when it was bought by its current owner, Howard Kalmenson. Station estimates count about 1 million listeners daily in Los Angeles and Orange counties. KWKW also broadcasts all Dodger baseball games. KLVE (FM) and KTNQ (AM) are both owned by KLVE Radio Broadcasting, Inc. Station statistics approximate weekly combined audiences at well over 1 million. KKHJ, one of the most recent enterprises, began in April 1990. Another station, Radio Express, broadcasts from Mexico City and transmits to Los Angeles via KXPRES.

In addition to broadcast media, dissemination of information and advertisement takes place through a variety of media genres and enterprises, and a wide range of Latino/Chicano magazines, radio stations, and public information–related businesses has developed. Additionally, there has been more development in Spanish-speaking and Hispanic-oriented special interest departments in the mainstream print media, entertainment and recording industries, and advertising and public relations enterprises. The Hispanic Academy of Media Arts and Sciences (HAMAS) and the Hispanic Musicians Association were organized in the early 1980s. The number of academic and scholarly publications related to Chicanos and Latinos in the United States has increased regularly during the past decade.

In spite of the continuous diversification and integration of the media, the entertainment industry, academia, and the government and private sectors in general, an important question remains: to what extent will the Latino subculture assimilate into the mainstream? Some will answer that this will never occur to the extent it has with other U.S. minorities. Mexico is simply too close—geographically, historically, economically, and in the final analysis, culturally.

Chapter 3

A Chronicle of Musical Life
Los Angeles, 1945–90

> I go home and I get fed . . . not just food, but life. My life. My family, my neighborhood, my culture, and true inspiration. I go home and my dad's listening to Mexican music—all kinds of Mexican music—*corridos revolucionarios,* Javier Solís, Alberto Vásquez, Rocío Dúrcal, Vicente Fernández, Jorge Negrete, now, Linda Ronstadt—you name it. It's his music and his reality . . . his *value.* That's what the whole trip is . . . the trip home—a jump into my own reality—or as Danny Valdez might say, "A Real Reality."
>
> Arroz con pollo, carne asada, Sunday's Mass, my mother's rightful nagging, and my father's explosions . . . Reflection . . .
>
> —STEVE LOZA

As World War II was coming to an end, musical life in the Mexican community of Los Angeles continued to be active. Performances by local musicians and other entertainers, films, and theatrical presentations from various Latin American countries were an integral part of the musical scene.

Available sources documenting this musical period include newspapers, popular magazines, and literature. In addition, oral histories of the major participants can be particularly useful, supplementing newspaper accounts with detailed, critical information about the artists and their artistic enterprises. The principal oral history source for this chapter was a series of interviews with Lalo Guerrero (see chap. 4 for a profile of Guerrero).

The principal documentary source for the information presented in this chapter was *La Opinión,* a Spanish-language newspaper published in Los Angeles since 1926 and the oldest Spanish-language newspaper in the United States. Founded in 1913 by Ignacio Lozano, Sr., *La Opinión* originally headquartered in San Antonio, Texas, under the name *La Prensa.* Ignacio Lozano, Jr., became editor-in-chief in 1953, and his son, José Ignacio Lozano, is the paper's current publisher. *La Opinión* is now the nation's fastest-growing newspaper.

A section of the newspaper called "Mundo Artístico y Social" included articles on music, theater, dance, and film. Weekly and daily columns reviewed not only what was being imported from Mexico to entertain the Mexican community but also local productions. The paper also included advertisements for current entertainment in the Los Angeles area in general. Reading the pages of *La Opinión* gives a sense of the interaction of world politics, local events, and internationally distributed Latin music and film in the Los Angeles Mexican community. The changing concerns of the newspaper during the years following World War II also reflect the changing profile of the Spanish-speaking community. The newspaper originally served Mexicans who were established in Los Angeles and involved with the local artistic scene. The current readership is primarily new immigrants from various Latin American countries who are interested in the international Latin music scene and who are not necessarily familiar with the local musical network of bands and performers.

1945–50

An example of *La Opinión*'s coverage of popular entertainment in Spanish is an article in the 7 January 1945 edition announcing "la pareja ideal" (the ideal couple)—Jorge Negrete and María Elena Márquez, who had become popular in the film *Así se quiere en Jalisco*. The pair was being featured again in the motion picture *Rebelde* showing at the Teatro Monterrey on Whittier Boulevard. Negrete, an internationally recognized Mexican singer, had recently performed in Havana and then returned to Mexico, where he was preparing for another tour to Puerto Rico in February. During his previous visit to Puerto Rico he had donated the proceeds of his concert to the U.S. National War Fund.

The popular Mexican singer Tito Guízar appeared at one of the *serenatas* that took place on Sundays at the Placita adjacent to Olvera Street in downtown Los Angeles. Another popular Mexican singer, Celia Martínez, appeared at the Embassy Auditorium in November 1944. *La Opinión* simultaneously headlined the "Tercer Ataque a Tokio [third attack on Tokyo]."

Interest in the contemporary music of the period often focused on Latin American composers visiting Los Angeles. The Brazilian composer Hector Villa-Lobos conducted a classic work by Werner Janssen as well as his own music in a program at the Philharmonic Auditorium on 26 November 1944. A music critic commented on the prolific style of Villa-Lobos, writing that his "música ha invadido el mundo en estos últimos años [his music has invaded the world in recent years]" (*La Opinión*, 26 Nov. 1944:5). Violinist Nicasio Jurado presented a concert at the Philharmonic Auditorium on 22 January 1945, where he performed works of Henry Eccles, Bach, Gluck, and Debussy.

Mexican composer Carlos Chávez, whom *La Opinión* described as "uno de los más grandes valores musicales de México [one of the greatest musical talents of Mexico]" (7 Jan. 1945:3), conducted a concert on 11 January 1945 at the Philharmonic. The concert was devoted exclusively to Chávez's music, performed by the Los Angeles Philharmonic Orchestra. The concert was well received by the public; in the January 14 issue of *La Opinión,* Samuel Martí, the Mexican violinist and musicologist, commended Chávez's performance. Martí wrote, "sus ritmos y melodías emocionaron y entusiasmaron poderosamente al conocedor público que las escuchó [his rhythms and melodies moved and captivated the audience]" (3). Martí was also founder of "Conciertos Martí," chamber recitals that increased recognition of Mexican artistic values in the United States and transmitted American artistic endeavors to Mexico.

From late November to early January the Padua Hills Theatre in Claremont staged a six-week engagement of "Las Posadas," musical acts or drama that depicted religious observances during the nine days before Christmas traditionally celebrated by Mexicans.

Dance artists appearing at the Philharmonic Auditorium included Argentinita and Pilar López, accompanied by the widely recognized Spanish guitarist Carlos Montoya. At Teatro Liberty, located downtown, the Mexican film *Soy puro mexicano* was screened for a limited appearance. The film featured actor Pedro Armendáriz and a special appearance by Mexican singer Pedro Vargas, who interpreted songs by composers Ernesto Cortázar and Pedro Galindo.

On 3 February 1945 *La Opinión* contained, among other things, an article discussing Frank Sinatra's musical success through substantial radio exposure, an advertisement announcing the Spanish guitarist Andrés Segovia's upcoming concert at the Philharmonic, and a full-page ad announcing fourteen Mexican artists in six "actos espectaculares." Featured in these acts were Andrés Huesca y Sus Costeños, who interpreted musical forms such as *canciones,* rumbas, *bailes,* and *sones;* Los Cantantes de América; Sally Camacho; T. Chispa Tapón; and Lino Carrillo.

A headline on February 8 announced "Roosevelt, Churchill, y Stalin en el Mar Negro [Roosevelt, Churchill and Stalin in the Black Sea]." On February 11, Mexican composer and singer Lucrecia Teruel, recently arrived from Mexico, made her debut in Los Angeles on a Spanish-language radio program hosted by David Orozco. Samuel Martí, mentioned previously, gave a violin recital at El Monte High School in El Monte, an eastside suburb of Los Angeles, for an audience of more than five hundred aficionados. Various Mexican films were being screened in Los Angeles, including *Ay Jalisco no te rajes,* named after the well-known *ranchera* song and starring Jorge Negrete.

The syndicated radio program "Cadena de las Américas" was broadcast from New York to Los Angeles each Sunday, Wednesday, and Thursday. Eva Garza, better known as La Novia de la Canción, was contracted to sing on these shows. The Mexican singer Miguelito García, from Chihuahua, Mexico, who was featured on the show "El Despertador," was also popular on local radio.

A romantic musical film, *Caballo y rey,* distributed by Azteca Films, was being screened at the Mason Theater on Soto Street. The film score featured popular music including rumbas and "bellas canciones." *La Opinión* ran several favorable reviews of the film. In the Teatros Quinn cinema chain, Jorge Negrete and Armando Ledesma were starring in *El peñón de las ánimas,* described in one review as "una bella comi-musical en la que se establece hermosa comupetencia entre la música folklórica mexicana y la argentina [a lovely musical comedy that establishes beautiful competitive interchange between Mexican and Argentinian folk music]" (*La Opinión,* 12 March 1945:5).

On February 25 a new musical organization, Patronato Cultural Mexicano (Mexican Cultural Patronage), announced its formation, proposing to institutionalize recognition of traditional Mexican artistic values. Additionally, the organization planned to facilitate grants to promote the development of new artists of Mexican origin. According to an article in *La Opinión,* the new organization:

> . . . tiende a resolver uno de los problemas más serios de todos los padres de familia, el de orientar en una forma accesible y práctica a nuestra juventud y hacerle consciente de su propio valor y responsabilidad para la comunidad. Por esta razón todo aquel de ascendencia mexicana debe por patriotismo y amor propio hacer acto de presencia en los festivales del Patronato y a darle todo su apoyo moral y económico.
>
> [. . . it aims to resolve one of the most serious problems of all parents, that of educating our young people in an accessible and practical manner and making them aware of their own value and responsibility to the community. For this reason, anyone of Mexican heritage should, out of patriotism and self-respect, assist the festivities of the organization by giving it complete moral and financial support.] (*La Opinión* 4 March 1945:4)

Festival recitals were planned for March 10 and 11 at Garfield and Polytechnic High Schools.

During the same period a Festival Cultural was organized by the Mexican American Movement (MAM), a Mexican-American student and young adult association, to raise funds for a recreational park for Mexican children and display the Mexican community's artistic talents. On March 23 at the Embassy Auditorium the American Anti-Prejudice Society, Inc., produced the Trío Mexicano in a Concierto Internacional, directed by the Rev. C. Townsend Tucker. Singer Tito Guízar presented another concert in Los Angeles at the Orpheum Theater in March 1945.

Las Hermanas Padilla had continued to sing and record and also toured extensively throughout the 1940s, performing in Venezuela, Mexico, and New York, where they were known as the "Mexican Andrews Sisters." They were the first California *dueto* to become popular in Mexico and later appeared on national television, attracting a large American following. Originally recording for Vocalion Records, they were subsequently contracted by Discos Columbia under an agreement to record thirty-two records per year.

During the bracero program of the 1940s, the Mexican Consulate, which provided Mexican entertainment for the workers, asked the Padilla sisters to sing at the bracero camps. The duet's popularity increased with the introduction of the jukebox (*sinfonola*) in clubs, bars, and restaurants throughout the Mexican sectors of the city. The *sinfonolas* often contained more 78 r.p.m. records by the Padilla sisters than by any other artists. The Padillas also performed at the Million Dollar Theater, where they were featured in American variety shows along with such stars as Red Skelton, Abbot and Costello, and the Ink Spots. (The American variety format continued until 1949, when management at the Million Dollar changed.)

In 1945 Margarita Padilla married Mexican composer Víctor Cordero, who had not yet attained the international fame that would eventually come his way for his immortal *corridos* such as "Juan Charrasqueado" and "Gabino Barrera." The couple met through Silvestre Vargas, the director of the renowned Mariachi Vargas de Tecalitlán. A year later, María Padilla married Memo Quintero, a violinist with the Mariachi Vargas. After their marriage, María and Memo began performing and recording together. They recorded on Azteca Records, founded by Trinidad Pelaiz, and became known as Dueto Azteca. Pelaiz's career in the music industry had begun with Mauricio Calderón, owner of La Casa de Música. On Calderón's death, Pelaiz assumed management of the record store and incorporated the Azteca label. When Dueto Azteca began to record on Imperial and Columbia records, the Azteca label was discontinued.

Las Hermanas Padilla's musical activity subsided after their marriages in the mid-1940s, but the Mexican public continued to listen to their records for many years thereafter. After the death of Víctor Cordero, Margarita continued to live in Mexico City; María and Memo (who died in 1987) settled close to East Los Angeles in Montebello. One of the duet's last public performances was at the Teatro Blanquita in East Los Angeles (Boyle Heights) in a program billed as "Homenaje Artístico a las Hermanas

Padilla" [artistic homage to the Padilla sisters] in November 1980 (Sonnichsen 1984).

Movies starring Jorge Negrete continued to be screened throughout the Spanish-speaking quarters of Los Angeles during 1946, two major films being *Tierra de pasiones* and *Perjura*. Celso Vega y Sus Muchachos broadcast from New York on the CBS radio syndicate. On June 6, *La Opinión* announced that a "nueva película de espíritu patriótico en que interviene Ricardo Montalbán será estrenada el lunes [a new film with patriotic spirit featuring Ricardo Montalbán will be premiered on Monday]" (5). The Revista Típica Mexicana, a musical extravaganza featuring a variety of popular musical styles from Mexico and choreographed by Miguel Lerdo de Tejada, Jr., appeared at the Shrine Auditorium.

On June 13 the Mexican film star María Félix was appearing in the film *La Monja Alférez* at Teatro Monterrey. An advertisement in *La Opinión* announced the appearance of Chuy Reyes and his orchestra along with thirty-five Latin American artists. Titled "La Revista Musical de las Américas" [Musical Review of the Americas], the show ran from June 12 through June 16 at the Wilshire Ebell Theater and featured artists such as Luz García, "exponente del ritmo" [exponent of rhythm], and Cuban singer Bertica Serrano. A headline in *La Opinión* on the final day of the review read, "Amenaza a los Mexicanos de Los Angeles el K.K.K. [K.K.K. Threatens the Mexicans of Los Angeles]."

Scheduled for 15 August 1947 at the Hollywood Bowl was a major concert by bandleader Xavier Cugat, "El Rey de la Rumba," and his *orquesta típica* performing a variety of Latin American music that he had arranged during his recent tour through Latin America. The Mexican tenor Urcelay, comedian Mario Moreno (Cantinflas), and the renowned Mexican composer Agustín Lara accompanied Cugat.

Carlos Molina and his orchestra appeared at the Aragon Cafe in Ocean Park on August 15 through August 17. Molina played a significant role in introducing the tango and rumba to Californians. Reviews of the concert raved about the high quality of the Latin American musical interpretations and the standing-room-only crowd. *La Opinión* announced the performance of the official Vatican choir at the Hollywood Bowl on September 21 and 22.

During the summer of 1947, free Sunday concerts took place at various parks in Los Angeles, many of them organized to appeal to the Latin population of the city. On Sunday, August 24, for example, an *orquesta típica* under the direction of José Córdova Cantú performed at Griffith Park while a symphonic band performed at Exposition Park.

In August a special program celebrated the anniversary of the founding of the Mexican Civil Rights Association. Coordinated by Margo Albert, a prominent actress in the Mexican community, the program featured the Latin orchestra of locally popular bandleader Phil Carreón.

La Fiesta de la Canción was produced on September 11 in the Mason Theater to recognize Latin artists in Los Angeles and to present musical achievement awards based on the results of a song contest. Participating artists included Carmen Estrabeau, Rodolfo Hoyos, Lupita Cavazos, Loló Pardinas, Fernando Rosas, Aurora Muñoz, Carolina López, María L. Vásquez, Profesor Carlos de Hoyos, Hermanas Mendoza, Ignacio Flores Galindo, and Manuel García Matus (Matos?).

Carlos Chía and the orchestra of Phil Carreón celebrated Mexican independence day (September 15) at the Avalon Cafe. On September 29 the Mason Theater presented a musical review that included artists Ana María González, Los Tex Mex, Rosalinda, Vivian and Corina Díaz, and Alejandro Montenegro. After performing at the same theater in October, guitarist Ortiz Villacorta recorded a number of his original compositions for a Hollywood recording company.

On 7 February 1949, *La Opinión* reported on the successful progress of La Orquesta de la Iglesia de Santa Isabel, formed under the direction of Francisco Valadez. Community support was sought and rehearsals were scheduled for Wednesdays, Thursdays, and Fridays at the church, which was located at Boyle Avenue and Opal Street.

The Trio Janitzio returned to the Wilshire Ebell Theater for a five-day concert engagement from February 11 through February 15. Appearing along with the Mexican trio was Celso Hurtado and his internationally recognized marimba orchestra from Guatemala. Dancers Tavo y Esperanza and pianist Celso de Soyos also performed. During the same period local radio presented "El Programa Todds" with soprano Lupita Cavazos and tenor Juan Enríquez, accompanied by Carlos Chía's highly respected orchestra. *La Opinión* described the program as "uno de los más bien combinados programas de radio que se han puesto en las estaciones locales [one of the best integrated radio programs that have been aired in the local stations]."

The headline of the February 18 edition of *La Opinión* read "Eisenhower previene a la nación [Eisenhower Warns the Nation]." A program of "música hispana," predominantly Mexican, was presented at the Menorah Center at 961 Alma Street in East Los Angeles on February 23. Councilman Edward Roybal, the principal speaker, directed his comments to the Mexican community of Los Angeles.

On Friday, February 20, the front page of *La Opinión* carried the headline, "México enviará braceros a E.E.U.U [Mexico will send Braceros to U.S.]." Las Hermanitas Mendoza returned to Los Angeles from New York, where they had been performing at the Flamingo and El Chico clubs.

During their appearance at the latter, they met Jorge Negrete and Carlos Arruza, both of whom were visiting New York City. Las Hermanitas Mendoza had begun to sing boleros and attained such success that they revised their repertoire to include only boleros. The sisters were also particularly admired for their traditional dress of "la china poblana."

On Sunday, February 29, local Mexican tenor Rubén Reyes was appearing at the Avedon Ballroom. Reyes recorded exclusively for the Taxco Recording Company. On March 10, at the Million Dollar Theater, El Trío Janitzio, Las Mascotitas, and Pancho, Margarita, and Celso de Soyos were warmly received. On the same date, a newspaper article announced that Mexican actor Pedro Armendáriz had been given the leading role in the film *Juan Charrasqueado,* based on the well-known Mexican *corrido* composed by Víctor Cordero.

El "pianista jarocho," Chuy Reyes, who was performing nightly at Ciros, was profiled in the March 14 edition of *La Opinión:* "Prolífico lleno de ardor, sabe arreglar la música afrocubana en jazz moderno [Prolific and passionate, he has command of arranging Afro-Cuban music in the modern jazz style]" (5). Reyes was a talented musician from the Huastec region of Mexico. In 1925, at the age of five, his parents brought him to Mexico City. Two years later he was enrolled at the Conservatorio de México and subsequently received a scholarship for five years of musical study in Germany. His American debut came in 1933 at the Chicago World's Fair. In 1940 he organized his own orchestra and was contracted by Earl Carroll to work in the Hollywood Theater for two years. Reyes later appeared at the Mocambo Club and El Copacabana in Chicago. He also scored films, such as *Panamérica, Rhumba Rhythm,* and *Freddy, Step Out.*

Don Ramón Cruz hosted a bilingual program of Latin American music Monday through Friday evenings on KXLA in Pasadena. It is believed that Cruz was instrumental in the development of singer Andy Russell's musical career.

Mexican tenor Pedro Vargas came to Los Angeles in July 1949 to appear at the Mason Theater, at Twelfth and Main streets, for a short engagement. Immensely popular throughout Latin America, Vargas's orchestra played arrangements that reflected his musical versatility. A full-page ad in *La Opinión* listed the artists performing at the Mason Theater concert: Heriberto Alcalá, Adelina García, Armandita Chirot, Las Hermanas Flores, Beatriz y Mando, Luz Jardey, and Gloria Sánchez.

Guitarist Luis Elorriaga gave a concert at a theater located at 4775 Vancouver Avenue that was acclaimed as a great success. Pianist Leonel de León, tenor Juan de Dios Orantez, and violinist Abraham Chávez (who later became director of the El Paso Symphony) also performed. The film *Angelitos negros,* a musical starring Pedro Infante and Emilia Guiu, was presented at the Mason Theater. Radio, film, and television actress and singer Dora Del Rio broadcast for Voz de América (Voice of America) and also recorded for various record companies in Latin America. Showing at Teatro California was the film *Maclovia,* starring María Félix and Pedro Armendáriz.

On Saturday, 13 August 1949, the Dueto Fresquez Durán sang at a benefit concert for La Iglesia de María Auxiliadora on Darwin Street and 20th Avenue. Another benefit concert, this one for La Iglesia de Talpa, took place at Teatro Mayor on Monday, August 22. La Banda de Música de Talpa performed for a week at the theater. A July 2 concert of Mexican music at Hollenbeck Park, located on 4th and St. Louis streets, featured singer José Córdova Cantú accompanied by a mariachi and other performers. Throngs of aficionados filled the small park.

María Luisa Landín, accompanied by Fernando M. López, appeared July 12 at the Redondo Barn Ballroom, Redondo Beach. Tony Alvarez's orchestra and singers Rudy Martín, Pancho Morales, and Trío de Chito Montoya were also on the program.

Juan Aguilar

Teaching at Mt. Saint Mary's College in 1949 was Juan Aguilar (Juan Aguilar y Adame), who also served as organist at St. Vibiana Cathedral in downtown Los Angeles. Born in 1883 at Pueblo de Cosío near Aguascalientes, Mexico, Aguilar studied piano at Mexico City with Miramontes and composition with Godínez (composer of *Marcha Zacatecas*); he settled in Guadalajara.

> To escape the ravages of the revolution, he took his young family to Chihuahua, Chihuahua, in 1916, then to El Paso, Texas, in 1917. The next year he emigrated to Los Angeles where he found immediate employment as pianist in the nine-member Pryor Moore instrumental ensemble that played nightly at Boos Bros. Cafeteria until the outbreak of World War II. He composed prolifically throughout his entire career, and was recognized as a virtuoso organist as early as June 30, 1920, when he played at the dedication of the new organ in San Gabriel Church, Los Angeles. His works, which were constantly being performed during his 35 years in Los Angeles, should be catalogued and analyzed in a dissertation or thesis. (*Pacific Coast Musician,* quoted in Stevenson 1988a:36)
>
> In the March 17, 1945, issue of PCM [*Pacific Coast Musician*], these Juan Aguilar compositions were listed: *Easter Mass* and *Regina caeli,* sung in the Sistine Chapel at Rome; *Moorish Suite* for orchestra, two movements of which were conducted by Sir Henry Wood at

Hollywood Bowl, July 20, 1934 (March-Fanfare; Asturiana); Viking's Daughter (cantata); and film scores for *Thunder over Mexico* and *Viva Villa*. The October 5, 1946, issue cites him as a resident of Santa Monica with studio at 223 South Broadway in Central Los Angeles. He died September 15, 1953, at the address . . . [of] his daughter Beatriz. (Stevenson 1988a:36)

The 1950s

From 18 June to 2 July 1950, Trío Los Panchos appeared in Los Angeles at the Mayan Theater. According to a *La Opinión* critic, the trio was received extremely well by Angelinos, and their expressive harmony brought to the public "los hondos sentimientos de sus canciones. En la interpretación de los músicos folklóricos hispanoamericanos ponen todo su corazón y alma de grandes artistas [the deep feelings of their songs. In the interpretation of the Hispanic-American folkloric musicians, they put all the heart and soul of the great artists they are]" (22 June 1950). Other artists featured at the same concert were Rubén Reyes, Helia Casanova, Fanny Jordón, Rocío y Julio, Lili Mar, Roberto y Sus Muñecas, and Teppy.

Radio station XEGM, which aired Mexican music, advertised in the June 25 edition of *La Opinión* a program featuring Mexican singer Amalia Mendoza with José Ayala. Miguelito Valdez, the sensational Cuban singer, performed at the Avedon Ballroom on July 7. Enjoying his recent hit "Babalú," Valdez presented a show of *valses,* sambas, rumbas, and American (U.S.) songs. The film *El miedo llegó a Jalisco,* starring Argentine tango singer Emilio Tuero, was showing at that time. Songs that he interpreted in the film included "Dilo tú," "Serenata," "Sueño," "Torrente," and "No puede ser."

Appearing for El Día de Campo at Mountain Park in Verdugo Hills on Sunday, July 13, was the orchestra of Esteban Grajeda, one of the more popular trumpeters in Mexico. The film *Tú sólo tú,* starring Rosita Quintana and Luis Aguilar, was showing at the Maya and Mason theaters. Also featured in the variety shows produced at Teatro Maya was tenor Tibo Luna on July 24. *La Opinión* published an article announcing a performance of the Concert Rehearsal Group consisting of violinist Irving Geller, cellist Rosalia Smith, and pianist Lionel de León.

Baritone Daniel Estrada sang in the Santuario de Guadalupe on December 12. Mexican composer Agustín Lara played the leading role in the motion picture *Mujeres en mi vida,* which was being screened at the Mason Theater. The annual Las Posadas was produced at the Padua Hills Theater. Singer Rubén Reyes was scheduled to perform on December 21 at Teatro Maya, interpreting his most recent musical creations. Opera baritone Rodolfo Hoyos also appeared at the Teatro Maya on that date, at a posthumous tribute and benefit for the journalist Gabriel Navarro, where Hoyos sang two of Navarro's compositions.

A local Christmas program was aired on the radio network Voz de Sud América; headlining the review of entertainers were Fernando Rosas and Tily López. The popular Martín Becerra, whose radio career lasted more than thirty years, was featured on radio station KWKW in the program "Hogar de Regalos." The show featured musical variety, especially Mexican music, and aired Mondays through Saturdays from 10:30 A.M. to noon. On 1 January 1951 the Tournament of Roses Parade was broadcast for the first time in Spanish by radio station KALI and NBC-affiliate television channel 4, hosted by David Orozco and Angel Lerma.

To celebrate El Día de la Raza on 9 October 1952, a group of local artists participated in Fiesta de la Raza at the Bronson House, located at 3127 Pleasant Street. Organized by singer Daniel Estrada, the festival featured artists Romualdo Tirado, Rodolfo Hoyos, Petrita Santa Cruz, and Orlando and Alma L. Beltrán. Councilman Edward Roybal addressed the audience.

A front-page headline in *La Opinión* on 10 October 1952 read, "Truman es la voz de Stevenson, dice Ike" [Truman Is the Voice of Stevenson, Says Ike]." Also on the front page was a photo of Dwight Eisenhower wearing a charro suit,[1] sombrero, and a sarape during his visit to San Diego, California. The marriage of Mexican stars Jorge Negrete and María Félix in Mexico City was also announced that day.

An article in the November 2 issue of *La Opinión* hailed singer Leticia Cárdenas as "una de las más populares danzantes de boleros de esta metrópolis. . . . Esta cantante ha sabido conquistarse al público con su voz y su personalidad, tanto en el teatro, en la radio, en la televisión como en el cine [one of the most popular dancers of the bolero in this city. . . . This singer has conquered the public with her voice and her personality, as much in theatre, radio, and television as in film]." Violinist Samuel Martí played a concert in the City Terrace section of East Los Angeles. Las Hermanas Pallais, a group of Mexican singers who were performing primarily in Los Angeles, appeared on a Saturday evening television program on KHJ called "Momentos Alegres," produced and hosted by Eddie Rodríguez. The show was first broadcast in the fall of 1952 and continued into 1953 for thirty-two weeks. It was sponsored by Bulldog Beer. Rodríguez had also written, produced, and hosted KHJ's "Spanish Theater Hour" in 1951, which featured movies in Spanish and out of which evolved the "Momentos Alegres" program.

Tenor Armando Silva was a rising talent and appeared at numerous concerts and nightclubs throughout the city. *Martín Corona,* starring Mexican singer Pedro Infante with Sarita Montiel, was screened at Teatro Monterrey. *Que te ha dado esa mujer,* featuring Infante and Luis Aguilar, was showing at Teatro Unique. Tenor José Gallegos was scheduled for the "Momentos Alegres" television show in December.

Of all the theaters that have featured Chicano-related programs, one of the most important is the Million Dollar Theater, which has become an institution in Los Angeles, one nearly synonymous with Mexican culture. The majority of the films shown there are Mexican, and the live stage shows feature primarily Mexican artists. Indeed, Chelo, a popular Mexican female singer who performed at the theater in 1985, recently declared that the entertainment house remains symbolic to this day: "It's still a very prestigious place. The greatest dream of a lot of performers, both well-known and the lesser known, is to perform at the Million Dollar" (Geyer 1984:38; see 38–40 for an excellent ethnographic profile of the Million Dollar's social and artistic ambience).

The Million Dollar Theater was founded in 1918 by Sid Grauman (who also founded Hollywood's Grauman's Chinese Theater). Originally used for movies and stage shows in English, during the 1950s the ornate entertainment house, with its high ceilings, chandeliers, and winding staircases, began catering to the Latino community and became legendary throughout Latin America. Personalities booked at the Million Dollar during that era included such Mexican stars as Pedro Infante, Dolores del Río, Pedro Armendáriz, José Alfredo Jiménez, Augustín Lara, and María Félix.

In the 1950s the Million Dollar sponsored major events and showcases. Scheduled for February 1953 were artists such as well-known actor Freddie Fernández, composer/pianist Chucho Zarzosa, and singers Adelina García and Virginia Barrera. In March, Luis Aguilar appeared at the Million Dollar: "el famoso gallo giro . . . con un conjunto artístico sin precedente en los foros de este coliseo [the famous black and white rooster . . . with an artistic ensemble unprecedented on the stage of this theater]" (*La Opinión* 6 March 1953). Los Mexicanos and Evangelina Elizondo were also featured in the program. Singer Sylvia Alvarez performed with composer Víctor Cordero at the Million Dollar on March 15.

"El Hijo del Pueblo," José Alfredo Jiménez, soon to be Mexico's most popular singer/composer, sang at the Million Dollar, accompanied by Mariachi Los Tecolotes, Tun Tún, Tibo Luna, Lolinda Raquel, Chonga y Chabela, and Leticia Cárdenas.

The Teatro Unique screened *Carne de Presidio,* starring Pedro Armendáriz, in March 1953. *La Loca,* a film featuring Argentine singer Libertad Lamarque, was shown at Teatro Monterrey. Singer Kathy Jurado received the Golden Globe award in recognition of her success. Meanwhile, a headline in the March 6 *La Opinión* announced, "José Stalin ha muerto" [Joseph Stalin Dead].

The movie *Sombrero,* starring Ricardo Montalbán, was showing at the

Paramount Theater at Hill and Sixth streets in downtown Los Angeles. Other actors in the Hollywood production included Pier Angeli, Vittorio, Cyd Charisse, Yvonne de Carlo, and Rick Jason. Angel Infante and his well-known brother, Pedro, appeared in a film screened at the Teatro California, *Por ellas aunque mal paguen.* Isabel Alba played the leading role in the musical comedy *En el mes de mayo,* which was running at the Padua Hills Theater in Claremont.

A week of "Variedades de Alta Calidad" began in early October 1953 at the Million Dollar Theater, featuring Los Hermanos Martínez Gil. A local reporter wrote, "Los famosos cancioneros vienen de la ciudad de México, después de una temporada de grandes éxitos, para deleitar el público angelino [The famous singers are coming from Mexico City following a season of great hits, to entertain the Los Angeles public]" (*La Opinión* 5 October 1953:7). Appearing at the Teatro Maya were Sarita Montiel, Agustín Lara, and Raul Martínez in the film *¿Por qué ya no me quieres?*

Plans for a festival at the Philharmonic Auditorium to raise funds for the Plaza Monumental de la Basílica de Guadalupe were under way in October 1953. The Orquesta Típica Mexicana gave the final concert of its 1954 season at Lincoln Park on October 10. The highly respected and popular group was directed by Professor José Córdova Cantú and performed a variety of Mexican and Spanish music. Featured singers with the orchestra were tenor Alfredo Margo and soprano Alicia Márquez.

Carlos Crespo, who had performed with his trio in October at the Villa México at the Los Angeles County Fair in Pomona, was preparing for an extensive tour. Crespo composed such songs as "Hipócrita," "Callejera," "Un corazón," "La Raza," "El París," and "Mercador de los rancheros." Accompanying Crespo were two local talents, Juanito Sarabia and Alfonso Guzmán. Two prestigious groups, Los Ki-Karos and Los Martínez Gil, appeared on November 14. An article in the November 7 *La Opinión* described the two groups as "exponentes notables de la canción mexicana, la cual han llevado a través de todos los países de habla española, prestigiando con su actuación a México y su música [noted exponents of the Mexican song, which they have taken throughout all the Spanish-speaking countries, giving prestige to Mexico and its music through their performance]."

Scheduled for 29 January 1954 in the January 29–February 4 issue of *T.V. Guide* was the debut of the television show "Fandango" on local CBS station KNXT. Produced by brothers Eddie and Pete Rodríguez, the program was sponsored by Rheinegold Beer and hosted by Mauricio Jara. Eddie Rodríguez also wrote the show. Marimbist Federico Salvatti and his band appeared on the premiere. The program continued into 1955 and featured various musical artists including Rudy Macías and his orchestra, Adelina García, Andy Russell, Los Flamingos, Manny López and his ensemble, Eddie Cano, Lalo Guerrero, Sarita Montiel, Natalie Wood, the Bobby Amos Orchestra, and the Sammy Mendoza Orchestra, among many others. Another television program of the same period was Lupita Beltrán's "Latin Time," which aired Sundays on KCOP. The show first appeared in the mid-1950s and featured entertainers such as Rita Holguín, composer Lalo Guerrero and his orchestra, and Aura San Juan (Ríos-Bustamante and Castillo 1986:173).

Tenor Julian Olivas, who had been associated with the San Carlos Opera, died on 31 March 1955. Mariachi Aguila de Tecalitlán appeared at the Granada Cafe on Saturday and Sunday evenings. The owner of the Granada Cafe, a man named Chávez, had traveled to Tecalitlán, Jalisco, Mexico, to arrange for the mariachi to perform for his clientele. Featured at the Million Dollar were singer/actress Sarita Montiel, Luis Pérez Meza, and the Mariachi Aguilar. *Escuela de vagabundo,* starring Miroslava and Pedro Infante, was showing at Teatro California.

A headline in *La Opinión* on 14 April 1955 read, "La vacuna contra la polio en Los Angeles [Vaccine Fights Polio in L.A.]." A three-part Fiesta Primaveral was planned by the Asociación Artística for April 22. The first part of the festival aired on Rafael Trujillo's radio program; the second part was a series of concerts featuring pianist Leonel de León, violinist Orlando Beltrán, baritone Carlos Macías, and Trío de Los Chicos; and the third part was the musical review "Amanecer Ranchero."

On 16 April 1955 a scholarship benefit dance, the "Baile Pro-Beca," was held at the Shrine Auditorium. The orchestras of Tony "Chi" Reyes and Phil Carreón performed. Sponsored by the United Latin American Clubs of Southern California and inspired by Councilman Edward Roybal, the scholarship, known as "La Beca Armando Castro," was dedicated to the memory of a young boy who had lost his life.

The motion picture *Que bravas son las costeñas,* starring Mexican-American singer Andy Russell and Evangelina Elizondo, was showing in the city during May 1955. Russell and Elizondo were also scheduled to make a live appearance during the film screening at the Million Dollar Theater. By this time Russell had become an internationally recognized singer and film star (see chap. 4 for a profile of Russell).

The Nightclub Circuit

Little published material exists documenting the musical life of local Mexican and Chicano musicians, the nightclub circuit, the locally popular musical forms sung and danced, or the state of the recording industry, especially during the 1940s and 1950s. To fill this gap, the next portion of this chapter relies heavily on information extracted from an oral history interview

I conducted with Lalo Guerrero, who proved to be a valuable source of information on these topics (see chap. 4 for a detailed profile of Guerrero).

On arriving in Los Angeles from Tucson, Arizona, in 1937 to pursue a more active musical career, Guerrero began working at the La Bamba nightclub, one of the more popular clubs among Mexicans in Los Angeles, located downtown at Macy and Spring streets. In addition to its Mexican clientele, many Hollywood personalities frequented La Bamba. Today, a parking lot fills the space where the building that housed the club once stood. Guerrero's trio performed among the tables during breaks between the main sets, which featured floor shows with a large orchestra directed by Chuy Pérez. At the time, the tango and its main interpreter, Carlos Gardel, were in vogue. Also popular were a variety of Cuban musical forms including *son, guajira,* rumba, and conga. Pérez's orchestra was musically proficient and sophisticated. The director played violin, clarinet, and *bandoneón* (an accordion used in Argentine popular music styles and characteristic of the tango). A nineteen-year-old musician named Pedro Arcaraz played piano; Alberto Pérez, brother of leader Chuy, was the drummer; and an Anglo-American played marimba. Fronting the floor shows was singer Bobby Ramos, accompanied by Guerrero's group. After singing a set, Ramos would change roles and work as a waiter, a frequent custom among young, developing singers at the time.

According to Guerrero, about 98 percent of the clientele who patronized Latin clubs in Los Angeles from 1937 to World War II were Mexican Americans. The bracero program had not yet begun, so the number of Mexican immigrants was negligible compared to the number of Mexican/ Chicano residents:

> La gente que estaba aquí era gente que habiá emigrado o méxico-americanos que eran de los Californianos viejos, los Californianos que aquí nacieron, padres y abuelos, y gente que emigró como mis padres que emigraron en los años de 1910 a 15; entonces se componía aquí la población latina de 98 por ciento gente mexicana o méxico-americana. No había como hoy en estos tiempos la aglomeración de razas latinas de diferentes países, y La Bamba era uno de los centros más bonitos, más populares. Estaba en la esquina de Macy y Spring, y allí iba mucho americano también y era un lugar de mucha clase.
> [The people who were here were people who had emigrated, or Mexican Americans who were the old Californians, the Californians who were born here, parents and grandparents, and people who emigrated, as my own parents did, in the years 1910 to 1915. At that time the Latin population consisted of 98 percent Mexican or Mexican-American people. In those days we did not have the large number of

Latin Americans from different countries, and La Bamba was one of the more attractive and popular clubs. It was on the corner of Macy and Spring, and many Anglo Americans frequented it; it was a place with class.]

Lalo mentioned other Hollywood clubs—Mocambo, El Trocadero, and Ciro's. A group led by Felipe López, a trumpeter originally from Phoenix, Arizona, performed at El Trocadero. Pianist Jerry Galian, originally from Mexico, also played there regularly, leading an orchestra that included saxophone and bongos. During the late 1930s Bobby Ramos directed an orchestra at Ciro's, a club that became quite popular after La Bamba closed in 1949. These orchestras specialized in the mambo and tropical music for dancing.

The Club Brazil, located on Broadway Avenue in downtown Los Angeles, contracted east coast orchestras such as that of Machito, the Cuban bandleader based in New York City. La Casa Olvera, adjacent to Olvera Street in the downtown district, was also a profitable business. Located directly on Olvera Street were the Cafe Caliente and El Paseo (the latter still exists). El Patio was another entertainment spot, located on Spring Street near Olvera. All these clubs hired Latin ensembles on a regular basis. In addition to presenting dance bands, most of them scheduled flamenco dance shows, which featured a couple performing the Spanish dance, and ballroom dance in an embellished style, the male leading the female in numerous aerial routines. Tuxedos and elegant gowns were the customary dress for these ballroom settings. Guerrero remembered this period from the late 1930s to the late 1940s as "los golden years de la música latina y de los músicos aquí [the golden years of Latin music and musicians here]." He recalled the musicians whom he had worked with and respected—Felipe López, Chuy Pérez, Pedro Alcaraz, and Poncho Cera, among others.

Mexican musicians in these Latin nightclubs reproduced Cuban musical styles by imitating recorded arrangements. Hits of the era included "Para vivo me voy" and the rumba "El combanchero." Artists like Benny Moré from Cuba and Rafael Hernández from Puerto Rico were very popular throughout Latin America and in Los Angeles. Hernández composed "El combanchero," "Perfume de gardenia," and "Jibarito." Mexican music and artists, however, were always included in the standard repertoire and were very popular. Tunes such as "Noche de ronda" and "Solamente una vez," both composed by Agustín Lara, were especially popular in the 1930s and became international standards that are still performed today.

In addition to the available records, stock arrangements and scores were often ordered from New York City or Mexico City. One problem besetting Los Angeles musicians was the trade regulation that forbade the importa-

tion of records from Mexico. Therefore, songs were often transmitted by
word of mouth and by one band hearing the music of another. For this reason, independent record companies formed in Los Angeles, many of which
eventually prospered and had a lasting impact on the Mexican population
of the city.

Guerrero recalled another popular club, El Zarape, located on Sunset
Boulevard, where he worked during the late 1930s; years later it was renamed El Continental. The club featured the orchestra of Nino Menéndez,
a local Cuban pianist and composer who wrote the popular song "Ojos
verdes." Menéndez still lives in Los Angeles.

> Un gran artista, un gran pianista. . . . El compuso unas cosas muy
> bonitas pero le hizo famoso una canción. Ahorita está grande, bas-
> tante grande. Quisiera yo verlo porque fue amigo mío en ese tiempo
> cuando yo tocaba en El Zarape allí en las mesas. Era muy amable
> y aunque el era pianista y el director allí, nos trataba a nosotros los
> cancioneros muy bien. Platicábamos con él, tomábamos una copa y
> platicaba mucho de Cuba, y me gustaría ahora que está aquí verlo otra
> vez. Vi una foto de él en un periódico hace poquito. Ya está grande,
> se ve de algunos. Bueno, yo tengo 68 años, Nino ha de tener sus 75,
> 78. Quiero que lo busques porque. . . . Es uno de los grandes de todo
> el tiempo, de los compositores grandes que hubo en esos años como
> Agustín Lara, Gonzalo Curiel. . . . Guty Cárdenas. . . . Miguel Prado.
> [A great artist, a great pianist. . . . He composed some very beautiful
> things, but he became famous with one song. Today he is old, quite
> old. I wish I could see him because he was a good friend in those
> days, when I played at El Zarape (at the tables). He was very friendly,
> and even though he was the pianist and the director, he treated us
> singers very well. We would chat with him, have a drink together,
> and he talked a lot about Cuba, and I would like to see him again
> now that he is here. I saw his picture in a newspaper not long ago.
> He looks older, quite a few years. Well, I'm sixty-eight, Nino must
> be around seventy-five, seventy-eight. I wish you would try to locate
> him because he is one of the greats of all time, of the great composers
> of those times, such as Agustín Lara, Gonzalo Curiel, Guty Cárdenas,
> Miguel Prado.]

During the 1940s and the war era, many clubs frequented by the Mexican population closed or changed ownership. The war years brought new
forms of musical expression that coincided with a new mode of awareness emerging among many Mexican Americans. New styles of music, such
as the big band sound, heavily influenced the musical culture of young
Chicanos, especially within the pachuco cult of Los Angeles. It was dur-

ing this period that Lalo Guerrero, for example, composed such songs as "Chuco suave" (which incorporated the *Caló* dialect of Spanish popular among pachucos), "Marijuana Boogie," and "Vamos a bailar," in which musical forms fused the rhythmic structures of swing, rumba, and jazz. Hybridization pervaded the culture in language, music, dance, politics, and patriotism.

In 1945 a club called El Sombrero opened on Main and 15th streets in central Los Angeles. Performing on the ground floor was the group of Don Tosti, a local Mexican-American bassist (originally from El Paso) who at one time had played with Tommy Dorsey's orchestra. Tily López and his orchestra played on the second floor of the club. Tosti, whose real name was Edmundo Martínez Tostado, eventually became quite well known locally through a single his group recorded called "Pachuco Boogie." The other two members of the Don Tosti Trio, drummer Raul Díaz and pianist Eddie Cano, also performed on that recording (Cano is profiled in chap.4).

El Babalú on Sixth Street, El Janitzio, La Capital, and Italian Village were other clubs that catered to the Mexican population in the postwar years. Italian Village featured the Latin music of trombonist Chico Sesma and his group. Sesma later became well known throughout the city because of his Latin music radio shows. New styles, new clientele, and new demographic patterns brought considerable change to the nightclub circuit. Guerrero recalled the difference in the tropical music environment, commenting that "lo que es ahora salsa es lo que tocaban; entonces, ya cuando volví yo a Los Angeles en '45, ya me encontré a new scene. . . . New people que era Don Tosti, que era Chico Sesma, que era Tily López . . . otros elementos en orquestas. [What they now call salsa is what they were playing; so when I returned to Los Angeles in '45, I encountered a new scene . . . new people like Don Tosti, Chico Sesma, Tily López . . . and other musicians in the orchestras]." Many of the younger musicians had studied music and were instrumental in the reinterpretation of musical forms and new musical styles.

When he returned to Los Angeles in 1945, after five years in San Diego performing for the USO, Guerrero performed again at La Bamba, this time as lead vocalist with Alfonso Fernández's orchestra. In 1948 he began recording on the Imperial label and became very popular in Los Angeles and other areas of the Southwest. He eventually left Fernández's orchestra and formed his own group. Although he fronted the new orchestra, he was not trained in arranging or notating music, so he employed Pedro Alcaraz, who had been playing piano with Chuy Pérez. Guerrero's group debuted at El Acapulco, a club in the Olvera Street vicinity. After that engagement, the orchestra was contracted by La Capital, the first major Latin club to open in East Los Angeles. The owner, Sam Tamboni, named the club La

Capital because the decor was reminiscent of Mexico City, with paintings of the Angel de la Independencia and the eagle devouring the serpent from the Mexican flag. Guerrero also performed at El Janitzio (located near the Million Dollar), which had a large, shell-shaped bandstand painted in gold. A balcony surrounded the stage, and a dance floor was located below. The owner of El Janitzio, a local Mexican American named Eddie Guerrero, had been a musician before becoming a nightclub owner.

Business negotiations were conducted in both Spanish and English. A bilingual, bicultural atmosphere pervaded the nightclub scene. When asked whether the war had indeed led to change in the cultural awareness and political self-determination of the community in relation to its musical life, Guerrero responded with his own analysis:

> Muy buen punto que has hecho. Sí es cierto, es cierto. No se me había ocurrido. Pero después de la guerra sí nos sentimos todos los latinos, los mexicanos que éramos la mayoría, nos sentimos ya like we belonged here. Teníamos derechos, porque mucha de nuestra gente fue a servir en el servicio militar y muchos murieron, se quedaron allá. Entonces el mismo anglo, como dicen ahora, también nos aceptaban más. Ya sentíamos nosotros más confianza y fue una regeneración, o como renacimiento. . . .
>
> Fue cuando empezó a despertar la raza porque antes de eso no teníamos representación de nada en ninguna parte. Después de la guerra sí ya tuvimos más aceptación, y pudimos ya tener más libertad para hacer muchas cosas, y fue cuando ya salió Eduardo Roybal que encabezó el City Council.
>
> [You've made a very good point, and yes, it's true. It had not occurred to me, but after the war we all felt that we were Latinos. Those of us who were Mexicans were the majority, and we felt like we belonged here. We had rights, for many of our people had served in the military service and many died, they stayed over there. So the same Anglo, as they say now, also accepted us more. By then we had more confidence, and it was a regeneration, or something like a rebirth.
>
> That was when *la Raza* began to wake up because before that we had no representation anywhere. After the war we did have more acceptance and we could now have more freedom to do many things, and that is when Edward Roybal emerged as a leader in the City Council.]

Eastward Ho

Eventually, musical activity became more intense among Mexicans and Chicanos in the east side of Los Angeles. Numerous clubs and record shops opened in the area as the population began to reflect the postwar emigration of non-Mexicans, or "white flight," and the constant immigration of Mexicans.

> What happened is, La Capital was the first place to open in East L.A., and I remember I had my band and I was hired to go there, and a lot of musicians, you know, guys like Jerry Galian [also played there]. . . . In the meantime, another little place opened in East L.A., which is a cute little place que se llamaba La Noche [which was named La Noche]. You ask Eddie Cano. Did you ever interview Eddie Cano?
> . . . Eddie Cano. The first time I saw him and heard him, he was a young kid, playing like crazy, real good. There were four young guys playing great music in a little nightclub que se llamaba La Noche, and if I'm not mistaken it was on Rowan Avenue, off of Brooklyn.

Cano's group performed mostly Latin music at La Noche, although it also played jazz. Bob Hernández played saxophone; there were also a trumpet player, a drummer, and a bassist. Guerrero added that "they were all young dudes . . . they were the new wave coming on and they were really good."

Soon after, eastside clubs proliferated.

> Since the clubs in the West Side started dying off . . . the musicians that had not wanted to come to East L.A., because they thought it was a step down . . . were practically forced to come back because there was not too much happening on the west side, 'cause the Latin scene had passed—the rumba and the tango, the conga and all that. The music changed, and now in East L.A. we were playing *danzones*. We were copying Mexico. We were playing *sones,* boleros, and *guarachas* and mambos and cha cha chá, and the Raza still wanted a polka here and there.

New eastside clubs included El Club Ballón on Atlantic Boulevard near Whittier Boulevard, which featured bandleader Manny López. After performing there for a number of years, López opened his own Manny López Club at a nearby location on Atlantic Boulevard south of Whittier. The Paramount Ballroom on Brooklyn Avenue and Agnes' Place, located on the corner of Soto and Brooklyn, also opened. Near Lincoln Park was a club called La Casita, where Memo Mata first performed for the public, becoming one of the most popular bandleaders in East Los Angeles. Guerrero reminisced about Mata's musical talent: "Memo Mata is a very fine arranger. There's something very good about Memo that I admire. He was a *cancionero*—trios, *guitarrista*. He didn't know a note of music—I mean writing, reading. But he decided he was going to learn, and he started to learn; and he turned out to be one of the best arrangers in L.A. In a period of two or three years he was writing and arranging and he had his own band. I admire him for that because few people do that."

While Mata was performing at La Casita, a trio called Los Chucos, led by Sal Meza, was playing at Agnes' Place. Tony's Inn, which had been in business before Guerrero's engagement at La Capital, was owned and operated by Torinio Reza. Los Muchachos de los Escalantes, featuring Manilú Escalante on trumpet and Blanca Escalante in the floor show, played there. Years later, Guerrero purchased Tony's Inn and converted it into his own club, called Lalo's.

Meanwhile, local producers began to hold dances featuring Latin music at the Hollywood Palladium. Although the Palladium usually promoted swing bands, it instituted "Latin Holidays" featuring east coast artists such as Celia Cruz and Tito Puente. Later, groups from Mexico such as Sonora Santanera and that of Luis Alcaraz performed there. Most of the local ballroom show promoters, such as Chico Sesma and Richard Ceja, were Chicanos. Guerrero described Ceja as "a record man. He had been in records for years . . . good friend. . . . He was the man who was bringing all these groups from New York, and they were popular. When they would come, La Raza, la Chicanada would pack the Palladium." There were a few Cubans or Puerto Ricans among the large Mexican audiences, but those groups did not constitute a large percentage of the Latino population.

In addition to being a promoter of the Palladium Latin shows, Chico Sesma was a well-known musician and radio disc jockey in the Los Angeles Mexican community. Guerrero recalled that at one time Sesma "was playing mostly at the Italian Village downtown on Sixth and Olive . . . a trombonist and a very fine arranger. Mostly *charanga, pachanga,* mambo. Mexican from L.A.; and he had a radio program on the air for a long time where he would announce in English, 'cause he spoke English very well; but he played all Latin music. It was a very popular radio show." Guerrero also mentioned another important radio personality, Vance Graham, who broadcast a Latin music show during the 1950s.

Guerrero purchased Tony's Inn, renamed it Lalo's, and operated it for twelve years. His own group performed at the club and played mambo, Tex-Mex, cha cha chá, some swing, polka, and *danzones.* Guerrero sang, Pete Alcaraz did the musical arrangements, and Tony Fachudo performed on trumpet. Fachudo toured Japan with Pérez Prado and eventually died of kidney failure.

Adjacent to Guerrero's club was another Latin club, Beto's, owned by a Mexican German. The Latin Lover was also located on Whittier Boulevard; it was run by Mitch Rodríguez, brother of Ray Rodríguez, who owned the Paramount Ballroom in Hollywood. (The latter Rodríguez is not to be confused with the popular bandleader of the 1970s and 1980s also named Ray Rodríguez.)

Another prominent musician during the 1950s was Miguel Sánchez, a highly rated flautist like his brother Alfonso Sánchez Chavaleis. Also part of the same musical network was Cuban flautist Issi Morales, who performed regularly at Tony's Inn. Guerrero recalled: "These groups are the ones that made the L.A. scene jump. He [Morales] lived here at the time and he was marvelous. And that's why I want to mention these people, because [they were] very outstanding musicians, not only local, but we had a lot of them that came from out of town." Guerrero continued to comment on the mix of Latin musicians:

> Yeah, in the bands . . . not in the population. We'd have good mixture . . . We had a good mixture of people; like Mincho Serra was a very fine Cuban sax man and arranger—marvelous. And of course, Issi Morales, Lalo's brother, and many others. . . . There was always one or two Cubans or Puerto Ricans. There was Pollito Casadín . . . es Veracruzano, pero parece Puerto Riqueño. . . . ¡Oye Chico! ¡Todos Muchachos! [. . . he's from Veracruz, but he seems Puerto Rican . . . (with his expressions such as) "¡Oye Chico! ¡Todos Muchachos!"]

During the 1950s numerous artists from Mexico City performed at the Hollywood Palladium, such as Lobo y Melón and Sonora Santanera, both of whom specialized in tropical, Caribbean music. Luis Alcaraz's big band, which played both Latin and swing music, was also frequently featured. Pérez Prado's band, which consisted primarily of Mexican musicians, was becoming internationally known throughout Mexico, Cuba, the rest of Latin America, and in Europe.

Guerrero would often contract these international acts that were visiting Los Angeles to perform at his club. Luis Alcaraz and Carlos Campos (who specialized in the Cuban *danzón* musical style) both performed at Lalo's on their unscheduled nights as part of their Los Angeles itineraries. Guerrero earned a considerable profit from such ventures, charging a ten-dollar cover and usually filling the house to more than capacity. Furthermore, such appearances lent his club some added prestige.

The rise and fall of so many clubs in East Los Angeles reflected the difficulty of establishing and maintaining such a business before and after the war years, when the economy was in constant flux, especially in the Mexican quarters of the city. Guerrero, for example, was unable to finance the purchase of his own club through his earnings from playing in the club circuit. He explained how he was able to start Lalo's:

> Of course, I worked for a long time and made good money, but you know musicians aren't able to save very much . . . not because they can't, it's just that they won't. You know, we're bohemios. . . . I made it from my recording with Pancho López, when I did the parody

to "The Ballad of Pancho López." It was off of the Davy Crockett theme. I made two verses, one in English and one in Spanish, and we didn't get clearance to do it. It was a local record company called Discos Colonial de [of] Manuel Acuña, mi compadre [my close friend], who is still working together [with me]. We didn't get clearance from Disney 'cause we figured, what the hell, we'll make this little parody I wrote; it was a funny version of "Davy Crockett." I was poking fun at Davy Crockett, especially de Texas y the Alamo and all of that. So we did, and we figured we'll sell four or five thousand records and make a few bucks. But Jim Amechi, who was at that time the disc jockey and Don Amechi's brother . . . you know, the actor, Don Amechi? Well, Jim Amechi was a disc jockey on KLAC, very popular. He got ahold of our record and he put it on the air on KLAC, and the thing took off, man. It took off, it became a national hit [Lalo sings some of the melody]. It made the charts . . . the one in English. And of course the one in Spanish was a big hit in Latin America, so I also made some great royalties over there. But that's where I got money to buy my club, because just the first month that the record went out, I remember my cut of it was 98,000 dollars just the first month, and this was in the middle '50s. Like I said, we did it with this local company, and what happens?

. . . We thought we were going to sell three or four thousand records and nobody's gonna pay attention; and we got caught. And they made an appointment for us to come to Walt Disney Studios, which belonged to their publishing companies, Wonderland Music Company; they controlled it. So we went in, myself and my partners—two partners of the record company. And Mr. Disney himself was in the office with his attorneys, and they said, "Mr. Guerrero, we called to see if you have clearance," and I thought, "God, they are going to nail me to the cross, a powerful man like that—he already had Disneyland." Well, he was great, he was a wonderful gentleman. He says, "Look, Mr. Guerrero, your lyric is very clever, very clever, very cute. . . . So you wrote a great lyric and it's going very well, so all we want you to do is give us 50 percent for our music and you can have 50 percent for the lyric—you accept that? Or else we'll have to go to court and we'll take everything." He was very smart . . . he didn't give me much choice, you know. I said, "Listen, Mr. Disney, you are very gracious. I know you could take it all if you wanted to; we didn't get clearance, but I'll be very happy to sign a contract for 50 percent." And I did, I signed the contract for 50 percent. But that was enough, you know, what the heck. Yeah, they pushed it, and that's where I got the money and bought that club. Oh yeah, they

made good money out of that thing—they'd already made it off Davy
Crockett. So that's where I got the money for the club, for I really
didn't have any money to speak of. I lived well, but I had a family,
I had my wife and two kids; but that's where I got the money all of
a sudden, in a lump sum. . . . And I bought the building from Tony
Reza, Toribio Reza there on Brooklyn, and I remodeled it . . . and
went into business, and I was there for thirteen years. [Guerrero sold
the club in 1970 and moved to Palm Springs, where he still performs
on an occasional basis.]

The Recording Industry

The recording industry that contracted with Mexican artists in Los Angeles immediately after World War II was a lucrative business, especially for
the owners. Although the artists did not fare as well financially, the local
industry was perhaps their only vehicle for gaining radio and market attention. U.S. laws prevented Mexican companies from recording in the
United States. During the 1940s, therefore, the local companies such as
Imperial, Vocalion, Azteca, Tri-color, and Aguila recorded Mexican artists. Los Madrugadores (originally Los Hermanos Sánchez), the *ranchera*
group Chicho y Chencho, Fernando Rosas, Lalo Guerrero, El Trío Imperial (with whom Guerrero was a soloist), and El Conjunto Los Costeños,
in addition to many other well-organized duets and groups, recorded on
the Imperial label. After earning considerable profits on their initial investment in recording Mexican artists, the two owners of Imperial shifted their
emphasis to black artists who performed rhythm and blues. Fats Domino
and T-Bone Walker became top-sellers on the Imperial label. Imperial became so successful in the black music market that it deleted the Mexican
recording catalog. Guerrero described the resentment among Mexican artists, but he also explained the financial compromises:

> They canceled all of us Chicanos out. They threw the Chicanos out
> because they were making too much off the blacks. . . .
> There was [resentment], but you see, things in those days were
> economically bad. You know what I was paid for a record, 78 r.p.m.,
> two sides? I got paid fifty dollars a side, one hundred dollars a record.
> In a neat session I'd do two records, so I'd make two hundred dol-
> lars a session, and they wouldn't pay us royalties . . . hey, we argued
> about royalties. "No, no royalties," and rather than not record at all,
> we went along . . . because I was making a name, that was what I
> cared about, but they were paying us fifty bucks a side, two hun-
> dred dollars a session, and they were making hundreds of thousands.

I found out later that they were making hundreds of thousands of dollars on my records—not only mine, but the others, Los Madrugadores and other people. Anselmo Alvarado recorded there too . . . very popular at the time. [The recordings] were all original compositions, and that's where I did all the music with *Zoot Suit* on Imperial Records. [I recorded that with] my own little group, five-piece, and they made a mint and we only got two hundred dollars . . . for two records. But what the heck, every time I'd get two hundred dollars I'd buy my wife a washing machine, a dryer; you know, it was good for me 'cause we weren't making that much money. So there was a resentment that they didn't pay us what we should be getting and they were. I didn't realize how much money they were making until years later when Manuel Acuña, who was the A&R [artists and repertoire] man there, told me. He says, "You know how much they used to make on your records? One of your records would produce as much as two or three hundred thousand dollars," and I was getting two hundred dollars. Ha!

Manuel was the one who got the groups who write the arrangements, who would get the session together, who would direct the session, and he'd get paid so much. But those guys made a fortune . . . to the extent that after they got the black groups, they went higher and they dropped all the Latinos or the Chicanos, and then they sold the label to, I believe it was Liberty first and eventually it ended up with Capitol, and they sold it [the label] for a million dollars; something that started with us Chicanos . . . that little hole in the wall on Western Avenue . . . they sold it for a million dollars, which in those years was a lot of money.

Other record companies that featured Mexican artists in Los Angeles between the years 1945 and 1954 included Tri-Color, Taxco, Aguila, Bribiesca Bros., and Azteca. Tri-Color and Aguila were owned by Mauricio Garten; Bribiesca Bros. was operated by José Bribiesca, who also owned a photography shop located on First Street across from Los Angeles City Hall. The owner of Azteca, Trinidad Pelaiz, originally from Mexico, was ninety-two years old in 1985. These companies featured Mexican artists exclusively. They did not record other Latino or U.S. mainstream artists.

One of the people recording with Taxco records at the time was singer Rubén Reyes, who became one of the more successful local artists. Originally from Monterrey, Mexico, Reyes came to Los Angeles and soon became popular for his renditions of Don Tosti's "Cuando yo vine aquí" and another song titled "Yo soy el aventurero." Guerrero recalled the "boy wonder": "He was marvelous. He was seventeen years old, and boy, they exploited that kid. He was here alone with no brothers, sisters, mother, nothing; and the people that controlled the record company and everything . . . that guy would pack the ballrooms up and down the coast. He must have earned millions of dollars, and he used to get—whatever they gave him; but he was happy, he was from Mexico and he was seventeen years old, so if they gave him five hundred dollars, oh, he was thrilled." Reyes resides in Los Angeles to this day. His popularity diminished after he stopped recording during the 1950s.

By the mid-1950s, Mexican record companies had acquired rights to export merchandise to the United States. Local recording companies began to decline because of the large quantity and marketability of the Mexican imports. U.S.-based companies such as Columbia, its affiliate Caytronics, RCA Victor, and Capitol began to record and contract Mexican artists such as María Victoria, Fernando Fernández, Pedro Vargas, and Luis Alcaraz.

Guerrero also mentioned the importance of the Million Dollar Theater during the 1940s and 1950s. Recording artists from Mexico such as Pedro Infante, Luis Aguilar, Jorge Negrete, Lucha Reyes, and many others appeared regularly at the Million Dollar and other local theaters, such as the Mason. These theaters provided the largest live audiences at that time, although they operated on a scale much smaller than that of present-day productions at the Universal Amphitheater and other major concert houses. Such performances enhanced local record business immensely.

In addition to being involved in the local recording industry, which had become an integral element of the musical life of Mexicans and Mexican Americans in Los Angeles, the singer-musician-composer Guerrero developed business relationships with various Los Angeles–based music distributors and music stores, especially in the downtown sector and the East Side. From Schireson Brothers, located on Broadway and Fourth Street, Guerrero bought percussion instruments such as *guiros,* claves, and maracas, in addition to stock arrangements published in Mexico City or New York City. The American Music Company, located downtown, also supplied arrangements. For guitars Guerrero patronized Candelas, on Brooklyn Avenue in East Los Angeles, which does business to this day under the same ownership. Other important businesses located in the East Side were Philips Music in Boyle Heights and Millan Music on East First Street, both of which sold records and musical instruments.

The Swing Era

Although a mainstream style, swing music had considerable impact on the Mexican population in Los Angeles during the late 1930s and throughout the 1940s and 1950s. One exception to the marginal exposure received locally and nationally by most Mexican-American swing musicians was

Andy Russell. Named Andrés Rábago at birth, Russell adopted his angli-
cized stage name and became an international star, selling eight million
records during the 1940s and early 1950s (see his profile in chap.4).

Swing became especially popular among Los Angeles zoot-suiters during the 1940s. Dances not only were places for socializing but also typified
the way young Mexican Americans adapted to and assimilated different
styles. Along with the tropical music of the Caribbean and traditional
Mexican popular music, the bands of Cab Calloway, Jimmy Dorsey, Glenn
Miller, and Duke Ellington became symbolic vehicles of change and adaptation.

Jump Blues

In an article titled "The View from the Sixth Street Bridge: The History of
Chicano Rock," Rubén Guevara, an important contemporary figure in the
"Eastside Renaissance" of music, formulates various theories concerning
the development and adaptation of different musical styles and preferences
among Mexican Americans in Los Angeles. Guevara's historical perspective traces his own musical life and enculturation in Los Angeles since the
1940s: "In East L.A., as in so many other places, the link between swing
and early R&B and rock 'n roll was jump blues. Jump evolved in the thirties
from Harlem bands like those of Cab Calloway and the Kansas City groups
of Count Basie and Louis Jordan. In Los Angeles the leading early prac-
titioners were Roy Milton and The Solid Senders" (Guevara 1985:115).
By the end of World War II Roy Milton had achieved national prominence with his hit "R.M. Blues," recorded on Specialty Records. He was
among the many swing artists who became popular among Mexicans in
Los Angeles.

The zoot suit era of the 1940s was characterized not only by the popularization of swing but also by an assortment of Latin styles including
mambo, rumba, and *danzón,* all Cuban imports, often via Mexico. As noted
previously, Mexican music was also popular among zoot-suiters. Swing
and tropical rhythms were more popular among the zoot suit "cult," which
adopted particular styles of dress, language (the *Caló* dialect of Spanish),
music, and dance. Zoot-suiters patronized particular entertainment spots
and formed social groups that eventually became known as gangs. Many
speculate that the pachuco gang evolved as a defense mechanism in response to the Zoot Suit riots.

A growing number of blacks were settling in Los Angeles in search of
better-paying war industry jobs. The availability of low-rent housing in the
Mexican neighborhoods of east and south-central Los Angeles prompted
many blacks to settle there. Conversely, as Anglos became economically

mobile they moved away from those neighborhoods: "Blacks and Chicanos, isolated together, began to interact and, in large numbers, they listened to the same radio stations. For instance, there was Hunter Hancock ("Ol' H.H.") on KFVD. He had a show on Sundays called "Harlem Matinee" that featured records by Louis Jordan, Lionel Hampton, and locals Roy Milton, Joe and Jimmy Liggins, and Johnny Otis" (Guevara 1985:116).

Otis, originally from Tulsa, moved to Los Angeles in 1943. By the end of World War II he had become one of the major proponents of "jump blues," the name given to this pre–rock and roll swing style derived from blues. Guevara notes:

> When Johnny first played the Angeles Hall in 1948, introducing black jump blues to the Eastside, he caused quite a sensation. His swing didn't just swing. It jumped! And the Eastside jumped right along with him. Chicano jump bands began to form—the first was the Pachuco Boogie Boys led by Raúl Díaz and Don Tosti. They had a local hit, "Pachuco Boogie," which consisted of a jump type shuffle with either Raúl or Don rapping in Caló [pachuco street slang: half Spanish, half English] about getting ready to go out on a date. Very funny stuff and another candidate for the title of the first rap record. (Guevara 1985:117)

Guevara lists the following Los Angeles–based record companies as some of the more significant in the distribution of the R&B style during the 1940s: Art Rupe's Specialty Records, Jules Bihari Modern and 4 Star, Exclusive, Aladdin, and the aforementioned Imperial.

Guevara's analysis derives primarily from his personal musical development, which, like that of many Chicanos enculturated in urban Los Angeles, was integrally related to the black music experience, for musical as well as economic reasons. (These concepts are discussed in more detail in chap. 5.)[2]

With the 1950s came the Korean War, the bracero program, and more Mexican deportations. The period also witnessed the emergence and development of rock and roll in the United States, and the Mexican quarters of Los Angeles—especially the East Side—were no exception. Guevara notes the role of radio disc jockeys, who often played particular local and regional records that eventually became national hits. In 1952, for example, Hunter Hancock aired an instrumental single titled "Pachuco Hop" by black saxophonist Chuck Higgins. Hancock later became a disc jockey at KGFJ radio, the first station to broadcast exclusively the music of black artists seven days per week. "A massive audience in East L.A. tuned in on

each and every one of those days. At about the same time D.J.s like Art
Laboe and Dick 'Huggy Boy' Hugg started playing jump and doo wop on
the radio" (Guevara 1985:117).

Besides Chuck Higgins, other major influences were black saxophonists Joe Houston and Big Jay McNeely. Chicano saxophonists Li'l Bobby
Rey and Chuck Rio (whose real name was Danny Flores) emulated their
styles but also added their own particular Mexican and Latin-based stylistic idioms. "Corrido Rock," recorded by the Masked Phantom Band in
the mid-1950s and featuring Rey, is a good example. The instrumental
arrangement consists of two saxophones playing a *norteño*-styled riff in
harmony, superimposed on a supporting fast rock beat. Rey also recorded
"Alley Oop" with the Hollywood Argyles, and Chuck Rio, as a member
of the Champs, achieved national attention with his own composition and
instrumental hit "Tequila" in 1958. The song rose to the number one spot
on the national rating charts.

Another important figure during the 1950s was Li'l Julian Herrera.
Hungarian by birth (according to one source) but raised by Mexican-
American parents in East Los Angeles, he became perhaps the first major
eastside R&B singer.[3] His vocal style was heavily influenced by Jesse Belwin
and Johnny Ace. Herrera was given major public exposure at the El Monte
Legion Stadium by Johnny Otis, with whom he co-composed "Lonely,
Lonely Nights," a local hit. Guevara describes the tune as "an elegant and
beautiful doo wop ballad, very much in the ballad style, but something
about it—the accent, the voice, the attitude—made it different. It was
Chicano rock" (Guevara 1985:118). Guevara gives the following ethnographic description of the Chicano musical ambience during the late 1950s
and early 1960s at the El Monte Legion Stadium:

> A typical weekend dance at the Legion would pack in crowds that
> were 90 percent Chicano, 10 percent Anglo. The dancers sported
> khaki pants with a Sir Guy shirt and a charcoal gray suit coat, one
> button roll, and spit-shined French-toed shoes. The girls had stacked
> hair and wore white shoes called "bunnies," black tight short skirts,
> and feathered earrings. A lot of Anglo kids copied not only the styles
> but the dances, the most popular of which were the Pachuco Hop,
> Hully Gully and the Corrido Rock.
>
> Of all the dances, the Corrido was the wildest, sort of an early
> form of slam dancing. Two or three lines would form, people arm-in-
> arm, with each line consisting of 150 to 250 people. With the band
> blasting away at a breakneck rocking tempo, the lines took four steps
> forward and four steps back, eventually slamming into each other
> (but making sure that no one got hurt). The *corrido* is a Mexican

traditional folk story/song and dance that goes back to at least the mid-1800s, still very popular at weddings and dances today.

An evening at the Legion always ended with tight, slow dancing, called scrunching, usually to ballads by locals like "Handsome" Mel Williams or Vernon Green and the Medallions. After the dance, it was out to the parking lot for the grand finale. Where's the party? *¿Quién tiene pisto? ¿Mota?* Who's got the booze? Weed? Rumors would fly all night as to which gangs were going to throw *chingasos*—come to blows. The Jesters Car Club from Boyle Heights, which dominated the Eastside, would parade around the parking lot in their lavender, maroon, or gray primered cars, wearing T-Timer shades (blue or green colored glass in square wire frames). In what was an inviolable ritual every weekend, the police would eventually break everything up and we'd caravan back to the Foster's Freeze at Whittier and Mott or to Johnny's at Whittier and Ditman. (Guevara 1985:118)

The Salsa Infusion

Music based on Caribbean rhythms, especially Afro-Cuban, has been very popular within the Mexican community in Los Angeles since the "rumba craze" of the 1930s (see Roberts 1979). Recent immigrants constituted a large portion of the Mexican population, and the community continued to transfer familiar forms popular in Mexico. These musical forms included *música tropical,* the Afro-Cuban form that, in New York City, would become known as *salsa* after the 1950s. The urban Mexican-American audience in Los Angeles expanded its musical horizons as it adapted to U.S. media and record dissemination and became aficionados of the early salsa bandleaders emanating from Cuba, New York City, and Puerto Rico. During the 1940s and 1950s these included Machito (a Cuban based in New York), Tito Rodríguez (a Puerto Rican), Tito Puente (a New Yorker), and Pérez Prado (a Cuban who had spent time in Mexico).

In addition to the many nightclubs and ballrooms mentioned by Lalo Guerrero, an assortment of other places catered to tropical music audiences in various sectors of Los Angeles. Band leader Tito Puente confirmed Guevara's (1985) estimate that during the 1950s his audiences in Los Angeles were about 90 percent Mexican (see Loza 1983a).

Musician Eytan ben Sheviya describes Los Angeles as a stronghold for Latin music since the 1930s.

From the late 1930s right up to the early 1960s "Latin" music was as popular with the U.S. public as any other popular music of the day. Dance studios were everywhere and classes on rhumba, cha cha chá, mambo, and merengue were packed. . . .

Changing demographics have played a large role in the salsa scene here in Los Angeles. With such a large Mexican-American population, Los Angeles has always been a stronghold for Latin music. Several of the most popular venues for Latin music in the '40s and '50s—the Hollywood Palladium, Virginia's (across from MacArthur) and El Paseo on Olvera Street—are still open today.[4] And the movie industry always drew the top performers from Latin countries hoping for a break in pictures. (Sheviya 1983:40)

One individual synonymous with Latin dance music throughout the 1950s and 1960s was the previously cited Lionel Sesma, known professionally and through radio as "Chico" Sesma. Mexican American and a product of Roosevelt High School in the Boyle Heights section of Los Angeles's East Side, he began his musical profession as a trombonist in the local orchestras of Tily López and Sal Cervantes, both popular Mexican-American bandleaders. He then toured extensively with the big bands of Johnny Richards, Pete Rugalo, Kenny Baker, and Russ Morgan.

It was in radio, however, that Sesma made his initial and long-standing impact, especially on the Mexican-American population of Los Angeles. In 1949 he was hired by radio station KOWL to produce and host a bilingual program. Originally, he aired about two Latin music recordings per half hour, which were usually chosen from discs of Tito Puente, Benny Moré, Machito, Tito Rodríguez, Pérez Prado, or other such internationally popular artists of the period. The rest of the broadcast material consisted of other popular music, including that of Billy Eckstine, Herb Jeffreys, Jimmy Lunceford, Billie Holiday, Dinah Washington, and Sarah Vaughn. After three months on the air, Sesma converted the radio show to an all Latin music format.

In 1956, KOWL was changed to KDAY, and Sesma was featured as one of four disc jockeys headlining the station. The others were Joe Adams, Jim Ameche, and Frank Evans. In 1958 Sesma changed jobs and began a radio program at KALI, an all Spanish-language station where he stayed until 1967. There, he continued his bilingual format of airing contemporary Latin dance music.

The other major impact that Chico Sesma made on musical activity in Los Angeles was his long-standing production of the "Latin Holidays." Designed as Latin ballroom dances, the first took place in 1953 at the Zenda Ballroom. In 1954 Sesma changed the location of these monthly, semiannual, or annual dance concerts to the Hollywood Palladium, where they became a twenty-year popular tradition, especially among Mexican Americans, until 1973. Among the many artists featured at the Latin Holidays were Celia Cruz and Sonora Matancera (for whom this was their first appearance in Los Angeles), Tito Puente, Machito, René Touzet, Orlando Marín, Benny Moré, Miguelito Valdez, Orquesta Aragón, Sonora Santanera, Sonia López, Cal Tjader, George Shearing, Jack Costanzo, Vicentico Valdez, and Pérez Prado. At the dances Sesma would also feature the music of local orchestras and solo artists such as Eddie Cano, Bobby Montez, Manny López, Johnny Martínez, Tony Martínez, and Tito Rivera and his Havana Mambo Orchestra.

In May 1979 Sesma again began to broadcast a program at KALI as part of an arrangement with New York–based Fania Records, which specialized in salsa. The show lasted until May 1982.

Since the 1960s, tropical music and salsa musicians have continued to perform in Los Angeles, and many Mexican Americans have become avid fans of such styles. Clubs and widely promoted dance concerts at various venues (e.g., the Hollywood Palladium, the Los Angeles Sports Arena, and the Los Angeles Convention Center) have continually featured artists such as Eddie Palmieri, Tito Puente, Celia Cruz, Sonora Mantancera, Johnny Pacheco, El Gran Combo, Sonora Ponceña, Oscar De León, Justo Betancourt, Ray Barreto, Wilfrido Vargas, and Lalo Rodríguez, among many others. Supporting this ambience have been specific radio stations catering to aficionados of salsa and Latin music (these are discussed later in this chapter).

Jazz, Latin Jazz, and Fusion

Because jazz, Latin jazz, and fusion are often interrelated with respect to the musicians performing them, many artists have crossed such boundaries during the past forty years. The appendix to this chapter lists many of the Chicano and other Latino musicians who have performed in this network of diversity, interchanging musical styles from be-bop and Latin jazz to modern fusion, often within a complex borrowing from various Latin styles.

The performance contexts of these musicians, among the many others of relative experience, have ranged from small clubs to recording and from "jam" sessions to tours with internationally acclaimed artists. Jazz, Latin jazz, and modern "fusion" styles have often been referred to by musicians as "progressive" styles. Regardless of the nomenclature, these particular genres and combinations of music have held an intense place in the musical life of Mexican Americans in Los Angeles, as they have in so many parts of the world.

Vikki Carr

Born Florencia Bisenta de Casillas Martínez Cardona in El Paso, Texas, Vikki Carr is the eldest of seven children. Her father, Carlos Cardona, was a construction worker. Carr was raised in the San Gabriel Valley, in the east portion of Los Angeles county, and attended Rosemead High School during the 1950s. It was there that she began studying music and playing leading roles in the school's musical productions. While still in high school she also began to sing on weekends with local bands. On graduation she was offered a job as soloist with the Pepe Callahan Mexican-Irish Band and opened as "Carlita" at the Chi-Chi Club in Palm Springs. This opportunity led to additional tours to Reno, Las Vegas, Tahoe, and Hawaii. Following this initial public exposure in the early 1960s she changed her stage name to Vikki Carr. Soon afterward she recorded her first demo and was signed to a long-term contract with Liberty Records. Following a highly successful tour to Australia, with a hit record "He's a Rebel," Carr joined the "Ray Anthony" television series as the featured vocalist.

In terms of international recognition and financial success, Vikki Carr is one of the most successful Mexican-American vocalists to date, male or female. She has headlined the world's most prestigious nightclubs and has sung to sold-out audiences in Las Vegas, New York, the Netherlands, Germany, Spain, France, England, Australia, and Japan. She joined Danny Kaye in a three-week tour of military bases in Vietnam, which she described as one of her more rewarding experiences. In 1972 she was honored as "Singer of the Year" by the American Guild of Variety Artists.

Carr also has done musical comedy throughout the country, including such shows as *South Pacific, The Unsinkable Molly Brown,* and *I'm Getting My Act Together and Taking It on the Road,* and has made numerous dramatic television appearances. In 1967 she performed for Queen Elizabeth II and the next year appeared in her own "Vikki Carr Show" at the London Palladium. Carr has performed for state dinners and other events at the White House—for President Richard Nixon's inaugural celebration, as two-time national chairwoman of the American Lung Association's annual Christmas-seal drive, and as part of a televised White House Christmas show during the term of President Ronald Reagan. In 1990 Carr sang at the inauguration of the Richard M. Nixon Library, where presidents Bush, Reagan, Ford, and Nixon were in attendance.

Carr's recording credits are among her most impressive credentials. She has recorded over fifty best-selling albums, both in English and Spanish. Her list of single hits in the United States includes "It Must Be Him" (which earned her a Grammy Award nomination in 1967 and which had been a major hit for her in Britain that same year before being rereleased in the U.S.), "With Pen in Hand" (1969 Grammy nominee), and "Can't Take My Eyes Off You." During one period, Carr had two albums and two singles among the nation's top 100 records. She has had recording contracts with Liberty, Columbia, and CBS International.

Vikki Carr's first personal appearance in her grandparents' native Mexico took place in 1972 at the Hotel Aristos in Mexico City. After subsequently hosting two Mexican television specials, she received the Visiting Entertainer of the Year Award. Since then, Carr's career has focused on singing in Mexico and the rest of Latin America. Since her recording of "Y el amor" in 1980, she has accumulated fourteen gold records for her albums recorded in Spanish, all on the CBS International label. She received a Grammy Award for the Mexican-American category in 1986 for her LP *Simplemente mujer*. In 1989 the single "Mala suerte" from her album titled *Esos hombres* (released in 1988) became a major hit throughout Latin America and the Hispanic areas of the United States. She was awarded another Grammy in 1992 in the Latin Pop category.

In 1971, with funds earned from a television commercial for milk, Carr established the Vikki Carr Scholarship Foundation to award higher education scholarships to young Mexican Americans. The foundation has awarded scholarships to approximately 170 students for attendance at universities and colleges throughout the United States. In recognition of her many philanthropic endeavors, Carr received the *Los Angeles Times* Woman of the Year Award in 1970 and the Hispanic Women's Council Hispanic Woman of the Year Award in 1984. She has also received honorary doctorates from St. Edwards University and from the University of San Diego (the latter in law).

The Mariachi Tradition

The mariachi has been popular in Los Angeles since it became the vogue of Mexican radio during the 1930s. As immigration has continuously increased, so has the growth of mariachis. Perhaps the most well-known symbol of Mexican music, scores of mariachis perform at restaurants, clubs, weddings, civil functions, holiday celebrations, and a variety of other occasions. Because so many Mexican *ranchera* singers are popular in Los Angeles, mariachis have been a mainstay of musical accompaniment for that genre in addition to performing their traditional genre—the *son jalisciense* (see Pearlman 1988).

Additionally, popular singers of the mariachi style from Mexico regularly appear in concert at major venues such as the Pico Rivera Sports Arena, the Universal Amphitheater, the Los Angeles Sports Arena, the Greek Theater, the Million Dollar Theater, the Hollywood Bowl, and numerous community parks and concert halls. Such artists have included José Alfredo Jiménez, Jorge Negrete, Pedro Infante, Lola Beltrán, Lucha Villa, Luis Aguilar, Vicente Fernández, Miguel Aceves Mejía, Juan Gabriel, Rocío Dúrcal, and Aída Cuevas.

Of the two most recognized mariachis in Los Angeles, the Mariachi Los

Camperos de Nati Cano and the Mariachi Los Galleros de Pedro Rey, the former has enjoyed the greatest popularity. Established in 1961, Los Camperos was rated by aficionados of the art form as being among the most proficient and stylized mariachis in both Mexico and the United States. Nati (Natividad) Cano, the director of the mariachi, is originally from the small town of Ahuisculco in the state of Jalisco, Mexico, and studied mariachi music with his father and violin at the Academia de Música in Guadalajara. In 1953 he went to the border city of Mexicali, Baja California, where he played with Mariachi Chapala, eventually becoming the group's musical director. In 1957 the mariachi relocated to Los Angeles, where it began to perform at the Granada Restaurant club on Broadway Avenue in the downtown district. In 1961 Cano accepted an offer to perform with a mariachi that backed a variety of musical acts at the Million Dollar Theater, including Mexican artists such as Lola Beltrán, Pedro Vargas, Miguel Aceves Mejía, and numerous others. When the director of that mariachi died in an auto accident, Cano was named the new director and the group's name was changed. Mariachi Los Camperos de Nati Cano thus emerged and continued to perform as a highly popular act at the Million Dollar Theater. By 1962 Los Camperos were performing at Catalina Island, where they developed a unique road show that they took on future tours. In 1963 the mariachi headlined with Pedro Vargas at Carnegie Hall in New York City. Between 1962 and 1967 the group performed in Las Vegas and shared billing with Harry James, Ray Anthony, and Della Reese. In addition to its Las Vegas show, the group performed on an entertainment circuit that included extended tours to Lake Tahoe, Hawaii, and New York.

In 1967, in collaboration with other members of Los Camperos and Francisco Fauce, then owner of the Million Dollar Theater, Cano extended his entrepreneurial role by opening La Fonda Restaurant, which became the permanent home of Los Camperos. Eventually, Cano became principal owner. La Fonda de Los Camperos quickly became one of the most popular night spots among residents and international tourists alike. Especially innovative was Cano's concept of a mariachi "show," complete with traditional-style dancers, a diverse musical repertoire of both commercially popular and dexterously demanding arrangements, and dinner service. Los Camperos has performed for some 2½ million patrons at La Fonda over the past twenty-three years.

Cano has continuously employed some of the most proficient mariachi musicians from Mexico to play in Los Camperos. The mariachi has recorded various LPs in addition to making its regular appearances at La Fonda (six nights a week) and other locales throughout the U.S. Southwest and Canada. The group has performed in different locations for presidents Jimmy Carter, Gerald Ford, Ronald Reagan, and George Bush, as well as for numerous other national and international dignitaries. In 1988 and 1989 the group made several television appearances with Linda Ronstadt, including spots on NBC's "Tonight Show," the 1988 Grammy Awards show, and the HBO (Home Box Office) cable network's "¡Caliente y Picante!" special, in addition to touring California with her. Los Camperos have been featured at the major mariachi festivals in the Southwest, including those of Tucson, Universal Studios in Los Angeles, and San Diego. Nati Cano has become a principal consultant for the annual Tucson International Mariachi Conference. In 1990 he was awarded the National Endowment for the Arts National Heritage Award, a national honor bestowed annually on accomplished artists in the United States. In 1991 Cano and his Mariachi Los Camperos again recorded with Linda Ronstadt on her second LP of Mexican music, *Más Canciones*. The recording also featured Mariachi Vargas de Tecalitlán. Mariachi Los Camperos de Nati Cano toured extensively with Ronstadt throughout the United States in 1991. In 1992 Cano began work on a solo album by Mariachi Los Camperos, with Ronstadt as associate producer.

Mariachi Los Galleros de Pedro Rey is another very popular and long-standing mariachi also affiliated with a popular restaurant in Los Angeles County—El Rey, in Montebello. Principally owned by family members of the mariachi (the Hernández brothers), the restaurant was opened by director Pedro Hernández (a.k.a. Pedro Rey) and other investors in 1976. Before organizing Los Galleros in 1970, Pedro Hernández had performed with both Mariachi Vargas de Tecalitlán in Mexico and Mariachi Los Camperos de Nati Cano in Los Angeles.

The history of Mariachi Los Galleros covers five generations of the Hernández family. The origin of this legacy can be traced back to Don Esteban Hernández, who was born in La Cofradía, Jalisco, in 1924. There, in Jalisco, he was influenced by his father and maternal grandfather, both musicians. By the age of eight he was performing in his father's mariachi, Los Aguilas de Chapala. Hernández married in 1940, and he and his wife, Maria Eva, bore eight children. All six sons became mariachi musicians.

In the early 1940s Hernández, along with brothers Miguel, José, and Leopoldo Sosa, formed Mariachi Chapala, named after their native city in Jalisco. In 1944 and 1945 the group toured Tijuana; in 1946 and 1948 it was hired to perform at Jeanette's, a popular Los Angeles nightclub catering to the Mexican population. As noted previously, the mariachi was based in Mexicali during the early 1950s and relocated to Los Angeles in 1957 (both periods of Nati Cano's tenure as musical director). Esteban Hernández continued as a member of Mariachi Chapala until 1961. Hernández's oldest son, Pedro, who was born in Chapala, never performed with the mariachi and spent the periods from 1946 and 1970 playing both trumpet and guitar with the leading mariachis in Mexicali, Tijuana, Los Angeles (i.e., Mariachi Los Camperos in 1967), and Mexico City. In 1966 he arrived in the latter city to become a member of Mariachi Vargas de Tecalitlán, the most highly recognized mariachi in Mexico. In 1970 he returned to Los Angeles, where he formed Mariachi Los Galleros de Pedro Rey. After holding contracts at restaurants such as El Chapala in Woodland Hills, El Gato in the San Fernando Valley, the Million Dollar Theater, La Carioca in Boyle Heights, and the Palacio Azteca (located in downtown Los Angeles beneath the Million Dollar Theater), Hernández opened in El Rey.[5]

Mariachi Los Galleros has recorded various LPs and regularly performs dinner shows at El Rey six nights per week. The mariachi has also performed at the major mariachi festivals in the Southwest, including those of Tucson and Universal Studios.

José Hernández, one of the Hernández brothers who performed with Los Galleros, left the group to form and direct Mariachi Sol de México. In 1986, in the tradition of the show mariachi, he opened a restaurant, Cielito Lindo, in South El Monte, another eastside suburb of Los Angeles.

Among the hundreds of mariachis that have performed in Los Angeles through the past forty years, some of the more recent ones include Mariachi América, Mariachi Mi Tierra, Mariachi Los Angeles, Mariachi Azteca, Mariachi Atotonilco, Mariachi Imperial, Mariachi Las Rosas, and Mariachi Continental.

During the early 1970s student mariachi groups formed at various universities in Los Angeles. Because of the prominent mariachi culture in Los Angeles, many college students, both Mexican American and non-Mexican, began to experiment with the mariachi style. The first such mariachi, Uclatlán, was formed in 1961 at the UCLA Institute of Ethnomusicology and was directed by Jesús Sánchez, a traditional mariachi musician from Zacoalco, Jalisco. Participants included graduate students Don Borcherdt and James Koetting, Professor Timothy Harding from California State University, Los Angeles, and numerous other students and community musicians. The group was later directed by one of its original members, Mark Fogelquist, a graduate of the UCLA ethnomusicology program who wrote a master's thesis on the *son jalisciense* (1975). Eventually, in the mid-1970s, the group ceased to be university-affiliated and became a professional ensemble, competing with the many mariachis in Los Angeles. A second mariachi, Nuevo Uclatlán, was established and directed by Daniel Sheehy in 1976 as part of the UCLA ethnomusicology curriculum to continue the study group concept. Both Uclatláns still exist and perform throughout southern California. The original Uclatlán has actually become one of the premier mariachis in southern California. It, too, is based at its own restaurant (El Mariachi, in Orange County) and has adopted the show format. Uclatlán, whose musical director from 1984 to 1991 was Juan Manuel Cortez, is headed by Mark Fogelquist, who still performs with the group along with his brother Jim, another original member from the group's UCLA period. The mariachi has performed, toured, and recorded extensively (five LPs), features a variety of challenging arrangements, and has accompanied major recording artists. Mariachi Nuevo Uclatlán was directed for a period by Hector Aguíñiga; since 1981 it has been headed by Steven Pearlman, who received his Ph.D. in anthropology at UCLA and wrote his doctoral dissertation on mariachi music in Los Angeles (Pearlman 1988).

Other academically based mariachis have included Mariachi Calstatitlán from California State University, Los Angeles; Mariachi Mexicapán, which originated at Roosevelt High School under the direction of Joaquín Soto and evolved into one of the more popular professional mariachis; a student mariachi at California State Polytechnic University, Pomona; and Mariachi Aztlán from California State University, Northridge. In the fall of 1989, the student mariachi ensemble was reactivated at UCLA's Department of Ethnomusicology. Hired to direct the class were Nati Cano and Juan Manuel Cortez. At the high school and junior high school level, mariachis were formed at various schools throughout Los Angeles, especially in the city's eastside and other Latino sectors.

Mariachi festivals have become popular in several locales throughout the Southwest. The San Antonio, Texas, festival began in 1982 and the Tucson festival in 1983. The Universal Studios Hollywood mariachi festival originated in 1985 and continues on an annual basis. At UCLA the Mexican Arts Series staged a "minifestival" in April 1990, billed as Feria de Mariachi, which was later televised as the anchor location for a Cinco de Mayo special on KCBS. The Mariachi Los Camperos de Nati Cano and Uclatlán de Mark Fogelquist participated, the new UCLA student mariachi group debuted, and the UCLA Grupo Folklórico interpreted a variety of traditional dances. The Mexican Arts Series introduced instructional elements into its 1991 festival. In June 1990 a major production was staged at the Hollywood Bowl. Promoted as Mariachi U.S.A., the afternoon festival featured Vikki Carr, Linda Ronstadt, Mariachi Vargas de Tecalitlán (from Mexico City), Mariachi Los Camperos de Nati Cano, Mariachi Sol de México de José Hernandez, and Mariachi Las Campañas de América (from San Antonio, Texas). The festival was again staged in 1991 featuring the mariachis Vargas de Tecalitlán, Sol de México, Los Galleros, and Las Campañas de América. Featured singers included Lucha Villa and Little Joe. Rodri Rodríguez, producer of Mariachi U.S.A., continued the annual festival into 1992.

Another phenomenon of mariachi culture in Los Angeles is its incor-

poration into the Roman Catholic Mass. The concept of the Misa Panamericana or Misa de Mariachi originated in 1966 in Cuernavaca, Mexico.
Folk genres and mariachi expression were adapted to the sung parts of
the Mass. The Misa Panamericana was first performed in Los Angeles in
1968 at Saint Joseph's Church in downtown Los Angeles on the feast day
of Our Lady of Guadalupe, December 12. Mariachi Imperial, directed by
Gabriel Leyva, performed the music. The mariachi Mass continued to be
performed weekly at Saint Joseph's, Saint Basil's, and at the Olvera Street
La Placita church. At the latter, a mass on the feast day of Our Lady of
Guadalupe in 1984 was accompanied by more than fifty mariachi groups
performing inside the church. Numerous other local parishes also continue
to offer mariachi masses for the Spanish-speaking population.

As in Mexico, the mariachi in Los Angeles has demanded stylistic dexterity. Mariachi ensembles are required to maintain an extensive repertoire
of Mexican traditional folk music in addition to interpretations of current
popular music. Mariachis are also expected to perform other popular Latin
styles. For example, Los Camperos, Los Galleros, Mariachi Sol de México,
and Uclatlán have adapted a variety of popular songs from Latin America
and the United States to their repertoires, thus appealing to a more diverse
market.

In recent years, one of the major impacts of the mariachi tradition in
Los Angeles has been singer Linda Ronstadt's recording and performance
of Mexican music. Her 1988 LP *Canciones de mi padre* has become both
an anomaly and a milestone in the music industry. Recorded in Los Angeles, the LP employed the musical accompaniment of members of three
mariachis based in Los Angeles: Los Camperos de Nati Cano, Los Galleros de Pedro Rey, and Mariachi Sol de México de José Hernández. The
fourth mariachi involved in the recording, Mexico-based Mariachi Vargas
de Tecalitlán, has generally been recognized as the most long-standing and
successful group in the history of mariachi music. Mariachi Vargas accompanied Ronstadt on her national tour featuring the music of the album.
The group's director, Rubén Fuentes, arranged and conducted the music
of *Canciones de mi padre*. Additionally, José Hernández (director of Mariachi Sol de México) provided assistance and coordination in the musical
production of the recording. Also featured on the album and in its many
related concerts afterward was vocalist, composer, and actor Daniel Valdez. The LP received a 1989 Grammy Award in the Mexican-American
category. Her second album of Mexican music, *Más Canciones,* was released
in November 1991.

Although originally from Tucson, Arizona, Ronstadt has produced most
of her recordings and conducted her enterprises from the Los Angeles area
since 1969, when she was still a member of the Stone Ponies. An eclec-

tic artist who has explored various genres of popular music, she began
to experiment with the mariachi style in the PBS television production
of Luis Valdez's *Corridos* (filmed in San Francisco in 1985) and by guest
appearances with mariachis at the annual Tucson International Mariachi
Conference. (The rest is history!) Nati Cano has expressed on numerous
occasions throughout Los Angeles and on national television that Linda
Ronstadt has done more than revive the mariachi tradition for both old
and new audiences; she has brought to the mariachi style an even larger,
international level of commercial recognition and diffusion.

Other Mexican/Latino Styles in Los Angeles

Another segment of the musical network and local music industry in Los
Angeles that deserves mention consists of the groups that cater exclusively to the city's Latino community, especially Mexicans. These largely
immigrant bands, generally consisting of four or more members, perform
popular music sung in Spanish and usually recorded by Latin American or
Spanish artists. They also record original material on local labels and have
established a considerable following. The actual musical genres performed
include ballads, *cumbias* (a style originally from Colombia and popular
throughout Latin America), and many dance rhythms related to the Mexican *ranchera* and *norteño* styles (often with a basic polka or waltz rhythm).
Among the repertoire of some of these ensembles is even a style called a *chicana*. Instrumentation consists of keyboards (quite frequently electric
organ or synthesizer), electric guitar, electric bass, drum set, and some
Latin percussion. Performance style is often modeled on the many popular
groups in Mexico such as Los Bukis, Los Humildes, Los Yonics, and Los
Freddys.

In 1985, two students in a class I taught at UCLA conducted a small-
scale research project on this general musical ambience in Los Angeles (the
father of one of the students was involved in the local industry). I found
their thoughts on the subject insightful.

> There do exist musicians who focus on the Latino population exclu-
> sively. The process by which these groups and individuals find their
> audience and forge prosperous careers within the selective . . . Los
> Angeles and southwestern U.S. Latino communities is [indeed inter-
> esting, and we will refer to the Los Angeles experience as] "Latin
> L.A.'s mainstream sound."
>
> The "pop" music of East L.A. and its neighboring Latino areas
> has very traditional elements of Mexican music, and its popularity
> with little doubt is due to high numbers of Mexican immigrants now
> living in this community. The rhythms are familiar patterns found

in mariachi and ranchera songs. Added to these sounds are small amounts of mild rock and romantic ballads. And of course, the music is strictly sung in Spanish. This is due to audience demand. A recent event illustrative of this demand took place at the Universal Amphitheater when a romantic singer from Mexico, Emmanuel, sang an American tune in English. The reaction from his L.A. crowd was vocally negative, with loud boos and shouts of "solamente español."

Today there are over two hundred of these Latino bands playing the Los Angeles area. Some of the most notable for popularity and for the way they typify the mainstream Latino sound are Los Diablos, Los Bondadosos, El Chicali, La Leyenda, and El Padrino. (Hernández and Preciado, 1985)

It should be noted that whether one is referring to these styles or to salsa and other tropical dance music, there has traditionally existed in Los Angeles an interplay among Latin American immigrant musicians in a diversity of contexts. Both immigrant Mexicans and U.S.-born Mexican Americans have performed various styles of music with Cubans, Puerto Ricans, Central Americans, Colombians, and musicians from many other Latin American countries. As immigration patterns have continued to create constantly changing modes of acculturation among Latinos in Los Angeles, their music has adapted.

The internationally marketed contemporary styles and artists imported from Latin America and Spain are part of this Latino complex. Popular singers such as Julio Iglesias (Spain), José José (Mexico), Rafael (Spain), Emmanuel (Mexico), and José Luis Rodríguez (Venezuela) conduct concert schedules and recording promotions throughout Latin America, the United States, and Europe and are in constant demand at major commercial concert halls and arenas throughout Los Angeles.

It is also important to recognize the impact of the various Mexican traditional musical styles (in addition to the mariachi tradition) in numerous locations in Los Angeles. These styles, which cater to Mexican immigrants as well as Mexican Americans born in the United States and other Latinos, include the *trío* (in the style of Trío Los Panchos), the *norteño* (the northern Mexican style accented by the use of accordion), the *jarocho* (a style originally from the Mexican state of Veracruz and especially popular among Mexican *folklórico* dance groups in Los Angeles), and the marimba orchestra (originally from Guatemala and the Mexican states of Chiapas, Oaxaca, and Guerrero).

The Eastside Sound

During the 1960s, bands and individual artists that symbolized the absorption and adaptation of particular musical styles into the musical expression of the eastside community dominated the musical life of Chicanos in Los Angeles. Popular bands such as Thee Midniters, The Village Callers, Cannibal and the Headhunters, The Ambertones, El Chicano, and Tierra were just a few of the hundreds of groups that performed during the 1960s and 1970s, most of which never attained national recognition. The band phenomenon became somewhat of a cult and ritual process in East Los Angeles, and the musicians were symbolic shamans who led their audiences in their inborn passion for musical expression and life.

An "eastside sound," or Chicano style, developed, based on borrowed, adapted genres such as rhythm and blues, soul, rock, funk, salsa, and Mexican traditional forms. In 1980 Luis Rodríguez of Los Angeles wrote a two-part article that appeared in *L.A. Weekly* (1980a, b) and the Los Angeles–based Chicano magazine *Q-VO* (1980c). Comparing the eastside bands to media-created idols such as the Beatles, the Rolling Stones, Little Richard, or Chuck Berry, Rodríguez described the prolific symbolism of the eastside musicians.

> They were heroes and heroines of lowrider car clubs, street gangs, and high school teens. Their records were sold as soon as they came out and whenever they made appearances they crowded dance halls and concerts. Who were they?
>
> They were the rock artists based in East Los Angeles. They were part of a phenomenon known on the West Coast as the "Eastside Sound." It has spanned over twenty years of Chicano musical development.
>
> They were Latin, they were rhythm and blues, they were soul, and they defied categories. The music was a localized fusion of Mexican and American influences. Yet they have been largely ignored.
>
> The ensuing struggle to bring them out of the barrio, record them, and get them to national prominence is a story of glory and tragedy: a story often told in the annals of the record business. (Rodríguez 1980c:27–28)

One of the tragic stories was that of musician Ritchie Valens, whose real name was Richard Valenzuela. After achieving national recognition at the age of seventeen with hits like "Donna" and a rock and roll version of the traditional Mexican *huapango* "La Bamba," the young Chicano was killed in a 1959 plane crash on a snow-covered cornfield in Iowa. Valenzuela had been on tour with rock and roll stars Buddy Holly and J. P. "Big Bopper" Richardson, who died in the same plane crash.

Ritchie Valens came from the barrio of Pacoima in the San Fernando Valley of Los Angeles County. He was discovered by producer Bob Keane and recorded on the latter's record label, Del-Fi Records. In addition to "Donna" and "La Bamba," Valens also had national hit singles with "Come On, Let's Go," "That's My Little Susie," and "Little Girl" (the latter two posthumously). In his brief but significant career, Valens recorded numerous singles and two albums. A third album, *Ritchie Valens in Concert at Pacoima Jr. High,* combined a live concert recording with several work tapes that were never completed for release (Dawson and Keane 1981a).

John Ovalle, owner of the Record Inn in East Los Angeles (and profiled in chap. 4), said of Valens, "A lot of Chicanos copied other people's material. Only one guy really produced more of what Chicanos know —Ritchie Valens. When he did his music the whole world copied him" (Rodríguez 1980c:28). What could have been a sensational impact—a Chicano entering into the mainstream recording industry—was vanquished with the death of Valens. Besides Vikki Carr, there would be no other Chicano recording artist of national prominence for many years. Although a few hits would arise in pocket episodes, no enduring artist would surface until Los Lobos del Este de Los Angeles (profiled in chap. 5) arrived on the national scene in 1984—ten years after their inception in East Los Angeles. *La Bamba,* a film written and directed by Luis Valdez and based on the life of Ritchie Valens, premiered in 1987. The musical score featured the music of Carlos Santana, Bo Diddley, and most notably Los Lobos, whose recording of "La Bamba" reached the number one spot on the national pop music charts, almost thirty years after Valens had done the original version. In the same period that the film was released, Beverly Mendheim published her book *Ritchie Valens: First Latino Rocker* (1987).

Rodríguez (1980a, b, c) interrupts his historical chronicle with a discussion of the early eastside music industry. In addition to producer Bob Keane of the Del-Fi Record Company, who recorded Valens and other Chicano musicians, the other major figure in 1958 was Eddie Davis, who negotiated record productions of eastside groups for the next twenty years. By selling a chain of restaurants and other businesses, Davis accumulated the necessary capital to incorporate his own record manufacturing firm, Faro Productions, in 1958. Three labels emerged from his original investment: Faro, Linda, and Rampart.

By 1962 Davis, in partnership with Billy Cárdenas, owned a nightclub, the Rhythm Room in Fullerton. Weekend dances at the club and at the Rainbow Gardens in Pomona featured local talent (the latter hosted dances promoted by radio station KRLA and emceed by disc jockeys Bob

Eubanks and Dick Moreland). Rodríguez notes that "one of the bands was called The Mixtures, a rarity for the time because they were mixed Chicano, black and anglo musicians" (Rodríguez 1980a:29). Billy Cárdenas, who managed several East Los Angeles bands, brought in various groups to be featured at the two clubs. Cárdenas introduced his clientele to such bands as The Jaguars, The Premiers, The Romancers, and The Salas Brothers.

Rudy and Steve Salas were thirteen and eleven years old, respectively, when they made their first recording. They eventually became the core of the nationally popular eastside group Tierra. The journey to that point, however, was a long one. As young boys, they performed for family re-unions where they sang Mexican *rancheras* and *boleros*. In an interview that Luis Rodríguez conducted with both Eddie Davis and the two Salas brothers, they recalled some of the early events in their careers:

> Rudy: One day, this guy heard us at a playground. He talked to our parents and started booking us at some of the bazaars.
>
> Steve: Then we met Mario Paniagua, who had a band called The Percussions. They were into rock and wanted us to sing. We didn't know anything in English so we had to learn.
>
> Rudy: Through him we met Cárdenas. We changed the name of the band to The Jaguars. Eddie Davis saw us and said he wanted to record us.
>
> Davis: At that time Motown was very popular. But these bands had something unique about them. . . a different sound. I got turned on to that sound. I guess because of their own ethnic background they were locked into a different kind of rhythm.

Davis then began using the Rhythm Room as a rehearsal studio and constructed a remote recording facility within the building. Various bands began to review musical material and to speculate on viable recording ventures. Davis's Rampart Records produced a 45 r.p.m. single by the Salas Brothers called "Darling," the first commercial record to come out of that studio. The recording was the first of many from eastside artists recorded and produced locally through Davis's initiative. As the proprietor of the Rampart label, he "was now becoming part of a whole record buying public on the Eastside of Los Angeles that other companies were ignoring" (Rodríguez 1980c:29).

Rodríguez also alludes to the importance of Ramón Jiménez, popularized in the musical network of East Los Angeles as Li'l Ray. At the age of fourteen Jiménez left his family, which included twelve siblings, and migrated to Los Angeles from Delano to pursue a singing career. He confided to Rodríguez, "The opportunities at home were limited. I mean you can pick grapes, cotton, or work at a shoe store" (1980a:29). Jiménez had already established a professional singing career in Delano and Bakersfield. After settling in Los Angeles, he was able to sing at Los Angeles venues like the popular El Monte Legion Stadium, accompanying such nationally recognized acts as The Penguins, Don and Dewey, Johnny Otis, Jacki Wilson, Brook Benton, and The Coasters.

Jiménez became a vocalist with the original Midniters band but gradually emerged as a vocal soloist frontlining his own group. He was soon offered a recording contract from Motown Records, which he accepted. At the time Motown was moving its headquarters from Detroit to Los Angeles. Somehow, communication deteriorated during the transition, and Li'l Ray was never recorded by Motown. Another potentially lucrative opportunity became a disappointment when, shortly after an agreement had been secured for Jiménez to record with internationally recognized rhythm and blues artist Sam Cooke, Cooke was killed in a Los Angeles motel. Li'l Ray did achieve regional success in southern California with his recording of "I (Who Have Nothing)" on Davis's Rampart label.

Other eastside groups that attained popularity during the same period included The Premiers, whose rendition of "Farmer John," a song originally recorded by Don and Dewey, received substantial radio airplay in 1963. Their recording was rated in the country's top twenty. Warner Brothers Records became interested in The Premiers and negotiated a contract, which was the first time a major record company produced a band from East Los Angeles. Another eastside band, The Blendells, who had success with the record "La La La La La," was contracted by Reprise Records, another major recording company.

As he had with so many other eastside bands, Eddie Davis produced the initial recordings of both The Premiers and The Blendells. In the words of Rudy Benavides, "Eddie became the 'Godfather of the Eastside Sound'" (Rodríguez 1980c:69). Rodríguez explains further: "Street kids playing music was the concept. Max Ubállez remembers that soon afterward other bands were being created out of barrio musicians: The Heartbreakers, The Emeralds and the most popular band of East L.A., Thee Midniters." Uballez, an original member of Thee Midniters, proceeded to relate the following story to Rodríguez: "One time The Romancers played at the Catholic Youth Center on the corner of Brooklyn and Gage in East L.A. We met this guy, Eddie Torres, who says to us, 'Can you help some guys out? They are a bunch of hoods, always in trouble.' Well we all were. So we helped them out. These guys became Thee Midniters. Soon it began to snowball. It grew a lot quicker than we realized. Before we knew it we had dances all over town."

Thee Midniters

From 1964 to 1970 Thee Midniters were considered by many to be the most significant rock and roll band to emanate from the Mexican community in Los Angeles. In a *Goldmine* article, David Reyes and Tom Waldman noted that, "although releasing only four albums, Thee Midniters left behind a repertoire of ballads and rockers that are strong testimony to the talent this eight-piece group possessed. The experience of performing hundreds of concerts enabled the band to develop a smooth and polished stage presence. This also earned them respect, particularly among Latino rock fans in Southern California" (Reyes and Waldman 1982:176).

Thee Midniters evolved from a nucleus group called The Gentiles. Members included lead singer Willie García, trombonist Romeo Prado, and saxophonist Larry Rendon. In 1963 the group became known as Benny and the Midnighters, named after *conguero* (conga player) and manager Benny Savaillos. Eventually, the group changed the name to Thee Midniters, using the spelling "Thee" to avoid being confused with another band popular at that time, Hank Ballard and The Midnighters. At one point, three of the eastside's foremost vocalists were singing together in the band: Cannibal (of Cannibal and the Headhunters), Li'l Ray Jiménez, and Willie García (Willie G.).

Soon after an important rock and roll concert at Salesian High School in 1964, Eddie Torres (who had become manager of Thee Midniters) negotiated a record contract with Chatahoochee Records, a small Hollywood label. The song "Land of a Thousand Dances," which Thee Midniters performed at the Salesian show, became the group's first single and was released in 1964, attaining number sixty-seven on the Billboard charts. Regionally, the record was a major hit, reaching number ten on radio station KFWB in Los Angeles during January and February 1965.

Although Thee Midniters enjoyed extensive popularity throughout southern California, record sales were never highly profitable. During the latter part of 1964 the group embarked on an intense six-year concert tour. "It was not unusual for Thee Midniters to play four places a night at locales all over Southern California. Even in the early days their success as a live band was evident" (Reyes and Waldman 1982:176).

Tailored suits (similar to those of the then-popular Beatles) and group choreography were essential elements in the band's stage show. In 1965 the group recorded its first studio single, an up-tempo rock-style instrumental titled "Whittier Boulevard." "The song quickly became an anthem for young latinos in Southern California, partly because the title named one of East Los Angeles' most popular cruising spots" (Reyes and Waldman 1982:176). As a result, the band's first album, *Thee Midniters,* did very well. The album included "Whittier Boulevard," and eleven other songs, among them "Empty Heart," "Slow Down," "Stubborn Kind of Fellow," and "I Need Someone."

In 1966 Eddie Torres incorporated Whittier Records, and all of the subsequent Midniters's recordings were released on that label. The first such LP was *Love Special Delivery*. The majority of the musical material was composed by lead vocalist Willie García and bassist Jimmy Espinoza. Production and arranging was a group effort. Other albums were titled *Thee Midniters Unlimited* (1967) and *Giants* (1968), the latter a greatest hits compilation (except for two tracks sung by new vocalist Al Anaya, who replaced Willie García). Reyes and Waldman assessed the late 1960s in terms of the group's musical style and competitive quality in relation to major popular artists:

> Some of the best rock songs ever done by Thee Midniters came out in 1967. "Everybody Needs Somebody," a cover of the Solomon Burke tune, was a searing replication featuring Willie's soul screams and a lightning solo on guitar by George Dominguez. "Jump, Jive and Harmonize" is a wild rock song that begins with a bluesy guitar riff and moves along on some of the loudest drumming Danny Lamont ever did. These two singles represented the capabilities of Thee Midniters to produce exceptional hard rock. At their best the group rivaled the Standells and Paul Revere and the Raiders in this area. (Reyes and Waldman 1982:176–77)

In the same *Goldmine* article, bassist Jimmy Espinoza recalled the musical ambience of the band's material: "On the *Thee Midniters Unlimited* album (1967) we were starting to sail on our own."

> This is borne out by the fact that there are eight originals and only four covers on the record. By this time Thee Midniters were able to reproduce any of the rock sounds of the day, including psychedelia and hard blues, and make them their own. "Never Knew U Had It So Bad," arguably the band's greatest rock song, sounded like the San Francisco groups, '60s punk, and The Rolling Stones all under one roof. Ballads still received high priority with the group, and "Dreaming Casually" ranks with their best efforts on the slow side. For an outrageously eclectic representation of '60s rock, *Thee Midniters Unlimited* can hardly be topped. (Reyes and Waldman 1982:177)

Thee Midniters released the single "Chicano Power" in 1969. Interestingly, in light of the intensity of the Chicano political movement at the time, the tune was an instrumental; it was also the group's last recording.

Throughout most of the year the band performed regularly at the Mardi Gras club adjacent to MacArthur Park near downtown Los Angeles. Failure to obtain a major recording contract, however, coupled with some internal tension, led to the demise of Thee Midniters in 1970.

Cannibal and the Headhunters, a group that would eventually achieve national popularity, emerged from the same network of young eastside musicians. The group was not an instrumental band; instead, the format was that of a vocal quartet patterned after such Motown acts as The Miracles and The Temptations. Reflecting their origin in the Ramona Gardens Housing Project, the members used their street names of Scar, Yo-yo, Rabbit, and Cannibal. Their major success was the song "Land of a Thousand Dances" which in 1965 made the nation's top-forty listing. (The same song was recorded by Thee Midniters in 1964.) During the same year Cannibal and the Headhunters became the opening act for the Beatles' historic second U.S. tour. The Columbia Records subsidiary, Date Records, secured a contract with the group, but another hit record never materialized.

Another local band that demonstrated great potential in the popular market was The Village Callers. Consisting of six men and one woman, the group was managed by Héctor Rivera; in 1967 it recorded "Hector," an original song named after him. Eddie Davis again was the recording entrepreneur for another eastside group and produced The Village Callers's first album, which included "Hector" (the LP was a recording of a live show at the Bunny Club in Pico Rivera). Problems ensued when Liberty Records began negotiations that included the use of the "Hector" recording, which Davis had produced. Court proceedings followed, and the infighting had a negative effect on eastside artists.

Following Willie G.'s association with Thee Midniters, Eddie Davis teamed the talented singer with Li'l Ray Jiménez and billed them together in a group called God's Children. Davis arranged a contract with Uni Records (a company that was also recording the popular Hugh Masekela), and the group recorded the song "Hey Does Somebody Care." The song ranked in the top five in New Orleans. According to Davis, however, Willie G.'s manager prohibited the singer from traveling to New Orleans to promote the record. After additional complications, Li'l Ray left the project. Davis then contacted MCA Records to promote Willie G. with a female singer named Lydia. Although a substantial amount was invested in promotion, the enterprise never became very popular. Willie then joined the San Francisco–based Chicano group Malo, which disbanded soon thereafter. In 1966 Davis and Rudy Benavides produced the Rampart Records LP *Golden Treasures—Volume One: West Coast East Side Review,* which consisted of twenty tracks of East Los Angeles bands popular from

1963 to 1965, including Cannibal and the Headhunters, The Premiers, The Blendells, Li'l Ray, the Salas Brothers, The Pagents, The Atlantics, Mark and the Escorts, Ronnie & The Pomona Casuals, The Sisters, Frankie Olvera, The Mixtures, Thee Enchantments, The Jaguars, The Heartbreakers, the Ambertones, Alfred & Joe, The Romancers, The Slauson Brothers, and The Blue Satins. Volume two followed in 1969 and also included twenty tracks covering the years 1965 through 1968, including some of the groups from volume one plus Thee Royal Checkmates, Thee Midniters, The Aldermen, Thee Epics, Sammy Lee and the Summits, Thee Flurtations, The Eastside All Stars, The Back Seat, Sunday Funnies, David and Ruben, Thee Runabouts, Thee Impalas, and East Side Kids. At a later date, a reissue of volumes one and two of the Rampart Records production was distributed by American Pie with a simplified title, *East Side Revue.*

In an interview conducted by Luis Rodríguez, Davis expressed his sentiments stating, "There are three people I felt should have been international stars . . . I mean as big as Frank Sinatra. They are Steve Salas, Li'l Ray, and Willie García" (Rodríguez 1980b:76). Among the many albums that Eddie Davis produced, one included his thoughts in its liner notes (from El Chicano's 1970 LP *Viva Tirado,* MCA Records):

> The Chicano movement that is taking place within the United States at this time is unique. The wants of the Mexican American are so simple and the principle of their movement is so basic and pure that it is, in fact, the very essence of what the United States of America is all about. All they want is to enjoy the heritage that the migrating forefathers of all of us born in America intended their offspring to have: EQUAL OPPORTUNITY AND INDIVIDUAL RESPECT BASED SOLELY UPON PERSONAL QUALIFICATION.

El Chicano

In 1970, the year of the East Los Angeles Moratorium and the high school blowouts, political unrest and cultural reawakening manifested themselves through artistic expression, especially among young Chicanos. In that year one of the most popular and symbolic groups emerged—El Chicano.

Originally assembled as the V.I.P.s, the group recorded a rendition of a tune by jazz composer Gerald Wilson, "Viva Tirado." Wilson had written the instrumental piece in homage to the art of bullfighting and Mexican *matador* (bullfighter) José Ramón Tirado.[6] Billy Watson, who had engineered an informal recording of the composition, presented the version to Eddie Davis and Rudy Benavides. Both considered it a potential hit but suggested a different name for the group because of the Latin quality of the musical arrangement. As Rodríguez observes, "It was 1970. Chicano consciousness was on the rise. Santana had already made big featuring the

Latin-fusion sound" (1980c:76). Soon the name was changed to El Chicano, and the single and album *Viva Tirado* were released. Davis included the following recollection in the album's (1970) liner notes: "When Watson brought me the sampling of what he had produced, I heard the ultimate of that feeling that has always turned me on" (Rodríguez 1980c:76).

"Viva Tirado" became a local hit within twelve weeks after being aired on radio stations such as KGFJ and KHJ. It remained the number one record for thirteen consecutive weeks. It also attained top radio ratings in Baltimore, New York, the South, and the Midwest. Rodríguez (1980a) notes that the record also became historically significant in the recording industry because it was the first single to attain positions in all popular music categories except country and western. Believing "Viva Tirado" to be the national hit that would finally propel the eastside sound into nationwide exposure, Davis invested his finances and energy in the project. He reorganized his Rampart label and established Gordo Enterprises, advertising the theme "Chicanos Are Happening! The Sound of the New Generation."

Davis also contacted some of the acts that he had previously helped produce, such as The Salas Brothers and The Jaguars, who had joined forces to become The Six-Pac. Davis recorded the new group in addition to Willie G.'s single "Brown Baby." Promotion for the assorted recordings was intensified in conjunction with the El Chicano momentum.

Problems surfaced again for Davis. The original V.I.P.s had decided not to proceed with the El Chicano project. Davis therefore formed a new group, but after the success of "Viva Tirado" both the new record company (MCA) and the V.I.P.s demanded the original format, and the latter group formally became El Chicano. Davis continued to produce the group along with its first album. While Davis was promoting the group on the East Coast, El Chicano began dialogue with another producer in Los Angeles who offered a different direction for the band. Frustrated, Davis withdrew from the project in which he had invested so much hope. The year was 1971, and Davis began a five-year semiretirement from the record business.

El Chicano continued to record and perform. One of the more successful local hits was an interpretation of the traditional Mexican bolero "Sabor a mi," sung by female lead vocalist Ersi Arvizu and recorded on the *Revolución* LP in 1971. The recording became known in some eastside quarters as "the eastside anthem," and to this day it is still remembered as one of the most important musical legacies of its period in East Los Angeles. Another interesting endeavor of the group was the recording of a new piece titled "Gringo en México," a track on the 1974 *El Chicano V* album. Composed by songwriter Wendy Waldman, the arrangement incorporated a mariachi and bilingual lyrics. Although El Chicano recorded five albums on the MCA label, the group never produced another national hit.

In 1976 Davis reappeared on the scene after being approached by bassist Héctor González to record a band he had recently assembled. The group consisted of instrumentalists and female vocalists. With the help of Rudy Benavides, Davis recorded the group on his reactivated Rampart label. The band became known as The Eastside Connection and featured Bertha Oropeza as lead vocalist. Another group that Davis began to produce was Skylite, featuring Harry and Dolores Scorzo, former members of East-side Connection. Both groups, composed of Chicanos, Anglos, blacks, and women, were more integrated ensembles than many of the previous Davis affiliates.

Tierra

Of all the bands to emerge from East Los Angeles, Tierra is one of the more successful. Fronted by Rudy and Steve Salas, formerly known as The Salas Brothers (whom Davis had also produced), the group was formed in 1973 after Rudy had performed as a guitarist and vocalist for short periods with El Chicano and with a group called Maya. In the band's first year it recorded its first LP, *Tierra,* on the Twentieth Century record label. Another member of the group at that time was David Torres, Jr., who played piano and trumpet and was one of the band's principal composer-arrangers. Although a local product, having attended Garfield High School, Torres also studied music at the Berklee School of Music in Boston. Also with Tierra in the early to mid-1970s were Rudy Villa (reeds), Kenny Román (drums and Latin percussion), Conrad Lozano (bass), Aaron Ballesteros (drums and vocals), Alfred Rubalcava (bass), and Leon Bisquera (keyboards). In 1975 the group recorded the LP *Stranded* on the Salsoul Records label.

One of the outstanding aspects of Tierra during its early years was its sty-listic innovations, both musical and thematic. On the group's first LP, for example, a mix of R&B, rock, salsa, and ballads characterized the album. Especially notable were two specific recordings: "Gema," a bolero highly popularized throughout Latin America by Mexican singer Javier Solís, was reinterpreted in a variated, rock-influenced format utilizing interesting references to traditional Mexican styles. As was El Chicano's rendition in 1971 of "Sabor a mi" (also recorded by Solís and Eydie Gorme, among others), Tierra's "Gema" was one of the first such adaptations of Mexican music recorded among the various bands of East Los Angeles. The other highly innovative cut on the album was "Barrio Suite," a multi-themed composition by Steve Salas, Rudy Salas, and David Torres. The lyrics and musical contours of the piece specifically referred to the Chicano experience of the early 1970s. Social statement, idealism, and musical experimenta-tion weaved an interesting combination of sound, thought, and sentiment. Other innovative examples from the album include "La Feria," a bilingual salsa-rock mix (originally composed for and premiered at the first Feria de la Raza festival, held at California State University, Los Angeles, in 1971), and the track "Tierra," an arrangement that invokes subtly placed motifs referring to Mexican folk and indigenous culture. The record also exhibits a substantial amount of David Torres's fluid, progressive jazz–influenced piano offerings.

Eventually, Tierra expanded with the addition of El Chicano's original *conguero*, Andrés Baeza. In 1978 Joey Guerra, who had been playing with another eastside group, Changing Times, replaced Torres on piano. Also featured were Bobby Navarrete on saxophone, Steve Falomir on electric bass, Phillip Madayag on drums, and Roberto Loya on trumpet. The group played regularly for two years at Rudy's Pasta House on Olympic Boulevard in East Los Angeles, a club with a diverse musical history over the past thirty years.

In 1979 Tierra recorded the single "Gonna Find Her," which became a radio hit in Los Angeles and throughout the Southwest. This was a self-financed project, as was their subsequent recording of a ballad called "Together," originally recorded by The Intruders. This single, featuring Steve Salas on lead vocals, reached a position in the top 100 on a national scale, and the group was offered a contract with Boardwalk Records. The LP *City Nights* was released in 1980, featuring the latter two tracks in addition to "Memories." With an album to Tierra's credit, their song "Together" reached number eighteen on the national top-forty charts. Among the guest artists performing on the album was Willie Bobo (*timbales*), who had also been involved in the production of two of the band's recordings ("Gonna Find Her" and "Time to Dance"). Internationally, "Together" achieved the number thirty position in the Radio Free Europe top-forty charts and received extensive airplay in Japan. The group also recorded a Spanish version of the song that was quite successful in Mexico.

The year 1981 was monumental for Tierra in terms of national and international recognition and industry success. The group appeared on numerous television programs, including "American Bandstand," "Soul Train," "Solid Gold," "The Toni Tenille Show," and the "American Music Awards." An east coast tour of the United States included concerts at the Ritz and Carnegie Hall in New York City. Press coverage was extensive throughout the country but especially in East Los Angeles and the Southwest. Tierra was featured in almost every major Latino publication in articles, interviews, and advertisements, and "Together" earned the prestigious platinum record award, in recognition of over one million records sold.

Although the members of Tierra considered it difficult to classify their diverse music, the group's sound was often associated with the black R&B sound of many top-forty groups popular at the time throughout the country (Earth, Wind, and Fire; The Commodores; Stevie Wonder). When the group performed live, black audiences, familiar with the group only through radio, were often surprised to find its members were not black. In addition to the heavy R&B influence on the group's musical style, Latin music, especially salsa, was another essential ingredient. Tierra has strived to maintain a strong Chicano cultural identity. They have performed at various high schools and community events throughout the East Los Angeles area. In an interview conducted by Andrew J. Quiñones for *Q-VO* magazine, pianist Joey Guerra offered the following thoughts about the concept of identity:

> All of us in the band grew up with the attitude, because the media and society in general had told us that we were below other people. Part of the obsession we had to make it was just to be able to prove them wrong; and yes we can do something. . . . It's inspiring, especially to the kids, to see another of their own kind making it. It gives them the idea that, yeah, maybe I can make it too because he did it. We try to tell them that we're not going to confess we have all the answers or that we have the formula in life, but one of the main things is to keep trying. Just keep trying regardless if you're Chicano, regardless of what you are, if you have the ability. . . .
>
> There was also something musically important that we were trying to get across, the idea that this band is a cultural band, so to speak. We're a Chicano band and there's a lot of influences that we have aside from the zoot suit being symbolic with our people. It was also the idea, too, that we were incorporating the 1940's music, and that's always been something that's been part of our culture. The theme from the album *City Nights* was about people and the lifestyle of the people that live at night, which is also part of the Chicano culture too; you know, the lowriding thing, the dancing thing, the romance thing. The zoot suit thing was to be able to show that there were also cultural elements involved; you will notice if you listen to the album. (Quiñones 1981:8)

A second Boardwalk LP, *Together Again*, followed in 1982 with considerably less commercial success than its predecessor. In 1983 one of Tierra's principal producers, Neil Bogart, died, while the group was still on the rise. Mike Jiménez, the young eastside singer who had led his own group, Nice 'n Easy, was recruited as an additional singer, and the band recorded another album, *Bad City Boys*. Again, the minimal commercial success acheived was not what had been anticipated, and Tierra has produced no other national hit since "Together." The group's production organization, however, has been able to maintain a busy performance

schedule throughout the United States, especially the S[...]
band continues to perform and record. In 1990 Tierra b[...]
and produce a concert/show in various venues titled "La [...]
Revue," including major concerts at the Celebrity Theat[...]
at UCLA's Royce Hall. In addition to spotlighting Tie[...]
tured the two other most recognized eastside groups of the 1960s and
1970s—Thee Midniters and El Chicano.

The New Wave

As the year 1980 approached, a change occurred in the music industry
that greatly affected the musical life of young, maturing Chicanos in Los
Angeles. Disco music had become the most popular musical product for
that group as well as the epitome of nightclubs and fashion vogue. During the early to mid-1970s many top-forty bands flourished throughout
East Los Angeles, and a complex network of musicians and performances
developed.

> I remember. I was part of it. I can still see the Garfield and Salesian
> High School auditoriums jam-packed with young people from the
> Eastside coming to listen to the "Battle of the Bands" featuring
> groups such as Ace, Best of Friends, We the People, The Mob, Changing Times, Nice 'n Easy, Fast Co., Power House, Clean Slate, Fantasy, Shining Star, Sabor, and Sophistafunk. Other bands playing in
> the Eastside club circuit were Yesterday's Dreams, Loose Caboose,
> Babyface, The Counts (later Cauldron), Sly, Slick and Wicked, Thee
> Midniters, and of course, Tierra.
>
> The bands of East Los Angeles in the period of 1970 to 1978
> were playing at clubs, weddings (mostly Mexican/Chicano wedding
> receptions) and high school dances. The "battles" were usually staged
> by small, local producers from the Eastside itself. One such producer
> was Joe Sandoval, well known among all the bands, who used to
> distribute flyers of his productions on Whittier Boulevard during
> the "cruising" of Friday and Saturday nights. For all of the criticism
> that the Eastside received during that time, a real social network or
> "cult" had developed. The lowriders, their style, and forms of communication were the essentials of a sub-culture in the U.S.—Chicano
> culture.
>
> As the "cult" was unique, so was the music. Most of it was black
> R&B, Top-forty inspired by such groups as The Commodores, Earth,
> Wind, and Fire, Stevie Wonder, Tower of Power, and the Ohio
> Players. Gradually it adapted to the disco lights and dance style in-

fluenced by The Bee Gees, Donna Summer, K.C. and the Sunshine Band, and A Taste of Honey. Always popular by demand were the "oldies," Mexican standards and corridos, cumbias, and salsa, which also left their mark. Eventually, as punk rock and new wave came in, D.J.s began to dominate the dances, clubs, and receptions with their record collections and light shows, and usually for a much more reasonable price than charged by the bands. Combined with other factors the Eastside bands began to disappear and it is now at a point where many of the veterans of the period refer to it as an "era." (Loza 1983a)

A club circuit existed alongside the eastside band network of the 1970s. Some of the many clubs featuring eastside top-forty bands included The Gold Dust on Garfield Avenue in Montebello, The King's Table on Rosemead Boulevard in Pico Rivera, Monterey West on Atlantic Boulevard in East Los Angeles, Nero's on Slauson Boulevard in Commerce, Rudy's Pasta House on Olympic Boulevard in East Los Angeles, and the Mardi Gras on Wilshire Boulevard near downtown Los Angeles across from MacArthur Park.

"Battles of the bands" occurred periodically at different high schools, auditoriums, and public parks. Students at Salesian High School in Boyle Heights sponsored such battles, many of which in their earlier forms were called rock and roll shows. A program from a 1975 show ("Salesian Rock 'n Roll Shows '75") reflects the variety and high quality of the productions. The show was produced and directed by Bill Taggart, a leading figure in the development of many eastside musicians. Tony García was Bill Taggart's student and protégé; García eventually replaced Taggart as band director at Salesian High School. García expressed his belief that Taggart has not received sufficient credit for his contributions to eastside education and musical productions (personal communication, Tony García, April 1985).

Taggart's Salesian rock and roll show program provides information on the various eastside bands that purchased advertisement space in the forty-page booklet. The groups that advertised, all with photographs, included Boozer, Mixed Company, Batch, The Delgado Brothers, Wade Geary, Evil, The Mob, Kupersztych, Easy Piece, T.B.R., Shh-Boom, Rage, Unison, Sudden Urge, Ace, Brushfire, Cornerstone, Free Country, Blaze, Odd 'n Ends, Sky, Eko, Tierra, Juicy Roy, El Chicano, Bones, Bobby Rodríguez, Johnny Gamboa, and Pepe Gamboa. Ads for Cronen's Music Center, located on Beverly Boulevard in Montebello, occupied a significant amount of space in the program. In association with Cronen's, Taggart provided band consultation and career guidance and training for original groups.

Although the club circuit is not as active now as it was during the

1970s, several clubs and groups are still in operation, many under new management and with different names. Some of the more recent popular club bands have been Cool Breeze, Azusa, and Images. Salsa has experienced moderate growth in popularity, reinforced by highly frequented clubs such as Candilejas (Hollywood), Steven's (Commerce), Casa Blanca (Hollywood), Club Riviera (Eagle Rock), and Club Caché (Silver Lake). A few eastside clubs feature D.J.s and salsa on alternate nights, for example, Quiet Cannon and Club Visage (formerly Sugar Daddy's, La Pantera Rosa, and The Gold Dust), both in Montebello on Garfield Avenue. Johnny Martínez is a popular bandleader whose salsa group performs in various Latin clubs throughout Los Angeles, especially in the East Side. The list of Latin music groups and artists popular either now or in the recent past includes Azucita y Su Orquesta, Azúcar, Niño de Jesús, Miguel Cruz and Skins, Johnny Nelson and His Orchestra, Típica Antillana (directed by Danilo Lozano), Ray Rodríguez, Rudy Macías, Eddie Cano, Paul López, Ralfi Pagán, Bobby Rodríguez, Rudy Regalado y Chévere, Adrián Monjes, and Poncho Sánchez (a Grammy Award nominee in 1985, 1991, 1992). Two popular groups that have featured female vocalists are Califas and UCLATINO. Califas featured lead vocalist Irma Rangel and performed a variety of Mexican, Caribbean, and Brazilian dance music. (Eddie Cano is profiled in chap. 4; Irma Rangel and Poncho Sánchez are profiled in chap. 5.) UCLATINO, directed by the author, was organized in 1980 at UCLA as the successor to the Uclatlán mariachi and still performs as a Latin American music study group. UCLATINO has become quite popular throughout southern California, has toured Mexico, New Zealand, and across California, and has featured guest artists such as Tito Puente, Poncho Sánchez, Irma Rangel, Claire Fischer, Lalo Guerrero, Dolores De Angelo, Miguel Delgado, Danilo Lozano, David Torres, Airto, and Flora Purim.

Contributing to the musical awareness of Los Angeles Chicanos was the success of Luis Valdez's play *Zoot Suit,* which was staged at the Mark Taper Forum at the Music Center in downtown Los Angeles and at the Aquarius Theater in Hollywood (also on Broadway in New York) during the late 1970s. Much of the music in the play was composed by Lalo Guerrero and Daniel Valdez; the score recalled the musical ambience of the war period in Los Angeles and the pachuco subculture. The motion picture *Zoot Suit,* a Universal Studios production under the direction of its creator, Luis Valdez, appeared in 1982 and starred Edward James Olmos and Daniel Valdez. Shorty Rogers's musical score utilized the big band format in both swing and Latin styles. Musical selections adhered to the original theater production.

Luis Valdez also wrote and directed the musical play *Corridos.* The original version was staged by Teatro Campesino in 1972 and then in Los Angeles in 1973. An adaption was first produced in San Juan Bautista in 1982 and arrived in Los Angeles after highly successful, award-winning runs in San Francisco and San Diego. In Los Angeles the play ran for four weeks at the Variety Arts Theater of early Hollywood fame in the downtown district. Musical director of the production was Francisco González; Miguel Delgado was choreographer as well as a member of the cast. Other performers featured in the play included Luis Valdez, Jorge Galván, Leticia Ibarra, Sal López, Alma Martínez, Irma Rangel, Diane Rodríguez, and Robert Vega. In 1985 *Corridos* was filmed in San Francisco as a PBS television special.

An important event in 1985 was the recording of the song "Cantaré, Cantarás" at A & M Recording Studios in Hollywood. The song was performed by a group of internationally recognized Spanish-singing vocalists from throughout Latin America, Spain, and the United States. Representing Los Angeles were singer Vikki Carr, actor Ricardo Montalbán, and comic Cheech Marín. The recording was released on the Discos CBS International label.

As interest in East Los Angeles musical activity has intensified, older out-of-press recordings have been recompiled and continue to sell, especially those of 1960s eastside rock productions and artists (just as 1960s rock and roll in general is once again popular in the mainstream U.S. music industry). Such interest has also directed attention toward young eastside bands involved with more contemporary styles of rock and other musical forms. Tierra is an example of one of the older groups that became associated with the modern wave because of its high point of national recognition in 1982. El Chicano has also continued to record and tour, although sporadically.

Groups such as The Brat, Los Illegals, The Undertakers, and Los Cruzados (formerly called The Plugz) are some more recent examples of musical expression emanating from Los Angeles Chicanos. Their style has relied on the punk rock and new wave movements, although certain musical nuances and literary styles still relate to aspects of the historically unique Chicano/Mexican musical tradition. Hybrid quality is quite evident, therefore, in the modern musical styles of these groups, many of which have received substantial attention in the media.[7]

Punk rock originated as a popular musical movement in England during the late 1970s among the lower socioeconomic strata, especially ghetto youth. The new musical form was often referred to as violent expression, its words and rhythms frequently espousing abstract ideals of anarchy, contradiction, and rebellion as a masked cry for change or for social, political, and cultural revolution.

New wave evolved from punk and continued to critique society, but in a more esoteric fashion. In lieu of the primal musical references of punk, new wave employed danceable beats and recording techniques utilizing synthesized sound and electronic clap tracks. Whereas punk may have been too brash for much of the record-buying public, new wave proved to be a popular alternative and quickly encountered success and a diverse market in the United States. New wave in the Chicano community of Los Angeles offered musicians and aficionados a vehicle for social statement and at the same time the potential for penetration into a new market (Bakaler et al. 1985:2). Chicano bands in Los Angeles that have employed the new wave concept include Los Cruzados (The Plugz), Felix and the Katz, Odd Squad, The Undertakers, Loli Lux and the Bears, The Brat, and Los Illegals.

One of the first record labels to feature eastside Latino new wave was Fatima Records, owned by Tito Larriva, a member of The Plugz, a band that greatly influenced other young Chicano groups such as The Undertakers, Los Illegals, and The Brat. All these bands played frequently at the Vex Club. Fatima Records's initial pressing of The Brat's first record, "Attitudes," was appraised by *New Vinyl Times* as one of the top local releases in Los Angeles in 1982. Also recorded on Fatima was Kenny and the Electrics, a reggae-style band from Guadalajara, Mexico.

Rubén Guevara and the Eastside Renaissance

As musical activity and reference to the Chicano musical legacy continued to evolve in East Los Angeles, the concept of an "Eastside Renaissance" emerged. For years, murals, literature, theater, and politics had been viewed as the cultural spearheads of the Chicano movement. Finally, music began to be examined in terms of the community's self-determination; music had been the assumed, yet underestimated, quintessential symbol of power, behavior, and culture.

Rubén Guevara, a musician and producer, was largely responsible for the concept of the Eastside Renaissance; in fact, he coined the phrase. Born in Boyle Heights and raised throughout Los Angeles, Guevara frontlined Frank Zappa's Ruben and the Jets for several years during the 1970s. In 1968 Zappa recorded a concept album with the Mothers of Invention entitled *Cruisin' with Ruben and the Jets,* a parody of an East Los Angeles doo-wop band. Zappa decided to stage the concept in 1972 and hired Guevara to front a new group using the Ruben and the Jets format. The group, consisting mostly of Chicanos from East Los Angeles, recorded two albums and went on tour, opening concerts for Zappa. In 1983 Guevara initiated the production of three LP compilations on his own Zyanya record label, distributed through Rhino Records. One album was a recompilation of the eastside musical scenario of the 1960s (mentioned above) titled *The History of Latino Rock: Volume 1, The Eastside Sound,* which included the following tracks: "La Bamba" and "Donna" by Ritchie Valens; "My Heart Cries" by The Romancers; "Farmer John" by The Premiers; "La La La La La" by The Blendells; and "That's All" and "Whittier Boulevard" by Thee Midniters. Another album was a greatest hits compilation of Thee Midniters, and the third LP, a compilation of local contemporary groups titled *Los Angelinos: The Eastside Renaissance,* reflects the variety of musical styles manifested by eastside Chicanos. Represented on diverse tracks, for example, are R&B-based arrangements by The Royal Gents and the group Mestizo, which in addition to drawing on R&B adapts its own version of "Chicano salsa." "El Corrido to End Barrio Warfare" by Los Perros presents a traditional Mexican genre adapted to a specific Los Angeles social problem, and Califas offers a salsa-blended, culturally lyricized "La Música de la Gente" (analyzed in chap. 5), an expression of Latino solidarity through music. New wave or contemporary rock styles are employed by The Brat, Felix and the Katz, and The Plugz. The latter group's two cuts on the album are described as a "unique blend of Tex-Mex and hard core punk" and are sung in a bilingual format. Last, "Los Angelinos" contains one track by producer Guevara's group Con Safos, whose name is an expression common among eastside Chicanos, frequently spray-painted on graffiti-covered walls as C/S. Although there is no literal translation, *con safos* might be the equivalent of expressing a defiant "so what" attitude or the idea of "safe" or "don't mess with it."[8] Guevara has extended the meaning of the phrase as a defiant symbol of Chicano self-determination, self-reliance, and self-realization, or, in effect, self-empowerment. With that definition in mind, he composed "C/S" as a reflection of the Chicano experience in Los Angeles, a composite of an urban, historical struggle.

"C/S"

L.A.
City of the Angels.
Founded in 1781 by Felipe de Neve
And settled by
      Mexican Pobladores.
      Blacks, Mestizos, Mulatos, Indios
El Pueblo de Nuestra Señora La
      Reina de Los Angeles
      de Porciúncula,
L.A.
City of the Angels.

We came to work your fields
    our plenty.
We made you rich—you paid us
    pennies.
We laid your railroad over trails
    that once were ours.
We taught you how to mine
    your gold,
Rope your cattle and irrigate
    your land.
Your land?
Con Safos
March, 1942, it was "Taps" for
    the "Japs."
You put them all in concentration
    camps.
Who was left to scrape your goat?
The Mexicans. Why not? We were
    your favorite joke.
Three thousand years of
    civilization:
Olmec—Maya—Toltec—Aztec
Three thousand years of
    civilization
To wind up in L.A.
A people in damnation.
Vatos [*sic*] Locos. Damn right!
Vatos Locos. Die or fight!
Go 'head Clover, sign your treaty
    of Guadalupe Hidalgo,
A "Treaty" that was supposed to
    guarantee equality.
Go 'head Vatos Locos,
Children of Aztlan.
Spray your metallic blood
'Til all the walls come down.
Con Safos. Look at me.
Con Safos. Know me.
Con Safos. Listen to me!
I am somebody!
I am!

I am somebody!
Yo Soy!
Con Safos
Listen to what the walls have to say!
Viva Los Angeles!
Viva mi tierra!
Long live L.A.! (Cerco Blanco
                    Music/Bug [ASCAP])

In reviewing "Los Angelinos," Andy Van de Voorde (1983) observed that "because major labels have been more amenable about signing L.A. bands in the Eighties than they were in the Sixties, at least three groups that would have qualified for inclusion on the LP—Los Illegals, Tierra, and Los Lobos—are ineligible for the compilation effort."

As part of his efforts to promote the Zyanya LP releases and the concept of the Eastside Renaissance, Guevara staged a series of revues featuring artists who were part of the recording project and produced shows at the Club Lingerie in Hollywood and at UCLA as part of the 1985 Mexican Arts Symposium. The UCLA show included Aztec dancers performing simultaneously with "break" dancers in order to reflect the ancient and the modern, in addition to the female vocal trio Las Angelinas (conceived and produced by Guevara), who interpret R&B songs, oldies, and boleros that have been popular among Chicanos over the past forty years. The trio consisted of Irma Rangel (lead vocalist for Califas), Jeri González or Suzie Esquivél-Armijo, and Dolores De Angelo.

Other groups that began to emerge in the late 1980s included bands such as The Alienz and Los Rock Angels, both of which incorporated Mexican and other Latin musical concepts into a basic rock and R&B format. Also active were Feel-ix, Umbral, the Wild Cards, and the Lost Soul Rebels. Chicano musicians in Los Angeles generally faced a completely new and constantly evolving market. Also confronted with this constant flux were musicians of the punk, new wave, and "post-punk" eras who had already become involved with the new music industry through various recording contracts, for instance, John Avila (Oingo Boingo), Tito Larriva (Los Cruzados), Jeanette Jurado (Exposé), and the youthful Bobby Ross Avila. The Chicano rap group Kid Frost released the LP *Hispanic Causing Panic* in 1990 on the Virgin Records label. Included in it was the market hit "La Raza," which attained substantial airplay and was themed on the tune "Viva Tirado" popularized by El Chicano in 1970 and composed by Gerald Wilson. Kid Frost was also involved in the release of the rap project *Latin Alliance* in 1991. Another group to emerge in the market in 1991 was A Lighter Shade of Brown, which released an album entitled *Brown &*

Proud on the Pump Records label. As with Kid Frost's, their rap style was bilingual, in English and Spanish.

Whether or not the 1980s truly signified a rebirth of East Los Angeles bands, the period was certainly a rebirth for the group Los Lobos. Their first album, *Just Another Band from East L.A.,* was released in 1978 through New Vista Records, a local label. After adopting a rock and roll/Mexican/ *norteño* format in lieu of exclusively Mexican and other Latin American folk music, the group received a 1983 Grammy Award in the newly devised category of Mexican-American recordings. The *norteño*-style traditional song titled "Anselma" was one cut from Los Lobos' first Slash label LP, distributed and marketed through Warner Brothers. Another album, *How Will the Wolf Survive?* followed within a year, in addition to two commercial music videos. In 1987 a third Slash LP was released, titled *By the Light of the Moon,* which was rated the number two pop/rock album of the year by *Los Angeles Times* critic Robert Hillburn. In 1989 Los Lobos released an album (also on the Slash/Warner label) composed of Mexican folk songs, similar to their initial local LP of 1978. With this recording the group was voted another Grammy Award by the National Academy of Recording Arts and Sciences.

The National Academy of Recordings Arts and Sciences expanded its Latin category for the Grammy Awards into three different style categories in 1983. These included Latin pop, tropical, and Mexican American. The latter style category allowed for Mexican-based styles from both south and north of the Mexican-U.S. border, contingent on their distribution in the United States (that is, ethnicity of the artists is not a factor for eligibility, only the location of the recording's sales). Following Los Lobos' initial award in the Mexican-American category, artists receiving the recognition in subsequent years included Sheena Easton and Luis Miguel (1984) for their duet "Me gustas tal como eres" (the Grammy Award for this duet resulted in controversy among local Mexican-American musicians, and a protest ensued); Vikki Carr (1985) for her LP *Simplemente mujer;* Flaco Jiménez (1986) for *Ay te dejo en San Antonio;* Los Tigres del Norte (1987) for *¡Gracias! América sin fronteras;* Linda Ronstadt (1988) for *Canciones de mi padre;* and Los Lobos (1989) for *La pistola y el corazón.*

In 1988 Los Premios "Bravo" were initiated as annual awards specifically designed to recognize musical artists popularized through Spanish-language radio in the United States. Interestingly, among the various categories were "Crossover" and "Mexican American."

Another form of awards instituted to recognize Latinos in music were those established by Nosotros, the association developed to enhance the artistic careers of Latino entertainers. Eventually called the Golden Eagle Awards, these began in 1970 and were given to a variety of artists in the entertainment industry. Recipients of the award in the area of music have included Valentín Robles (1977); Andy Russell (1979); Charro, Chris Móntez, and Tierra (1981); Freddy Fender and Lisa López (1982); Pedro Vargas, Julio Iglesias, Anacani, and Herb Alpert (1983); Irene Cara and Rita Moreno (1984); Tony Orlando and Lalo Schifrin (1985); Trío Calaveras and Mark Allen Trujillo (1987); José Feliciano, Las Hermanas Padilla, and Los Lobos (1988); Lalo Guerrero and Vikki Carr (1989); Gloria Estefan, Emmanuel, and Martica (1990); Celia Cruz and Tito Puente (1991); and Carlos Santana (1992).

Institutional and Media Development

Another politically symbolic element that coincided with the concept of the Eastside Renaissance was the organization of the Hispanic Musicians Association (HMA) in 1984, composed largely of eastside Latino musicians, mostly Chicanos. The first president of the association was pianist Eddie Cano, and the vice-president was saxophonist Tony García. Singer Jeri González was secretary, and saxophonist Adolfo Martínez was the first treasurer. The goals of the organization included performance networking, educational development, and the increased viability of the Latin musician within American Federation of Musicians Local 47. A board of directors was convened, and the organization's first fundraiser was held at the Casa Rivera in Pico Rivera (which was also the association's meeting place). In 1991 the HMA released an LP of its big band orchestra entitled *California Salsa* on the Sea Breeze label (this ensemble has been renamed the HMA Salsa/Jazz Orchestra).

The role of local television, especially the Univisión affiliate KMEX, has also been developing in Los Angeles. Although few international musical shows are produced locally, the OTI (Organización Televisión Iberoamericana) Song Festival regional competition is hosted annually by the station. Local arrangers and musicians are contracted for the production, which features California composers of songs in Spanish or Portuguese. Chicano composers, however, have not responded greatly, perhaps because of the requirement of Spanish or Portuguese lyrics in addition to other considerations. In 1984, in collaboration with the author, television station KMEX also produced a week-long series (as part of its daily "Los Angeles Ahora" program) focusing on the music of Mexican Americans in Los Angeles. In addition to myself, those appearing on the show included Lalo Guerrero, former radio personality Martín Becerra, Irma Rangel, Marcos Loya, and César Rosas of Los Lobos. In the same year, Los Angeles public television station KCET, a PBS affiliate, taped a four-part performance series celebrating the impact of Latin music on styles popular in the United States and exhibiting the diversity of Latin artists based there. Titled "Sound Festival," the series was produced by Mexican-American filmmaker José Luis Ruiz and featured artists José Feliciano, Flora Purim, Airto Moreira, Tierra, Sheila Escobedo (Sheila E.), Ray Barreto, and Tito Puente.

The role of Mexican-American music in film has recently begun to emerge on a larger scale. Both Los Lobos and Carlos Santana were involved in the score to the Columbia motion picture *La Bamba,* and various Los Angeles musical artists were employed in the filming of *Old Gringo* by the same studio. Universal's *Zoot Suit* included the music of Lalo Guerrero with vocal interpretations by Daniel Valdez. Since 1980 Raúl Pérez has been the director of music administration at Columbia Pictures.

On radio, various interesting shows catering especially to the Latino/ Chicano audience have been developed within the past twenty years. One of the most prominent has been the highly popular "Alma del Barrio," broadcast for the past eighteen years on KXLU, a station operated by Loyola Marymount University. The program specializes in salsa; one of its founding disc jockeys was Enrique Soto, who later in the 1980s hosted a Latin jazz show on jazz station KKGO (which converted to a classical format in 1989). Other "Alma del Barrio" disc jockeys who have extensively promoted Latin music in Los Angeles have included Eddie López, Carmen Rosado, Blanca Sandoval, Nina Linart, Vanessa Sulam, Albert Price, and Tony Cruz. In the 1970s (beginning in 1972) Richard Leos hosted a Sunday and Monday evening radio show featuring Latin jazz and salsa on KBCA. The program received the top listening ratings for the station through the Pulse radio survey service. Another Latin music radio program that began in the mid-1980s was "Canto Tropical" on KPFK, hosted by Héctor Reséndez and Kathy Díaz, among others. In 1984 the "Sancho Show" began on KPCC, a radio station broadcast from Pasadena City College. Hosted by Daniel Castro (Sancho) and geared toward younger people, the program featured music of Chicanos, ranging from Thee Midniters to Poncho Sánchez. One of Castro's objectives has been to encourage education. In 1989 an annual Chicano Music Award was initiated through the program. Lalo Guerrero was the first recipient of the award, and in 1990 the honor was given to the members of Don Tosti's Pachuco Boogie Band of the 1950s, including Tosti, Raúl Díaz, and Eddie Cano (the latter posthumously). Another radio show featuring Latin music, "Jazz on the Latin Side," was begun by disc jockey/journalist José Rizo on KLON in 1990.

Additional musical development has taken place in the educational community. The previously described university mariachi study groups are but one example of the many folkloric classes at the primary, secondary, and university levels. Mexican *ballets folklóricos* and other folk ensembles of

Mexican dance and music have proliferated. Enrollment in university classes related to Mexican and Chicano folklore has grown substantially as a consequence of the late-1960s Chicano movement and the maintenance of that movement. In 1985 I taught the first class at UCLA to explore the music of the Chicano, titled "Chicano/Latino Music in the United States."

In recent years, educational institutions have established individual and cooperative programs examining Mexican/Chicano artistic expression. Such intensified interest has resulted in a variety of symposia, conferences, and publications designed to integrate performance, education, and research. Such institutions as Plaza de la Raza and the Los Angeles Art and Music School, both located in Los Angeles's East Side, have gained notable momentum in the development of educational programs in the arts. Some local universities have also initiated art programs related to the Mexican/ Chicano experience. UCLA has been a leader in the latter effort. In 1980 a major film festival, "Cine sin fronteras" ("Film without Borders"), was organized principally by graduate students and sponsored by the University's College of Fine Arts. The following year the College of Fine Arts and the Department of Music sponsored a conference on the music of Mexico and the Chicano Southwest titled "Music of Mexico: Yesterday, Today, and Tomorrow." In 1982 a group of graduate students, again sponsored by the College of Fine Arts along with administrative support from the Chicano Studies Research Center, designed the Mexican Arts Symposium, which explores the juncture of the Mexican and Chicano in terms of artistic expression. Events were first presented in April and May 1983. Now called the Mexican Arts Series (as of 1986), the program, which combines performance and scholarship, recently completed its tenth consecutive year representing a total of over seventy events.[9]

Another academic institution that has developed extensive musical programming relative to the Mexican American has been East Los Angeles College. Henry Cobos, professor of music at the college, has spearheaded numerous projects: the formulation of a Cultural Arts Committee; a concert by the National Symphony of Mexico; a concert by the Mexican Arts Chamber Symphony featuring a violin concerto composed and performed by Manuel Enríquez; various recitals by chamber groups or soloists from Mexico; two appearances by the Ballet Folklórico Nacional from Mexico City; and a concert by the University Choir of the Universidad Nacional Autónoma de México (UNAM), directed by Gabriel Saldívar, Jr.

Born and raised in El Paso, Texas, Henry Cobos studied piano at the Eastman School in Rochester, New York, where he received bachelor's and master's degrees in music. In January 1969 he became a full-time professor at East Los Angeles College, where he also chaired the Music Department from 1975 to 1984. As of 1990, he still served as vice-chair of the department and as the chair of the Cultural Arts Committee.

Various other individuals are actively engaged in related academic/musical activities at the university level in the Los Angeles area. Fermín Herrera, a professor of anthropology and Chicano studies, has taught at California State University, Northridge, since 1971. He also is a harp specialist in the Mexican *jarocho* style and has led a *jarocho* musical group composed of members of his family (brothers, sister, sons, and daughters) since 1973. The group, called Conjunto Hueyapan, has become widely known throughout southern California. Other academicians of Mexican-American or other backgrounds involved in teaching and/or research related to Latin American music in general include the following: Robert Stevenson, UCLA professor of music, one of the most prolific scholars in Latin American musicology; Charles Fierro, a pianist who teaches at California State University, Northridge; Beto Ruiz, director of Mariachi Aztlán at the same university; Timothy Harding, professor of history at California State University, Los Angeles, who has taught courses in Latin American music, helped organize an international festival of Latin American music in 1981, and is a harpist specializing in Latin American styles; Danilo Lozano, instructor of flute and survey courses in Latin, jazz, and popular music at Whittier College and California State Polytechnic University, Pomona; Raymond López, piano instructor at East Los Angeles College; Aurelio de la Vega, professor of music and composer in residence at California State University, Northridge; Raymond Torres-Santos, composer and professor of music at California State University, San Bernadino; Nancy Fierro, a pianist teaching at Mount San Antonio College; and Adrián Ruiz, instructor of piano at the University of Southern California (USC) during the mid-1970s. In the fall of 1991, Mexican composer Manuel Enríquez was a visiting professor at UCLA.

Emerging composers of Mexican descent who have been active as alumni of academic institutions in the Los Angeles area include the following, among others: Víctor Saucedo (bachelor's degree in music education and composition, USC, and Ph.D. in music composition, UCLA); José Antonio Ramírez (bachelor's degree in music, California State University, Los Angeles, in addition to studies at the UNAM Conservatory of Music in Mexico City); and David Reyes, originally from Pomona and an alumnus of Immaculate Heart College, where he studied composition. Raymond Torres-Santos, originally from Puerto Rico, received his doctoral degree in music theory and composition from UCLA.

An organization that merits attention is Sinfónica del Barrio, directed by Peter Quesada. Among its other aims, this community symphony orchestra seeks to represent the young multicultural population of Los Angeles, especially the Latino sector, and to incorporate music teachers active in the community into a performance context. In addition, the orchestra interprets the symphonic repertoire of Mexico and other Latin countries. Soloists featured with the Sinfónica del Barrio have included Gustavo Romero (piano), Carlos Elías (violin), Adrián Ruiz (piano), Danilo Lozano (flute), Ingrid Kwo (violin), and Joseph González (guitar).

In the fall of 1991, the Mexican government sponsored an art exhibit entitled "Mexico: Splendors of Thirty Centuries" at the Los Angeles County Museum of Art. The exhibit had previously toured to New York and San Antonio. In conjunction with the exhibit, the Mexican government and local groups in Los Angeles organized a diversity of activities related to Mexican culture and promoted as "Mexico: A Work of Art." Among these activities was a concert series of chamber music and musicians from Mexico. Mexican composer Manuel Enríquez programmed the concerts throughout Los Angeles. Venues included the California Institute for the Arts, UCLA, East Los Angeles College, Los Angeles County Museum of Art, Whittier College, Santa Monica Public Library, Forest Lawn Memorial Park, Plaza de la Raza, California State University at Northridge, Instituto Cultural Mexicano de Los Angeles, California State University at Long Beach, College of the Canyons, Occidental College, L'Hermitage Foundation, Loyola Marymount University, and the Gene Autry Museum.

On 29 September 1991, the Los Angeles Philharmonic presented a concert of Mexican symphonic music at the Hollywood Bowl in a program billed as "Fiesta Mexicana." Guest conducting the orchestra was Enrique Diemecke, director of the National Symphony Orchestra of Mexico. The concert was also scheduled in coordination with the "Mexico: A Work of Art" and "Artes de Mexico" projects.

Two scholarships specifically designated for the study of music in the Mexican-American/Hispanic community were established during the 1980s. In 1981 the Hispanic Women's Council created the Nati Cano Music Scholarship, dedicated to and underwritten by Nati Cano, director of Mariachi Los Camperos and owner of La Fonda Restaurant. Since its inception, the Nati Cano Scholarship Foundation has awarded funds to numerous student musicians for the advancement of their musical studies. The Ritchie Valens Music Scholarship, instituted by the Youth Opportunity Foundation, an organization of business and political leaders, has also awarded a significant amount of scholarships to young musicians showing strong potential in music. Mexican-American/Latino recipients of UCLA's prestigious Frank Sinatra Award in music have included Raúl Pérez (vocalist), Garrett Saracho (pianist), Pamela Córdova (vocalist), Steve Loza (arranging/orchestration), Jorge Arciniega (trumpet), and Raymond Torres-Santos (arranging/orchestration).

Although not geared specifically to musical education, in 1989 the newly formed National Hispanic Arts, Education, and Media Institute produced a benefit concert to raise funds for the development of educational leadership conferences for Mexican-American youths of Los Angeles. On August 2 two television specials were taped for cable television network HBO (Home Box Office). The all-star lineup included Rubén Blades y Son del Solar, Celia Cruz, Mariachi Los Camperos de Nati Cano, Jerry Garcia, Esteban "Steve" Jordan, Tito Puente, Linda Ronstadt, Poncho Sánchez, Carlos Santana, and Daniel Valdez. The show was coordinated by film producer Moctezuma Esparza, and Rubén Guevara served as musical director. Los Angeles City Councilman Richard Alatorre was honorary concert chair. Taped twice the same evening, the concert aired in the fall of 1989.

In the winter of 1990, Plaza de la Raza, a cultural art center located in the Lincoln Heights section of Los Angeles, organized "Chicano Musicworks," a competition/festival of original music. Coordinated by choreographer Miguel Delgado, the project was part of the center's "Nuevo L.A." arts series. Chicano/Mexican composers living in the state of California were eligible to enter, and entrance categories included any style of music—rock, Mexican traditional forms, jazz, Latin, art music (classical), and experimental. Close to 300 entries were submitted. An awards concert took place on 29 June 1990, where the finalists performed live and the results of the competition were announced. Awards, presented in four categories, were bestowed on Víctor Saucedo (classical), José G. Saldana (folk/traditional), Rodrigo González (contemporary Latin and progressive styles), and Michael Villanueva (contemporary pop).

It was a pleasure for me to chair the Plaza de la Raza Musicworks project and its panel of judges, and it gave me great satisfaction to see such an event take place. The members of Los Lobos served as honorary chairs; the band was scheduled to videotape a public service announcement to promote the festival on Spanish-language television station KVEA. Serving on the panel of judges were John Avila (Oingo Boingo); Nati Cano (Mariachi Los Camperos); Daniel Castro (Sancho Show, KPCC); Henry Cobos (professor of music, East Los Angeles College); Celia Cruz; Bobby Espinoza (El Chicano); Jimmy Espinoza (Thee Midniters); Mark Fogelquist (Mariachi Uclatlán); Tony García (musician/teacher); Lalo Guerrero (composer/performer); Rubén Guevara (Con Safos, Ruben and the Jets, writer); José Hernández (Mariachi Sol de México); Fermín Herrera (California State University, Northridge); Willie Herrón (Los Illegals, artist); Tito Larriva (Los Cruzados); Danilo Lozano (Whittier College and California State

University, Pomona); Isabel Miranda (California State University, Northridge); Raúl Pérez (Columbia Studios); Tito Puente; Héctor Reséndez (Canto Tropical, KPFK); Alfredo Rubalcava (American Federation of Musicians Local 47); Rudy Salas (Tierra); Poncho Sánchez; Chico Sesma; Robert Stevenson (professor of music, UCLA); Daniel Sheehy (National Endowment for the Arts, Folk Arts); David Torres (musician/composer); and Elizabeth Waldo (composer/musician).

Conclusion

From *La Opinión*'s coverage of musical activity in the 1940s through the emergence of a so-called Eastside Renaissance in the 1980s, a diversity of patterns has been created by music makers and music users representing the Mexican tradition in Los Angeles. This tradition has encompassed maintenance and promotion of various bicultural instances of adaptive musical expression and innovation. From the adjustments to and use of early radio and the recording industry in the 1930s to the nightclub circuits of the 1940s through the 1970s, the Mexican American in Los Angeles has consistently relied on and relished the meaning of music. It has been adapted to social issues, political movements, and to the eternal quests for love and spiritual ideals.

It is possible to view the various examples from Lalo Guerrero, the ever-evolving mariachi culture, and the eastside bands of the Chicano movement era to Poncho Sánchez, new wave, Los Lobos, and the adapting Grammy Awards as some of the beacons of a specific musical history and culture. But the historical contours and consequences of the post–World War II musical life of the Mexican/Chicano people of Los Angeles illustrate much more. The period also symbolizes, in a variety of forms and contexts, the persistence of a subculture through the process of maintenance, change, and adaptation. Intercultural cooperation developed through a fascinating and complex matrix of interdependence, ethnic identity, and cultural survival.

Appendix: Jazz and Fusion Musicians

Justo Almario: saxophonist, originally from Colombia, who has performed with Freddy Hubbard, Poncho Sánchez, Bobby Rodríguez, Alex Acuña, and many other international artists, in addition to being a very active studio musician and leading his own fusion group.

Jorge Arciniega: a jazz and Latin music trumpeter.

Aaron Ballesteros: drummer/songwriter who has played with groups ranging from the Royal Checkmates and Tierra to Thee Midniters.

Ramón Banda: percussionist *(timbalero)* for Poncho Sánchez.

Tony Banda: bassist for Poncho Sánchez.

Víctor Barrientos: drummer/percussionist who has performed a diversity of music, from top-forty rock and soul to Latin to fusion and other modern styles.

Ray Bojórquez: performed with Gerald Wilson during the 1960s on alto and tenor saxophones and flute.

Eddie Cano: profiled in chapter 4, he achieved international acclaim as a stylist in Latin jazz.

Sal Chico: bandleader active in the Latin club and dance circuit in the 1960s.

Luis Conte: of Cuban heritage, he has done extensive studio work and has recorded and performed with Poncho Sánchez, Claire Fisher, Billy Childs, Diane Reeves, Diana Ross, Tania María, Joe Sample, Herb Alpert, Helen Reddy, Boz Scaggs, Doc Severinsen, Al Dimeola, Madonna, and numerous other major artists. He also recorded two solo LPs, *Black Forest* and *La Cocina Caliente*.

Henry De Vega: alto saxophonist and member of Gerald Wilson's orchestra in the 1960s and 1970s.

Ramón Flores: trumpet player and arranger originally from Mexico who has performed extensively on Latin music dates, in recording sessions, and with a variety of major industry artists.

Sam García: pianist who has performed with many popular and Latin music groups.

Tony García: a woodwind player who has performed in a variety of contexts from jazz to Latin to rock, in addition to being involved in music education. He received a bachelor's degree in music from California State University, Los Angeles.

Jeri González: vocalist who worked for many years with the group Chico and various other groups; she has also recorded extensively.

Lou González: trumpet player active in Latin, jazz, and commercial music.

Frank "Chico" Guerrero: percussionist active in film and recording studios since the 1950s.

Mike Gutiérrez: timbalero and percussionist active since the 1950s, especially in Latin music.

Joey Heredia: drummer who has performed with Billy Childs, Diane Reeves, Tania María, Hubert Laws, Joe Farrel, Freddie Hubbard, Lani Hall, Herb Alpert, Eddie Cano, Joe Sample, Stevie Wonder, and Sergio Mendez, among many other international artists; he is the son of Adelina García, the aforementioned international vocalist and film star popular in Los Angeles during the 1940s (see Flans 1990).

George Hernández: Cuban pianist and arranger who became involved in the Los Angeles Latin music network, especially during the 1950s. He eventually worked extensively in Las Vegas and on Broadway as an arranger for numerous show bands and orchestras.

Robert Huerta: trombonist who played in Gerald Wilson's first big band in 1944.

Federico Lanuza: pianist from San Diego who worked in Los Angeles throughout the 1970s and 1980s. Among the artists and groups he performed with were Mongo Santamaría, Changing Times, and UCLATINO. He received a bachelor's degree in music from UCLA and has composed music for various musical plays.

Rubén León: saxophonist who performed with Miguelito Valdez, Charlie Barnett, and Eddie Cano. Interestingly, his other profession was psychology, in which he earned a doctorate.

Manny López: vibraphonist and practitioner of Latin music styles, especially active in the 1960s.

Paul López: a 1942 graduate of Roosevelt High School, he studied at the Juilliard School of Music in New York and at the Pablo Casals Conservatory in Puerto Rico. In 1946–47 he performed as a trumpet player with Woody Herman, Stan Kenton, and Al Donahue. In 1948 he left Los Angeles for Chicago, where he played with Freddy Slack. Later that year he moved to New York City, where he remained for five years. There, he worked as a trumpet player, arranger, and composer with various musicians and orchestras, including Miguelito Valdez (for two years), Noro Morales, Tito Rodríguez, Boyd Raeburn, Max Roach, Billy Taylor, and Curly Russell. In 1947 he was listed in one of the *Downbeat* jazz polls. In 1955 López returned to Los Angeles, working simultaneously in Las Vegas show bands, where he performed behind artists such as Frank Sinatra, Nat King Cole, Louis Armstrong, Peggy Lee, Sammy Davis, Jr., Dinah Washington, and the Hines Twins. In 1967–68 he played in the experimental big band of Don Ellis, and currently he teaches arranging classes at the Dick Grove Music School in the Van Nuys area of Los Angeles.

Marcos Loya: the guitarist and director of the group Califas, Loya has worked with popular music star Madonna on LPs and music videos, namely, "Isla Bonita" and the *Like a Prayer* album. He has also performed in many stage plays, including Luis Valdez's *Corridos,* and he composed the music for the Los Angeles Theatre Center (LATC) produced *La Víctima;* his musical score was nominated for a Los Angeles Theatre Critics' Award. He has performed and recorded with Daniel Valdez and recorded on the sound track for the Columbia Pictures film *Old Gringo,* and in 1990 he became musical director for KMEX television's weekly *El Show de Paul Rodríguez.* During the summer of 1990 Loya composed and performed for the play *August 29,* another production of the LATC Latino Lab. He recorded his first solo album in 1991.

Willie Loya: Latin percussionist for the group Califas, Daniel Valdez's ensemble, and numerous other groups.

Danilo Lozano: of Cuban heritage and raised in the Boyle Heights section of East Los Angeles, he is a master classical flautist and practitioner of Latin, jazz, and other modern categories, having recorded extensively with various artists and as a soloist. He received a bachelor's degree in music from the University of Southern California and a master's degree from UCLA.

John Madrid: a virtuoso in the art of lead trumpet, Madrid played with the big bands of Buddy Rich, Stan Kenton, Woody Herman, and Louis Bellson, in addition to Blood, Sweat and Tears and Boz Scaggs. He also spent considerable time performing in show orchestras in Hawaii and Las Vegas, especially with singer Wayne Newton. Madrid was an alumnus of Montebello High School. He died in 1990.

Sal Márquez: trumpeter widely recognized for his performance and recordings with rock artist Frank Zappa; he established his own jazz quartet in 1990. Much in demand as a studio musician, Márquez premiered with the newly assembled band led by Branford Marsalis on the "Tonight Show" hosted by Jay Leno on NBC Television in May 1992.

Adolfo Martínez: received his degree in music from California State University, Los Angeles, and currently is music director at Belvedere Junior High School, where he began a highly popular student mariachi, Mariachi Olímpico. An adept saxophonist/flautist, Martínez has performed with the group Chico for twelve years, in addition to playing with Willie Bobo and on various studio and film score dates.

Johnny Martínez: originally from Chicago, his salsa band has been active in Los Angeles since the 1950s. He has recorded his own LPs and has arranged and composed a large assortment of repertoire, in addition to having performed in the major salsa clubs in Los Angeles.

Rubén McFall: played trumpet with the big bands of Woody Herman (during the 1950s) and later Gerald Wilson. He was featured with Wilson's band on the recording of "La Macarena."

Oscar Meza: bassist who has performed a variety of Latin music, jazz, and studio work. He was with the New York Philharmonic for two years and has performed with many major artists, including Tito Puente and Ray Barretto. He also holds a masters degree in philosophy.

Adrián Monjes: drummer/percussionist who has led various Latin/jazz/fusion ensembles both locally and on tours abroad.

Bobby Móntez: vibraphonist who led his own Latin ensemble in the 1950s and 1960s.

Henry Mora: trombonist/arranger active in the salsa scene.

Tony (Anthony) Ortega: a jazz and studio saxophonist who recorded in the 1960s and performed with the orchestras of Lionel Hampton, Gerald Wilson, Nelson Riddle, Percy Faith, Frank Sinatra, and Frank Zappa, among many others.

Romeo Prado: trombonist/arranger and one of the original members of Thee Midniters.

Fred Ramírez: Pianist who has performed with a variety of popular and Latin music ensembles including that of Willie Bobo.

Alex Rodríguez: a highly talented artist who played trumpet with the big bands of Lionel Hampton, Woody Herman, Stan Kenton, and Gerald Wilson, in addition to leading his own jazz combos.

Bobby Rodríguez: trumpeter who has led and recorded with his own ensembles, resulting in two LPs, *Simply Macrame* and *Tell an Amigo.* He has performed with Quincy Jones, the Brothers Johnson, Ike and Tina Turner, Maurice White, Lalo Schifrin, Willie Bobo, Tierra, The Emotions, Chaka Kahn, Ray Charles, Gerald Wilson, Poncho Sánchez, Louis Bellson, Don Ellis, and in earlier periods, the East

Los Angeles groups The Etalons and The Counts, among many others.

David Romero: Latin percussionist of Puerto Rican heritage, originally from New Jersey, who has been a regular member of the Califas and Poncho Sánchez ensembles.

Poncho Sánchez: conguero and international exponent of Latin jazz (profiled in chap. 5).

Garrett Saracho: pianist who recorded his own LP, *En Medio* (1973), on the Impulse label.

Alfonso Smith: conguero who has performed with numerous groups in addition to leading his own Latin band.

Eddie Talamantes: Latin percussionist who performed with numerous ensembles, including that of Eddie Cano.

David Torres: prolific East Los Angeles musician, composer, and arranger who was an original member of the group Tierra. He played with Johnny Martínez, Califas, and Ray Camacho and as of 1990 was pianist for Poncho Sánchez.

Don Tosti: (whose real name is Edmundo Martínez Tostado) studied music at Roosevelt High School and Los Angeles City College. He performed as a bassist with the big bands of Jimmy Dorsey, Charlie Barnett, Les Brown, Jack Teagarten, and Bobby Shirwood. Eventually, he led his own band called the Pachuco Boogie Boys, which included Eddie Cano on piano and Raúl Díaz on drums. Tosti also did considerable work as an arranger for the popular Los Angeles–based Mexican singer Rubén Reyes.

Charlie Tovar: conguero who has performed with numerous eastside groups, including Los Lobos on their initial, local LP.

David Troncoso: bassist who has recorded his own LP and was a regular member of Eddie Cano's Latin jazz group.

Roland Vásquez: originally from Pasadena, Vásquez is a drummer who has led his own group, Urban Ensemble. He has recorded three solo LPs, including *Urban Ensemble* and *The Tides of Time.* He was also a member of Claire Fisher and Salsa Picante, where he played with fellow percussionists Alex Acuña, Poncho Sánchez, and Luis Conte.

Art Velasco: trombonist for Poncho Sánchez's ensemble who has also performed extensively in the Latin music scene, for example, with Tito Puente, Rudy Regalado, and many others. He has also played substantially in the studios and on numerous recording dates.

Notes

1. The charro suit, worn by a Mexican *charro* (cowboy), consists of a short jacket, string tie, studded pants, and usually a sombrero. The charro suit, or *traje de charro,* is the traditional dress of the mariachi.

2. Recently, Guevara has been interested in the influence of Latin musical styles

on the development of rock. Guevara referred me to Marsh (1984). Guevara (1990) also addresses this issue.

3. Guevara noted (personal communication) that he described Herrera as Hungarian-born according to information provided by Johnny Otis. See Guevara (1990).

4. Virginia's has closed since the publication of Sheviya's article.

5. The information on Mariachi Los Galleros de Pedro Rey is largely extracted from unpublished notes written and provided by Philip Sonnichsen. Pedro Hernández (a.k.a. Pedro Rey) has verified the data.

6. Wilson, an internationally renowned jazz arranger, composer, trumpeter, bandleader, university lecturer, and disc jockey, lives in Los Angeles and is married to a Mexican woman. He is a great aficionado of bullfighting, especially in Mexico.

7. Musical groups such as The Brat, Los Illegals, and Los Lobos (all profiled in chap. 5) have received extensive media coverage in various articles that have also surveyed the historical development of rock bands in East Los Angeles. See especially Diamond (1984a, b); "Cultura Chicana: Los Angeles," in *La Opinión* (Suplemento Cultural, no. 11, 13 July 1980); Van de Voorde (1983); "East L.A." (*New Vinyl Times*); Macías (1982); Waller (1981); "A Twist—East L.A. Visits Roxy" (*Los Angeles Times,* 14 Feb. 1981); Diamond (1981); Snowdon (1984b); and the important article by Luis Rodríguez (1980b, c).

8. The "safety" interpretation of *con safos* is from Rubén Guevara (personal communication).

9. The Mexican Arts Series has featured several musical forums: a panel discussion of the Chicano experience in music (1983); a concert featuring Mexican composers Mario Lavista and Julio Estrada and Chicano composer and UCLA music student Frederico Lanuza at East Los Angeles College (1983); performances by Los Lobos del Este de Los Angeles and Lalo Guerrero (1983); panel discussions by distinguished scholars on Mexican musicology and the Chicano experience in music (1983); a film screening of *Zoot Suit* with guest commentary by Luis Valdez (1984); two concerts featuring the music of Mexican composers Manuel Enríquez and Lucía Alvarez, and the Cuarteto de Cuerdas Latinoamericano (1984); folk music presentations by Los Jaraneros from Mexico City and Don Félix Trejo, an interpreter of the corrido (1984); and four performances of the Mexican Arts Chamber Symphony under the direction of Abraham Chávez, conductor of the El Paso Symphony (1985–87). The concerts included symphonic pieces and concertos by Mexican composers Ponce, Galindo, Halffter, and Enríquez and featured soloists Johana Harris-Heggie, Danilo Lozano, and Joseph González, in addition to compositions by UCLA graduate music students Raymond Torres-Santos and Pablo Furman; a musical composite concert of music from East Los Angeles titled "The Eastside Revue" produced by Rubén Guevara (1985); a concert featuring UCLATINO with guest artist Poncho Sánchez (1985); a restaging of an excerpt from Luis Valdez's *Corridos* in conjunction with UCLA's Wight Gallery exhibition of the works by Mexican photographer Agustín Víctor Casasola (1985); two fundraising concerts featuring Linda Ronstadt, Mariachi Los Camperos de Nati Cano, Tito Puente, UCLATINO, Poncho Sánchez, Mariachi Uclatlán, and Vikki Carr (1988–89); a concert and recording session by the National Symphony Orchestra

of Mexico with guest conductor Abraham Chávez (1988); a staging of *Una Pasto-rela* (based on a traditional *pastorela*) directed and adapted by Francisco González at the San Fernando Mission (1989); two mariachi festivals (1989, 1991); a co-sponsorship of a Chicano Pop Legends Revue at Royce Hall featuring Tierra, El Chicano, and Thee Midniters (1990); and the commission of a piece for string quartet, piano, and mezzo-soprano by composer Thomas Pasatieri based on the poetic texts of "Canciones del Barrio" by Chicano poet José Montoya (the con-cert at which the piece premiered was billed as "A Mexican/Chicano Encounter in Chamber Music" and was part of the series produced in conjunction with the Mexican government's "Mexico: A Work of Art" project in the fall of 1991).

Antonio Coronel demonstrating a traditional dance for author/photographer Charles Lummis (circa 1888). Courtesy of Seaver Center for Western History Research, Natural History Museum of Los Angeles County.

Sisters Luisa and Rosa Villa, singers of Mexican songs who recorded for Charles Lummis (1904). Courtesy of the Southwest Museum, Los Angeles. Photo N:35531/P33398A.

Rosendo Uruchurto recording on wax cylinder for Charles Lummis in 1904. Courtesy of the Southwest Museum, Los Angeles. Photo N:24310.

Writer, photographer, and collector of songs Charles S. Lummis at his desk in Los Angeles (1902). Courtesy of the Southwest Museum, Los Angeles. Photo N:24381.

A *salterio* (psaltery) ensemble of Los Angeles (circa early 1900s). Courtesy of the Southwest Museum, Los Angeles. Photo N:35529/P40035.

Pedro G. González, Los Angeles radio personality and promoter during the 1920s and 1930s, (circa 1934). Courtesy of Zachary Salem Collection.

"El Despertador y Los Chicos," performers on KFOX radio (circa 1932). Left to right: La Prieta Caldera, Víctor Sánchez, Tina León (front row, seated), Beto "El Romántico," host Tony Sáenz ("El Despertador," standing at microphone), Fernando Linares (back row, seated). Others unknown. Courtesy of Zachary Salem Collection.

At right are Las Hermanas Padilla, popular singers in Los Angeles throughout the 1940s. At center is Mexican singer Pedro Vargas and at left are Las Hermanas Julian (circa 1940, Mason Theater). Courtesy of Philip Sonnichsen Collection.

Manuel Acuña, active since the 1920s until his death in 1990 as a music arranger and in the area of Artists and Repertoire (A&R) for various record companies that included a Mexican catalogue. Courtesy of Alma A. Lucastic.

Adelina García performing on live radio for station XEW during the period of her career when she was based in Mexico City. She relocated permanently to Los Angeles in 1938 and made her first recording there (with Columbia) in 1939.

Conductor Sal Cervantes and his big band orchestra perform at the Royal Palms Hotel (circa 1938). Musicians include singer Lily Ramos, Bobby Gil (piano), Ray Ramos (lead alto saxophone), Chico Sesma (trombone), and Paul López (lead trumpet). Courtesy of Chico Sesma Collection.

The La Bamba nightclub, located on Macy and Spring streets, (circa 1946). Lalo Guerrero (with maracas) sang for the ensemble led by drummer Alfonso Fernández. Also performing were Manny Cerecedes (piano), José Salais (trumpet), and Russell De Salvo (accordion). Courtesy of Lalo Guerrero Collection.

DON TOSTI & TRIO

Don Tosti and the Pachuco Boogie Boys (circa 1948). Clockwise from left: Bob Hernández, Don Tosti, Raúl Díaz, Eddie Cano. Courtesy of Don Tosti Collection.

At the Avedon Ballroom (circa early 1950s). From left: Phil Carreón, Rubén Reyes, Don Tosti. Tosti, who was a leader of his own groups, was a music arranger for singer Reyes. Carreón was a bandleader active in Los Angeles. Courtesy of Don Tosti Collection.

Chico Sesma (far right) directs his orchestra during a live broadcast of the KNXT television show "Fandango" (1955–56), produced by Pete and Eddie Rodriguez. Photo courtesy of Chico Sesma Collection.

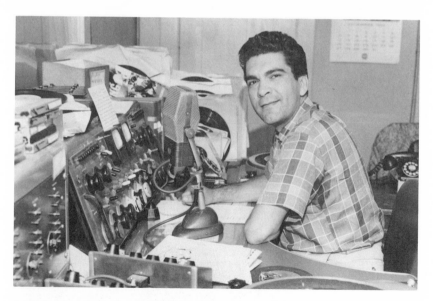

Latin music disc jockey, musician, and promoter Chico Sesma at radio station KALI (circa 1965). Courtesy of Chico Sesma Collection.

Marquee announcing the appearance of Orquesta Aragón, the highly popular Cuban *charanga*, at the Hollywood Palladium in 1958. Produced by Chico Sesma, the evening was billed as "Una Noche Aragón" and also featured the music of the Johnny Martínez Orchestra and the Bobby Montez Quintet. Courtesy of Chico Sesma Collection.

Bandleader Tito Puente performs at a Chico Sesma "Latin Holiday" production (circa 1957). Courtesy of Chico Sesma Collection.

Chico Sesma's Hollywood Palladium concert/dances (1958). Accompanying the very popular singer Celia Cruz was the Orquesta Nuevo Ritmo de Cuba, which featured musicians Pupi Lagarreta, Rolando Lozano, and Cuco Martínez. Courtesy of Chico Sesma Collection.

Los Angeles–based bandleader Manny López (right center) performs with vocalist Nita Cruz at the Hollywood Palladium (circa 1961). Courtesy of Chico Sesma Collection.

CALENDAR

NOVEMBER 25, 1984

MILLION DOLL

EL PIPORRO

GRAN Variedad

CONJUNTO MICHOACA

DEL 16 al 25 DE

Un Espectáculo Fantástico

The Million Dollar Theatre in downtown Los Angeles has been the mecca of Latin entertainment in Southern California for 34 years. When it stages lively variety shows featuring top talent direct from Mexico City, thousands of Latinos turn it into a family outing. It becomes a fantastic spectacle. Anne Geyer reports on the current show and some of the crowd. Page 38.

Anne Geyer's feature article in the *Los Angeles Times* "Calendar" section reviewed some of the history and the contemporary musical ambience of the Million Dollar Theater in downtown Los Angeles. Copyright 1989, *Los Angeles Times*. Reprinted by permission. Photo by Max Dryden.

Bassist Oscar Meza at a rehearsal of his ensemble, The Sixth Sun (circa 1973). Courtesy of Tony García Collection.

Vikki Carr. Courtesy of Dale Olson & Associates, Inc. Harry Langdon Photography, © 1982.

Trombonist Art Velasco and saxophonist Tony García (circa 1976). Courtesy of Tony García Collection.

Mariachi Los Camperos de Nati Cano. Courtesy of Nati Cano, La Fonda Restaurant.

Mariachi Los Galleros de Pedro Rey. Courtesy of Pedro Hernández, El Rey Restaurant.

Mariachi Sol de México de José Hernández. Courtesy of José Hernández, Cielito Lindo Restaurant.

Mariachi Uclatán de Mark Fogelquist. Juan Manuel Cortez, musical director. Courtesy of Mark Fogelquist, El Mariachi Restaurant.

Reissued Ritchie Valens LP containing the hits "La Bamba," "Donna," and "Come On Let's Go," among others. Del-Fi Records 1958, 1959. Distributed by Rhino Records Inc., 1981. RNDF200. Used by permission.

Publicity photo of Linda Ronstadt promoting her 1988 Grammy Award–winning LP *Canciones de mi padre,* recorded in Los Angeles. Also featured on the album were Daniel Valdez, Mariachi Vargas Tecalitlán, and Los Angeles–based mariachis Los Camperos de Nati Cano, Los Galleros de Pedro Rey, and Sol de México de José Hernández. Used by permission, Elektra/Asylum Records.

Li'l Ray Jiménez. Photo in Salesian High School Rock and Roll Show Program, courtesy of Mike Jiménez. Used by permission, Salesian High School.

Thee Midniters. Courtesy of Minerva Amaro Collection.

Front cover of *Golden Treasures, vol. 1: West Coast East Side Revue,* the first of two volumes produced by Eddie Davis and Rudy Benavides and released through Davis's Rampart Records label (1966, 1969). Used by permission, Eddie Davis.

Salesian High School yearbook photo (1962) of the school's Mustang Band directed by Bill Taggart. Courtesy of Tony García Collection. Used by permission, Salesian High School.

Ace, one of the most active bands in the 1970s eastside circuit (circa 1975). Courtesy of Salesian High School.

El Chicano. Courtesy of MCA Records.

El Chicano LP featuring the hit title track "Viva Tirado" (1970). Used by permission, MCA Records.

Tierra's 1980 *City Nights* LP, which included the platinum record single "Together."
Used by permission, Christopher Whorf, Art Director. Boardwalk Records, Inc.,
FW 36995. © 1980.

Mike Jiménez and Steve Salas singing for Tierra in 1983 during a television taping of "Sound Festival," a PBS series of Latin music produced by José Luis Ruiz. Courtesy of KCET, Public Broadcasting System. Photo by Mitzi Trumbo.

Cleanslate, one of the many eastside top-forty bands of the late 1970s. Author appears at upper left (circa 1978). From the author's collection.

Rubén Guevara, producer, musician and writer. Courtesy of Rubén Guevara.

Album cover of *Los Angelinos: The Eastside Renaissance* (1983). Produced by Rubén Guevara on the Zyanya label, the LP included the music of ten diverse Chicano groups active in eastside Los Angeles. Used by permission, Rhino Records. RNLP 062.

Edward James Olmos performs Luis Valdez's *Zoot Suit* at the Mark Taper forum (circa 1978). Music and dance highlighted the play. Courtesy of Mark Taper Forum. Photo by Jay Thompson.

Poster promoting "Noche Mexicana," a benefit concert and part of the 1988 UCLA Mexican Arts Series. Clockwise from top: Linda Ronstadt, Daniel Valdez, Poncho Sánchez, and Tito Puente. Also performing were the UCLA Latin music ensemble UCLATINO and special honorees Nati Cano (Mariachi Los Camperos) and Lalo Guerrero. Funds raised from the concert were used to produce a subsequent concert by the Mexican National Symphony Orchestra and its recording of three concertos under the direction of guest conductor Abraham Chávez. Courtesy of UCLA Mexican Arts Series. Artwork by Ignacio Gómez.

Scene from the Columbia Pictures film *La Bamba*, featuring actor Lou Diamond Phillips in the role of Ritchie Valens. Written and directed by Luis Valdez, the film was a major box office success and generated Los Lobos' double-platinum hit remake of Valens's version of "La Bamba." Photo (from *La Bamba*, © 1987) courtesy of Columbia Pictures Industries, Inc.

Program cover of Plaza de la Raza's 1990 Chicano Musicworks competition for composers. Courtesy of Plaza de la Raza. Artwork by Willie Herrón.

First place winners, finalists, judges, and administrators of the 1990 Chicano Musicworks project sponsored by Plaza de la Raza. At front center is project coordinator Miguel Delgado. Courtesy of Plaza de la Raza.

Musicworks panel of judges: (top row) Rubén Guevara, Bobby Espinoza, Rudy Salas, Al Rubalcava, Héctor Reséndez, Luis Garza; (middle row) Jimmy Espinoza, Steve Loza (chair), Gema Sandoval (executive director, Plaza de la Raza), Danilo Lozano, Tony García, Chico Sesma; (bottom row) Tito Larriva, John Avila, Willie Herrón. Courtesy of Board of Directors, Plaza de la Raza.

Part II
Ethnography

Chapter 4

Profiles of the Artists
The War Veterans

The kid was born in Mexico, and went back to visit after being raised in L.A. for most of his life. Sitting in front of his grandfather, he began to stir the *atole*, doing by rote what seemed to come naturally from many years before. His *abuelo* asked him a question in Spanish. The boy responded by saying that he had forgotten his Spanish. The old man then said, "You have forgotten to speak Spanish, but you still remember how to stir the *atole*."

—TRADITIONAL MEXICAN FOLKTALE

In October of 1984 I conducted and videotaped a series of nine interviews with fifteen Mexican-American musicians and entrepreneurs associated with the musical culture of Los Angeles since the mid-1940s. In this chapter and the next I present the data from the interviews in a narrative form, encompassing a cross-section of the individuals who constitute the focus of this book. Four of the ethnographic profiles are followed by brief musical analyses of selected songs of the artists.

The individuals interviewed ranged from twenty-four to sixty-eight years of age. I chose the interview subjects because they were, or had been, actively involved in the Mexican-American musical life of Los Angeles. Some were born in Los Angeles, and others immigrated from Mexico. All of them considered their art form central to their careers and actively strove to work consistently as professional artists. A questionnaire was developed and administered, in a conversational manner, to each informant. The ethnographic data show varying degrees of assimilation.

The interviews are intended to be the basis for an ethnography of the musical life of Los Angeles in the postwar years. The interviews add a personal dimension that provides a framework of responses and attitudes based on a common set of inquiries. This framework can then be used in a comparative analysis to assess the diversity of musical activity among the

Mexican Americans of Los Angeles. Although the nine interviews represent contrasting musical directions, a different nine might be even more diverse. The present nine interviews, therefore, do not completely portray the musical life of the Mexican American in Los Angeles, but they do document the activity of a selected group of musicians who represent a particular musical movement.

I have written a narrative profile of each artist based on the videotaped interview. The interview generally took place in the artist's home, but in three cases the artist requested a different location. Teresa Covarrubias asked to be interviewed at a McDonald's restaurant on Whittier Boulevard in East Los Angeles because she had spent a great deal of time there composing music and thinking about her musical career. Lalo Guerrero, who lives in Palm Springs, California, was interviewed at my parents' home during one of his trips to Los Angeles. The occasion was a memorable reunion between a popular and legendary artist and some of his longtime aficionados. The members of Los Lobos were interviewed on the roof of the Palmer Building in Hollywood after videotaping a performance to be aired on German television.

Videotaping the interviews not only provided a visual dimension to the narrative data but also illustrated to the interviewees how their thoughts would serve as primary documentation. The musicians were quite enthusiastic about a study of Chicano music, and they viewed contributing to such a project as an important and honorable task. Additionally, many of the artists knew me on a professional or personal basis and felt comfortable throughout the process.

John Ovalle: Selling Records on Whittier Boulevard

For many years, John Ovalle was the proprietor of the Record Inn, located on Whittier Boulevard in East Los Angeles. He died in October 1987, two years after I interviewed him. He merchandised records there since 1974 to a clientele that was almost exclusively Mexican American. His inventory ranged from the local Mexican/Chicano artists and top-forty rhythm and blues categories to Latin music and the current new wave and punk rock groups. Through his years of operating a small store in the midst of Chicano culture, John observed a plethora of trends and marketing techniques in the record industry. He also witnessed a categorical uniqueness in the musical preferences and mentality of the Chicano market.

John was born in Gallup, New Mexico, and was raised in the Colorado Rockies. In 1932 he came to Los Angeles, where he received his education and began working in machine shops as a young man. Discharged from the armed forces in 1948, he started working in the record industry as a wholesale distributor. During that year John also decided to enroll at the Los Angeles Conservatory of Music. He graduated with a certificate in music after completing studies in music theory, orchestration, and performance on acoustic bass.

As a child John played the piano in his parents' home. As he grew older he also learned to play the guitar, but he did not have formal instruction until he entered the conservatory following military service. His parents enjoyed classical music; at the same time, they listened to a great deal of Mexican music, such as traditional artists and folkloric genres. Los Hermanos Torres were among their favorites, in addition to some of the big band music so popular during the 1930s and 1940s. John's own interest in the popular jazz styles of the era began with recordings of Count Basie's orchestra. His parents often referred to that particular genre of jazz music as "devil music," and cautioned him, "Don't buy that—that's dead music." Another profound influence during the period were the Latin forms such as the *danzón*[1] and rumba.[2] To John's parents, Latin music did not represent "devil music" as did the blues and jazz, even though they were also popular at the time in Latin quarters throughout the country.

The elements that first attracted John to jazz included "good progressions of music [that] make you think further up ahead." Performing *corridos*[3] is not as challenging in a technical sense, for most *corrido* forms are based on two or three chords. In playing jazz he had more opportunity to experiment because jazz chordal language provides a more expansive harmonic palate. Early in his career he wanted to become an arranger in the style of jazz artist Pete Rugalo, but John realized that the financial opportunities for jazz musicians within his particular network of musical employment would not support a career. He therefore began to work with a diversity of musical groups that included western bands, blues bands, and classical music ensembles.

The Los Angeles Conservatory of Music was located on Pico Boulevard and Figueroa Avenue. (The school was eventually closed, and the building is now a dance ballroom.) While John was a student there he had to perform professionally to receive academic credit. In those days he played for three dollars a night at a variety of clubs and functions with bands that played show tunes, dance music, western music, bluegrass, and blues. The conservatory did not offer classes related to Mexican music, but the students played everything else.

John became involved in the record industry because he had always enjoyed the record phenomenon. He decided to open his own record shop on East First Street while attending the conservatory. He operated that business for about four years until Aliso Village, a nearby residential area, was destroyed for development in the area. Having lost the majority of his customers, John became a wholesale record distributor while continuing to work as a musician at night.

The principal product in John's record distributorship was popular, commercial music. His record clientele were primarily wholesale buyers who represented a variety of record stores throughout the Los Angeles area, especially in the East Side. His warehouse specialized in rhythm and blues and included approximately two hundred different labels. These were not the major labels such as RCA and Columbia but rather records produced by companies such as Specialty, Do Tone, Avco, and Atlantic. Additionally, John's manager, the owner of the distributorship, employed many of the local disc jockeys. John explained the situation: "And of course, we had every disc jockey in Los Angeles working for my boss. You've heard of the payola. Well, they weren't on payola, they were on straight salary. That's why they weren't doing nothing wrong. It was paying them for a service and it was R&B, jazz . . . and then there was about six playing spirituals. So we had everything covered."

John's company distributed the records of some of the most popular rhythm and blues artists of the 1950s, including Little Richard, Fats Domino, The Penguins, and many others. His clientele included the Record Rack, located at the intersection of Whittier and Atlantic boulevards in East Los Angeles, Newberry's, Cress, and the department stores in the eastside area. The company also worked with Mr. Mayan's Music on First Street and Brooklyn Avenue, Nelly's on First Street and Boyle Avenue, and a number of shops on Spring Street and North Broadway downtown.

Although John was marketing mostly black rhythm and blues music, his company had three different lines of Mexican records. Because the company also catered to the juke box market, a small percentage of Mexican recordings would usually be inserted into the machine menu. "So when we took them a Little Richard or Fats Domino, we also took them a Lalo Guerrero, a Beto Villa . . . and all of the juke boxes would buy them by the hundreds."

John found that the older generation of Mexican Americans preferred traditional Mexican music. The younger generation, however, was partial to rhythm and blues styles and to what John referred to as the "doo-wop" style, eventually called "oldies" among Chicanos. John sold a substantial amount of this music throughout the 1950s and 1960s. Much of the music sold well in his shop, but the recording artists were never offered contracts with major recording companies; hence, few became popular outside East Los Angeles. Some companies, such as Pan American in Chicago, did try to market Mexican and Chicano artists in other regions of the United States, but most of these have since been consolidated into larger companies.

Because the highly concentrated Chicano population in the East Side was purchasing and listening to large quantities of black rhythm and blues music, performers there began to be influenced by that particular sound in their own musical expression:

The ones that were imitating in the East L.A. area were small groups: two, three, four, or five guys, no more than that . . . Alfred and Joe, The Amber Tones, Atlantis, Blue Satin, Cannibal and the Head-hunters (they had a little six or seven [piece group] and he was on Mercury, I remember that), Doug Saldana, the Chapman's, The Blendells, Frankie Ortega (he was an individual singer; he was backed by the groups), The Heartbreakers (they were four boys), the Jaguars (they were also four), and Little Junior Herrera (he was a singer by himself and he recorded on about four different labels). The one that he got his biggest break on was Johnny Otis's label "Dig," (and that was Johnny Otis's band backing him up), and Li'l Ray, Mark and the Escorts, The Mixtures, Oscar Saldana (he had a band, a nine-piece band), The Pageants, The Premiers, The Romancers, and Rosie and the Originals. It was The Originals, and Rosie was singing with them; she's from Escondido. They sent the tape over here, and that's the worst record made because they did it at home. But when it got here, they took it to the Huggy Boy Show and they played it, just the dub, and it was a smash overnight. So they says, "Forget it, we'll take it right off this dub and make the masters." Now whenever you hear the vibrations of the guitar and the garage and the whole thing— that's the national anthem of R&B. The Salas Brothers later became Tierra; [there were also] the Slauson Brothers, and there was another group of girls from the south part of town called The Sisters. Now all these kids were imitating the R&B, but they were adding a little something. . . . When they started getting more instruments, they started Latin rhythm—not as you hear with Tito Puente, but it's a made-up rhythm of the kids that are trying to play Latin . . . Lupe and all those type of things, but they gave it a little different flavor, little different harmonies, and that's what made them great with the Chicanos, because . . . they didn't want to hear Maria Callas singing a big thing when they had somebody here to do it for them on the classic or any other form.

At that time in Los Angeles, the Mexican-American population was not highly involved as performers in local mainstream classical music activities. There were, however, important exceptions. A trained singer named don Rodolfo Hoyos had sung with opera tenor Enrico Caruso at the Metro-politan Opera house in New York. A Mexican who resided in Los Angeles,

Hoyos operated a studio on Second Street and Broadway in downtown Los Angeles. He recorded for Columbia Masterworks, and Caruso recorded with RCA Victor; John cited this difference as the reason why the two singers were never able to record together. Another highly talented singer, Carlos Ramírez, came to Los Angeles in the late 1930s. "But when he got to Hollywood they spoiled him. He got into the movies with Lana Turner and so forth—Gilbert Roland and the whole trip." The Mexican composer Carlos Chávez was also an important figure at the time, but the general involvement of Chicanos with classical music was minimal, because it was not the music they were performing. On the basis of music appreciation, however, art music enjoyed a high degree of respect within the Mexican/Chicano culture.

Because local artists lacked substantial financial resources, various eastside investors or the artists themselves produced and marketed the recordings on many small labels that are now defunct. "I can't remember all the labels that were available that they created themselves. All those records are now deleted from the catalogs as somebody else bought the masters or reissued on another label and they just keep rolling along. I wish somebody would come up with the money, because it takes a lot of money to create a good catalog. Of course, they only sell in California, Arizona, New Mexico, part of Texas, and a few in Chicago. The rest of the country don't want to hear about them."

The late 1940s were highlighted by various local recording artists in the Chicano community, including such personalities as the Torres Brothers and Eddie Cano, who was then playing with the Don Tosti Trio. Tosti's repertoire was wide, ranging from boleros to jazz. Memo Mata was another popular musician who led a big band, as was Phil Carreón, who recorded a diversity of music from both the United States and Mexico. Vikki Carr was singing with Carreón's band at the time. Carr may have also sung quite often with Trini López in El Paso, returning on occasion to the city of her birth to perform.

Musical activity among Mexicans in El Paso was intense. *Tejanos,* or Mexican Americans from Texas, often produced and disseminated records more rapidly and on a larger scale than Chicano artists in Los Angeles. For example, the Tejano Ernie Casares, who was a member of Glenn Miller's orchestra, was one of the first Chicano big band musicians. "All the guys from Texas—they beat us to the punch, because there was Ernie Casares, then came Sonny Osuna with these two songs—went national: 'Sonny' and 'Talk to Me.' They were on the Tear Drop label."

Although the song "Sonny" was a national hit for Sonny Osuna, it was written by Chris Móntez, a Chicano from Los Angeles who for years sang in the club circuits of the city. The nationally successful Freddie

Fender, whose real name was Andrés Baldemar Huerta, was also from Texas. Another highly successful Tejano group was the Country Roland Band, which played country and western style. The leader of the group, Rolando García, was accompanied by his son and three daughters. In addition to country and western, García's band also performed traditional Mexican songs such as "La Barca de Oro": "Nick Lesando is on the piano and he [sings] with a twang in his voice. It's fantastic how he does it." The music of the Tejanos has been marketed throughout the Mexican/Chicano population of Los Angeles, but the urban sound of the music from Los Angeles is not as appealing to the Tejanos. As John put it, "The punk type of thing—they don't like it over there . . . they don't like it."

In the 1960s and 1970s new stylistic elements defined the music of such Chicano groups as Thee Midniters, El Chicano, Cannibal and the Headhunters, and eventually, Tierra. Doo-wop music and other pop forms gradually declined in popularity. For a long period, however, many groups continued to perform these "oldies," so their musical style still influenced the direction of Chicano musical expression. The Salas Brothers were exemplary. After performing under various names for many years in the eastside circuit, they finally attained national success with the group concept of Tierra. John sold their single "Together" steadily for two or three months (circa 1980) before it even had radio play, selling 500 copies a week. He ascribed this paradox to the fact that young Chicanos were exposed to the recording through their local socialization and entertainment network: "Why? Because somebody got it, played it at home, they came and bought it, they played it at the house. I was selling records from here to El Centro, San Bernardino, all the area here, and Fresno, Bakersfield . . . and the record wasn't even on the radio yet. They only had one single. We finally got on the air and it went."

Eventually, the single was included on the album released about one year later under the title *City Nights* on Boardwalk Records. The album's production was delayed because there was not enough money in the original local production to manufacture a complete album. As the single generated more profit, a percentage of the money was invested in the production and recording of the album, which went "platinum" in its first year, selling more than one million copies.

During this era, many eastside groups persistently failed to achieve the national recognition enjoyed by black R&B artists such as Michael Jackson, Stevie Wonder, or the group Earth, Wind, and Fire. John offered the following reason: "Because they didn't have the money to spend on the promotion that Motown has; or they didn't have the money that Columbia has. Don't forget, Columbia releases maybe thirty singles a week and five or six albums every week."

Dominant companies like Columbia and Motown were not generally interested in recording the Chicano artists: "They didn't trust them. Not until the last few years has Columbia taken El Chicano and taken other groups. But RCA is still trembling, yet they have one of the largest Mexican catalogs in the world. That, they've taken a big way back from the company that was releasing [them]." The record companies "didn't trust them" in that they were not optimistic about the potential market for Chicano artists and therefore did not make initial investments. Another problem lay in the demographic patterns of Chicanos compared to blacks—the latter reside in most sectors of the United States, whereas Chicanos are mainly concentrated in the Southwest.

John also emphasized that "if a record makes it . . . it will sell all over," meaning that successful records need not be tailored to the Latin market. Entrepreneurs would call him to propose the marketing of hit recordings in Spanish, such as the music of Stevie Wonder, saying, "We want to catch the Latino trade." John responded, "Forget it, because if a Hispanic wants to buy, he wants to buy it this way by Stevie Wonder and he wants it by Stevie Wonder."

Success within the music industry therefore entailed some compromises for the Chicano musician. John has seen how artists such as Vikki Carr and Andy Russell compromised in certain artistic or cultural aspects to enter the cultural mainstream. Such a dilemma affected all Chicano artists, even those of the later eras like the rhythm and blues players:

> They had to compromise to begin with. I don't know about Vikki; but I know all the rest had to—just the R&Bs. And right now, if you go to a label, they'll say, "Okay, we'll do it under these conditions, that it has your name on it and the producer's name on it as composer and the A&R man as something, and when your royalties come in, you won't get not even one tenth percent of what you should get. That's a compromise. You have him do this, you have him do that, and they all get their name on the record label and you wind up with nothing . . . that's what happened then.

Vikki Carr and Andy Russell appear to have achieved a longer lasting international popularity than the younger Tierra because they

> cater to the older Anglo that will buy the album, take it home. If it sounds bad after a couple of years, he'll go buy it again. Not with the kids that are buying Tierra. In a week they'll miss an album and they will never buy another one, because by that weekend somebody else came up with the Go Gos or whatever. They just go with the trend. The difference of one week on the pop album has a lot to do with

it. Two weeks, three weeks, boom. That's why the Michael Jackson *Thriller* has all these sales, because it was good and everybody bought it. There'll never be another album like that. Johnny Mathis—he sells all the time, and you don't hear him on the air. But who's buying it? Over forty.

"Chicano"-labeled groups such as Tierra, which has consciously affiliated itself with the Chicano and Latino movements in the United States, may have placed themselves in a "can't win" situation:

> A group like El Chicano and all of these groups that are trying to make it . . . they're from the valley of Chicanos—they're dead now. Nobody hears about them. Nobody buys their records; yet they're playing. But the ones that will sell forever is the old Andy Russell, Vikki Carr; but don't forget the Lalo Guerrero. He's sticking with his Ardillitas,[4] and I don't blame him because he can't sell here one-tenth [of a *ranchera*] in the whole United States, but he'll sell "Las Ardillitas" in Mexico and all the South American countries; add them up to one hundred times more over there . . . but he's sticking with it.

The dilemma is further reinforced by the fact that a group such as Tierra, although strongly aligned with the Chicano/Latino community, does not exclusively perform in the Spanish language (although the group did record a translated copy of "Together"). Marketing, distribution, and live performance therefore become more of a barrier in Latin America, a difficulty further exacerbated by the group's lack of bicultural business representation.

Even in John's record store, recordings of Chicano artists who were not current were difficult to obtain. The primary problem is that many of these recordings are no longer pressed; such is the case with numerous records of Andy Russell, El Chicano, Little Ray Jiménez, and Cannibal and the Headhunters. John tries to purchase and stock collections or reissues of Chicano artists whenever possible. He cited Malo, a Chicano San Francisco–based Latin rock group popular during the 1970s, as an example: "Like Malo—three years, no album, no 8-track, no nothing . . . but they told me that a guy in Canada had seventy-eight 8-tracks of Malo, so I contacted the man. I told him, 'You bring them across this side and ship (them) to the United States. I'll send you an American money order and cashier's check, and then you can ship. I'll pay for the freight here. . . .' They lasted me ten days; a guy took five."

Many records by Chicano artists that were once popular in the community are no longer available, but the market still seems to exist, as in the case of the Malo record. For this reason, the reissues of recordings by Thee

Midniters and Ritchie Valens, the Eastside Sound Volumes (1–12), and the Rhino Record project always sold well at the Record Inn. One persistent problem, however, was availability of stock. Another example of this discrepancy between supply and demand is Ersi Arvizu's vocal rendition of the Mexican bolero standard "Sabor a Mí," one of the East Side's "anthems," which was recorded by El Chicano. When John could obtain copies of the record, it still sold—long after it first appeared, twenty years ago.

During the era of the popular San Francisco–based groups Santana, Malo, and Azteca, when Chicano artists' records were distributed to John's shop they were advertised heavily before they were released:

> The distributor called us and says, "We have a new album by Malo."— Malo, Carlos Santana, or whoever it was coming out on a certain date. Well, we asked them for some kind of picture, or something to put on the window. But we told all the customers that were coming in, "Next Friday we're going to have Thee Midniters; we're going to have Carlos Santana," or whatever it was. Now when the record came out they were waiting for it, and we'd have a long list. . . . Believe me, they moved out that day, two days, three days. We got to replace the order right away to make sure we had our stock in good demand. It's not like now. Now they hear it on the air for a week or two and then they finally buy a single and when they finally get to it they listen to it here. Then, what came out new—it sold then. If there was a Beto Villa, Lalo Guerrero, Thee Midniters, or Miguel Aceves [Mejía], or whoever came out, it sold then.

Young eastside Chicanos today tend to be consumers of the various musical styles aired on English-language radio. Genres include music reminiscent of 1950s rock and roll, oldies, Motown (rhythm and blues), current heavy metal, and new wave. If Mexican music is purchased, the same young people will buy such records "only when it's their parents' or grandparents' birthday." Current "hit" artists' albums displayed in front of the cashier counter included those by Culture Club, Soft Cell, Dawn Patrol, Sergio Mendez, The Blasters, Lionel Ritchie, Supertramp, Rod Stewart, Back Street, Runaway, Pure Magic, Silvester, Baxter Robertson, Melissa Manchester, Alabama, The Bongos, Michael Jackson, Hall and Oates, Champaign, Shalomar (for *Dancing in the Street*), Cesar, Rescue, and Los Illegals. Another shelf displayed oldies recordings such as Little Richard, The Dells, Mary Wells, and The Stylistics. Above these were located a limited variety of Latin music by artists such as Machito and Andy Russell.

On the other side of the store, John's stock was almost exclusively records and tapes from Mexico and other parts of Latin America—Puerto Rico, Cuba, and a few from South America. Among the many records in stock, some of the best sellers were those of Las Damas, Los Barones Internacionales, and *"los conjuntos norteños."* In characterizing the *norteño* music from Mexico and the Texas border region, John distinguished the style from local Chicano music: *"Conjunto norteño* is the country boy, real country. He'll never give that up. Whether you take his right arm, or you take his green card, he won't give up his music. That's norteño. It's a real folkloric music."

Those who continue to purchase the records and tapes of Mexican music are primarily Mexican-born immigrants who continue to listen to and maintain that musical tradition. Conversely, many of the young immigrants come to the Record Inn to purchase current hard rock recordings, in spite of the fact that many of them do not comprehend the English lyrics: "They'll come in and they don't even speak English. But they'll come and say, 'Vengo buscando una roka pesada,' and they act like they're playing a guitar and [that] means heavy metal. And then the girls come in asking for 'música loca'; that's also rock. They are young, maybe up to thirty years old . . . usually city folks. When you get the little braceritos, ranchero, he goes back home and he'll never change."

Concerning the next phase of musical trends among young Chicanos of the East Side, John expects to witness a recycling of nostalgic styles and innovation:

> They're going back into the next R&B, and they might go back to the doo-wops. Because, don't forget, it's not so much the music on the doo-wops, it's a message of the words in the song. A guy sees a girl, he dedicates it on "Flaco de Oro" como se llama "Huggy Boy." "I Got Eyes for You," from Chato to Nena, then she answers him, "I like you too." Then he writes back to her, like writing, but they don't write. They dedicate songs. I think that's coming back. I hope it does . . . 'cause that will last forever. It's been twenty or thirty years since that's happened, in big, and it might come back. Time will tell, because musically speaking, the groups now are not doing what they were doing twenty-five, thirty years ago. They may have better sound because they have better equipment. First time I saw Lightning Hopkins, he flipped me over. He was playing a shoe box guitar. Now you have these guitars with twenty thousand wires going out to pedals, and wangs and this and that, you know. You go see Segovia, you hear guitar playing. He had no amplifier; has a speaker in the front of him where he talks. But it's not amplification to his guitar.

Regarding his own future, John described his personal plans and sentiments, as well as his aspirations and models for local Chicano artists:

I would like to keep going for a while, but my health is not too good. So I'm going to have to find somebody that can take it over. But what they can't take over is what I got up here [pointing to his head]. Once you lived through it, you'll never forget it. And the musicians I played with, the guys I played with, the people I know in the record industry from high to low—I can never replace it. What I would like to tell the kids and old guys that want to get into the business: You have to study. It doesn't come easy. Because, you know, three-fourths of it doesn't come easy if you're a rock and roll star. You have to study, practice, and don't be so noisy, because once it gets so loud that they only have one volume—that's distortion as heck. I like some of the stuff that comes out right now. I do. Take Los Lobos. They're very original. That's why I'm helping them. I'm giving them songs that they can do. They go out and do "Under the Boardwalk" and then they come and do "Anselma." . . . And they got a Grammy. You know who they beat out? Vicente Fernández, José José, all the stars from Mexico. And they can do it. They are going to be number one. Now they'll be leaving for Europe again next month, I think. They're in Ventura right now, but they'll be going again and they are going to be number one for a long while. A long, long while because they're catering to everybody. They come to your house; you want corridos, polkas, or whatever you want—they'll play them. And then somebody comes up and says, "Why don't you play us this?" Boom, they'll play it, too. A doo-wop, an R&B, whatever—and they'll go to another club the following day—what the club wants—and they'll give it to them exactly.

John agreed that Los Lobos represents a salient musical reflection of the Chicano eastside community in Los Angeles: "It's a mixture. You can say a Mexican only likes 'La Cucaracha' or 'El Rancho Grande' and that's all, like they portray us in the movies. But from Chávez, 'Pirámide del Sol'— did you ever listen to it? . . . 'La Pirámide del Sol' is Chávez—beautiful."[5]

Postscript: In 1988 Los Lobos dedicated their Grammy Award–winning LP *La pistola y el corazón* to the memory of John Ovalle.

Andy Russell: Crooner from Boyle Heights

Andy Russell's singing career spans two complete continents. He began as a drummer and singer with such acts as the first Stan Kenton Orchestra, Johnny Richards, Gus Arnheim, and Alvino Rey. Early in his career Russell signed with Capitol Records and recorded songs in both English and Spanish, including "Bésame Mucho," which became the first of his eight different million-sellers. Russell's other hits included "Magic is the Moonlight," "Laughing on the Outside," "Amor," and "What a Difference a Day Makes." Russell became a national sensation like his contemporaries Frank Sinatra and Perry Como. Relocating to Mexico City in the early 1950s, Andy became the host of the popular Argentine television show, "El Show de Andy Russell," which aired from 1956 to 1965. During those years he also appeared in several motion pictures and toured extensively throughout Latin America, winning awards such as "The Pioneer of Argentine Television," "The Showman of the Americas," and in 1974 the "Eagle of the Americas," bestowed on him by Mexican journalists.

Andy describes himself as having "100 percent Mexican blood." His mother was originally from Chihuahua, Mexico, and his father emigrated to the United States from the Mexican state of Durango. Andy was born in Los Angeles on 16 September (the date that commemorates Mexico's independence from Spain) in 1919. His real name is Andrés Rábago Pérez. He and his seven brothers and two sisters were raised in the Boyle Heights section of East Los Angeles.

Although he spoke Spanish with his parents, Andy referred to his childhood command of the language as "very bad." Andy's parents spoke primarily Spanish and never learned practical English. As do the children in many bilingual families, he answered his parents in English when they conversed with him in Spanish and would tell his mother, "Por favor, hábleme en inglés" [please speak to me in English]. His eventual interest in American mainstream music joined with his strong Mexican linguistic and cultural background, so that he has always thought of himself as a mixture of Mexican and American.

Andy's father worked as an extra in Hollywood films, where he earned a substantial income. He had an assorted wardrobe for the variety of calls he received (e.g., a Mexican bandit outfit and an American Indian costume). Andy's mother was, in his words, "a wonderful mother and housewife."

The issue of displacement and Mexican identity was different for Andy as a child compared to what it is for many young Chicanos today: "In those days, I was just one of the guys. We had Russian people, we had Jewish kids, we had Mexican kids, we had the blacks, we never noticed things like that. Today it seems to be such a big thing. The only time I'd feel a little embarrassed was at lunch hour—we'd sit down at the bench to get our lunches. Everybody would open up their sandwich, and all of a sudden, I'd open up mine and my mother would put burritos in mine. And everybody would say, 'What is that?'"

Andy never experienced feelings of inferiority or displacement in society, school, or with respect to his professional ambitions: "I'm a very cocky little Mexican kid from the East Side, and I never had those feelings. I always feel that it's up to the person. You know, I would tell everybody, I'd say, 'I'm Mexican,' and they'd say, 'No Andy, you must be Spanish.' I'd say, 'No, I'm Mexican . . .' and they'd say, 'No Andy, but you're so light.' And I'd say, 'No, no, I'm Mexican. My father's Mexican. My mother's Mexican. . . .'"

At home Andy's parents listened to Mexican music, while his brothers and sisters listened to music from the United States. Andy related to American music first: "When I was a kid, Bing Crosby was my idol. I was just a little kid, and I'd listen to all the American things. I loved everything American. Musically, I didn't understand the Mexican music. My mother would talk to me about mariachi. I'd listen to Benny Goodman. I wanted all my life to be something important in the American atmosphere."

Andy had wanted to be a singer since he was a young boy. One of Andy's earliest influences was Jack Leonard, who sang with the Tommy Dorsey Orchestra. Andy also admired Benny Goodman, Dorsey, Glenn Miller, and Frank Sinatra. While he was still in high school Andy began singing with Don Ramon's band, which played primarily in the east side of Los Angeles. The members of the band were Mexicans and Mexican Americans; many of them, including Andy, eventually played with the Stan Kenton Orchestra. He had been singing with different groups throughout the East Side before he started studying drums out of necessity:

> They said to me one night and broke my heart, they says, "Andy, we can't afford to have you as just a singer. You've got to play some instrument." I said, "But, gee, I'm a singer." And they said, "Yeah, we're paying you two dollars, two-fifty a night and it's too much. You know, the guys wanna split the rest of the money." So I said, "What can I learn in a hurry so I can join the band? . . . Drums would be the easiest thing." So I got a bunch of the old records and started to learn to play drums. Down in the cellar I'd learn to play drums and keep good time. This was when I was in junior high and I was learning to play drums. Later on I got a teacher to teach me how to read, and before you knew it, I took drums seriously and I became one of the top drummers on the east side of L.A.—swing drummers. And I was playing drums with all these bands and then I'd sing.

Andy's high school experience was positive. He felt that he had studied with many fine teachers there. He was musically active, playing with the ROTC marching band (which entertained at football games and street parades), the jazz band, and the high school symphony orchestra under the direction of Harry Gruppengetter, who was a strict music teacher. After that experience Andy was offered more professional opportunities, in part because he had learned to read music playing in the orchestra.

When he left high school in 1939 Andy joined the band of Gus Arnheim, who had already employed such beginning artists as Bing Crosby and Woody Herman. In order to legally employ Andy and to allow the underage singer to work and tour out of state, Arnheim arranged adoption papers and became Andy's legal guardian. Arnheim suggested to Andy that he sing with the band on a bilingual basis. Andy replied, "No, Gus, my Spanish is very bad; I'm embarrassed." Arnheim finally convinced Andy that it was a good idea on a business level because, in his words, "If you do something different, the people are going to take notice." So Andy started singing songs in both English and Spanish: "People would kind of stop dancing, and they'd come up the bandstand and they'd get close and they'd say, 'Look, he's singing in another language,' and they took notice right away."

Andy was eventually offered a contract to record for Capitol Records in Hollywood, and he decided to take Arnheim's advice "to do something different." He chose to record a bilingual version of the Mexican standard "Bésame Mucho." The recording became a million-seller in the United States. That record release was a watershed for Andy: "That's where my whole life started. I was known as the bilingual singer in this country. After that came 'Amor, Amor,' . . . [singing], 'What a Difference a Day Makes,' and a whole bunch of those big hit songs; they were all million-sellers in this country. So I was very happy that I had that Spanish, that Latin background."

Up until the time of his recording of "Bésame Mucho" Andy had played with Stan Kenton's orchestra as a drummer and singer; he also performed in the same capacity with Johnny Richard's band and Alvino Rey and the King Sisters. It was during his association with Ray that he began recording for Capitol Records. "That's when I recorded 'Bésame Mucho.' From there on I left the drums and never touched them again [chuckles]." Andy also remembered the time he was offered the opportunity to replace drummer Buddy Rich in the Tommy Dorsey band. Dorsey personally made the offer to Andy while in town to perform at the Hollywood Paladium. Andy was interested in singing with the orchestra and told Dorsey, "I know that I can sing as good as your guy, and you'll save money 'cause I'll be playing drums and singing, too." Dorsey declined the dual counteroffer, explaining that he could not release his singer. Andy therefore declined Dorsey's offer. Dorsey's singer was young Frank Sinatra.

Andy changed his name from Rábago to Russell early in his career:

> I went on the road as the drummer and singer and he [Gus Arnheim] and I had to sign adoption papers to get out of the state of California. He was my father for a while. . . . When I was in Memphis, Tennessee,

I was working at the Peabody Hotel, and all the people were running to the bandstand whenever I'd play a drum solo, or whenever
I'd do a vocal, in English and in Spanish. And this bandleader, this
very famous bandleader who discovered Bing Crosby, was looking
at all these people looking at me. He says, "This kid is beginning to
become big with my band." So he talked to me; he says, "Andy, I've
got to tell you something. The name Rábago has got to go [laughs],
Rábago's gotta go." I says, "What do you mean?" He says, "I've gotta
change your name. Rábago hasn't got that ring to it, you know?"
I says, "But that's my name." He says, "Look, we'll keep Andy, all
right?" I says, "Okay. So what would you call me then?" He says, "I
used to have a singer, a famous singer, a fella that took Bing Crosby's
place years ago. His name was Russell Colombo, one of the famous
singers of that era. I'm gonna call you Russell—Andy Russell." I says,
"Yeah, that doesn't sound too bad." So right from there, from Memphis, Tennessee, there and Fort Worth, Texas, it was Andy Russell,
my new singing sensation, you know? So they changed the name to
Russell and he said that Rábago was just not a good name. At that
time everybody changed their name, Jack Benny, everybody had to
change their names.

Because he was singing bilingually, Andy felt that the public would
know his background by the Spanish songs in his repertoire. He did not
know at the time whether Arnheim was concerned about the nonmarket-
ability or the ethnic sound of the name (which was not particularly easy to
pronounce). In any case, it would have been difficult in the early 1940s to
use a Spanish surname. "Whenever you're a Mexican, if you're a Martínez,
a Rodríguez, a González, whatever it is, they always put you in a certain
fold, you know? 'He's a Latin singer, so let's give him a guitar and let him
sing only Mexican songs.' And I didn't want to do that. I didn't want to be
a guy with a Mexican hat. I wanted to be a pop singer."

   In effect, partly because of the stereotyping that existed at the time,
Andy compromised on the issue. Also, in that particular era (and even
today), name changing was common among performers, so that whether
names have been changed for ethnic reasons cannot always be determined.
In spite of the commercial name change, however, Andy's legal name is
still Andrés Rábago. He also felt that he would not have to make the same
compromise today: "It's a whole different [story] today. Rábago would
probably be a big thing today, or 'Rubaygo' [laughs]. Today, it's a different
thing. You can keep the same name. It's wonderful. It's a different world.
It's a different era completely."

   Andy did, however, remember the negative era:

I went to a fountain once at one of the 5 and 10s at Fort Worth, Texas, and I'd start drinking water, and everybody was standing around looking at me. I says, "My gosh, what did I do? Everybody's looking at me with a dirty look." And it said, "Colored Fountain." And I thought, "What would they say if they knew I was Mexican? You know? They won't let the black people drink from that fountain. What would they say if they knew I was Mexican?" And, thank goodness that they just didn't know. But I had that little complex in there, too, hidden. Hidden, but I'd always tell everybody I was Mexican, always.

Although he recognized the prejudice that existed in society, Andy was never the actual focus of racism. In his words, "I would sing in perfect English. I could pass for a gringo, exactly." Andy did not identify with the zoot suiters in the days of the zoot suit riots in Los Angeles, the physical confrontations involving pachucos during the 1940s:

I was embarrassed for that era, with that zoot suit stuff. I was really embarrassed. I think it was horrible, you know? Just terrible. . . .

In fact, I hated the word . . . it's terrible to say. . . . I'll probably make some enemies, but I'm gonna be frank and out in front. I hated the word "Chicano" at that time, 'cause at that time it was that, "He's nothing but a Chicano, you know?" That was a terrible word at that time. Yeah, "Pachuco" or "Chicano," you know? That's a horrible word. I says, "I'm not Chicano. I'm Mexican American. First I'm Mexican because my mother and dad are Mexican and I'm Mexican, and I'm American 'cause I was born here. I'm a Mexican American, I'm not a Chicano, you know?" I just didn't like that word. It stuck with me. I don't like it even today. I'm sorry, I don't like it. . . . Just don't like the sound.

Andy represents a paradox in the gap between the bicultural experience and the mainstream. Innovations or new trends may stem from an ethnic source, but many aspects of that ethnicity need to be glossed over so that the entertainment industry might be willing to risk marketing it to a mainstream audience. His own stereotype provided the recording and entertainment industry with a financially lucrative product based on an attractive "gimmick":

In our country, in the USA, as long as it's making money—and I've seen it in so many businesses—as long as you're making money, they don't care what you do or what you are. So at that time I was new, something new for them and making money, because "Bésame Mucho," a Mexican song, became number one in this country. "Amor,

Amor" [singing] became number one in this country with my record. [Also singing] "What a Difference a Day Makes." So you see, they didn't care. They said, "This is our Mexican-American singer." Now, for Capitol Records, I'm very proud to say that I was the first one that opened up their international market, 'cause they only sold records in this country. They didn't have a market outside of this country. I was the one that opened up their market in Latin America and in Mexico.

In the 1950s, after achieving national success in the United States, Andy went to Mexico. What was originally planned as a temporary move became an almost twenty-year residence in and association with Mexico and other parts of Latin America. His initial reason for leaving was personal. He and his wife were divorcing, and he was being advised by the Church and the Hollywood community not to proceed with the divorce: "The Catholic Church was after me because I was married in a Catholic Church. 'You can't do that,' he says . . . 'you just got the award of being the best couple in Hollywood.' I was getting pressure from Louella Parsons. All the Hollywood people were calling."

When he arrived in Mexico, thousands of people greeted him at the airport. A new level of success unfolded: "All of a sudden, my life—a complete turnabout from English to Spanish. I got into Mexico, got into the theater; we broke the records at the theater. I did my television show; it became the number one show; the number one radio show. I made a movie; it became the number one movie. Everything happened."

Another factor that Andy confronted in Mexico was his facility in the Spanish language. Although he spoke fluently, he felt his Spanish at the time was inadequate. "My Spanish was eastside, very bad, you know; so I was very embarrassed. So I got with friends and everything to help me with words, help me with different things. How to pronounce this and so and so. Before you know it, I was making movies and I became a Mexican idol, all over Latin America and Argentina, Venezuela, every place. I was the number one box office in all these countries in Spanish. So I have the two lives, in English and in Spanish."

Andy found his roots in Mexico; encouraged by the success that he attained, he decided to remain there. He married a Mexican woman and they had a son. During his Latin American career he toured extensively in Mexico, Argentina, Cuba, Venezuela, and other countries.

I'll never forget. I was at the Dune Television, and doing the [Havana] Hilton there, and I'd work Cuba about every six months . . . and I was there right when Castro came in, and I was one of the fools celebrating in the streets of Cuba, you know, because "Cuba's gonna be free now, it's gonna be so wonderful; this man is in here to free Cuba." So I was there celebrating with everybody. I'll never forget it. It was just a beautiful celebration. But you see what's happened now. A country that had the greatest music in the history of Latin music from Cuba, you know? Now they're just closed in completely.

Andy was also invited many times to perform in Spain. He sang for Franco on three different occasions and received awards from him, including that of "Barcelonés Honorario" and "Mayorquín Honorario." Traveling outside the United States gave him the opportunity to observe a political and cultural environment that contrasted with that of his place of birth. His experience outside the United States affected his political views about being both Mexican and "a member of a marginal society in the United States."

The truth is that I was very, very much confused, for traveling and living in all those countries all over Latin America. I'll tell you one example. When I went to Spain, I saw the most wonderful, peaceful country. And it's terrible to say, but I'm gonna say exactly . . . a dictator was then the head of the country, which was Francisco Franco. And I wondered, I says, "My God, isn't this great? All this great, wonderful freedom that they've got. . . ." I was always so confused with politics and everything because we'd always talk about the dictators, the bad guy, and so and so, and we've learned this in our country all my life. But I was in Spain. I'll never forget the wonderful, peaceful country that I was living in while I was in Spain. And everything was so beautiful. They just took care of the tourists so beautifully, and it was just a wonderful country, and lots of freedom. And here was a country being run by Mr. Franco. Then, when Mr. Franco passes away—this is what confuses me—he passed away, then democracy came in very strong. Now, the killings in the streets started, all the problems all over, and I says, "Well, how come? I don't understand it. Democracy is supposed to give us freedom and liberty and happiness with the people. . . ." It isn't the same way. There was killings in the streets. I used to walk at three and four in the morning through alleys in Spain. Never any problems when Franco was there. Today they say, "No, Andy. No camines en las calles a esa hora [don't walk in the streets at this hour] . . . Don't walk. . . ." Why? So, you stop to think, what is it? I come to our country now. We abuse our freedom in our country because we overdo it. We overdo this freedom. . . .

But . . . there's nothing like the USA. You've got to go around to those countries, to Bolivia, to Argentina, to Mexico. You'll never find—you haven't got the freedom in Mexico that you've got here.

You wouldn't dare say anything against the government of Mexico, or you're found in an alley the next day, or you're thrown out of the country. You haven't got that freedom. In this country you can do everything you want; in fact, a little too much [laughs], you know?

Although he advocates maintaining biculturalism, like that promoted by the Chicano movement, Andy stressed the importance of first learning English to interact with U.S. legal, social, and economic institutions. He also feels that a bilingual society in the Southwest would be a definite advantage for the population at large.

Regarding stylistic trends, the recording industry, and the Mexican-American musical experience, Andy foresees a positive future. The current popularity of the different Latin rhythms and music, especially in New York City, indicates a significant influence of the Latin community throughout the United States. The success of the East Los Angeles–based group Tierra is an important example of Chicanos "breaking the market." Chicana Linda Rondstadt's recent venture into the nostalgic music of the big band era is equally liberating. "Years ago, they'd say, 'You play your Mexican music.' Today, that market is open for all of us."

Postscript: Andy Russell died on April 16, 1992, in Sun City, Arizona, where he had recently retired. He was seventy-two years old.

Eddie Cano: Memories of a Pianist

Eddie Cano, an internationally recognized Latin jazz pianist, is a native of East Los Angeles. On 30 January 1988, a little over three years after my interview with him, he died unexpectedly at the age of sixty (although he had recently undergone a successful heart operation). His father was originally from Chihuahua, Mexico, and his mother, of Mexican descent, was from Pomona, California. He was raised in the area that used to be called Chávez Ravine, or "Palo Verde," as it was sometimes known by the people who lived there. It is also the area that became Dodger Stadium. When the dwellers of the ravine were forced to move, his family moved to the East Side and have lived there to this day. When Eddie later married, he moved to El Sereno and later to South Pasadena.

Music was always present in the house when Eddie was growing up. His father greatly appreciated classical music, and his grandfather had been a professional musician, having performed as a member of the Sinfónica Nacional de México (National Symphony Orchestra of Mexico). In addition, all his uncles played music, although not professionally. Because he was raised in a Mexican neighborhood, he was exposed to a large amount of Mexican music. When he was a child, he particularly enjoyed his family's Sunday visits to his grandfather's house. There, a group of men, perhaps six or seven, would play Mexican music together on the front porch. They played *corridos,* waltzes, polkas, and other forms.

Eddie did not hear many stories about Mexico at home, but all conversation was in Spanish. His parents were both bilingual, as was his grandmother; when he spoke to her in English, she responded in Spanish. At school, however, children were not allowed to speak Spanish in the fourth through sixth grades. As a child, he thought that particular regulation was wrong, and he still feels that way.

Eddie felt no particular displacement where he lived because Chávez Ravine was overwhelmingly populated by Mexican families. Among hundreds of Mexican households, there were perhaps two black families, a German family, and two Italian families. Feelings of displacement first arose when he joined the army. He once went to the dance halls on Ocean Park Pier, near Venice, and was not allowed to enter, even though he was in uniform. At another time, he and a fellow musician, Bob Hernández, were driving up the coast of California. They stopped at a restaurant and were surprised to see a sign that read, "No Mexicans or Dogs Allowed." That was Eddie's first experience with such a situation, and it affected him greatly. He has never experienced that type of discrimination in the music industry, however. Charles Mingus, a highly respected black musician with whom he worked in 1945, once said to him that in music there is no color and no race and that the only question in music is whether you can do the job.

The Los Angeles Zoot Suit Riots and their consequences are unpleasant memories for Eddie. His family lived near the Naval Reserve Armory on Chávez Ravine Road, and he walked by the facility regularly. On one occasion, he and his cousin were confronted, assailed by some sailors, and stripped of their pants. Eddie and his cousin, however, were wearing jeans—not zoot suits. As unpleasant and unjust as the experience was, he felt both the sailors and the zoot suiters were guilty of inciting the confrontations.

During his childhood, the musical atmosphere within his household did not conform to the majority pattern in the barrio. Although Eddie awakened on many mornings to the music of Mexican radio programs from surrounding homes, his father did not listen to popular music. Even though his father played guitar and at one time had worked with a Spanish dancer, popular music "wasn't really his thing. My dad would listen to classical, opera—that was his bag."

Eddie began to study piano at the age of five. He studied with Mr. Cessens at Page Military Academy for twelve years. His parents strongly encouraged and supported his musical development and interest in the arts.

It was a thing of every week, practicing every day. When you start that young, you really don't know whether you like it or not. You're doing things because it becomes part of your life. You get up in the morning, you brush your teeth, and you sit down at the piano and you practice for half an hour. You come home from school, you just sit down and practice, and when my dad would come home . . . every day.

And every Sunday we'd go over to my grandfather's house, and the minute I'd walk in . . . "OK into the room," into his room . . . either playing piano or doing solfeo, or when I got on the bass and [started] talking music. But again, strictly classical; no shortcuts, no nothing; strictly classical. And I thought to myself all the time, "Oh, God . . . I'm bilingual, we speak English. Why is he telling me these things in French and in Spanish and German?" I really wasn't into music. I was just doing what I was told; but thank God I was born with it.

Thus, it was not such a major accomplishment on his part to learn music in this fashion, although he did study earnestly. His grandfather's encouragement, suggestions, and instruction made his subsequent course of study at the Los Angeles Conservatory of Music less difficult.

While in grammar school Eddie became interested in the regional folk dances of Mexico and studied with a group directed by one of the teachers. He continued to dance with the group while in junior high school. He also became a member of the school orchestra. Because there were already a number of piano students in the group, the director offered Eddie the string bass position. Within a year he had learned to play the instrument proficiently, in part because he had already learned to read bass clef through his piano training. When he entered Lincoln High School he became interested in performing in the high school orchestra, but the piano and bass positions had already been filled. Eddie accepted the thirteenth chair trombone position, and his parents purchased a trombone for him. By the time he graduated from high school, he was playing first chair.

It was during high school that Eddie decided to become a professional musician:

My first job was with the high school band. The piano player got sick and couldn't make it, so I played the job and we got paid with a turkey apiece. I was so impressed with that. I came home and I woke up my mom, and I said, "Mom, I'm going to be a musician." And at that point I made up my mind that's what I was going to do—be a musician. I hadn't been interested in the dance band at Lincoln High School. They had a super jazz band there, but after that job, I talked to the teacher there, a man named Dozier, about getting into the band, and within a year I got my first professional job. In that job is where I learned about improvisation, about having to play tunes in three, four different keys, memorizing and knowing all the standards, and being able to play Latin, play jazz, play this, play that, whatever.

Eddie's uncle, one of his father's younger brothers, first exposed him to the music of Duke Ellington. At the time, he was studying the bass and became infatuated with the musicality of Jimmy Bladen, who played bass in Ellington's orchestra. The orchestra's arrangement of "Jack the Bear" became one of his favorites. Later, he was highly impressed with tenor saxophonist Coleman Hawkins's recording of "After Hours" with Larry Parrish on piano (ca. 1943). The period of Eddie's exposure to the jazz world was, as he put it, "the first time I really listened to anything."

In 1943 Eddie was also playing with a band managed by Joe García, a local promoter, for Saturday night dances at the Royal Palms Hotel. Led by Izzy Izar, the band was quite popular in Los Angeles and played a variety of arrangements that included music of Glenn Miller's band, popular standards of the era, boleros,[6] and rumbas. There were also numerous clubs in East Los Angeles that promoted exclusively Latin music in the style that was being imported from Cuba and Puerto Rico. At that time, however, a large number of the mostly Mexican-American Latino clients were bilingual. This clientele therefore preferred to frequent clubs that presented both Latin and American (especially swing) dance music. "I worked clubs in East L.A. where we played both types of music. You had to."

In 1945 Eddie entered the army. He was stationed at Fort MacArthur in San Pedro, California, which at that time served as an induction and separation center. When he was assigned to the service band, he was asked to play the string bass in the symphony orchestra and concert band and the piano in the dance band. The trombone position was filled in the marching band, so Eddie was instructed by the warrant officer to play glockenspiel. While in the army, Eddie attended the Los Angeles Conservatory of Music in 1946, the same school that John Ovalle attended two years later. He finished the complete course of study in six months.

After leaving the army, Eddie worked with numerous groups, traveling extensively to Hawaii, Canada, San Francisco, and eventually back to New York with Tony Martínez in 1955. Los Angeles, his home, was still the center of both his family life and much of his professional career as a musician, arranger, and composer.

By 1947 the zoot suit had become a stylized dress vogue and a symbol of the Zoot Suit Riots for many Chicanos in Los Angeles. During that era Eddie played with Don Tosti, a Mexican-American bass player who led a group with a local radio hit called "Pachuco Boogie." Eddie had met Tosti while the latter was working with Charlie Barnett's band. Along with drummer Raúl Díaz, Eddie and Don recorded a set of tunes that Eddie referred to as "the real zoot-suit type of thing." In addition to "Pachuco Boogie," the group also recorded "Las Ruedas de la Nana" and several other numbers that reflected the era.

Eddie's piano style was greatly influenced by two musicians who became his close and inspirational friends—Errol Gardner and Noro Morales. He was attracted to Gardner's jazz style, whereas he thought Morales was "the greatest Latin pianist ever." Eddie first heard Morales, originally from Puerto Rico, during the late 1940s, just before Eddie ventured to New York. Eddie was working with Tony Martínez's group at Slapsi Maxi's, a nightclub in the Wilshire district. One evening the renowned Cuban singer Miguelito Valdez came into the club and heard Eddie playing with the orchestra:

> About two weeks later . . . Tony got a telegram: "Need a piano player, please send me yours." So Tony says, "You want to go to New York?" . . . and I said, "Of course I do"; so that was my opportunity. I joined the band (of Valdez) in Minneapolis and stayed with the band almost two years. I got to see my idol, Noro Morales, and of course, all of the other groups of the time. César Concepción, Machito . . . that was a beautiful era because that was when Charlie Parker was coming up and the guys would go in and work with Machito's band. That was when they were finally getting Latin and jazz together. Dexter Gordon, Flip Phillips, Dizzy, Miles Davis, Howard McGee . . . of course, Charlie Parker. That was when it was really happening back there.

After playing piano with Miguelito Valdez for two years, Eddie returned to Los Angeles and began working with Bobby Ramos at a club named Ciro's. Ramos had started the first Latin music television show to be produced in Los Angeles. The Los Angeles base of Ramos's group remained at Ciro's, and Eddie played at the club for two years.

One of the most memorable and inspiring experiences in Eddie's career was his association with Cal Tjader, the Latin-style vibraphonist who died in 1982. Eddie was working again with Tony Martínez during the mid-1950s. Tjader worked with pianist George Shearing's ensemble, and whenever he was in Los Angeles he would come to hear Tony's group. Tjader "sat in" with Eddie one evening and two weeks later contacted Tony, offering Eddie a recording date with Tjader's own group. The recording group also included Al McKibbon on bass and Armando Peraza on bongos and congas (Peraza later played with Carlos Santana). The session was a success, and the resulting album did quite well in the Latin jazz market. In later years, Eddie continued to collaborate with Cal Tjader, sometimes doing arrangements for his larger ensemble. Eddie even composed a tune that Tjader recorded titled "Cal's Pals," which was rerecorded by Poncho Sánchez in 1984.

Eddie recorded his first solo album in 1956. After preparing arrangements of some of his original compositions, he contracted a group for the recording session that included Larry Bonker on vibes, Tommy Tedesco on guitar, Eddie Aparicio on timbales, Bill Richmond on drums, Tony Reyes on bass, Jack Costanzo on congas, and himself on piano. He recorded a "demo" tape on a home tape recorder and then, at the suggestion of Larry Bonker, presented the recording to Shorty Rogers at RCA Victor. Rogers was one of the leading arrangers in Hollywood at the time and had done numerous arrangements for Stan Kenton, Count Basie, and his own big bands. He enjoyed the demo and arranged a recording contract through RCA. It gave Eddie great pleasure to have unlimited artistic freedom on his first album as well as on subsequent recordings, although at times there were companies that wanted him to produce more commercial music:

> When I was with Reprise . . . I got my biggest thing with "Taste of Honey." And later, as the company was growing, they had the idea that they wanted me to do commercial things which really just didn't make it. That's when I left the company. We did an album of the "Sound of Music" [the motion picture]. . . . They wanted me to do the entire score. We went ahead and did the score, but I kept fighting it all the time. I told them, "How many tunes do you remember from the 'Sound of Music'?" "Well, there's 'Do Re Mi,' 'The Sound of Music.' . . ." I says, "Right. And what else? Who's heard of 'The Lonely Goat?' 'The Lonely Goat Herd'?" But that's what they wanted. At the time, that's what was selling. I wasn't into a complete jazz bag or a complete Latin thing. Latin jazz was what I wanted to do, what I've always done. That's my bag. So from there I went with Dunhill and we did exactly what we wanted to do. I never had any problems except that one incident. But mostly it was whatever we wanted to do. Certain limitations, you know, but nobody would say, "Oh, you can't do that." Never, never did I have that problem.

Eddie remained involved with his community and culture, primarily because his family is very close, particularly his mother's side of the family, with whom he grew up. On both sides, he was raised with "the feeling of roots with your family." He has always loved Los Angeles and southern California, but the most important factor has been that whenever he returns home he is returning to his family. Los Angeles is also the place that has given him some of his greatest opportunities. He was very lucky in working at an early age with Izzy Izar's band, where he had the opportunity to learn the art of improvisation and the business of working in nightclubs and where he was able to express himself artistically. "It was a 'joint,' but you were free to do anything you wanted musically." Eddie also had fond memories of his career in Los Angeles, such as the records he did with Don Tosti and with composer Les Baxter, which included "Ritual of the Savage" and "Quiet Village." When Eddie had the opportunity to conduct a thirty-piece orchestra for Nosotros for three consecutive years at the Hollywood Bowl, he considered himself "a young Mexican musician conducting at the Hollywood Bowl . . . it's not impossible, but for me it was a big thrill." The shows included appearances by major entertainers, such as Frank Sinatra. Going to New York was also exciting: ". . . going to New York, playing with Miguelito Valdez, sitting in with Tito's band, with Machito, with Noro Morales, José Curvelo, all of the groups. In Puerto Rico, working with all of the groups there, sitting in with them. There's no end to the great times that I've had in music."

Eddie believes that it has been difficult for the Chicano musician in Los Angeles to enter the mainstream music industry. For example, in Los Angeles there are Chicano musicians of excellent caliber, such as Rubén León, Tony Ortega, and Tony García, who are schooled in music and have excellent technique. The problem is that in Los Angeles, as in any city, there are musical "cliques." He referred to the Los Angeles Philharmonic Orchestra as one example of an organization that is not accessible to everyone. He commented:

> The symphony orchestra is locked up. . . . I think there's only one or two blacks. And I mean, they've had a hell of a time getting in there. In the studios, the motion picture studios, the Guerrero brothers, fantastic drummers . . . they did a lot of the stuff for "King Solomon's Mine," reading all of that stuff. How come they're not in there all of the time? Because this contractor had a friend he wanted to give more work [to] so therefore, the Chicanos, the browns, the blacks are kept down . . . which is a shame. It's a political thing . . . a money thing, not nepotism. They're not going to let you in. Why should they let you in? "You're not one of us."

Stratification in the music industry also results from contrasting value systems. When Eddie was a child, although he was primarily studying classical music, he also wanted to dedicate himself to other forms and styles such as jazz and Latin. This tendency is common among Chicanos: "Maybe it's our makeup. I shouldn't say that, because there's a lot of classical musicians in Mexico, but it has not been accessible to us. It's just like kids getting into athletics now because that's where the big bucks are at. It's a gamble, but if you make it, you make it big. In music, [with] a lot of the young kids, black and brown, and any other minority groups, the name of the game is money."

Many nonmainstream musicians, especially within minority communities, must rely on their musical ability to earn money from the beginning of their careers, often to help support their families. In contrast, many symphonic musicians are not obligated to work during their developing years and can therefore continue to focus on an art form that generally holds more prestige in this society and that eventually may even generate a fixed income. Within Eddie's generation and cultural network there were very few families who could afford to support their children after high school and college in terms of formal training and musical development: "Just because you graduated from high school doesn't make you eligible to go into the symphony orchestra. [In] the symphony orchestra, maybe the youngest musician there may be twenty-five or thirty years old. He's been playing all that time just to get into that symphony orchestra . . . and no big deal of having to earn a living. Whereas with the Mexicans, they did; with the blacks, they did."

Any existing value system also ensures that people's attitudes will create hierarchies among different musical styles and genres. The mariachi is an example; the complicated counterrhythms of the *sones*[7] are as viable a musical art as any other form. When Eddie was in high school, one of his music theory teachers once played a recording of a mariachi and instructed the class to notate the musical passage. Eddie remembered being not only impressed by the musicality but confused by the rhythmic complexity and performance technique. He realized then that this particular music required as much dedication as other styles in which he had been enculturated, such as classical, jazz, and Latin.

Until his later years Eddie did not have the patience required for teaching, although he did coach musicians. Some of the Latin musicians sought his advice and expertise in the jazz idiom, and jazz musicians likewise sought his help in some of the Latin patterns, equally his forte. Although he had no regular students, he did help various individuals on a limited basis and appreciated being able to contribute his knowledge.

Eddie's priorities during his last years were to just keep on playing. "I really enjoy playing. On good pianos, though, because you know what nightclub pianos are—horrible. Like last night, we worked with a super rhythm section—Poncho Sánchez on congas, David Troncoso on bass, Armand Grimaldi on drums, and it was just beautiful, fun. That's what music has always been to me; it's been fun. It's been good . . . very, very good to me."

Lalo Guerrero: Musician, Satirist, and Legend

Lalo Guerrero, a first-generation Mexican American, is a living legend among Chicanos of the Southwest and in Mexico. Perhaps more than anyone else performing today, he epitomizes the bicultural experience and expression of the Chicano musician. In September 1991, at the age of seventy-five, Guerrero received the National Heritage Award from the National Endowment for the Arts.

Lalo's father was born in La Paz, Baja California, and his mother in Santa Ana, Sonora. Emigrating to the United States in 1911, they settled in Tucson, Arizona, where his father worked for Pacific Railroad as a boilermaker. Lalo was born there in 1916. His parents spoke only Spanish, so the children did not learn English until they started school. They communicated with other schoolchildren in English and continued to speak Spanish in the home.

Lalo's mother contributed greatly to the musical atmosphere that prevailed in his family's household. Lalo was musically enculturated by listening to his mother play guitar and by learning how to play from her when he was fourteen or fifteen years old. She had learned to play the guitar and sing when she was a young girl. She sang quite beautifully, and she probably would have been a professional singer had she been born sixty years later. In the early 1920s, however, there were few substantial opportunities for women—and particularly Mexican women—to become professional entertainers. Lalo's mother danced as well as she played; she knew such traditional forms as the Spanish *jota aragoneza* and *paso doble*.

Lalo learned the music of Mexico from his mother. This included *rancheras,* traditional folk songs, and romantic songs. At the same time, his schooling exposed him to American culture, so that he began to assimilate a substantial amount of the American music that was popular during the 1930s, primarily through radio and motion pictures. He was influenced by Al Jolson, Russ Colombo, Rudy Vallee, and eventually Bing Crosby. Lalo maintained his Mexican music repertoire along with a variety of American tunes. Never having studied formally, Lalo learned everything by ear; of the hundreds of songs he has composed, he has written all the words and music (except in cases where he has borrowed the melodies of other songs, especially in his satires).

Lalo experienced some conflict about being Mexican as a child, particularly during his schooling. He attended school in a Tucson barrio that was inhabited completely by Mexicans. The children were not allowed to speak Spanish in the classroom, although they spoke nothing else on the playground. If they did speak Spanish in front of a teacher they were scolded, "apparently so that we would master the English language." He had very few Mexican-American teachers, and it was not until he entered junior high school that he attended school with Anglo-American students. "I felt a little out of place. It was given a negative connotation. . . . I had an inferiority complex because supposedly everything that was Mexican or Mexican-oriented was second-rate and pretty soon you got the feeling that you were second-rate."

Lalo wanted to sing and play contemporary American music of the era because feelings of displacement inhibited him from performing in the Spanish language. "I don't want to sound boastful, but I could sing and play in English the popular American songs of the day as well as any Anglo person." He wanted to succeed in the American music field more than in the Mexican field because he was living in the United States and wanted to be in the mainstream. Unfortunately, in that era (the 1930s—his high school years and after) there were few opportunities for Mexicans or those of Mexican descent to become popular singers. There was extensive discrimination, and even though he could perform as well as the Anglos, he could never get work because of his Mexican physical features. "They couldn't conceive of a Mexican, especially one who looks as Indian as I do, sitting up there and singing Bing Crosby songs. So naturally the Anglos would get the jobs. I'm talking about the nightclubs and the theaters and that kind of thing. And so I saw I wasn't going to make any money. I reverted to singing Mexican music."

So it was out of necessity that he continued to sing and perform in Spanish. This was the period of the Depression, and, in addition to discrimination, bad economic conditions also pressured him to perform in the Mexican sector: he needed the money. There were ample opportunities in Tucson at the time because of the large Mexican-American population. Among the many musicians with whom Lalo associated in Tucson was Gilbert Ronstadt, father of singer Linda Ronstadt.

Lalo performed in Mexican nightclubs, bars, and dance halls, playing with duos, trios, and four- or five-piece groups. He became interested in going to Mexico to have his songs recorded and published, especially because he was composing in Mexican musical styles. Eventually he went to Mexico City and was fortunate to have two songs recorded that later became very popular hits; they remain standards in the Mexican repertoire to this day. These were "Canción mexicana," recorded by Lucha Reyes, and "Nunca jamás," which was recorded by Los Panchos and Javier Solís.

Although Lalo's success in Mexico seemed imminent, he was disappointed by another kind of displacement when he attempted to become a performer there. He was Mexican American—a *pocho* to Mexicans, which meant a person born in the United States of Mexican descent who has assimilated American traits. Lalo stayed in Mexico for approximately one year, trying to attain musical success and credibility, but the stigma of being from the United States persisted among the Mexican entrepreneurs and other musicians. Lalo also sensed some resentment on the part of the Mexicans. "The Mexican people from Mexico have the feeling that we Mexicans who came to the United States were turncoats or traitors; and then, of course, being better off economically over here, there was a certain amount of jealousy, I suppose, which is natural, and I think that was the reason. To this day, we still have some of that."

When World War II began, Lalo left Mexico and went to San Diego, where he lived during the war, working as an aircraft mechanic. He joined a USO group there that included a band, singers, dancers, and comedians. The group toured extensively throughout the United States, entertaining the troops. It was during that era that Latin music became very popular in the country. The war caused a production shortage in publishing houses and record companies in addition to a lack of band leaders. The publishing companies extracted many songs and melodies from Mexico, the Caribbean, and South America to meet the demands of Tin Pan Alley. English lyrics were adapted to tunes originally from Mexico, which resulted in many hit songs of the 1940s, such as "What a Difference a Day Makes" ("Cuando vuelva a tu lado"), "Amapola," "Perfidia," "Green Eyes," and many more. Lalo performed all these Latin tunes on the USO tour.

Versatility was always a priority in Lalo's performance and compositional philosophy. In the 1940s, for example, he was writing songs that incorporated the Cuban forms popular at the time, such as the rumba and mambo, while at the same time he was writing other songs in the popular swing style of the big band era. Lalo adapted Spanish words to the swing numbers, and, along with the Latin forms, recorded them on Imperial Records. The recordings attained considerable popularity, particularly with the zoot suiters in Los Angeles. When Luis Valdez wrote the play *Zoot Suit* in the 1970s, he asked Lalo to adapt some of his music that had been discovered on old 78-rpm records of the era. Four of Lalo's songs were included in the stage and motion picture versions of *Zoot Suit*. He received royalties for music that he had composed thirty-five years before.

Los Angeles record companies profited from the Mexican community because music recorded in Mexico was generally unavailable in the United States. The local companies, including Imperial, Discos Tricolor, Aguila, and Azteca, recorded mostly Mexican and Chicano artists working in Los Angeles, including Lalo, Adelina García, Las Hermanas Padilla, Anselmo Alvarado, and Rubén Reyes. Because these record companies had no competition from Mexico, their records became popular throughout the Southwest.

Lalo recorded for Imperial Records, a company owned by Lutte Chat.

The company started in a small place on Western Avenue, recording Mexican artists and selling records in the border states. Chat was eventually so successful selling black music that he discontinued the Mexican catalog and exclusively recorded black artists such as Fats Domino and T-Bone Walker. Later he recorded Ricky Nelson and finally sold the Imperial label for about two million dollars. As a result of the sale, the master tapes of much of Lalo's material from the 1940s and 1950s are housed at Capitol Records in Los Angeles, waiting to be reissued. "We want to rerelease them in album form. There were a lot of very good novelty songs."

Although Lalo had never actually become a zoot suiter, he performed as a vocalist at the Mambo Club, which young Mexican Americans frequented dressed in zoot suits. Lalo himself never wore the zoot suit: "I never wore it because I was always introverted. Although I was a performer, I was a little shy. I had many friends among the zoot suiters and I learned to talk their language. Many of them would come over to dance where I played. They were strictly into swing. They hadn't gone in for the Latin music. This was before the mambo."

Los pachucos, or the zoot suiters, were attracted to the swing sound in a way that seemed to reflect the phenomenon of their *Caló* language, a slang form of Spanish that became their popular vernacular. It was at this point that Lalo also started to compose in the new Latin style, which was becoming popular even among the young zoot suiters. Instead of adapting his lyrics to swing, Lalo began to compose songs in the form of the popular Cuban *guaracha*, which incorporated Spanish verse in a more fluid and natural manner. In some songs he incorporated both styles: "Vamos a bailar" begins with a swing tempo, moves into a mambo, and then returns to swing. Lalo also used themes related to the cultural realities among Chicanos of the period and incorporated *Caló* into the lyrics. He even applied the theme of smoking marijuana in the song "Marijuana Boogie." "That plant has been around for ages; it was very popular in the days of Pancho Villa. Among the pachucos, zoot suiters, it was used very widely. They always had it. They always used to offer me some. Boogie woogie was very much in at the time. I said, 'Well, why not write something for these guys that identified with [it,' so I wrote] 'Marijuana Boogie.' They loved to do the swing because this was during the war and that was what was in. You remember how they used to do the jitterbug!" Lalo did not experience the zoot-suit riots in Los Angeles, however, for those occurred during the war, while he was in San Diego.

When Lalo moved to Los Angeles after the war, where he settled permanently, there was still no television, but there were many Latin clubs there—"El Sombrero," "El Babalú," "El Patio," "La Bamba," "La Casa Olvera," "La Capital," "El Bolero"—and they were filled most evenings with customers. Even on his group's night off, which was Monday, clubs would hire a substitute band. Groups from other cities were invited to Los Angeles clubs. Machito and Tito Puente, both bandleaders from New York City, brought their bands to Los Angeles to play their high-energy mambo and Cuban music. As television became more popular, many of the clubs closed, and those that remained operated only on Friday, Saturday, and Sunday, as they do to this day.

By this time, Mexican records were being sold in Los Angeles and other parts of the country. Groups from Mexico were becoming popular, including Pérez Prado,[8] Mariachi Vargas de Tecalitlán, and Luis Alcaraz. The Los Angeles market was becoming international, but it was only a "one-way" development. Although many artists came to Los Angeles from Mexico, Mexican artists from Los Angeles were not invited to Mexico. It was Lalo's opinion that to this day they are not accepted in Mexico, except for a few (e.g., Vikki Carr and Andy Russell).

Lalo did not make professional compromises, such as name changes, during his career. His features are unquestionably Mexican, so that even if he had changed his name, it would not have opened up any more opportunities. For years he did not know that Vikki Carr, for example, was Mexican American. Lalo knew Andy Russell in the 1940s, when Russell was internationally popular. Andy's appearance is not particularly Mexican, but he changed his name because that was something he had to do to "break into" the entertainment business. Lalo probably would have changed his own name had he looked less Mexican and "a little bit more *güero*" (a Spanish colloquialism referring to a person of light complexion). He wanted the success of an Andy Russell, whose appearance and name change were definite advantages.

Lalo had no trouble finding work in Los Angeles as long as he was performing in the field of Mexican entertainment. He is very satisfied with his success in Los Angeles, which began in 1948. He was quite popular on records for twelve years and composed many songs that became hits on the radio; he also owned his own nightclub. He appeared on a variety of television shows during that era, such as "Fandango," "Latin Time," and "Latin Cruise," hosted by Bobby Ramos, a very popular Mexican-American bandleader and singer. Although content with the exposure he received in Los Angeles, Lalo would still have enjoyed additional success in Mexico City. He did take occasional tours and professional dates in Mexico City, but only for short periods, because his family lived in Los Angeles and he could not afford to maintain a home in both countries. Very few Mexican-American artists, save Russell and Carr, have been successful in Mexico, "and there's been many, many good ones."

Lalo Guerrero is more well known among contemporary young Mexican Americans than someone like Andy Russell, also from East Los Angeles, because of his exposure and identification. Because Lalo performs for the younger people at various locations such as college campuses, they hear his music and consider him somewhat of a pioneer in the field of Chicano expression. He has written and recorded, for example, many songs that identify with the Chicano movement, such as *corridos* or ballads about César Chávez, Rubén Salazar, and other figures who symbolize the political struggle of Chicanos. Lalo has also adapted many American idols or heroes to the Mexican experience ("Elvis Pérez" in place of Elvis Presley and "Pancho Claus" instead of Santa Claus). Lalo has intended throughout his career to identify with his community, to which he feels he belongs. His base in the community centered on his nightclub, Lalo's, in East Los Angeles, which he operated for fourteen years.

Lalo accepts "Chicanismo" as a positive concept. He has never had problems with the term "Chicano." When he was a young boy during the 1920s and 1930s, his mother would always say with pride as she was singing or playing, "Soy pura chicana" or "Soy pura chicanita." Lalo therefore has never felt that the word carries a negative connotation.

Since the 1940s Lalo has been a singer, a composer, and a bandleader; he had an orchestra for many years that toured throughout the Southwest. The group played popular music: boleros, *danzones, guarachas,* mambos, and *cumbias.*[9] The instrumentation consisted of two trumpets, four saxophones, piano, bass, drums, congas, and Lalo as lead vocalist. His group, or *conjunto,* performed the most popular Latin music of the period. Lalo had several favorites among the many Mexican artists whose music was popular in Los Angeles—singers Jorge Negrete and Pedro Infante and songwriters Gonzalo Curiel, Agustín Lara, and Luis Alcaraz (who was also the bandleader of a very popular orchestra). Lalo also admired *ranchera* singers, such as Miguel Aceves Mejía and José Alfredo Jiménez, the "Agustín Lara [of] the *ranchera;* everything he wrote was a hit." Lalo was also inspired during his early years by Carlos Gardel, the legendary interpreter and composer of the Argentine tango. Later, the Puerto Rican composers Pedro Flores and Rafael Hernández had considerable influence on Lalo's style. From Cuba, Celia Cruz became an important symbol of musical expression to Lalo, as she did to so many people throughout Mexico and the Caribbean. The Cuban orchestra that often accompanied Celia Cruz (and still does to this day), La Sonora Matancera, also became one of Lalo's favorites, in addition to its Mexican counterpart, La Sonora Santanera.

The element of satire has always been prominent in Lalo's music:

I've always had a flair for writing comedy, and through the years, in Spanish, I had quite a few hits of novelty songs like "La mini-falda de reynalda," "La flaca," "Maruca," and "El güero aventado," many comical songs in Spanish. But I've written a lot of satirical things in English, but always with a Mexican flavor. Or I'll take a controversial subject that is a Mexican controversial subject and put it into a satirical song like . . . "No Way José," which is about the illegal alien problem, the undocumented worker problem. It seems that there's a very fine line between comedy and tragedy.

Although the social problem he writes about may indicate an unfortunate situation, Lalo attempts to extract the humorous aspects that project from "inside" the issue or personality. Both positive and negative attributes of a controversy therefore become humorous and thus quite human. Lalo writes these musical satires "as they come. I'm an opportunist . . . I jump on the subject. Sometimes I take criticism." His satirical songs gained popularity when he wrote "The Ballad of Pancho López" in 1955. Although it was financially successful for him, Lalo received considerable criticism from the Chicano community for presenting a Chicano stereotype in the lyrics. For this reason he no longer performs the song.

After the "Pancho López" feedback, Lalo realized that the community was correct in its critical response to the song: "It was kind of a putdown, but at the time I was hungry. I was starting and I needed the bread and maybe I shouldn't have done it, but I don't think it was really that bad. At that time the community was very sensitive about that. But I never did it again and I promise I won't do it anymore. The ones I do now . . . they're not derogatory in any way or stereotyping the Chicano. They're just about the Chicano situation."

Lalo has not been as sensitive or critical of the mainstream portrayal of Mexican and Chicano culture as other members of the Chicano community. An example is the controversy created when the song "Granada" was used as the theme song for Mexico during the opening ceremonies of the 1984 Olympic Games in Los Angeles. Although the song is based on a musical style of Spain and is dedicated to the Spanish city of Granada, it was written by a Mexican, Agustín Lara, so Lalo was not offended by the performance. At the same time, he pointed out that anyone turning on a television set to the Spanish-speaking stations and watching programs such as "Siempre en Domingo" will see musicians performing "poor imitations of rock and roll. Now if they were doing good rock and roll, I'd say all right. Why don't they do our music, Mexican music? . . . I can see a José José, a Juan Gabriel . . . marvelous . . . but you have all these groups who are playing bad rock and roll and that is what is dominating the whole scene down there."

In Mexico, especially Mexico City, increasingly more commercial American music is being played on the radio, on television, and in the nightclubs. Referring to the Chicanos in the United States, Lalo believes they are "more Mexican here than they are down in Mexico." To a varying extent, Mexicans in the United States appear to maintain traditions to a greater degree than do those who live in certain urban areas of Mexico, possibly because, since they are outside their native country, they wish to honor the culture and land of their parents.

Lalo is now semiretired and has lived in Palm Springs since 1974, where he entertains on a lighter schedule, performing about two nights a week. He still writes songs and parodies and records occasionally. For the past twenty years Lalo has been recording a series of children's records called "Las ardillitas" ("The Little Squirrels"). The records have been very popular in Mexico, where he recorded them (with the Mexican division of Capitol Records), and have become a tradition during the Christmas season. These recordings have cultivated many fans between the ages of five and twelve years, which gratifies him greatly. In 1991 Linda Ronstadt recorded Guerrero's "Canción mexicana" as part of *Más Canciones,* her second LP of Mexican music.

The recent attention given to music in the east side of Los Angeles and the idea of a "new wave" among Chicano musicians can be compared to what Lalo was involved in forty years ago. He appreciates many of the young musicians, including his son, Mark, a very talented rock songwriter who has recorded on the A&M and Capitol Records labels. Lalo is proud of his son, along with the young eastside musicians of today, whom he sees as part of a continuing tradition.

Examples of Musical Style

I selected three examples to illustrate Lalo Guerrero's musical style through forty years of his active musical life. "Canción mexicana," named after the genre itself, was composed in 1936 and was recorded for RCA Victor in 1940 by Lucha Reyes, one of the most popular *ranchera* singers of that time in Mexico. During the era of the zoot suiters Lalo also composed a *guaracha* (Afro-Cuban genre) called "Chucos suaves" (1944). The lyrics use the *Caló* dialect of Spanish that was popular within the pachuco cult. These songs illustrate how Lalo's lyrics blend satire and social reality. Complementing the two examples from his earlier period, the third one is a satirical commentary on the plight of the illegal alien, "No Way José."

The *canción ranchera* flourished during the 1930s and 1940s, especially with the inauguration of Mexico's first national radio broadcasting system, XEW. Its popularity was evident in the recordings of Mexican singers and film stars such as Pedro Infante and Jorge Negrete. José Alfredo Jiménez, a composer and singer who was perhaps the epitome of the *canción ranchera,* arrived on the artistic scene during the 1950s. He achieved such success with his recordings and compositions that he became a folk hero sentimentally referred to as "el hijo del pueblo" [the people's son] (see Gradante 1982). Jiménez was extremely popular within the Mexican/Chicano population of Los Angeles and continues to be internationally popular even after his death.

The first example, which follows the Lucha Reyes recording, shows that "Canción mexicana" combines the traditional *canción* form characteristic of the first half of the twentieth century and the popular, less strict *ranchera* style of the last thirty years. Guerrero's *canción* is, in effect, a compilation of different *canciones* and referential themes popular throughout Mexico, especially since the 1910 Revolution. Lalo interpolates the melodic themes and lyrics from standard Mexican *canciones,* such as "Cielito lindo" and "Adelita," in addition to a section of *son* structure. The mariachi accompaniment (Mariachi Tapatío) provides a typical stylistic framework for most of the song, which was originally composed by Guerrero. The interpolation of other song fragments causes the verse structure of "Canción mexicana" to deviate from the standard *canción* formula, which is usually a through-composed verse repeated a specific number of times. The verse structure is sung twice, followed by a borrowed fragment of "Cielito lindo"; the third verse is then sung and capitulated with an instrumental interlude based on the *son jalisciense* (a regional *son* style from the state of Jalisco), followed by a fourth verse. The arrangement then ends with a traditional interpretation of "Adelita." [10] (The transcription in example 1, as well as the others in this chapter and the next, is intended as a general melodic, harmonic, rhythmic guide to indicate song form and style. Dynamics and phrasing are usually not specifically marked, and the notations do not necessarily sound where written.)

"Canción mexicana"

Hoy que llena de emociones	Today full of emotion
Me encuentro con mi jarana	I'm here with my *jarana*
Voy a rendir homenaje	I am going to render homage
A la canción mexicana.	To the *canción mexicana*.
Voy a rendir homenaje	I am going to render homage
A la canción más jalona	To the hottest song,
La canción más primorosa	To the most beautiful song,
Que es la canción mexicana.	Which is the *canción mexicana*.
Pa' hacer pesos de a montones	To make a million bucks
No hay como el americano	There's nothing like the

	American
Pa' conquistar corazones	But to conquer hearts
No hay mejor que un mexicano.	There's nothing better than a Mexican.

Y como es que lo consigue	And how is it that he does it
Si no es cantando canciones	If it's not by singing songs
Como es el "Cielito lindo"	Like the song "Cielito Lindo"
Que alegra los corazones.	That makes hearts happy?

No hay otra cosa más linda	There's nothing more beautiful
Que en las mañanitas frías	Than to sing on a brisk morning
Cantarle a mi rancherita	To my little country girl
Mañanitas tapatías.	"Mañanitas Tapatías."

Que causan mucha alegría	What causes a lot of happiness
Y emoción al cuerpo mío	And emotion within this body of mine
Que los sones abajeños	Are the *sones* from the Lowlands
Del mariachi tapatío.	Of the mariachi from Jalisco.

Es la canción mexicana	It is the *canción mexicana*
La que se merece honor	That merits honor
Esa es la más primorosa	It is the most beautiful
Porque allí mienta el amor.	Because with it comes love.

Hay canciones extranjeras	There are foreign songs
Que alborotan la pasión	That excite the passion
Pero ni una se compara	But not one of them compares
Con esta dulce canción:	With this sweet *canción:*

"Que si Adelita quisiera ser mi novia	"If Adelita wanted to be my girlfriend
Y si Adelita fuera mi mujer	And if Adelita were my wife
Le compraría un vestido de seda	I would buy her a dress of silk
Para llevarla a bailar al cuartel."	To take her dancing at the barracks."

"Chucos suaves" is a *guaracha* that Guerrero composed in 1943 (see example 1). Based on traditional *clave*,[11] the composition is generically similar to the Afro-Cuban *son* style of the group Califas (later analyzed), although the texture sounds like a 1940s mambo.

Example 1

Vocal

Violins

Trumpet

Vihuela/
Guitar

F

Guitarrón

5

10

Hay   que   lle - no de e-mo -
Pa   'cer   pe - sos- *etc.*

Example 1 (cont.)

15
cio - nes me en - cuen - tro con mi ja - ra - na.

19
Voy a   ren - dir ho-me-na - je a la can-ción me-xi -

simile . . .

simile . . .

24
ca - na.   Voy a

simile . . .

simile . . .

Example 1 (cont.)

ren - dir ho - me - na - je   a la can - ción más ja - lo - na   la can-

simile . . .

simile . . .

D.C.

ción mas pri - mo   ro - sa que es la   can - ción me - xi - ca - na.

simile . . .

simile . . .

Example 1 (cont.)

Example 1 (cont.)

Example 1 (cont.)

Example 1 (cont.)

Example 1 (cont.)

98

Es la can-ción me-xi - ca-na la que se me-re-ce ho - nor.

simile . . .

103

E-sa es la más pri-mo-ro - sa por-que a-

simile . . .

simile . . .

107

llí mien-ta el a - mor.

simile . . .

simile . . .

Example 1 (cont.)

Example 1 (cont.)

The structural analysis of "Chucos suaves" provided here is based on a recent arrangement and recording produced for the motion picture *Zoot Suit* by Luis Valdez and filmed and tracked at Universal Studios. (See discography, appendix A.) Shorty Rogers's arrangement intentionally imitates the musical style of the 1940s, although audiotechnical aspects of the recording are contemporary in sound quality. Structured according to the Afro-Cuban *son* formula, "Chucos suaves" begins with eight measures of introduction accentuated by Latin percussion supported by a firm *clave* foundation and stylistically extended with a trombone pedal effect and a sustained Fm6 tonality, which establishes the song's key.

The verse structure of a *guaracha* is typically based on the four-line *coplas* (couplets) of the *son* and a repeated chorus *(estribillo)* section (see example 2).

"Chucos suaves"

Versos:	Verses:
Cada sábado en la noche (A)	Every Saturday night
Yo me voy a borlotear (B)	I go dancing
Con mi linda pachucona (A)	With my beautiful *pachucona* [girl]
Las caderas a menear. (B)	To shake those hips.
Ella le hace muy de aquella	She's really something
Cuando empieza a guarachar	When she starts to dance the *guaracha*
Y al compás de los timbale'	And to the rhythm of the timbales
Yo me siento patatear.	I really feel like dancing.
Estribillo:	Chorus:
Chucos suaves, baila rumba (A)	Fine dudes, dance the rumba
Baila la rumba y la zumba (A)	Dance the rumba and the *zumba*
Baila guaracha sabrosón (B)	Dance the tasty *guaracha*
Y el botecito y el danzón. (B)	And the *botecito* and the *danzón*.
Estribillo se repite	Repeat chorus
Carnal, pongase abusao	Get with it, brother
Ya los tiempos han cambiado	The times have changed
Usted está muy aguitao	You, sir, are very tired
Y hasta buti atravesao.	And even with the *buti*, out of step.

Example 2

Antes se bailaba el swing	They used to dance the swing
Boogie-woogie, jitterbug,	Boogie-woogie, or jitterbug
Pero esto ya torció	But all that has changed
Y esto es lo que sucedió.	And this is what is happening now.
Chucos suaves, baila rumba	Fine dudes, dance the rumba
Baila la rumba y la zumba	Dance the rumba and the *zumba*
Baila guaracha sabrosón	Dance the tasty *guaracha*
Y el botecito y el danzón.	And the *botecito* and the *danzón*.
Estribillo se repite	Repeat chorus

In the text of "Chucos suaves" the *Caló* dialect has been incorporated into the Spanish lyrics. *Caló* was used by the pachucos in Los Angeles during the 1940s and originated in quarters of Mexico City as a regional, urban dialect among the working class. The syllabic contours of particular words actually adapt to the *son* format in a manner quite characteristic of that genre's origin—the Caribbean. There, for example, many words ending in *ado* are often transformed to a one-syllable, fused phonetic of *a'o* (e.g., abusado = abusa'o and aguitado = aguita'o in the third verse). Similar phonetic transformations occur in the *Caló* dialect. Even the title, "Chucos suaves," uses terms derived from *Caló* expression. The word *chuco* is an abbreviation for *pachuco*, and the word *suave*, literally "smooth," is used as an adjective to mean "fine" or "cool." Other hybrid words in the text include the following: *de aquella, guarachear, petatear, abusao, cambiao, aguitao, buti,* and *atravesao*.

"No Way José" is one of Guerrero's more recent satirical expressions, written in response to the vast amount of controversy over undocumented workers, especially in California. The song is one of the most popular of Lalo's current repertoire, especially among the numerous politically active Chicanos throughout the Los Angeles community.

Guerrero employs the basic polka form in the composition of "No Way José," similar to the *norteño* Tex-Mex style (e.g., Los Lobos's "Anselma"). The transcription reproduced here is from a live performance by the composer, recorded during the interview with the author. Lalo sang the verse of the song and accompanied himself on guitar.[12]

The harmonic structure of the piece is based on a I-IV-V framework, quite similar to that of the Mexican *corrido* or polka. Melodically, the vocal phrasing deviates somewhat from typical polka-style singing, incorporating various motives from different American (U.S.) styles such as Broadway, ragtime, swing, vaudeville, and pop (see example 3).

Example 3

My name's Jo - sé Gon - zá - lez, I come from Mon-ter - rey, I came up to the bor - der one bright and sun-ny day. I told the im - mi - gra-tion man I go to U. S. A. He looked at me and laughed, this is what he say: "No way Jo - sé, no way you to to U. S. A. No way Jo - sé, if you don't got no pa - pers, you don't go to U. S. A."

The following notation is a transcription of the basic strophic melody and harmonic framework of Guerrero's live recording. The text is that of the first verse; the complete text is as follows. The satirical element in the text is self-explanatory.

"No Way José"

My name is José González
I come from Monterrey

I came up to the border
One bright and sunny day
I told the immigration man
I go to USA.
He looked at me and laughed
This is what he say.

No way, José
No way you go to USA.
No way, José
If you no got no papers,
You don't go to USA.

But I am very stubborn
And I jumped the fence next day
I took the Greyhound bus
And went to East L.A.
I wound up washing dishes
For fifty cents a day
I told the man "I want a raise"
This is what he say.

No way, José
No way you get a raise today
No way, José
If you don't got green card
You don't get a raise today.

I met a *señorita*
Her name was Sally Mae
I took her out to dinner
And to see a show one day
When I took her home that night
I asked her "Can I stay?"
She pushed me out the door,
This is what she say.

No way, José
No way, no way that you can stay
No way, José
But if you put ring on my finger
Then you can stay and play.

Caramba how I suffered
Until one lucky day

I met a man named Bruce
And this is what he say

I give you plenty money
And a place where you can stay
But then he tried to kiss me
I think that he was gay.

No way, no way
I think I go back to Monterrey

Notes

1. *Danzón* is a Cuban music and dance form that evolved from the *contradanza* and was especially performed by *charanga* orchestras during the 1940s and 1950s. The form incorporates both European and Afro-Cuban influences.

2. Originally developed during the latter part of the nineteenth century, notably in the province of Matanzas, the rumba was one of the first secular Afro-Cuban forms and one that became an essential bridge toward the development of various Afro-Cuban music and dance genres. Rumba is characterized by call and response singing, intricate drumming, and an intense, pantomiming dance.

3. The Mexican *corrido* is an epic narrative song form originally developed during the nineteenth century but especially used during the revolution of 1910. The narrative texts of typical *corridos* are based on legendary or historical themes; the stories usually relate to a person, place, or event. Traditional Spanish poetic forms, such as the *copla* and *décima,* are used.

4. "Las Ardillitas" (The Little Squirrels) is the name of a recording project that Lalo Guerrero has undertaken in recent years. It is a concept based on the "Chipmunks" music for children popular during the 1960s in the United States.

5. Although Ovalle uses the title "Pirámide del sol," he is referring to a ballet piece written by Mexican composer Carlos Chávez (1899–1979) in 1968.

6. The bolero is a musical form based on a usually romantic ballad text and a slow dance rhythm. Originally from Cuba, it became popular throughout Latin America, especially in Mexico.

7. In this case, *son* (plural *sones*) refers to Mexican regional folkloric genres of music that are characterized by song form and usually accompanied by dance.

8. Although he was originally from Cuba and versed in Cuban popular music styles, Prado lived and played in Mexico City. His orchestra was therefore commonly referred to as one of the Mexican bands.

9. The *cumbia* is a popular dance form originally from Colombia. It is one of the most popular dance forms throughout Latin America and the United States.

10. The "Adelita" instrumental theme even occurs at measure 121 in the trumpet part of the regular segment of "Canción mexicana."

11. The *clave* is the fundamental rhythmic pattern of most Afro-Cuban popular musical genres.

12. The song was recorded in a studio and originally released on an Ambiente Productions LP in 1983.

John Ovalle during the interview at the Record Inn. Videotape by Ramón Menéndez and Bill Dey. Photo transfer by James Cypherd, Department of Ethnomusicology and Systematic Musicology, UCLA.

Eddie Cano at the piano (1960). Courtesy of Chico Sesma Collection.

Eddie Cano and his quartet at the Biltmore shortly before his death in 1988. From left: Gary Cardile (Latin percussion), Aaron Ballesteros (drums/guitar), Eddie Cano (piano), David Troncoso (bass).

An Andy Russell LP (1982) representing the singer's many recordings in the Spanish language and his later career activity. Included on the album were standards such as "Bésame Mucho" and "Amor." Used by permission.

Andy Russell (center) joins singer Adelina García and her husband, percussionist José Heredia, at the Jesters restaurant in Hollywood following a broadcast of the KNXT "Fandango" television show (1955). Courtesy of Adelina García Collection.

Lalo Guerrero and José Lupe Fernández. Photo taken in 1939 in front of Cafe Caliente on Olvera Street. The duo serenaded outside the restaurant now known as El Paseo. Courtesy of Lalo Guerrero Collection.

Lalo Guerrero in a publicity photo issued by Imperial Records (circa 1955). Courtesy of Lalo Guerrero Collection.

Teresa Covarrubias. Courtesy of Teresa Covarrubias. Photo by Kristin Dahling.

Cover to a 1984 issue of the *L.A. Weekly* containing a Darcy Diamond article that assessed the new musical movements within the young popular culture of East Los Angeles. Pictured is the group The Brat with Teresa Covarrubias at center.

Poncho Sánchez. Courtesy of Poncho Sánchez.

Album cover of *Papa Gato*, Poncho Sánchez's sixth LP (fourth on the Concord/Picante label). The recording included a guest performance on all tracks by saxophonist/flutist Justo Almario.

Califas (from left): Joe Barragan, Rick Reyes, David Torres, Irma Rangel, Víctor Barrientos, Marcos Loya (director), and Willie Loya.

Film crew on location (1984) after an interview with Irma Rangel. From left: Rangel, Bill Day, and Ramón Menéndez. Photo by Steve Loza.

Los Illegals, 1984. Courtesy of Willie Herrón.

Album cover of Los Illegals 1983 *Internal Exile*. Heavily laden with social themes of immigration and intercultural conflict, the LP represented an innovative admixture of diverse urban and intercultural expression. ©1983, A&M records; used by permission.

Los Lobos' first LP, consisting of Mexican and other Latin American folk styles; it was released in 1977 on a local label. New Vista Records; used by permission

Los Lobos' album *How Will the Wolf Survive?* (1985). An interesting music video with an immigration theme adapted to the title track song enjoyed substantial national success on cable and network television. Used by permission, Slash/Warner Brothers Records. 25177-1.

La pistola y el corazón, a return
to Mexican folk music, released
in 1989, was Los Lobos' second Grammy Award–winning
record in the Mexican-American category. The song "Anselma" won the award in 1984.
Used by permission, Slash/
Warner Brothers Records, Inc.
25790-1. Artwork by George
Yépres; concept and design by
Louie Pérez.

Los Lobos celebrate award for best Mexican/American performance for "La Pistola y El Corazon."

Los Lobos members receive the 1990 Grammy Award. From left: David Hidalgo,
Louie Pérez, Conrad Lozano, César Rosas, and Steve Berlin. Copyright, 1990, *Los
Angeles Times*. Reprinted by permission. Photo by Jim Mendenhall.

Chapter 5

Papa's Got a Brand New Bag

Come here mama
And dig this crazy scene
Not too fancy
But it's fine and pretty clean
Ain't no drag
Papa's got a brand new bag

—JAMES BROWN

Teresa Covarrubias: The Wolf and the Lamb

Teresa Covarrubias is a singer/songwriter for the group The Brat, which is composed of young musicians from East Los Angeles. The group formed in 1979 and performed in clubs and for different functions throughout the Los Angeles area during the 1980s. They also completed two different record projects. The Brat's musical style has often been termed "punk" or "new wave," but Teresa is not particularly concerned with how her music is labeled. Compared to some of the older artists interviewed, Teresa was not so historically enculturated in the Mexican musical experience in Los Angeles, so she represents a new breed of young Chicano artists from the East Side.

Teresa is a third-generation Chicana who was born and raised in the Boyle Heights section of East Los Angeles. Her father was born in El Paso, Texas. He moved to Los Angeles, where he met Teresa's mother, who comes from there. Teresa attended Boyle Heights Elementary School and Resurrection School (a Catholic grammar school). She attended high school at Sacred Heart of Jesus in Lincoln Heights. She only recently discovered facts about her grandparents' backgrounds and something of their culture, although certain traditions have always been maintained in her home. English was spoken in the house; the Spanish that Teresa speaks she learned primarily during her years of high school Spanish classes.

Teresa's father was a welder, and her mother worked in the home, taking care of the children. Her parents used to enjoy Benny Goodman and other musicians of the big band era, but she was not exposed to very much Mexican music as a child, and her attitude toward it at that time was indifferent. "It wasn't until recently that I started getting into listening to *corridos* and stuff, and appreciating it for what it is."

Teresa's strongest musical influences were the records that her older brothers and sisters listened to: Bob Dylan, The Rolling Stones, The Beatles, The Who, and similar groups from the 1960s, especially those who wrote protest music. Most of her friends, in contrast, were listening to top-forty popular music aired by such radio stations as KHJ (which included disco, rhythm and blues, and rock hits).

Teresa did not become seriously involved with music until she was eighteen. Because the music that she had assimilated was that of the 1960s mainstream styles, she was not actually conscious of a relationship between music and Chicano culture. It was not until the seventh or eighth grade that she even realized her ethnicity and that she was "different from other people." As a child in East Los Angeles she associated with Mexican and Chicano children and was not aware of any systems of stratification that may have existed between cultures. She metaphorically commented, "I think it was when I went to Disneyland [that] I realized there was white people."

Teresa believes attending Catholic schools was a positive factor in her development. She considers the quality of education she received in the parochial schools to have been better than what she might have received in a public school. She also studied psychology at California State University, Los Angeles, for two years, while singing with The Brat. Teresa left the university, however, in favor of her musical ambitions, for she realized she could not fulfill both obligations.

While Teresa was in high school, she was more interested in "underground-type music" than in any other style:

> For example, like back in the seventies I was really into David Bowie and Brian Ferry, which weren't really popular back then. They had an underground cult following, but nothing that was mainstream. All my music, or the music I like, I've listened to from my brothers and sisters. The groups that they listen to kind of branched off and had all these other people coming from them, like T. Rex and stuff . . . and then I took off and found my own heroes that had to do with that music. It came from the same place. I guess I was really disillusioned with everything that was happening around here and I wanted to find something different. It becomes real boring, what people were into here; it seemed like a rut. People were just eating whatever they were showing on TV or listening to the radio and just accepting it as

being, "Hey, this is cool, whatever," and I wanted to find something that I liked that wasn't following the masses.

Her desire to seek out alternative music also led her to broaden her experiences in general: "I just got into it by reading, I guess. I used to do a lot of reading because I quit high school after two years. For two years I just kind of went wandering around. I used to, like, [take] buses everywhere, and just check things out. That's when I started to realize there was more to life than East L.A. and there was a whole other world out there."

Teresa did not finish high school at Sacred Heart of Jesus, but she eventually received her diploma by passing a state proficiency exam. She then entered California State University, Los Angeles, hoping to become a psychologist. It was during that period that she decided to meet people who were involved in certain musical styles and movements.

I always wanted to sing. If you like certain things, you're going to meet people that are into the same thing. So that's pretty much what happened . . . places I'd go, places I'd hang out. I met people who were into the same type of music I was, that wanted to do the same things, that played instruments, or sang or wrote, and we got together and things started happening. Most of the people that I met, that I know now, I met in nightclubs, all in Hollywood, because there's no nightclubs around here for kids to hang out. So I used to go to the West Side and go into clubs. I used to hang out there, like the Mask. And they used to throw a lot of shows in those old halls. They're still there, but they don't throw concerts anymore. I didn't know anybody around here who was into that until I started hanging out in the clubs, and then I met people in the clubs that lived around here, which surprised me, because I thought I was the only person. There used to be a lot of different bands. Half of them, I don't remember the names anymore. It was a lot of punk music, but I really didn't like them very much. I used to like some pop bands that came out of L.A. For a while, I got into pop music.

When she was a teenager Teresa sang in her high school glee club and in the choir that sang for Sunday Mass. She was also writing prose and short stories. It was not until she joined The Brat that she realized she could use her writing skills in the context of the band; she started writing lyrics and composing in collaboration with other musicians.

Teresa, Rudy Medina, and Sidney Medina are the core members of The Brat. Teresa met Rudy, who plays guitar, at the Starwood. He was performing in a group called Blaze, which played in a style similar to the Damned, the Sex Pistols, and other English punk bands. A few months later, Blaze disbanded and Rudy formed another group, The Brat. He asked Teresa to sing with the group along with his nephew Sidney, who plays bass. The three original members are still the central force of the band. An assortment of other musicians have been members of the group, but none on a permanent basis.

The Brat is basically a rock band, although many still describe Teresa's music as punk. "Punk is pretty passé right now. We were always labeled a punk band, but I don't think anyone really tripped on punk too much." Teresa has noticed that there seems to be a void now in the musical scenario for young musicians, especially those from the East Side. The "scene" happened and dispersed in three or four years. "There's not any bands out there that are really drawing an audience . . . right now, it's like a wasteland."

In Teresa's view, the growing interest in East L.A. bands, exemplified by articles published in 1985 in the major Los Angeles newspapers, was not matched by any increased musical activity. Although Teresa felt that it was beneficial coverage because the groups were labeled as "Chicano" and received attention in the press, she sensed that if the bands had not been Chicano and from East L.A., the media would not have been interested in this particular music. This "label," for example, actually helped The Brat and other groups such as Los Illegals, The Plugz, Odd Squad, and Felix and the Katz establish themselves as new acts in Los Angeles. The press in effect created the ethnic association:

> I don't think that anybody who was making music, coming out of East L.A., really had this concept of [an] East L.A. band, and this is what we're about and this is what we're trying to do. It was something that the West Side started buzzing about. They [the media] called it whatever they want to call it, because all the bands that are coming out of here are so different from one another. It's lucky if anyone's talking to each other at one time. I don't think anyone's ideas are the same at all. Everyone has these different ideas with what they're doing, what they want to do, why they're doing it, where they want to take it. Our music is different from Los Lobos, The Illegals, [or] any other band that's coming out of here. The only thing we have in common is where our parents came from.

Teresa also attributed current thoughts about an "Eastside Renaissance" to the media:

> I think the whole idea of an East L.A. Renaissance, whatever, is something that a newspaper made up. There's all these bands, by co-incidence . . . coming out of the same area. If anything, I find that a

lot of bands want to jump off that bandwagon, because they think that it's going to pigeonhole them in some way, and it kind of does sometimes . . . because we can start this whole little network here, like everyone knows we put out these records together. But you're kind of separating yourself from a whole other thing that's happening. And really, if you want to get your music out there, [if] you want to get the word out, whatever you're writing about or singing about, you've got to get on the radio. You've got to get mainstream radio play.

Teresa considers it a positive sign that the eastside bands are collaborating and that the Rhino Record series, produced by Rubén Guevara, has been an artistically productive project as well as a source of exposure for the groups involved. The only danger of such productions is the previously mentioned "pigeonhole" effect: "to get too into that and forget that there's a whole other audience out there is only hurting yourself." Attempting to enter the mainstream is not necessarily "selling out," and many bands in East Los Angeles are capable of attaining that type of mobility. "I think a lot of the music that's coming out is just as good as music that has been on radio right now . . . even better, because radio is pretty pathetic right now."

A worthwhile musical product demands hard work, especially if people are to understand the art form. The task entails generating work through performances, auditions, and public relations. For example, after hearing The Brat audition for different record companies over the past four years, some executives are finally beginning to understand the band's music outside its East L.A. context.

I think people create their own problems because they think of our band and all the other bands as an East L.A. band and they think there's some secret marketing technique that they have to apply when they're marketing an East L.A. band, and really, you market them like anybody else because our music isn't that different from any other rock and roll band that's playing. . . . Music is real simple. I think that it's just recently that they're starting to realize you market an East L.A. band like you market a band from Liverpool or anywhere else. The only way you're going to make it in the business is if you're good . . . and to say we're not making it because we're this or we're Chicanos, it's just like being a crybaby, being a *chillón;* because you've got to work hard. . . . Certainly there are injustices, and maybe you have to work a little harder than other people to get understood, [but] it all comes down to work. I've seen a lot of people trying and I think we're getting closer. The Illegals got signed; that was something.

Any demands by the music industry that Chicanos assimilate certain mainstream characteristics (for example, by changing their names or dyeing their hair blond) have not affected Teresa's image. She feels no commercial pressure to "Anglocize" her image; in fact, she seemed to detest the physical assimilation that in previous generations was common practice in Hollywood.

In regard to the consumer market, Teresa's goals and those of The Brat are simply to be heard by as many people as possible. She considers music a functional essential in society ("so people can hear it, dance to it, sing it") that is consumed aesthetically on the basis of sound and its variants. For example, the particular types of guitars, amplifiers, and sound equipment used constitute one level within a hierarchy of many components that help to distinguish The Brat's individual sound. Lyrics can also be a distinguishing feature. Teresa sometimes sings songs in both English and Spanish. "If it's good, it's not going to be a problem." She also believes that most of the audience attracted to the music of The Brat is probably "the type of kids who listen to radio."

The musical training of the other members of The Brat is quite different from Teresa's. Both Rudy and Sidney Medina have a classical background. They were trained in classical guitar and used to play duets together at recitals. They became interested in rock and roll at the start of the punk scene in the late 1970s. Rudy, who was twenty-seven years of age at the time of the interview, and Sidney, who was twenty-one, are both from East Los Angeles. Teresa commented, "Their parents are more hardcore than my parents. . . . [They] came over on the bracero program, and they're more traditionally Mexican than I am because they're first generation. They speak Spanish and their parents are ultra, ultra-traditional; they don't speak any English."

Rudy and Sidney took guitar lessons at a small music and art center on Third Street (the Los Angeles Art and Music School) where low-income families could send their children for instruction on a "sliding scale." Both Medinas continued to develop as musicians, and Rudy eventually studied at California State University, Los Angeles, graduating with a Bachelor of Arts in music. Sidney attended the same university but did not finish. Teresa described her two musical colleagues as "versatile, flexible, and influenced by what they hear around them," which is evident in the diverse and highly sophisticated music produced by the group.

Teresa is optimistic that the group will be offered a viable record contract. Money, however, is not easily accessible, and The Brat's individual artistry has limited its success in the record industry. "Everyone doesn't know if we'll go over well because of the type of music we're playing and the lyrical content, and they're not sure if people are going to be able to understand it. Like I said before, it took them four years to understand finally what we were trying to do and they are just real hesitant. It's just not real bubblegummy pop music that's easily digestible. It takes a little bit more thought."

Although The Brat has established a considerable name for itself, the group still lacks a major record. "Nobody knows what the band sounds like . . . it's a phantom." The group has generally been rejected by Los Angeles music aficionados. "There's a group of people in L.A. who more or less frequent clubs, and they decide who the L.A. bands are. And we've been playing in L.A. for six years and we've never gotten that support from the people in L.A. It's been really difficult for us." Teresa does not consider The Brat to be a one of the cult L.A. bands and believes that when a record is released nationally, an audience will more easily be generated.

The process of reinforcement within the eastside network of Chicanos has helped The Brat considerably: "Our band has been really lucky because all the people that we know on the eastside, all the people that we've done shows with, the creative community, has been real supportive. We've been struggling for six years and they're still really supportive, because they believe in what we're doing. They're always real encouraging."

Teresa hopes to do something for the Chicano community in Los Angeles by being a model of integrity for others to see. "I think the best thing we can do for the community is probably make it and just be a positive something that came out of East L.A."

Example of Musical Style

"The Wolf" is a hard rock tune written by Teresa Covarrubias and Rudy Medina. The essential rock flavor of "The Wolf" is characterized by a $\frac{4}{4}$ driving beat with typical heavy accents on the second and fourth beats of each measure. The basic form begins with an introduction followed by the main theme, which has both a verse and chorus section (measures 15 through 49). This order is repeated through all three strophic cycles, with a guitar solo interposed after each verse and chorus.

The lyrics of "The Wolf" refer metaphorically to the concept of a hegemony imposed over the masses by means of political, economic, and cultural exploitation. A Marxist analysis would interpret the song's text as a proletarian expression of the economic dialectic in society, symbolized by the wolf (the bourgeoisie) and the lamb (the proletariat). The metaphor also refers to ethnic and social stratification, however, so the more general and encompassing notion of cultural stratification is perhaps more appropriate than the Marxist one of economic stratification. The "lamb" refers specifically to the lower social class defined in terms of economic and political access. This is especially evident in the stanza alluding to borders and the history of land disputes and foreign intervention. This interpretation is reinforced by the last stanza and its allusion to "atrocious foreign policy."

"The Wolf"

Words: Teresa Covarrubias
Music: Rudy Medina

A star-spangled wolf comes,
Says that
This land was made for all
So hard to grasp the logic
Foaming from its rabid call.

You say this democracy
Believes in our equality
You lie!

Chorus:

The Wolf and the Lamb
The Wolf and the Lamb
We are the Lamb.

The country runs right through us
And it doesn't even blink an eye
Living off the poor man's labor
Sucking all our spirits dry.

We say this Democracy
Is laced with their Hypocrisy.
It's true!

The Wolf and the Lamb
The Wolf and the Lamb
We are the Lamb

Your claw of justice
Knows no boundary lines.
Tell me O Wolf of slaughter
How many peasants died?

With this one Democracy's
Atrocious foreign policy
Yeah!

The Wolf and the Lamb
The Wolf and the Lamb
We are the Lamb.

It is interesting to compare the verse structure of "The Wolf" with that of other examples in this chapter, many of which adhere to traditional, strict poetic verse structures from Latin America. Unlike them, "The Wolf" uses iambic rhythm, a standard English poetic pattern, in lieu of specific poetic formulas that dictate rhyme schemes, the number of syllables per line, and the groupings of stanzas. Whereas *coplas* and *décimas* are often incorporated into Latin American musical forms (e.g., *corridos, guajiras,* [1] *sones*), no such practice characterizes English song verse. Although rhyme schemes and even-numbered stanzas (e.g., the common four-line pattern) are frequently employed in English song verse, the deliberate application of formal poetic structures is a much less pervasive feature of English song styles than it is in Latin American genres. When improvisation does occur, as in gospel singing and rhythm and blues, strict poetic verse structure has not become traditional. Conversely, in Latin America, most improvised verse forms adhere to such poetic formulas even when such forms have developed as a result of multi-ethnic hybridization, that is, the intersection of styles from Europe, Africa, and the indigenous Americas.

The transcription given in example 4 demonstrates the basic strophic form of the song. Instrumentation consists of lead vocals, electric guitar, electric bass, and drum set. The arrangement continues after measure 46 with additional strophic verses, an extended guitar solo, and a final coda that reiterates the harmonic progression of the introductory section.

Poncho Sánchez: *Conguero*

Poncho Sánchez, a Latin percussion artist, has recorded eleven albums under his own name within the last twelve years, three of which have been nominated for a Grammy Award. He performed as a member of Cal Tjader's Latin jazz group for over seven years, touring throughout the world until Tjader's death in 1983. He represents a major constituent of the style generally referred to as Latin music, the blend of Afro-Cuban and other contemporary components such as salsa and Latin jazz. Among the artists who have performed on his recordings are Tito Puente, Freddie Hubbard, and Clare Fischer. Many musicians throughout the United States consider Poncho one of the most adept and creative young Latin recording artists.

Poncho is Chicano. His mother and father were born in Mexico and emigrated to Laredo, Texas, where Poncho was born and given the name Filoberto. When he was five years of age, his family moved to Norwalk, California, which is in the southeastern section of Los Angeles County. He still lives there with his wife, Stella, and two sons, Monguito and Tito (named after Cuban *conguero* Mongo Santamaría and *timbalero/salsero* Tito Puente, respectively).

Example 4

Example 4 (cont.)

Poncho's mother and father spoke primarily Spanish, but as the children grew older they started to answer their parents in English, because they had learned English in school, through the media, and in the neighborhood. Although the section of Norwalk where Poncho was raised was a Mexican/Chicano barrio, bilingualism was the norm.

> When I first moved out to California, four or five years old, I spoke nothing but Spanish, and we started to play with the neighbor kids and actually they started laughing 'cause we couldn't talk English. So they said, like in two weeks we had English down. We learned it real quick. They were actually making fun of us because we were speaking a different language. I feel that it's been kind of bad; at the same time, we spoke so much English, I forgot some of my Spanish. My mother and father always spoke Spanish in the house, but most of the time, we'd answer them in English. They didn't learn it as quick as we did.

Poncho's parents listened to "older, traditional Mexican music" when he was a child. His parents were quite busy earning a living and had little time for recreation. Poncho's father worked in the dry-cleaning business and continues to do so to this day. Poncho's mother stayed home and cared for Poncho and his ten brothers and sisters. It was primarily from his brothers and sisters that Poncho was exposed to large quantities of music, especially Latin music, when he was a youngster.

As a young child, Poncho listened to the records of Tito Puente, Machito, Joe Cuba, and Cal Tjader. At that time many Chicanos were not familiar with the particular styles of Latin music to which he was being enculturated, "because it's more like Cuban or Puerto Rican kind of music, or *música cubana*." Poncho learned to recognize musical and dance forms such as the mambo and the cha cha chá from the records of his brothers and sisters. He used to watch his sisters dance to the Chico Sesma Latin music radio program, which aired every night. "I just grew up listening to that thing, that type of music, and it stuck with me and I've always had a feeling for it . . . to play Latin music, or *salsa* or *música latina,* or Latin jazz, or whatever you want to call it; it feels real natural and it just feels good."

Poncho was also influenced by the Mexican music his parents liked. He respected the traditional forms and was sensitive to the understanding of the texts. "The traditional Mexican music, I could feel it. There's so much expression, so many feelings, you can really feel what they're talking about, and they sing about their lives and their women and their food; it's very flavorful. Same as *la música latina,* Cuban music—same thing. I think the Latin music has so much heart in it."

Poncho felt displaced in society because of differences in language, music, and culture in general: "Most Chicanos or Latinos go through things like that or periods of that, and I think that I probably did." Within that context of displacement, however, he tried to do what he felt was correct and practical, and "tried not to worry too much about what's going on around everywhere else." His parents inspired him in that respect: "My mother used to cook every day; she made *tortillas de mano* [hand-made tortillas] every day except for Sunday, because every Sunday they would go to church. Sunday would be her day out. My father would take her dancing. They still go every Sunday. They go to church in East L.A. and go to all the senior citizen *bailes* [dances]. I respect them so much for that. I think it's a beautiful thing. I think I've been very lucky with those kinds of parents."

He and his siblings also used to watch the Johnny Otis show on television, and rhythm and blues had a profound effect on the development of their musical tastes. He listened to the music of James Brown and Wilson Pickett. Poncho was never particularly attracted to rock: "I never really liked rock . . . for some reason . . . I just had this *salsa,* Latin jazz thing in my mind." Records, such as those of Cal Tjader, impressed him from the start, and hearing those recordings often at a young age helped him determine and dedicate himself to that musical direction. "That's why I've stuck with it so long. I used to watch the band across the street from my house, and I used to go sit there in the window and watch them practice all the time. It was regular R&B stuff, and they'd do a couple of Latin tunes."

Extensive exposure to Latin or salsa music in Poncho's home began when he was very young and continued until he began playing. Living in Los Angeles also affected the formation of his musical style:

As soon as I heard just the sound of the conga drum . . . I don't think [it would have hit me so fast] had I grown up in Laredo; I always had a feel for music, ever since I was a little kid, I had it in me. I think, yeah, moving to L.A. had a lot to do with it because there in L.A. you can grow up hearing a lot of different types of music. . . . The ones that stayed with me and the ones I really felt was the Latin thing and also the straight ahead jazz thing. I listened to all the great jazz musicians, too, when I was growing up—John Coltrane, Miles Davis, Count Basie, especially the be-bop musicians. That really played a part in my musical background.

The music that Poncho was absorbing produced a musical taste and direction that would eventually manifest themselves in a musical style. Poncho's early musical development is an example of a self-imposed mode of training motivated by persistent ambition.

I'm the only one in the family that ever took up music, although all my brothers and sisters were good dancers, and they always went to all the *bailes*. But nobody played an instrument or anything. When I

first started to play even my own family was saying, "You're not going
to be able to make it. You can't play that well, you're playing the same
thing over and over." When you're first learning, you're banging away
on the guitar until you get some help. I didn't get a lot of help from
my family. I had such a fire burning in me with the want to learn how
to do that.

He first started learning music when he started playing the guitar; afterward, he took up singing. "I was a singer, a straight stand-up singer in a
band for four years . . . . At that time we used to do all the James Brown
stuff [and] mostly all the popular soul music that was happening."
    The small band was composed of friends who lived in the same barrio
and who played guitars and drums. In addition to imitating the voice of
James Brown, Poncho also sang in the styles of Willie G. and Thee Midniters (from East L.A.), Otis Redding, and Wilson Pickett. After singing
and playing guitar with that small neighborhood band, Poncho met the
brothers Roy and Luis Echevarría, who both played saxophone. They invited Poncho to sing in their group, which their father, also a saxophonist,
directed. The ensemble played traditional forms popular among Mexicans
in Los Angeles: Tex-Mex, polkas, *corridos,* boleros, cha cha chás,[2] and *cumbias.* They performed most weekends, usually for weddings. One element
of the orchestra that attracted Poncho was the the group's interesting arrangements, particularly the horn parts. The group featured a lead vocalist
called "Little Jimmy," who eventually formed his own band, Little Jimmy
y Sus Vagabundos. Poncho also played with Little Jimmy's group, which
specialized in the traditional "Tejano" or Tex-Mex sound. That group recorded a 45-rpm disc of a song titled "Quiero Que Sepas," which became
a local hit. The band promoted the record on tour throughout southern
California, performing in Santa Barbara, Santa Maria, and San Diego.
    It was with Little Jimmy y Sus Vagabundos that Poncho began playing
the conga drums. He was still in high school at the time (ca. tenth grade)
and would play congas when the band played forms that stylistically ac-
commodated the instrument. "In this traditional Tejano band, they played
cumbias and cha chas from time to time, and that was when I would have
my chance; but yet going through all the traditional Tex-Mex music with
that style, like Little Joe and the Latineers, Sonny and the Sunlighters . . .
I still always had this Latin jazz thing in the back of my mind. I dug it and
I went through it and I still dig that. I knew it wasn't what I would end up
doing [the Tex-Mex] . . . [or] what I really wanted to do."
    After Poncho graduated from high school, he joined another local band
called Sabor. The band also performed for many weddings, but they played
a repertoire different from that of Little Jimmy's group, including more
progressive Latin and top-forty songs. The band members were other

musicians of his age, and, compared to the Echevarría group, they had more freedom in selecting tunes to perform; for example, they learned the music of Mongo Santamaría and Ray Barreto and the brassy rock style epitomized by the group Chicago. Sabor performed for casuals and in the local club circuit, catering especially to the Chicano clientele. The band became well established in the eastside musical network.

On various occasions, Sabor would perform in the "battles of the bands" that were organized around Los Angeles, mostly in the East Side, and produced by local Chicano promoters or organizations. Poncho and the other members of the band admired the leading eastside groups that participated, such as Thee Midniters and the Village Callers. The union organizations that produced these events were an integral part of the musical network. "There was definitely a clique going on with the whole Chicano scene, East L.A., the whole crowd there, the Big Union, the Little Union, and all the different *bailes* they had. I used to go to them all the time. We had our own little band going on all the time. [There] was a big turnout for us [when we played] with one of those bands."

Poncho worked with Sabor for about five years while he also worked a full-time job in a foundry; by that time, he was supporting his own family. It was during this period that Poncho's association with Cal Tjader began. An internationally acclaimed vibraphonist who specialized in Latin jazz, Tjader was one of Poncho's musical idols.

I went to see Cal Tjader one night at Concerts by the Sea (a club in Redondo Beach). About two weeks before I went to see him, we were playing at the International Club in Pico Rivera. It was called the Press Club [the Latin American Press Club] at the time. A guy walked in and said he was a personal friend of Cal's. I didn't really believe him. He said that he was going to tell Cal about me. About two weeks went by and Cal was in town and I went to go see him, and sure enough I walked into Concerts by the Sea, and this . . . his name was Ernie, he was an old Navy buddy of Cal's, was standing right there and talking to Cal. He was talking to him about me. He introduced me to Cal. The band he had at the time was getting ready to break up and . . . was going back to Chicago. Cal let me sit in that night. He liked the way I played and I got the job. That was about ten years ago. I worked with Cal Tjader for seven and a half years, until his death in Manila.

Tjader's death caused Poncho to reflect back on his own spiritual growth and artistry:

We had just gotten to Manila on a Monday and Cal passed away on a Tuesday. We were going to play at the Folk Art Center Friday, Saturday, and Sunday, that weekend, and it never happened. To say the least, it was a pretty bad experience. After we got back home, it took quite a while for me to get over it. It was very heavy for me. I didn't even feel like playing for awhile. Cal meant so much to me in my life. I was a big Cal Tjader fan even before I joined his band and I still am. I had the honor and the pleasure of working with him for seven and a half years, and I was on the last eight Cal Tjader albums. That played a big part in my life. I learned a lot from him about being on the road and music and everything. So it meant a lot to me and it took quite a while to get over it.

Poncho's association with Cal was a major component in his present success in the music industry. He now has his own band in addition to a recording contract with Concord Records (the same company for which Tjader was under contract). He has recorded nine albums with Concord. His first album, recorded in 1979 on the Discovery label, was simply titled "Poncho." He recorded another album, also as a leader, for Discovery before signing with Concord.

With respect to the issues of mainstream integration and marketability of Chicano/Latino musical expression, Poncho looks for a way to gain more exposure within the musical mainstream without compromising his musical and cultural style:

Entering the mainstream of the flow of all the big operations out there will always be a problem. I don't know exactly why, but I know it's going to be there . . . and it's going to be uphill and it always has been. . . .

It's good to see a lot of the old bands going back to the older traditional styles of sound. That's what I like in all types of music. I'm a purist and I like traditional, authentic music of all types. I think it's good and it should be able to be marketable, not only for Chicanos, but for all walks of life. There's a lot of Latino people in the U.S. . . . I went to Chicago with Cal Tjader. I had never been to Chicago. I was amazed how many [Latino] people are in Chicago. It's almost like L.A. And of course, New York, Miami, Texas, and Phoenix. I mean, it should be marketable. It would be good to see it happening; but of course, it's hard to say how to approach it or who or what to do . . .

I would like to see the Chicanos or the Latinos get in the big market as far as popularity, stardom, money, and all that stuff. But on the same thought, I think that a lot of people . . . will get up there, more or less. If I were to try to make big money and get in that big mainstream, I'm afraid that maybe I would have to start watering down my sound, style, or what I wear or what I do. . . . I want to wear a *guayabera*, whatever I feel, not because you should wear this little tie because that's what they're doing nowadays, and if you don't wear these kinds of whatever, you're not in the main thing. I'm afraid that I might have to be too commercial, and I don't want to do that. I want to play the way I feel.

Poncho calls himself a purist stylistically and is not interested in exploiting traditional forms by incorporating foreign or nonstylistic elements:

I play it the way I think it should be done. I'm a purist as far as the Latin jazz music goes, and I don't allow certain things in my band or certain sounds. I don't like loud guitars, rock drummers playing a back beat to a Latin groove; I don't go for that at all. That's like having a rock drummer playing with a Latin band. That doesn't do a thing for me. I like a *timbalero*, a conga player, a bongo player, and that's it. I think it should be left alone that way. You always do your own thing, although I definitely follow the lines and the patterns and the roads that Cal Tjader, Mongo Santamaría, Tito Rodríguez, Tito Puente and guys like that have left for us, or have set for us.

Poncho receives few studio calls because he does not read music; he therefore considers it important for young Chicano/Latino musicians to be versatile stylists and excellent sight-readers. On the other hand, he knows excellent, formally trained percussionists who "still don't get that many calls." He attributes the problem in part to the politics of business: "I believe there's a lot of . . . cliques in some recording companies. There definitely is that; I'm sure of that. I'm sure there are a lot of outfits that are not like that."

Poncho considers himself a part of the "Eastside Renaissance" in music:

I would definitely say I am part of that because I've grown up around all that; but yet I like to get other people involved in my music that weren't aware of our type of music. I mostly work jazz clubs, and most Latin bands work in salsa clubs or Latin clubs where they dance. I mostly work all the major jazz clubs in town. All different types of people go to those clubs. If you go to a salsa club, there's mostly just Latinos and they're *bailando* [dancing]. The clubs I play, you find all different types of people in there and I think it's great, because I'm letting everybody know what this is and what I'm doing; I think it's good. That's what I would like to do. If it comes up that way, yeah. Not that I'm really out there trying to do that for that particular reason. I'm out there because I love my music.

Irma Rangel: Angel Warrior

Irma Rangel was for some years the lead vocalist for one of the more popular Chicano musical groups in Los Angeles, Califas. From 1983 to 1984 she played a leading role with Luis Valdez's repertory company, Teatro Campesino, in the musical production "Corridos," which has been performed in San Francisco, San Diego, and Los Angeles. She currently leads her own music/dance group, Angel Warriors, a trio of performers that also features Susie Esquivel Armijo and Leticia Ibarra.

Irma was born and raised in Los Angeles (East Los Angeles, Santa Fe Springs, and Whittier). Her mother is originally from Sinaloa, Mexico, and her father was born in Texas. Irma's mother was the first of her family to emigrate to Los Angeles from Mexico; the majority of her family still lives in Mexico. For this reason, her family has maintained close contact with relatives there.

Irma gained an early exposure to Mexican musical traditions when her family celebrated holidays, fiestas, or special occasions such as baptisms and birthdays. Relatives were invited, and her parents took pleasure in planning a festive atmosphere to help break the monotony of daily work. Music played an integral part, and it was always Mexican music. Her father greatly appreciated female vocalists from Mexico, so Irma was exposed to Amalia Mendoza, María Victoria, Lydia Mendoza, Lucha Villa, and other singers. As a child she talked to the pictures of the women on the record jackets and sang along with the recordings. She also listened to Javier Solís, Pedro Infante, Trío Los Panchos, Beto Villa, and El Mariachi Vargas de Tecalitlán. Irma's visions of becoming a singer actually began during her early years, even before she was in school. She recalled that many of the neighborhood children would organize talent shows in their backyards, where the children would perform in showcases, each child singing, lipsynching, dancing, or doing acrobatics.

Irma grew up in a bilingual household. Her mother always spoke Spanish in the home, whereas her father used both languages (speaking Spanish with his spouse and English with his children). Irma most often speaks in English with her brothers and sisters. Most of the music she heard at home during her early childhood was sung in Spanish. She was exposed to American music with lyrics in English later within the broader social setting of school, television, and radio. The process of record collecting and musical assimilation began more overtly when Irma and her sister, a few years older than she, started listening to what are now referred to as "oldies" among Chicanos. These included the music of numerous rhythm and blues artists such as Martha and the Vandells, the Shirelles, and later Aretha Franklin, Tina Turner, and Patti Labelle. Irma also listened to male R&B

singers, but as a young, aspiring female singer, her dominant influences were female artists.

As a child, Irma sometimes felt displaced or inferior in the bicultural setting, even though she may not always have been conscious of it. She often felt ashamed of being Mexican; her ethnic background was evident because she spoke Spanish and had dark, Mexican physical features. Irma referred to the experience of displacement within her community as "peer pressure" from other children. When her family moved to Whittier, California, for example, she recalled, "They used to make fun of us because of who we were and because we had an accent; and it really wasn't heavy."

During her high school years Irma became more conscious of her background and began to develop her ethnic identity. She also wrote poetry, painted, and listened to different kinds of music, including American folk rock artists such as Laura Nyro and Judy Collins. Music became a medium of social expression for her in addition to being an artistic outlet. Irma became aware at a young age that she wanted "to make changes in this society for the betterment of all people." To affirm her bicultural experience, she decided to develop musically on a dual basis—American popular music and traditional Mexican and Latino genres.

Although Irma did adapt to certain mainstream musical styles, she still experienced a void when she tried to relate to high school musical or theatrical productions: "In high school I tried to go for the musical [laugh], theater type of stuff, but it was . . . taken over already by the Anglo students and the select few; it was like there was no room for some of us. There was very limited recreational activity that I remember where I could turn to in this particular area. So, I just . . . began taking junior college classes in high school, in subjects such as ethnic studies, and that just began to turn me on more."

Irma felt that the quality of her high school instruction did not prepare her for higher education. When she graduated from high school, she became more politically aware of the Chicano movement. Community politics became a part of her reawakening. She attended college in northern California, earning an Associate of Arts degree at D-Q University and a Bachelor of Arts in ethnic studies at California State University, Sacramento. (D-Q University is a school established with the specific goal of recruiting and educating American Indian and Chicano students.)

It was not until her college years that Irma had any formal instruction in music. She also studied Mexican *folklórico* dancing and Mexican indigenous forms: "I'm a *danzante;* it's in the Aztec style of dancing. I started at D-Q over ten years ago." Besides listening to the radio, records, and to live music, Irma also valued the feeling "from within" and the idea of singing with "*corazón, soul,* from the soul"; these became important concepts when she began to consider seriously a professional career in music. By meeting and corresponding with performers, she attempted to enculturate herself with as much cultural expression as possible related to her historical background and heritage.

Using emotional expression in interpreting a song was important in the development of Irma's individual style:

> The most important thing that comes to my mind . . . is the passion. I just would get this feeling inside and I know that I just wanted to put it out. It's a real emotional feeling and that comes from . . . it's almost a feeling of crying, of emoting, and it's not necessarily a sad feeling; it's just something that comes from the *corazón;* and to me, the way I see it, each song, each style of song, whether top forty or classical or any kind of Mexican or Latin style, blues, any of that . . . it all has its own heart, its own energy, its own little spirit to interpret. I think that it's an art to learn how to interpret with that heart or that energy, to make that song come alive with a pure feeling. For me, that's where it came from—the Mexican music, the Mexican movies, from the way my parents expressed themselves, and I've carried it through the English songs, the American styles.

Irma's first semiprofessional experience came during her college career in Sacramento, when she sang background vocals for a group called The Royal Chicano Air Force Band. The group performed Mexican *corridos, rancheras,* and boleros, as well as the newer *cumbias,* salsa, and top-forty songs. The band played extensively for the United Farm Workers and associated with many leaders of the Chicano community, including César Chávez and Dolores Huerta.

When Irma completed her studies at Sacramento, she returned to Los Angeles to continue her musical career. She began singing with a group called Xo-chi-pillis, which performed Mexican music, *cumbias,* and top forty. The group played for casuals such as weddings and occasionally in nightclubs.

Irma is connected to a network of Chicano musicians in Los Angeles who "pool together to help each other." Musicians often contact one another to recommend individuals for work or as substitutes in various musical groups. Women do not participate as actively as men in this network, however. Irma attributed the lower number of female musicians to male dominance in the music industry in general. When I asked her whether there is a particular reason why women—specifically, Chicanas—do not learn, for example, a musical instrument, she responded as follows: "I don't think it has to be that way, and it is changing. One way I'm changing it is by being out there, doing it and being sort of like a role model . . . to say, 'Look, I'm out here doing it and I'm a Chicana and I'm traditional . . . and some day I'll have my own personal *familia* . . . so if I can do it, you can do it.' You've got to find a balance with this."

During her involvement in the recording industry, Irma has seen the many problems that confront the Chicano/Chicana performer. To her, the major one is "just the ignorance of people not allowing the other cultural groups to share what they are." Irma feels that each cultural expression should be allowed to be part of the whole musical scenario, and she has dedicated herself as a performer to helping bring about that change. The rapidly growing Chicano population is a reason to expose more Chicanos on television, radio, and in concert halls, to perform as well as to educate. Marketability is also a problem. Bilingualism is not easily marketed in either the mainstream, English-speaking U.S. market or in the more marginal but expanding Spanish-speaking media network in the United States and Latin America. Moreover, "at this . . . time, a bilingual act is not selling because they're not making it a sellable product." A market, however, does exist within the Chicano community. "There's a market for anything that they allow there to be a market for . . . it's all a money game, is what it is, and they're going to have no choice in time but to have to listen to the voice of the Chicano community here in the L.A. area."

Capital resources exist, and "it's just a matter of time and community pressure." The series of albums called "The Eastside Renaissance" that was produced by Rubén Guevara through Rhino Records in 1984 is an example of the kind of project that is both educational and necessary. The record series demonstrated to the public that "there is this entirely different kind of vein of music that is living; it is happening right now and it's beautiful. It expands one's knowledge of what music is. To me, music is a healing power."

Irma was satisfied with the contribution that she and Califas made to the Rhino Records album, an original song track entitled "La música de la gente." The public's positive reaction to the album encouraged Califas to make plans to record a complete original album.

> I want to take it as far as I can as a performer until I can't sing anymore. I want to polish it, perfect it, teach it . . . as far as I can. I want to become a recording artist, and continue on stage. I want to do whatever I can to fulfill this mission that I have in life as a Chicana performer. I know that I can do it. I know that I will stand firm and will leave my impression or imprint in this society, and it will make changes for the betterment of all people.

Example of Musical Style

The music of the group Califas, which featured Irma, reflects the variety of musical styles within the young Chicano community. The group draws on traditional Latin American music from Mexico, the Caribbean, and South America. Califas performs a diverse repertoire of Latin American musical styles, ranging from Mexican *rancheras* and boleros to *norteños* and *huapangos*.[3] The group is influenced by salsa and its derivatives, in addition to the Colombian *cumbia* and the Brazilian samba and bossa nova. Each ensemble member has also played rock and rhythm and blues.

Califas's "La música de la gente," composed by the group's leader Marcos Loya in collaboration with Rangel, is an instrumental and stylistic hybrid. Essentially salsa, the piece incorporates various Afro-Cuban elements. For example, the introductory section is based on the traditional *guaguancó* structure.[4] The orchestration of the introductory *guaguancó* rhythm includes conga drums, timbales (*cáscara*),[5] claves, and flute. Califas has added a conch shell trumpet, which comes from the indigenous musical culture of Mesoamerica. The nuclear harmonic pattern of the introductory section adheres to the schematic shown in example 5.

The verse structure is a series of melodic variations sung with expressive rubato. The tempo is half as fast as the arrangement's subsequent up-tempo main body, enhancing the effect of the verse and evoking a certain pathos in the I-I[7] harmonic scheme. The introductory verse is as follows:

"La música de la gente"

Esta música que te tocamos	This music that we play
Es un sonido de todo el mundo	Is the sound of everyone
La idea nació del corazón	The idea was born
De los Chicanos con razón	From the heart of the Chicano
Para unir toda la gente	To unite all people
Con este ritmo ardiente.	With this ardent rhythm.
También queremos expresar	We also would like to express
Del pueblo se van escuchar	The voice of the people
Utilizando la música para	Using the music to
comunicar	communicate
La situación de nuestra	The situation of our people.
gente,	
Esta música que te tocamos	This music that we play
Es un sonido de todo el	Is the sound of everyone.
mundo.	
¡Oyela!	Listen!

Example 5

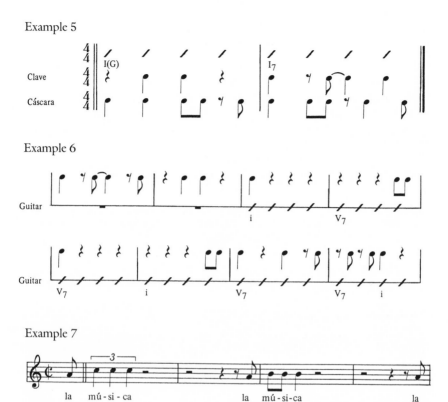

Example 6

Example 7

The introduction is performed in unison by the ensemble, with guitar arpeggios outlining the harmonic scheme that follows; it ends with a break that segues into the main body of the song. The rhythmic scheme of this typical break outlines a regular clave pattern in the first bar, as shown in example 6.

At this point, both the tempo and the modality abruptly change; the tempo transforms to a cut-time pace while the key modulates from G major to G minor.

An eight-bar flute fill follows, based on the same harmonic framework of the break, that of i-V^7—V^7-i. The chorus then enters with the sung melodic phrase "La música," adhering to the harmonic rhythmic scheme outlined in example 7.

Following the eight-bar chorus section is the main verse, as follows:

La música, la música
La música, la música.

Music, music
Music, music.

Hay músicos que tocan
Para curarse
Para curarse
Del corazón lastimado.

There are musicians who play
To heal themselves
To heal themselves
From a grieving heart.

Es una mala honda
Una mala honda
Siempre con la música
Se siente tranquilizado.

It's a bad scene
A very bad scene
With music you will always
Feel tranquility.

Chorus/Soloist:

La música/para curarse
La música/de la tristeza
La música/del corazón
  lastimado
La música para curar

Music/to heal yourself
Music/of sadness
Music/of a grieving heart

Music to heal

Somos del grupo Califas
y les expresamos
En una forma especial
Algo muy adentro.

We are the group Califas
And we express to you
In a special manner
Something from inside.

Muy adentro recibimos
De todo el mundo
Inspiraciones del mundo
Algo más profundo.

Deep inside we receive
From everyone
Inspiration from the world
Something so profound.

Chorus/Soloist:

La música/de todito el mundo
La música/hay que linda
  y querida
La música/de América Latina
La música/la tierra más fina

Music/from everyone
Music/so beautiful and
  loving
Music/of Latin America
Music/the finest land.

La música/Oiga pueblo Chicano

Music/Listen, Chicano
  people

La música/Eduquen a sus hijos

Music/Educate your
  children

La música/Andale hermana
  y hermano

Music/C'mon sister and
  brother

La música/Echale sus ¡gritos! ¡Ay!	Music/Shout it out! Hey!

Bridge:

Los ritmos y mensajes Son la fuerza de la gente	The rhythms and messages Are the strength of the people
Suelten sus gritos Andale, vente!	Let loose with your shouts C'mon, let's go!

Chorus/Soloist:

La música/del mundo	Music/of the world
La música/de México	Music/of Mexico
La música/del Africa	Music/of Africa
La música/Califas	Music/of Califas (California)

La música/del hermano
   cubanito
	Music/of my little Cuban
	   brother

La música/Puerto Rico	Music/of Puerto Rico
La música/Pueblos pobres	Music/of the poor people
La música/Como lo ves, ¡Ah!	Music/That's the way it is, Hey!

Bridge:

Las inspiraciones De todo el mundo Es algo tan profundo	The inspirations from everyone Are something so profound
La música La música es un sonido De todo el ¡mundo!	Music Music is the sound Of the whole world!

These stanzas use traditional *coplas* (couplets) as a basic format for the poetic structure, although they deviate from traditional *copla* form. Very few of the lines are octosyllabic, and few of the stanzas are constructed with *coplas*. Although flexibility is common in traditional *copla* verses and improvisation, the number of syllables in most of the lines in this example is not the result of the application of strict Spanish poetic structure. This music, generated by a group of young Chicanos in Los Angeles, demonstrates a comprehensive process of maintenance, change, and adaptation in traditional song structure. (These concepts are examined in chap. 5.)

Also of interest in "La música de la gente" are the chorus sections after the first and second verses. Although the phrases of the soloist are a predetermined part of the text, the singer improvises the delivery of the responses and interpolates them with varied rhythmic and melodic phrasing. Thus, the vocal style conforms to the characteristics of most *son* forms and structures.

Califas uses another innovation three times in this arrangement: rhythmically sustained bridge sections before the break sections are embellished with additional text sung with a recitative quality (refer to text section labeled "bridge"). The rhythmic structure of these bridge sections deviates somewhat from the nuclear pattern of the main verse. In lieu of the i-V[7]-V[7]-i repetitive progression, a sixteen-bar section based on a pattern reminiscent of the introductory *guaguancó* is inserted, embellished by arpeggiated flute figures constructed on the syncopated harmonic framework of the chordal *guajeo*,[6] played in the main body by the guitar and piano.

"La música de la gente" displays a hybrid form in terms of instrumentation and musical style. For example, the flute is played as in the traditional Cuban *charanga*[7] style, where it plays tutti with the rhythm section in breaks, provides constant melodic embellishment behind the vocal melody, and solos between *coros* (chorus sections). Another common stylistic trait is the flute solo during the *montuno*[8] section.

In deference to the traditional *son conjunto*[9] orchestration, Califas includes timbales, congas, and electric bass, all essential components of modern salsa—a form that has evolved from the styles performed by the traditional *son conjunto*. The result is a sonorous orchestration full of percussion and typical rhythms, layered with a lighter melodic and harmonic framework constructed by the *tres*[10] sounding twelve-string guitar and the *charanga*-styled flute. Irma Rangel provides a female vocal rendition of *son* form, which also adds to the unique timbre of Califas's musical texture.

The rhythmic structure of the main verse and *montuno* sections merits clarification. The rhythm makes use of reverse clave, characteristic of the *guaguancó* that comprises the introduction. The *tumbao*[11] (the basic bass and conga pattern noted in the following example) used in the main body, however, does not strictly conform to *guaguancó;* instead, a mambo feel is quite explicit, although the piece is not a mambo. Because of the combination of reverse clave and mambo, such an example is frequently referred to as *mambo-son*. In practical terminology, "La música de la gente" can be called a modern *son*-structured extension and adaptation of salsa styles. This hybrid musical example of a Chicano group represents an implementation and interpretation of traditional Afro-Cuban rhythms in a contemporary, fused style. The process implies more than an adaptation;

Example 8

it is a reinterpretation, in terms of both musical structure and symbolism (see example 8).

Los Illegals: Punk, Politics, and Latin Angst

At one point during the interview with the eastside rock group Los Illegals, the conversation turned to childhood food memories. The following comic exchange illustrates how the members have experienced their dual enculturations and how they have turned potentially negative experiences into positive ones through creative satire:

> *Willie:* I have a question, Sandra, before I lose my train of thought. Did you take bologna and Wonder Bread sandwiches to work, I mean to school, or did you take burritos wrapped [laughter] in wax paper . . . and then were you embarrassed to eat the burrito—and when you tried to unwrap it real fast the wax paper would stick to the burrito?
>
> *Sandra:* We would have a little bit of burritos and a little bit of bologna sandwiches, but to be honest with you, I would eat . . .
>
> *Willie:* No Wonder Bread?
>
> *Sandra:* I think so, yeah.
>
> *Willie:* Pan Bimbo, huh? [12]
>
> *Jesse:* I had Wonder Bread . . . with beans. Life was fine 'til I got to school, and that whole . . . it just blew everything. And then the bad images came up.
>
> *Willie:* Especially the bologna in a burrito, or the weenie, the weenie in the burrito.

On the jacket of Los Illegal's first album on A&M Records, Bob García describes the group as follows: "Los Illegals are five young Mexican Americans currently living and challenging the American dream on and in the streets of the barrio in East Los Angeles—a Hispanic haven for both legal and illegal aliens and refugees. Their debut album contains 12 song/poems dealing with subjects as diverse as lost loves, expectations, and identities. There are also songs of survival, hope, anger, youth violence and death. Fortunately, Los Illegals mean what they say" (1983).

Los Illegals are a diverse phenomenon, both musically and sociologically. Their name embodies the current cultural experience of Chicanos in Los Angeles. Confronted with such issues as the undocumented worker, urban crime, barrio slums, racism, and unemployment, Los Illegals have used their music to express the social web that has developed in the complex society of which they are products. They exemplify the potential of Chicano culture to convert the social dynamics of negative experience into positive energy and effect. The group's first album, *Internal Exile,* received the following review in *Caminos:*

> I've never claimed to be a fanatic about new wave artists, but the premier album by Los Illegals has got me wondering. With songs in English, Spanish, and textured in diverse melodies and rhythms, I'm not sure that one can classify this group with any particular nomenclature. One thing is for sure, though—there's some heavy social statement in this album, and my hat's off to these five young talented *atrevidos* [bold ones]. "El Lay" (L.A.), one of the many immigration-themed songs, portrays some dynamic poetry in Spanish which is even translated into English iambic rhythm—a lot of work and thought. "Secret Society" exhibits some magnificent singing ability by lead singer/composer/lyricist Willie Herrón. What these guys are doing with vocal rhythm is phenomenal. Again, a tip of my hat to them and their songs, especially "Guinea Pigs," "The Maze," "Wake Up John," "Not Another Homicide," "A-96," and "We Don't Need a Tan." Los Illegals have set out to say something, right from the heart and soul of East L.A. It's time for us to say something back. (Loza 1983d:53–54)

Los Illegals consisted of five members—Willie Herrón, Jesús (Jesse) Velo, Bill Reyes, Manuel Valdez, and Sandra Hahn—all of whom were born and raised in the east side of Los Angeles within a four-mile radius of one another. A former member, Antonio Valdez, recorded with the group on their first album.

Jesse Velo plays bass and sings background vocals for Los Illegals. Raised by his grandmother, he listened to Mexican music as a child, because that was the style his aunts and uncles enjoyed. He was also exposed to popular music of the 1950s and early 1960s, ranging from songs like "Tequila" to "Duke of Earl." Top-forty pop was also a factor in his musical enculturation from the late 1960s through the early 1970s. He attended Los Angeles public schools for his primary and secondary education and went on to work toward a college degree in sociology; although he compiled numerous class credits, he never completed the degree. After performing with many top-forty bands for several years, Jesse met Willie Herrón and participated in the formation of Los Illegals.

Willie Herrón sings, plays keyboards and saxophones, and provides a major portion of the leadership in the group. He is also recognized as one of the leading visual artists in the east side of Los Angeles. He has exhibited his murals and paintings throughout the city, in other parts of the country, and in Mexico. He became involved in art competitions at a young age, so his early training was primarily in painting and illustrating rather than in music.

> I really have never considered myself a musician, I've just considered myself an artist, and in the past four or five years I sort of chose to convey my artistic message through song, through music. And I did a lot of gigging, like top-forty groups and stuff, but most of the bands I was in during the sixties were all British groups, I mean British-influenced Chicano bands . . . we never played Latin music. We never played anything that was popular local, even though I grew up with a lot of modern salsa. Not too much like *norteño* or that kind of music. It was always like cha-cha-chás and mambos . . . those are the kind of things I remember when I was young. But most of my background has been and most of my interests have been in art, and I've just chosen to spearhead a concept which led to music, and I felt it would be really different to put this sort of a group together and challenge both the British influence on the English market as well as the Latin influence, just because I have been influenced by both.

Sandra Patricia Hahn is the newest member of Los Illegals. Raised in East Los Angeles, she is the second oldest of six children. Her family was poor. Her father was an illegal immigrant, but her mother had a green card. Because neither of them spoke English, language became a problem for the children: "Communication in English was a barrier to us, and there was a lot of struggle with that." When Sandra entered primary school, she spoke no English and had difficulty learning because most of her teachers did not speak Spanish. She started skipping school at a very early age.

> It was a lot of confusion communicating with teachers. So I dropped out and I was constantly ditching. At the age of eight I got a job at a bakery. They found out I was working without their consent, so they managed to drag me back into school. Through all my school years I was kind of a dropout, 'til finally some teachers took some interest in me and . . . I have an artistic background . . . so they kind of started pushing me towards becoming an artist or getting into that field. But I was pretty rebellious, so I just seemed to drift off into different directions; then I got into hairdressing, and then I pursued into that. I managed to have my business at eighteen and I kept that for awhile—'til twenty-one.

The status and role of women was a point of conflict between Sandra and her family, especially in relation to her family life as a young girl.

> Both my parents are from Mexico, and my mother was brought up real strict with the strict rule that a woman should be watching and feeding her man, and school wasn't as important to a woman. The most important thing was to get married and have children. Same thing with my father. So they kind of raised me in [a] real strict type of environment where I was very rebellious, and I thought . . . I don't want to get married and I certainly don't want to have children, and I don't want to cook for a man. These were things I honestly didn't believe in, but I thought . . . "Well, I really don't have a choice. This is the environment I'm set in," and I didn't know anything else, because we were confined to this environment and we really didn't have any friends or I didn't know anyone that really lived a different type of lifestyle.

When Sandra returned to school she became involved with various musical projects, recording small-scale experimental sound tracks with local groups. She then became interested in fashion designing and coordinated new lines for a modeling agency. She had been the hairdresser for Los Illegals when the group invited her to become a member as a keyboardist and vocalist.

Sandra's parents listened to a substantial amount of Mexican music, especially mariachi. Her father at one time played *guitarrón* in a mariachi. Her father said periodically, "This is *el son* that we want you all to learn." Sandra's mother used to enjoy the music of Mickey Lowrie, a Mexican bandleader popular throughout California. Her mother was "more into the cha cha and . . . more rhythm type of music . . . *bien loca*." Her mother's musical taste was "a little bit more diverse, 'cause she would . . . listen a little bit to Glenn Miller and a little bit of jazz. She was exposed to that." Additionally, her father appreciated classical music: "My father would turn the channel to classical music, and he would make us listen to it because he thought this was something we [should] all learn. But personally, I really enjoyed classical music, and that was the type of music I really enjoyed as a child. I just thought I was in heaven. I just thought, these are what I believe the angels would play for you when you walked into the heavenly gates."

As a child Sandra never actually thought in terms of what was popular or the "in thing." She listened to particular music for the enjoyment and did not "categorize . . . or dissect the music."

She did experience negative association with her musical heritage when she was a young girl. She was embarrassed when her Anglo schoolmates were exposed to the musical environment of her household: "When I did start making friends, I would bring them to my house and my parents would be playing their music, and all of a sudden they say, 'What's that?' And all of a sudden I'd realize . . . 'Oh, they're listening to that' . . . and I would change the station, because I didn't know . . . if I was embarrassed or I didn't want them to think that I was weird. . . . So right there it struck me . . . it was very *ranchera;* it was *norteño* I think it was, so to them it was really different. And I was really embarrassed."

In Sandra's mind, this embarrassment or displacement continued until she was about sixteen. At that age, she began to find out about and adopt eastside styles and trends, identifying with other *cholas*—young women who associated with car clubs or gangs and dressed in a distinctive style. "I started getting into this *chola* bit, or hanging around with the friends, and then I started to find that identity. Everyone, their parents, would listen to [Mexican music]. But we didn't sit around and listen to that type of music; we listened more to oldies."

Sandra had a negative association with Mexican culture during her childhood because she knew very little about her culture, and she feared other people's negative attitudes toward her and her family. What she did know about *Mexicanismo* she learned from her grandmother. "My parents never really talked about our culture, never talked about the music, where it came from. They never talked about anything like that. In fact, they would hide everything from us, even when they would bring uncles and cousins from Mexico, like under the blankets and stuff. We didn't know . . . 'Coyote—what's a coyote?'[13] . . . and they would keep everything from us. And I didn't care. I just wouldn't ask."

Her parents, however, did not intentionally attempt to assimilate into the culture of mainstream America. They told her: "'You're an American because you were born here, but you're from Mexican descent, and never be ashamed of your country. You're a Mexican.' Now, my mother would say, 'You're American, and then Mexican.' My father would say to all of us, 'You're Mexican, then American.' So it was like, well, I'm whatever, I guess I'm a melting pot here. But, I don't think they really tried to go either direction. I think . . . what was important to them was to give us an education and to learn, to adapt to the American culture."

Sandra has not resolved the conflict between her chosen profession and her family's idea of the more traditional role they think she should assume. As of the time of the interview, Sandra's parents were still unaware of her membership in Los Illegals. Sandra said that her parents "wouldn't accept it." She added, "To them, it's just something that you just don't do. I mean, there is no woman, unless you're a lead singer. . . . Since [I was] a little girl I had that natural ability to perform." Sandra's father, moreover, was also a musician at one time and has talked to Sandra about the difficulties of the profession. Her two brothers are also musicians, and they struggled considerably to attain moderate success within local musical networks. Their experience, somewhat of a disappointment to Sandra's parents, does not give them much optimism about her musical ambitions.

Bill Reyes, the percussionist for Los Illegals, was born and raised in Monterey Park, a suburb that borders East Los Angeles. His parents are bilingual Mexican Americans, born in the United States. His grandparents, although originally from Mexico, are also bilingual. Thus, Bill was raised speaking English almost exclusively. Bill's grandparents live on the corner of Floral Avenue and Branick Street in the east side of the city, only two miles from his parents' home.

> There's been music ever since I can remember. My parents were music lovers, and they introduced me to a wide range of musical styles at a very early age. I first got behind a drum kit at age eight and discovered Duke Ellington at age nine, Sinatra at age ten, and Grand Funk Railroad at age eleven. And it's been rock and roll [laughter] . . . so I'm still there; this is how I feel. I attended Don Bosco Technical Institute in Rosemead and graduated with an A.A. [Associate in Arts degree] in automotive technology, which you would never know it, because I really didn't pursue it heavily until later years. Those five years I spent at the institute were just filled with any kind of musical experiences I [could] grab. I had a long association with their music teacher, Gene Burns, and he just took me under his wing during those years and introduced me to orchestras, marching bands, which I had no interest in until he introduced me. And I became very heavily involved in that, arranging, composing things for drum sections and percussion ensembles. So, I have somewhat of a wide range of experience. After high school it was all the top-forty bands playing Salesian High School, the same circuit that Jesse played. The Monterey West, all those clubs down Whittier Boulevard. But it was beginning to be just a bit of a drag because it was turning into . . . late '79 it was getting to be more tedious than fun, and I was looking for something else to do.

Bill had neither a positive nor a negative association with tradition because of the way he was exposed to Mexican music within the confines of his parents' socialization. "When I hear mariachi music, I know what I remember; I remember being at my school where my dad was a principal in Pico Rivera at a very, very early age and hearing it. Like, they'd have celebrations, and I'd go to people's houses, I'd go to teachers' houses, the kids' houses, and [it would] be playing all over, continuously. And it's stuff that

I didn't hear at home. I'd heard whatever was on the radio . . . big band, jazz, pop, you know, soft, it was sixties stuff."

Bill became a member of Los Illegals after being introduced to Willie by his brother, Chris. Willie had met Chris while shopping for shoes at the store where Chris worked.

Several members of the group experienced biculturalism during their youth. One of the most interesting aspects of Jesse's life is his FBI record. He was issued a record while doing volunteer work with the United Farm Workers in local campaigns.

The thing that made me proud of it was that I sort of lived up to the rebelliousness that my grandmother, who was acting as my parent, taught me about her involvement in *la revolución mexicana*. And, together with that, I picked up a lot of the songs that were played. I mean, they were sweetened down versions by Nat King Cole of "La Adelita," but they were important in terms of the structure of it and in terms of the political and socioeconomic content of it. And so, together, that's the kind of stuff I grew up with, also on top of what I was learning in English. Because, you know, what's the *Mexicano-Americano* phrase, you know, the *pocho*, you're not a Mexican and you're not an American and so you're brought up with "Duke of Earl" on one hand and you're brought up with "La Adelita" on the other hand . . . "Las mañanitas" on one side, and who knows what on the other side, you know—"Peppermint Twist." And so, in my upbringing I was getting the feed from this side and the feed from this side and I was also getting it politically and socially in both ways. I'm real glad that that happened because I think I'm a much better person for it, simply because . . . I'm able to stand up and say what I feel that I wasn't musically. One of my first songs we wrote was called, "We Don't Need a Tan." Of course, the first audience we played it to was 80 percent Caucasian, but that didn't make a difference. At least they got the message. The *Mexicanos*, they come in later on and they start to pick up. We weren't doing essentially what Willie said earlier. Nothing that was totally, completely popular within the community, but it was for, by, and about the people in our community.

Willie experienced bicultural tension when he was a child, which he now expresses metaphorically through the concept of work and success.

A lot of my influence as I was growing up was, I had this real, labor sort of image in my brain just because I used to go like maybe twenty days out of the semester to school because I had to work. The reason why I had to work so much is because I too come from a big family. A broken home, so to speak, and also I was brought up, like a lot of us were brought up, by my grandparents. My grandparents had a lot to do with my upbringing and they owned also a *panade-ría* [bakery]. And so, I spent a lot of time working at the bakery, I mean, just literally sweating, to put shoes on my feet. And I always had this real strong drive for visual and mental and material success, because I didn't want to continue . . . I saw my grandparents, I saw my mom, my sisters, my aunts and uncles, I saw the whole family just laboring and, as I grew up, watched them age over the *tablero* [cutting board], just doing the *masa* [dough] bit. And it just wasn't for me. I just said, "Somebody's gotta break it. Somebody's gotta influence the next generation. Somebody's gotta do it." And I really felt strong, like, I mean, not to say at that time, I felt like I was, like I had that real special energy that may have come from who knows where. But I kind of felt that I was really the one that had to do it. Just because it was something that I just couldn't see going on. And so, I had a tendency to lean towards the arts at a really, really early age, because that was the thing that became real natural to me. And so, I think the arts sort of led me into everything and anything that had to do with being artistic. It was acting. It was fashion. It was music. It was painting. It was all of that stuff. And a lot of the music at that time was, I mean, like I had said earlier, was so diverse that you know, like in one day I was listening to real traditional Spanish music. And then I was listening to stuff that was sort of polka, with polka overtones. And then I was listening to stuff that we call European influenced. And then I was listening to rock and roll. And it was all, every day, I just listened to different types of music. A lot of soul was playing a big part in my life in the sixties. When Motown first started doing a lot of stuff, my sister, who's older than I, was really into just buying all the soul and all the Motown stuff. Not too much of the British . . . where I tended to lean towards more of the European influence at the time, which was being played on the radio. So I went from the radio to what the family was playing on the record player, from what my grandfather used to listen to, to "Santa María madre de Dios, sea tu nombre, dejate caer del cielo,"[14] to whatever, I mean, to the rosary every single night [laughter], every single night at three o'clock in the morning. Making *ojos de huey, chamucos, pan de huevo,*[15] [laughter] the whole bit. You know, so it was just real, it was mind bending and I was real confused. I mean, it was a confused state for a long time, and it kind of has eased off a lot . . . in the past ten years just because I think I've learned to really put things in a very peaceful perspective. I really let off a lot of frustration and a lot of things I held inside of me on our first LP. A lot of the material that was written had to do with the sweat shop, it had to do with being used as a decoy . . . for my grandfather to export illegal aliens, undocumented workers to help him in the *panadería* to work so they can earn a living to send back to their starving family. And a lot of them were uncles and cousins and third cousins. But they were all within the family and were just on the other side of the border. And so, there was a lot of influence there, just being under the blankets in the back of my grandfather's Cadillac, you know, and, when they ask you, "Where are you from?" just say you're a U.S. citizen. And meanwhile we had a couple of cousins or something under our feet covered with the blanket. You know, and we were like . . . without a t-shirt, just in flour sack underwear that my mom and my grandmother had made out of the *sacos de harina* [flour sacks]. So there was a lot of stuff, you know, a lot of stuff that was, that had a lot to do with how I am and what I am today. I have a lot of Spanish blood . . . my grandmother was American Indian . . . and my grandfather was from Mexico, from Chihuahua on my mom's side. And my great-grandfather was from Scotland. So it's all pretty mixed.

Such racial mixture is a point of pride. Jesse explained: "That goes to say that the *Mexicano* is the latest race, that we are a diverse mestizo, if you will. Americans call it mixture. Mestizo is a much better word. It loses a lot in its translation of what we are."

Jesse's musical enculturation when he was a child sprang from the music he heard in church and on the radio, which was a bilingual phenomenon for him.

You know, I was a walking commercial in elementary school, because that was the only thing I knew and that was the way to get around without getting my butt kicked. So that American radio, which wasn't totally American, because 15 percent of what we heard was *español*—Radio KALI, KWKW—just fused it; it just fused everything. And I became actually almost like one of our songs, you know. When he looks in the mirror, what does he see? You know . . . you're trapped between two cultures and your own way. But the way out of it was to fuse them and become who you want to be. It took many years for me to accept that, accept a lot of the things that they sent me to in elementary school and in junior high school.

In relation to biculturalism and the relationship between the Mexican experience and the American mainstream, Jesse's identity was controlled by others: "It's a role that I have been given solely because my parents chose to live that. But then again, what's the point? You got the dominant society that totally sends in their cultural air, you know, and dominates. It was like that even with the Aztecs dominating the Texcocos in the old times. And it happens everywhere. They just assimilate into the culture or keep a portion of it, or adapt with it, or change it, or fuse it and become something totally different."

The cultural domination that Jesse experienced most vividly when he went to school fostered feelings of displacement and inferiority. "All I can say is that life was wonderful until I got to school, and from then on, boy, everything went downhill. That's when I began to feel, when I got the indoctrination, and the education, and the George Washington bit with Christopher Columbus was here first, but you know, he was Italian anyway [laughter]; you know, that whole number."

Willie's exposure to Mexican history and to such figures as Benito Juárez was limited. He was taught "just about assassinations . . . who was assassinated; what Robin Hood of Mexico was invading the rich or whatever. I mean, those seem to be the only stories that seem to pop through—who's head was chopped off and put on a wall, as an example to the rest of the pueblo or things like that."

"Negative images" were nurtured by the media. According to Jesse:

The idea is that so many negative images from the movies we saw, the kind they teach you about in school, help people like me really start to doubt. You never see any positive Hispanics. And even today, a lot of the kids that go out in the circuit, they really don't want to see the Chicano-type groups, because they think, "Well, you know, it's like, they're not too hip, you know. They're short little fat dark guys with beards that play Latin scales with a cow bell." And that's the kind of thing that a lot of kids are starting to have a second thought about, the more—and I hate to sound pretentious about it—the more we get out there, the more the younger Chicanos that are just borderline . . . kind of like, "Yeah, I know I'm Chicano, but I'm not real happy, because the only Chicano bands I have to identify with, they're like the stereotypes you see on TV"—and we give them more of a positive image. We're here. We're Chicanos. We've got a degree of intelligence between us. Our music is a little crazy, but it's a fusion of both. And we tend to give that to the kids. It's something like we almost didn't get. We almost didn't get any of that at all when we were growing up. Certain groups would break into the national radio scene, and they would have a nice image and appeal to it. But the problem with that is that it's dated. And it just gets stuck with the mainstream and what was expected of them.

This limited portrayal of Mexicans was further enforced by the absence of role models during Willie's childhood:

Even the *indio,* even the Indian, was after some blood. It was always depicted. I mean, for some reason, when Zorro came out, let me tell you, I was in heaven.[16] It was like, finally, my God, somebody sees somebody; I mean that's positive! . . . You can really debate about that, because he was sort of—it was an American sort of idea, concept. But still, what it represented was somebody we could relate to. And there were no role models; none at all. Everybody was, there was always one way of doing everything, one way of looking, and there was always that state of confusion—"Well, where do I belong? What am I doing here?" But yet, for me it was very separate. My life at home, and my life in public, my social life was really, really different. And I really had little to no relationship, or I couldn't identify with a lot of the local situations, which at that time were, like, heavy gangs . . . the machismo of being a *cholo,* [17] tatoos; and my dad was like that, but for some reason, I just couldn't identify with it. It was just like something I just didn't want to be. And I was brought up with it, I mean, you know, the stabbings, the shootings, and having dinner and the gunshots coming through the window, and all of that. The cops breaking into the house in the middle of the night and dragging us all off with my mom screaming, and they're whacking her at the same time. All of that happened, and I just couldn't relate to a lot of it. It was like, "Why, why does this have to happen? Why is it like this?"

Jesse: All of this is reflected in our music. When I ran into this group, the first thing that I did is listen to it. And, my description of it then, and I love it, 'cause it was something totally new to me, it was like, Tito Puente takes LSD and hangs out with The Clash, or hangs out with existential Marxist theorists, if you want to talk extremes. But the idea of fusing those two that way, and not putting something in the middle that is just so acceptable from both sides, was real intriguing to me, and I loved it.

Willie: Yeah; I think it seems to have an interemotional approach, because you're combining cultures, you're combining ways, ideas that are alien to each other. You're taking them both, and you're mixing them together and coming out with some kind of palatable concoction of some sort.

Jesse: Also, the songs that we write, every single one, to this day, has to deal with some type of experience that has happened to one or all of us, at one point. On the last LP, "A-95," was the last time I saw my father for a long time. It was when he went to work, and the next thing you know, it's like, they took him away, they deported him on payday, and I hadn't seen him in months, you know? This is during the earlier raids in the late fifties, during the Eisenhower administration, when they were doing that whole raid number, and I didn't see him for months. You know, we lived on a sack of beans and potatoes . . . it takes twenty-five years for you to come around and be able to express yourself nationally, or actually internationally, through a recording. And then we come up with a song called "A-95," which was originally "I-95," which is your green card number that you have. And what we did with that particular tune, is we . . . took the inscription within the Statue of Liberty: "Send us your tired, your poor, your huddled masses," and we just turned it around. And we also fit it with the El Salvadoreans that are here now—the latest people to get beat on by the economics of this country and the politics of this country, sending the monies down there [and] the refugees, they're coming across, they're coming because they're getting guns that are killing them sent by this country. They're coming to the very country that's killing them, which is the irony of it all. And if it's irony on irony against the sarcastic inscription on there, you know the sarcastic reading of it.

Willie concluded, "It's like the name of the band and what we represent is not a concept. It's a way of life."

Whereas the majority of the group shared early feelings of harshness, bitterness, rejection, embarrassment, inferiority, and displacement, Bill experienced a somewhat different process of enculturation and social indoctrination without feeling that "hardcore displacement": "I really didn't, you know? These guys have shown me the dark side, 'cause after listening to them in the first few months, maybe the first couple of years, they had a lot to say. And I felt like, what did I miss out on? I missed out on something . . . So it's been quite an exchange of ideas, because I didn't go through that . . . I accepted everything; questioned a lot, but accepted."

Bill's parents were economically more stable than the families of Jesse, Willie, and Sandra, "but not by very much, because we're not well off. But . . . they saw to it that I did pursue private school and as good an education as they could provide. . . . It's like, I didn't have to work, but I had this urge to play, to work, and I stuck to the schooling. So when I came in the group, there was this, this whole new, whole new way of looking at it.

And I honestly felt like . . . shouldn't I have gone through that? What did I miss? So, I do a lot of listening, because there's a lot to learn."

All the members attested to the profound influence of language on their musical style during their enculturative childhood years. As Jesse put it, "had we not had a second language to deal with, or at least a larger influence of it in our lives, we'd probably be playing pop songs somewhere— brown faces playing pop songs, you know, with nothing but the content to sing about."

Modes of creativity and the motivation to succeed and to secure an audience are also factors in the development of musical style. Such specific musical aspects as rhythm, vocal nuances, and harmony often become attractive because they are associated with a particular style, such as rhythm and blues. Willie was influenced by one black artist's iconoclastic vocal style: "I think for me [it] was James Brown. I mean, he, to me, had the urgency, he had the passion . . . I heard just in his voice. I mean, and the *gritos* [screams], I really related to that, that *grito* he had, that [a scream in the background], he just made it; I mean, personally, that's how I really started and got into the R&B, was when I was first exposed [to] or around the James Brown sound."

Jesse singled out the concept of rhythm that particularly influenced him: "Not only that. A lot of the *Mexicanos* and Latinos, I guess, that are second-generation types, like we are, can identify with some of the primal rhythms that are involved in R&B music. You know, it's not real glitzy and sweet harmony. It's not like the Smothers Brothers are hanging their head down Tom Dooley. It grooves. We have that in us."

Jesse emphasizes the musical aspects of musical identity, which perhaps preempted the notions of political consciousness or of relating to the blacks economically.

This had nothing to do with brains—it was pure gut feeling. And for that reason alone we identified with it. We couldn't identify with some of the syntax, the way they spoke. It wasn't fitting with our type of syntax, you know, the Chicano's sort of slang that we use that is our hip, cool-type slang, a la go-go, whatever you want to call it. So we related on the primal rhythms of it, the urgencies of it, and some of the ballads were just so pretty, and we had nobody to identify with on that level anyway. Beach Boys to a degree, maybe 20 percent you'd like some of the sweet harmonies and some of the ideas of going to the drive-in; nothing else. And there just wasn't enough people out there that were Hispanic doing that kind of thing. So what do we do? Those of us that were used to assimilating into the culture assimilated and became the little brown guys throwing splits, acting like James

Brown. You still have it today. You have [Chicano] groups that get gold records doing stuff that black guys think are [blacks].

The urban, cosmopolitan personality of Los Angeles has given the Chicano musician more stylistic choices, so that the "primal rhythmic thing" that Jesse identified has been transformed from, for example, the *son jalisciense* to a conga drum, a trap set, an electric Jimi Hendrix guitar riff, or a James Brown *grito* within a particular urban ambience. According to Jesse:

> We're forced to live together through economic survival. Growing up in the projects, Willie and I have grown up in separate projects . . . where all the kids are out together. And there's blacks; a few whites; predominantly Chicano out there. And that just fused. And the music bouncing off the walls—everything from Marvin Gaye to Los Camperos, and everything . . . it just forced it to be what it is. And besides, L.A. is nothing but, it's like a big bowl of *menudo*[18] with everything else in it. So we have no choice but to just absorb each other's rhythms and patterns, if you will. . . .
>
> We're attracted to the "angst" in there, too . . . the availability of expressing yourself through urban anger. Just really letting it out, and being real expressive with it. And Willie has written a great deal of things in that particular mode, and we usually call Bill to give us some kind of a cue that is just so, like a strike of some sort here and there, instead of having a nice little drum fill. It's [imitating the sound]—something really sharp and angst and something that a lot of the kids will identify with.

Willie received minimal social reinforcement and minimal support from the network that provides work opportunities in music.

> For me it's been really difficult. I've had a lot of negativity from a lot of Anglos throughout most of my life where it comes to doing anything artistic or anything creative. My family's been the type that has never seen that as being anything profitable or anything with a very solid foundation. Not like a real technical kind of a trade, even though it really is . . . and it's something that sometimes you don't get a real immediate response. Sometimes, you know, some projects take really years and a lot of projects that I've been working on for a long time still haven't happened. . . . Lately it seems like . . . we've gotten a lot of support. And . . . it's like a full, two-drawer filing cabinet filled up with publications from throughout the United States, from Mexico, and from Europe. I mean publication after publication. They're interested in the band and exactly what the band is saying and that we're really saying something that may not be altogether

different, in a sense; but I think just that we're taking our stand and we're expressing something that is real rather than a gimmick. And so to a lot of the media, they find that very interesting, because we have our whole life to express, whether it was influenced through music or whether it was just mere experience . . . walking out the street and just, you know, seeing your brother laying in the alley, he was jumped by a rival gang, or something. I mean a lot of it has to do with the fact that it plays off the negative and it plays off the positive stereotypes. I mean, we have to realize lots of times, at least I do, that a lot of things that do happen that are newsworthy really fill the stereotypical image that a lot of people have of Hispanics or Latinos or Mexican Americans, especially in East Los Angeles. And so in that sense it almost works out in reverse; what turns out to be something negative about something is reevaluated, and it's turned into very positive energy through our music. It becomes not only entertaining, but very educational on the same level, and we're really fortunate to be able to express that.

So, a lot of the support has come by way of transferring over from negativity to positive energy through a lot of the stuff that we've read about ourselves . . . the way people in media, basically, see the band. But then, we've done lots of gigs where we were really surprised by the response from other people other than our own race. Even though, I mean all our ideas and everything, the way we've grown up . . . have come from our cultural experience. And so, there's been a lot of positive from that. I mean, we don't sell a lot of records, but I think it's something that will [happen], as the band continues and matures. I think we're very conscious of being very, very international. I think we've always had some sort of grasp, all of us, in our own upbringing and our own lifestyle, individually, and I think our music will always reflect that. I just think it's going to take time for us to create our own road, or 'til something just really turns over and we just have a niche in there. But I think as long as the group remains a unit, a strong group, the way we're starting off in the past three or four years, I think we'll be around a long time . . . and that's what's going to make us a great band . . . is longevity.

According to Jesse the group can actually gain leverage from the lack of reinforcement from the Los Angeles professional network and the music industry at large:

Using the negative to turn it into something positive has been something the band has always been able to use as leverage. An example is getting into the nightclub circuit, not just the local eastside circuit, but the Hollywood circuit that just about anyone can get in now. At one point we couldn't get in there just because of our name, and this was before a lot of the other groups came on that were Hispanics that were doing it. So you do your alternatives base. You get enough publicity generated from your own alternatives base. Good, positive publicity so that they really [generate] a following, and what works in this country of course is the dollar, like in anywhere else, [which] means that if we're gonna have a large draw and we play Joe Blow's club in West Hollywood, he's gonna make that much money. That's a negative thing that's being turned positive by the fact that, OK now, what I'm trying to say is that, because the papers let them know that there wasn't a chance for us to get in there, and because they were giving good reviews, and they also said how many, approximately so many hundred kids went to this particular date that they put on . . . let them realize what was happening. And because they said that we were underdogs, which we are and still continue to be as we continue to increase our role into an international level, we can leverage it and turn it over. That negativity [means] this band will probably never get its deals written in the *Calendar,* means that A&R people are starting to come about and say, "Oh really? And why?" And then they come out and check it out. So it's like, use it as leverage. Negative becomes positive, whether we like it or not . . . also, some people will call our music "bastardized music"—you know, "that's not Chicano music." Then you take it someplace else . . . "That's not rock and roll." You're just back in that whole bit. But the point is, they all remember it and they all are interested in it. Especially, once again, the European market, because to them, it's like it's new.

The members of the group received different kinds of musical training during their formative years. Bill had some early formal training:

I had a private teacher from age seven until age twelve. And then when I entered high school, I was taken under the wing of the music director, and it enhanced that knowledge that I had absolutely no experience, no training in Latin percussion. That was thrown on me when I joined a band at sixteen . . . we played nothing but Santana. And what that did was make me rely instantly on rhythms I had heard as a child, and I applied them. You know, I just had a set of timbales and bongos thrown at me . . . "Play these rhythms." It turned out, when I left that band I bought that same pair of timbales and they're here in the room and I'm continuing. But I don't have any training in that. I only know what I hear on the radio.

The band to which Bill referred was called Maceva, led by the Batista brothers. Robert Varela played timbales. When the *timbalero* was unable to perform at one of the group's gigs, Bill was told to play his part and hence began playing timbales. He went on to play with numerous groups on the east side of Los Angeles.

Willie had no formal musical training. He began to experiment by ear on the keyboards when he purchased his first Farfisa portable organ in 1964 at Cronen's Music Center in Montebello. He still plays by ear and did not actually start composing his own material until the mid-1970s. Sandra still uses no particular system of notation or of chord recognition. She would often mimic the conductor of the orchestra, directing the music of records with a small stick as a baton.

> My parents didn't believe that I should play music, or even waste my time in music, because I was supposed to get married and have children. So what I did was at the age of seventeen I bought a piano. It was all out of tune, and a couple of keys missing . . . for seventy dollars, and I started to play with it, just tinker with it. And then I bought myself a little Casio that was supposedly for me; it was like the big thing. And I just started playing with friends. I had no training whatsoever in music. So what I know now is just from playing with friends and experimenting with music.

As a female musician, Sandra often felt that she was perceived as a marginal component in a predominantly male musician's network. Her intense drive to perform, however, motivated her to learn keyboards and to gain acceptance among other musicians.

Sandra does use a few charts that display fingering positions "because I want to be progressive in a certain sound that I can't get just by majors or minors, but that's about it." Willie also consciously seeks innovation in his playing:

> So, I may think of maybe a bass pattern to go up the scale, and then I'll think of somebody else's part going down; and some of the notes meeting, and ending up harmonics, as they're moving and doing cross rhythms; things like that. But it's all been experimental—and like I said earlier—most of my formal training has been in art, and developing my creative abilities. And I think, in that sense, I can apply that directly to music. . . .
>
> I kind of see sounds and chords like I see colors. . . . So I think of songs in a very visual form . . . probably first. And then it's like, what would sound nice while that's happening.

The intriguing idea of music structure preceived in terms of visual concepts, layers, and colors coupled with a lack of formal training also provided Jesse with a conscious basis for innovation:

> The benefit of not having any formal training is that you tend to experiment out of habit. And you tend to come up with some great stuff. I had no formal training. I play bass guitar because the guitar that I learned off had some strings missing. Somebody gave it to me. That's not all. I'm also a left-handed person. I play right-handed 'cause I had no training. But because of it I'm able to just make up junk, food junk, otherwise I'd be in some jazz-fusion band playing the Baked Potato and I'd probably go out to pasture playing great licks, but I wouldn't be reaching a lot of people.

Informal training also affected Bill's playing: "The same thing. I play timbales backwards, bongos backwards, congas, everything. . . . I'm right-handed, but I don't play traditional because the guy that I saw, the guy that I learned from played that way. I had no choice. That's just the way he wanted to do it. [That was] Robert Varela."

The experiences of Los Illegals with the recording industry demonstrate how difficult it has been to define the market and develop effective marketing techniques for Chicano music.

> *Jesse:* The experience that we've had is the experience that they've had, and it's none. You're dealing with a giant megabillion-dollar industry, and a major label worldwide—[an] international label. Japan, Europe, *Mexicanos,* Latinos, Canadians, all involved in this particular label, with no experience on what to do with the type of group that we are. And we are, in essence, their guinea pig, and their tool to study. They have no background to search it. They can't go back to the sixties, you know, what Cannibal and the Headhunters did. And they can't go to the Santana thing, because it's not really the particular type of stuff we're doing. It's socioeconomical. It's political. It's not pop enough to be, really, like you know, [the] cute little kind of stuff that you can play on the radios easily. They're really shocked when they find that a good deal of our airplay is coming from Moscow, Idaho, and less of it in Los Angeles, which is a bigger Hispanic market. Then they're really pleased when we show them letters that are coming in from . . . there's this one sixteen-year-old kid in the projects in Arizona who's saying, "This particular song has really made me turn around." And what it is at this point, what we've learned, is that they don't know what to do with it. They don't know

enough about it, and we're teaching them. And that's more weight on our shoulders. We have to sit down sometimes with a representative of their artists' relations person, who is like the liaison between us and the company . . . and explain what it means, what's happening in Albuquerque and how it differs from what's happening in San Francisco, and the type of Hispanic population that's there . . . what they're into. The lowriders aren't going to obviously jump on one of our songs 'cause it doesn't sound like a lowrider song. But some of the college-educated kids in Nueva York will. And it's an education process for both of us, and it makes it twice as hard for the particular group; because not only we got to do our own business, we got to do our own writing and we have to educate the company, and tell them what kind of funds we need to back certain things up along the way. They need to know we're in town, and it's like, "Well, do we ask, do we advertise in the local *Mexicano* stations?" No, you got to go to second-generation types and let them know that it's in town. And you also have to, on the other side, go to the Caucasian college community. There in Austin, Texas, you don't just go to the Chicano side. You go to the university kids, too, and you have a smattering of the audiences like that. And this is stuff that we've had to teach them. And it's been really hard on all of us, because we've had to do twice the work.

Willie: We'll probably be doing our second LP on A&M, probably by the end of the year [1984]; if not, in January, the beginning of the year. But during the process of being in and out of the studio with our second LP, doing demos and trying out some European producers, we stumbled across some ideas of Mr. Quintana, who heads the Latin distribution section of A&M, he offered us [the opportunity] to do an album first for Latin America in Spanish. He was interested in some of our new material for our second LP. He had also offered us a package before we released *Internal Exile*. We told him at [that] time we felt that *Internal Exile* had to become our first, and then we would reconsider possibly doing a second LP specifically for the Latin American market, and not like *Internal Exile* . . . that kind of [LP] was just aimed at the U.S. market basically. And so, right now we're in the process of putting together some demo tapes, because we're not too sure if it's really going to work. José Quintana seems very, very positive about it. I mean, we have positive overtones, but we still have the underlying doubt that it still might not be the right time for the band to . . . try something that would cross over, so to speak. So, that's kind of where we're at. We're gonna try some tracks with Mr. Quintana, and if it works out then we will be doing our second LP specifically for a Latin American release, and not a U.S. release. That'll probably be our third album.

The second album will therefore be recorded in Spanish and, as Jesse emphasized,

> marketed that way also, with the knowledgeable people marketing it for Latins, as opposed to letting the regular A&M [people] handle it . . . A&M America—let's call it that. This'll get some of the real inherent, and the older *Mexicano* feelings and Latino feelings out of us. Through *baladas,* through actually sitting down and saying, "This is really another side that's been in there and embedded for so long." It's not going to be like real harsh—you know, "A-95," you know, "We Don't Need a Tan"—Los Illegals. But it's also going to be another part of us in here, in the *corazón.* We also anticipate doing, next year, another English release. So, we've got a lot of projects.

Since the interview that I conducted with Los Illegals in 1984, the group has basically disbanded, although Willie Herrón has organized various members for occasional performances. The group's second album was never released.

Example of Musical Style

The song "El Lay" by Los Illegals constitutes a structurally sophisticated and thematically progressive symbolic musical vehicle. Molded in a heterogeneous musical style incorporating nuances from punk and hard rock, reggae, Latin, and the Spanish language, the song reflects the urban diversity of Los Angeles and the "angst" referred to by Jesse Velo. Added to this cultural ambience is some explosive, highly urbanized political thought directed toward the exploited urban immigrant: the undocumented worker, or the illegal alien; the song's title, "El Lay," refers both to Los Angeles and to the slang expression for sexual intercourse, "a lay." Hopelessness and exploitation are thus conveyed through a metaphor that connotes an often casual, sometimes demeaning sexual lifestyle characterized by faceless, noncommittal sexual activity and promiscuity. The song describes the illegal alien's arrival in, employment in, and deportation from Los Angeles—to the song's authors, nothing more than "a lay."

"El Lay (L.A.)"

Verse 1:

Parado en la esquina	Standing on the corner,
Sin rumbo sin fin	Got nowhere to go,

Estoy en El Lay
No tengo donde ir
Un hombre se acercó
Mi nombre preguntó
Al no saber su lengua
Con el me llevó

I'm here in El Lay,
Got no place to stay
A man came up to me
And he asked me my name
Couldn't speak his language
So he took me away.

Refrain (Bridge):

¿Este es el precio
Que pagamos
Cuando llegamos
A este lado?
Jalamos y pagamos impuestos
Migra llega y nos da unos
  fregasos.

Is this the price
You have to pay
When you come
To the U.S.A.?
We came to work, we pay our taxes
Migra comes and they kick us on
  our asses

Chorus:

El Lay, L.A.
El Lay, L.A.
El Lay, L.A.
El Lay, L.A.

El Lay, L.A.
El Lay, L.A.
El Lay, L.A.
El Lay, L.A.

Verse 2:

En un camión
Sin vuelta me pusieron
Por lavar platos
En El Lay me deportaban
Mirar por el cristal,
Sentí pertenecer
Un millón illegales
No podemos fallar

He threw me on the bus,
That headed one way
I was being deported
For washing dishes in El Lay.
Looking out the window,
I felt that I belonged
A million illegals,
Can't all be wrong.

Refrain

Chorus

Verse 3:

Manos fijadas,
Al fin en la frontera
Le dije que quería,
Mejorar la vida
Familia sin futuro,

We ended at the border,
Hands above my head
I told him all I wanted,
Was a chance to get ahead
No future for my family

Falta de respeto   Can't even get respect
A donde fue   What happened to the liberty,
La libertad y la justicia?   And the justice that we get?

Refrain

Chorus

Musically, the piece is constructed on a framework of various rhythmic motives and a certain inflection of vocal/harmonic dissonance. The initial, principal motive is based on a tritone, and the combined reflexive emotions of tension, pathos, and rhythmic intensity are immediately personified by the ensemble, orchestrated with two electric guitars, synthesizer, drums (with assorted attachments, e.g., timbales), electric bass, and lead and chorus vocals. Example 9 shows the principal motive.

The motive is a unifying theme throughout the composition. In addition to its use as an initial, solo-structured "cry" at the first measure of the song, the motive occurs after each chorus section and as a reintroduction to the verse structure (the third verse) after the guitar, percussion, and synthesizer interludes end. The verse sections are sung over a two-measure chordal vamp—one measure the minor tonic and the other the diminished tonic—through an intensified, heavy rock beat.

The melodic contour of the text conforms symmetrically to the rhythmic and harmonic foundation, and the minor/diminished tonality reinforces the tense, textually thematic development, climaxing each verse with a bridge section based on the same refrain text after each of the three verses. Supporting the refrain bridge sections is a series of rhythmic breaks (see example 10).

In this refrain section, the vocal melody is a hybrid of sung voice and narration, structured on a monotonal melodic contour and variating no more than a whole tone in measured pitch.

The chorus sections following each refrain chant the words "El Lay" in a responsorial manner (literally a call and response pattern, the rhetorical questions posed in the refrain answered subtly yet agitatingly with "El Lay"). Underscoring and supporting the chorus sections is the rhythmic/harmonic framework shown in example 11.

The texture of "El Lay" is one of unifying forms. The timbre, for example, is characteristic of an organically interwoven ensemble of electronic instrumentation. The text, conceived through jagged contours of metaphor, satire, and symbolic contradiction, unites itself stylistically with the dissonant harmonic framework and the abrasive, hard-driving rhythmic structure. Vocal tone and pitch are produced with a diversity of rhyth-

Example 9

Principal motive:

Example 10

Example 11

mic/syllabic effect yet always conform to unifying rhythmic patterns and an aesthetically balanced order of transitions and variations, that is, the structurally different qualities of the verse, bridge, and chorus sections.

Los Lobos: Just Another Band from East L.A.

More than any of the other case studies analyzed here, Los Lobos reflect the musical diversity and processes of change, maintenance, and adaptation among the Mexican/Chicano peoples of Los Angeles. After ten years (1973 to 1983) of performing throughout the Los Angeles area and various parts of the Chicano Southwest, the group has attained international acclaim as a Mexican-style rock and roll band. Since their first album (*Just Another Band from East L.A.*, independently recorded and released in 1978 and produced by Luis Torres and David Sandoval), which consists exclusively of Mexican and other Latin American folk musical forms, they have entered the world of popular, mainsteam music, capturing considerable radio airtime in the process. Los Lobos recorded six more albums in 1983 (*And a Time to Dance*), 1985 (*How Will the Wolf Survive?*), 1987 (*By the Light of the Moon*), 1988 (*La pistola y el corazón*), 1990 (*The Neighborhood*), and 1992 (*Kiko*), all released on Slash Records, an affiliate of Warner Brothers Records, and they have toured as a headliner throughout Europe, the United States, Asia, Canada, and Australia. They have also toured with the groups U2 and The Grateful Dead. In 1984 Los Lobos received the internationally prestigious Grammy Award in the newly formed Mexican-

American category of recording artists. The Grammy was awarded for "Anselma," a *norteño*-styled song on the group's *And a Time to Dance* album. In 1987, the group collaborated on the major portion of the commercial soundtrack of the highly successful film *La Bamba*, based on the life of Ritchie Valens and written and directed by Luis Valdez. The title track, "La Bamba" (originally a Valens hit in 1959), was recorded by Los Lobos and in 1987 achieved the number one spot on the national charts in twenty-seven countries. In the United States it held that spot for three weeks and earned a double platinum record for selling over two million copies. It was also nominated for the Grammy Awards' Song of the Year category. (The band was also nominated for Best Rock Performance for "By the Light of the Moon.") Eight of the movie soundtrack's twelve recorded songs were performed by Los Lobos; the other four were recorded by Bo Diddley, Brian Setzer, Marshall Crenshaw, and Howard Huntsberry. In 1990 Los Lobos were voted by members of the National Academy of Recording Arts and Sciences to receive another Grammy Award for their 1989 album *La pistola y el corazón,* recorded completely in Spanish and largely comprising traditional Mexican folk songs.

Los Lobos consist of four young Chicanos: Louie Pérez, César Rosas, Conrad Lozano, and David Hidalgo. All born and enculturated within the confines of East Los Angeles, the four ranged in age from thirty to thirty-two years in 1984, when they were interviewed for this study. Louie and Conrad come from the same neighborhood, which is separated by a freeway from the barrio of César and David. After graduating from Garfield High School, where they met, they decided to form Los Lobos del Este de Los Angeles, the original, complete name of the group.

Louie Pérez plays trap set in addition to an array of string instruments including guitar, *jarana,* [19] and *requinto.* [20] "I've been with the band since 1974 (as with all of the members, since the formation of the group). I contribute to the composing and arranging [of] a lot of the songs." Louie's mother is originally from Wyoming, and his father is from Las Cruces, New Mexico. Both his parents moved to Los Angeles around 1926. Louie's father fought in the U.S. armed forces during World War II, and his mother worked for a number of years as a seamstress in downtown Los Angeles.

English was the primary language in Louie's household. His parents conversed with each other in English. Louie learned a substantial amount of Spanish as a child, however, in order to communicate with his grandmother, who lived with them.

Some of the earliest music he heard was what his sister listened to on the radio and on records, which differed from what his parents liked. "You listen to what's on the radio and what your parents are listening to . . . it was like two different worlds." Louie had no formal training nor any involvement with his high school band. "My mother bought me a guitar because I was interested in playing it. She got me a cheap guitar when I was about thirteen. I just kind of fooled around with it . . . bought records and tried to make sounds."

Louie first became involved with Mexican and Latin American folk music after he finished high school, in the early 1970s: "It was a collective kind of experience that we had. We all started to go toward listening to something that was a lot different. So what happened was that we all went back to our houses, to our mother's records, looking into all that stuff."

César's mother came from Guadalajara, Jalisco, and his father from La Purísima, Baja California. César was born in Hermosillo, Sonora, and the family emigrated to the United States in 1962. "I was raised around the Boyle Heights area—all parts of East L.A., and here I am. I play guitar, *bajo sexto,* [21] and do a little bit of writing for Los Lobos, my *camaradas.*"

In César's household, his family spoke exclusively Spanish. His early musical enculturation was a combination of *ranchera,* country, popular, and black music:

> My mother listened to all the *ranchera* singers like Lola Beltrán, Amalia Mendoza, and she watched the country and western shows on television that used to be on channel 13 and channel 9, Melody Ranch and The Ernest Tubb show. She would always have country music on radio, too. My sister, who was older than I, was listening to the current hits on the radio. I could remember as far back as when she brought home the single of Ray Charles's "Hit the Road, Jack." That was about the first time I ever saw a record.

César's first musical exposure was to the music his parents listened to, which included Miguel Aceves Mejía, Trío Tariácuri, and mariachi music. Because his mother was from the state of Jalisco, where the mariachi originated, mariachi music assumed a dominant presence in their household.

In 1962 César became interested in the popular music being disseminated through radio and other media:

> In 1962, I was about eight years old. It was the first time I saw an Elvis Presley movie. That's when I wanted to play guitar. It was a couple of years before The Beatles came to America; then I kind of picked up the guitar. . . .
>
> Actually, my older brother used to play guitar. He used to play Mexican music all the time and he was pretty good. I wanted to play guitar because I used to watch him. When he'd take off, I'd get his guitar. He used to tell me, "Don't touch the guitar or I'll break your neck," but I did anyway. . . .

I was self-taught. I didn't start getting serious about playing until I was in high school, really, which is kind of a little bit late. I learned at a local teen post. There was a music teacher there. They were offering guitar lessons, so I used to go down there like every Monday and Tuesday afternoon and take the guitar lessons, and once I could play a couple of chords, I'd buy some sheet music and stuff and play Beatle tunes . . . and a lot of soul music—Sam and Dave, and all the stax/volt stuff that was happening . . . Aretha Franklin. Later on I got a group together, a pretty big size group, and we had about five or six horns, keyboard, and all that stuff.

That particular group specialized mostly in the current rhythm and blues music of the period, particularly Tower of Power and James Brown. The top-forty band performed throughout the eastside club circuit. César was attracted to the soul and rhythm and blues music of the time "because it was cool. . . . The bass lines were great . . . harmonies, the whole thing." César did not attribute his affinity for black music to social or economic relevance. "I just liked it because I liked it. There was no barriers. I knew they were black."

At the same time, César was also listening to rock, especially English bands like The Rolling Stones, The Beatles, and The Animals. Jazz never had a great influence on him. As for salsa music, César remarked, "We got into that later a little bit. . . . Yeah, I do love it for what it is. I have all of Celia Cruz's albums . . . Pacheco . . . I'm aware of all that stuff. I love it."

Conrad Lozano plays electric bass, *guitarrón,* [22] and lead and background vocals for Los Lobos. "I'm the the bass player for the Lobos and I've done a lot of things in East Los Angeles. I've done community work. I've done things in the barrio. My pop was born in Santa Ana and my mom was from El Paso."

Conrad's parents did not listen specifically to Mexican music: "My parents were more into the 1940s stuff—big band stuff. I was just kind of in there and in-between; then I got into the music I liked." He and friends wanted to play music influenced by that of The Beatles and The Rolling Stones. In addition, one of his cousins was an aficionado of the music of Johnny Cash, which provided another dimension to the musical ambience of the Lozano home life.

Conrad's mother and father rarely spoke Spanish in the home, although they were bilingual. Conrad did recall that his parents sometimes used Spanish during anxious moments. "Whenever they'd get mad at me, they'd tell me something in Spanish and I would never understand." When Los Lobos began to sing traditional Mexican music in Spanish, Conrad recalled, "I just fell into it. It was something new to get into; it was something like brand new . . . something different."

David Hidalgo plays accordion, guitars, *jarana, requinto,* violin, steel guitar, *charango,*[23] and mandolin and also sings lead vocals with the group:

> Both my parents are from Arizona. My mom is from Gila Bend and her grandfather is from Sweden and my grandmother is from Sinaloa. On my pop's side, they're from Arizona and I'm not sure where before that. I know my father's folks were from Arizona also. Before that I don't know what happened. But anyway, I was born in Los Angeles, and I listened to everything else that every other kid did. It was The Beatles and The Stones that made me want to play guitar, and I took it up and I flew my folk's records. [The music my parents listened to was] probably *rancheras* and big band stuff. . . . I didn't have time for it; so I flew it. I regret it now because I like all that stuff. After a while you realize what's real and what lasts, so I went through the whole rock and roll trip and in about '73 this band came together. We started playing Mexican music—*Mexicano* music. It was just out of a need to do something different.

In the same way that César's development reflected the juxtaposition of different musical styles through radio and records, David was also influenced by everything that came through the media. "It's the same thing. All of us, like anybody . . . I heard all this stuff all around, I heard from the parents and from the parties. You heard *Mexicano* music, but at the same time I also heard Louie Prima, I heard Ink Spots, Louis Jordan, Joe Liggins, and I also heard on the radio The Beatles and The Stones, and the Motown thing was booming. I heard all kinds of stuff and it just all soaked in and I picked out what I liked. No matter what it was, it didn't matter."

Spanish was David's second language: "This band is where I started trying to learn how to speak Spanish. . . . English was spoken at home and I never learned it [Spanish]. When this band got together, we started learning folk music and I started getting interested, and I started learning myself because I wanted to."

At one point, all four members of Los Lobos ventured to Mexico to experience the country's regional cultures and music. They traveled as far as Veracruz, absorbing ideas, learning music, purchasing instruments, and generally enjoying the journey. They went to learn about their culture, the source of much of the music that they were re-creating and reinterpreting.

Being Mexican only occasionally created feelings of inferiority or displacement. Conrad's comments are exemplary: "I think being Mexican is a very strong thing for us; but I mean [not] being inferior—nothing like that. . . . Those things happen during junior high school. Those things happen there, but you grow up and you learn a little bit more. We were always proud . . . very proud. It was good. It was a very interesting thing. . . . We don't forget that . . . can't forget that."

All four members of the group had substantial exposure to gang culture during their youth because it was part of the fabric of their community. According to Louie, "The fact [was] we just lived where there was gang-related stuff all over. But somehow we made it and just kind of bypassed all of that and continued to develop ourselves . . . just music kind of kept us in line." César also remembered being exposed to gang culture without being completely involved with it. "We had a taste of all that stuff growing up. You can't help but do that. Two out of five of your buddies, man, were from the neighborhood barrio . . . you know, *ganga*, whatever. And so you kind of follow that a little bit. And after a while, you get your head beat in and stuff and you figure that maybe that's not for you; and because we had a love for music, we figure that either way . . . you grow out of it, man."

Mexican music was not only one step removed from their own experience, but it was also an anomaly in the East Los Angeles rock music scene at the time.

> *César:* We were involved in Mexican music . . . I'm saying that we're just a bunch of Mexicans that grew up in East L.A. It was 1973, and we started playing Mexican music because we felt that it was a good thing to do. We were the first East L.A. band—a group of East L.A. kids who embraced traditional music because we felt that it was something that was really important to do . . . important for all our peers, important to our culture, important to our community, and to awaken a lot of people and say, "Look, Mexican music is a beautiful thing and you shouldn't be ashamed of it."

The music of Los Lobos was at first related to the political symbolism of the Chicano movement, but later it took on a meaning of its own. Conrad commented, "The Chicano movement started it; but then the Chicano movement died, and we didn't." César expanded on the topic: "And when people put down their flags, we didn't carry the flag, we just carried the guitars." Conrad attributed the group's endurance to its dedication and the members' faith in each other. "We loved what we were doing. We are still together—the same dudes right here. We are still doing it." Louie added, "The artistic kind of thing that really turned us on was the music . . . music of our own culture. That's why we pursued it for so many years." David recalled the early trials and tribulations:

> The thing was . . . after we broke the ice and people decided that they could accept what we were doing, everybody was longing for what we were doing. Everybody had that need in them that hadn't been fulfilled or something. But we were playing this music that people said, "Oh yeah, that's what I grew up with," and so it started to click.

Like the first gig we played in Florence at the American Legion—
it was a *tamalada* and we only knew about five songs, and we kept
playing them over and over again. That was the first time that we
played somewhere where there was old folks, there was kids dancing,
there was teenagers, everybody was partying together. Before that it
was mostly for whatever crowd you were playing for. But we got all
these folks up and everybody was dancing. It was like "What is this?"
I never had that feeling before.

This new feeling made the experience important for the group. "We
were just doing it for the fun of it because we wanted to do it; but when
we saw the effect . . . we had on the people, we started getting a little bit
more into it and we started developing it."

The ethnic composition of their audience has diversified through the
years.

David: The people that were mostly interested in it were Chicano/
Mexicanos. Why? Because we played in our neighborhoods. See,
there's a lot of other people, white people, that enhanced this music
too. A lot of people started getting hip on this music after a while
too. Then you have all these college professors and all these people
of other backgrounds. What it is, is that they accepted it as an art
form. And these people, educated people who know something, or
can at least get beyond all the BS that's fed to them on TV and on
the radio, they start figuring, "Hey man, there's something going on
over there." They just go for the feeling. There's people that go from
the heart. That's where we come across to a lot of folks because they
don't speak our language, or Spanish, and a lot of times we throw a
lot of BS that they don't understand . . . but it's just [that] the heart
comes through and that's why all the stuff has been coming around.
Just like Arhoolie Records up in Berkeley. This white cat—but he's
sensitive to different styles of music—he's been taping . . . he's been
down in Louisiana for about thirty years. People are now saying, "Oh
yeah, there's Cajun music?" And he's trying to bring Mexican music
around too; because it's part of this one culture here in the United
States.

Los Lobos did not use the business networks within the Chicano subculture and among local promoters. In César's words, "When we played
Mexican music we were on our own—totally on our own. . . . We were
all away from Eddie Torres, from [Joe] Sandoval [East Los Angeles pro-
moters]—all those people." Los Lobos, in effect, presented themselves to
the Chicano community mostly through their own promotional efforts and

handled their own business negotiations. César continued, "This is very important. . . . When we played rock music and we decided to convert, if you will, to play this Mexican folk music, we were all by ourselves. We weren't playing the top-forty and swinging clubs anymore, predisco clubs. We were playing colleges, we were playing junior high schools, high schools, and it was just the word of mouth. People would call us to do gigs. So it was kind of like we were on our own."

Los Lobos presented a style that ranged from Latin American folk genres to modern rock and roll; that used instruments such as *guitarrón, vihuela, jarana,* and *charango;* and that represented a marginal musical culture and community—the Chicano community. Such eclecticism was not a standard formula for success.

> *David:* We believe in everything we've done so far. We were playing the folk music and we believed that it would take us somewhere else. It was always like an art to us. We always felt that it wasn't for the cantina, it wasn't for the barroom. This is beautiful music. This is our culture. We wanted to take it out and we wanted some people to hear it and check it out and enjoy it. Eventually, we ended up playing at a restaurant for two and a half years and getting tired of being a juke box; we just started jiving around, and around that time is when we got the accordion. The accordion wasn't planned. A friend of mine gave it to me, so I started picking it up. I brought it to the band, so César got a *bajo sexto,* Louie started playing the snare drum, and Conrad brought his electric bass. So from that point, it kind of led us into, "Well, we got an electric bass. How about an electric guitar? Pull it out again." So we started just jiving with that. And that felt good. And it started developing into something else. And at the same time that that was happening there was all this new music thing happening on the other side of town, over in Hollywood; well, all over the world, really. It was like punk, everything was going on, just breaking down barriers where everything was all jacked up. You couldn't get anywhere. All of a sudden people were ready for something new, so we felt what we were doing—we were starting to incorporate the electric instruments into our old music. We felt we had a place in there too. So we started pursuing it and that's how we ended up on that side of town [the west side]. We're just adventurous. It just happened.

> *Louie:* We've always been moved from the inside . . . our artistic progression. It always took us from playing backyard parties to playing Mexican folk music to be playing the music that we're doing now. We started off as radicals playing Mexican music before any other young people did. We bridged the generation gap . . . like Dave said,

all kinds of different-age people. So what we're doing now is because of the music that we've developed—that incorporates the Tex-Mex stuff and a lot of different traditional American styles. Again, we're causing another wave because it's something that no one else has done either.

The group's wide acceptance in Europe reflects the fact that, in Louie's words, "Europe has always supported American music . . . more so than what this country has in the past ten years. Because of what radio dictates over here . . . there's more commercialism. In Europe there's more flexibility. There's a little bit more of a cultural unity as far as the arts, and they're more sensitive to those things. And they like American music all the way from Elvis to what the bands are putting out."

The popularity of Flaco Jiménez in Europe is a good example. In David's opinion, "He's doing real good. Everybody knows about him. Everybody knows about Tex-Mex music . . . everybody over there is hip to it. They're ready. . . . Over here, everybody is waiting for the new thing to come from Europe."

The group has reacted with some caution to its recent phenomenal success. Conrad reflected that "We're still working at it. We're still laying the groundwork—all of us. We're not big stars." César added, "We just happen to get a little attention and it's working well and we're working at it, and that's about it."

Recalling that at particular periods throughout the last ten years he and his family "had to eat bologna sandwiches for breakfast, lunch, and dinner," Louie perceives both the contradictions and ideals of the "crazy, impossible dream":

> In some way you're telling yourself that, "Well, it's silly that some Mexican folk songs are going to be a number one on the *Billboard* chart." I understand there are certain limitations, but we always felt that we could elevate whatever we were doing at the time to a more visible position and it was through our own feelings that brought us to that music . . . and [to what] we are doing now. That whole artistic kind of progression that seemed to work in the past, that led our hearts to start doing what we are doing now. Fortunately, people find the honesty and sincerity in it and it's brought us this far, and it's just another level that we're at now that we have to pursue . . . and see it through.

Their families have been an important source of reinforcement and support for Los Lobos throughout their careers. Louie described it thus: "For our families, it's the only thing they ever knew. I think they all knew what they were getting into, and I think our families have always sensed a certain chemistry with this band—the same thing felt in us that brought us together. I think they find something real special in this too."

All four members are married and have children. Conrad explained the situation: "Our folks have been behind us all the way. Our folks have been behind us since we've been kids. But it's like we got new lives now. We have wives, we have children. It's a whole different thing. Our folks already understand where we've been through, what we're going through. It's the wives, and it's brand new to them. The kids are learning the new things."

Louie is aware of a particular spiritual adhesion that has bonded the four individuals together through so many years. "Now it seems like people are paying attention to what we're doing. And other people, aside from the people in our community and our families, are beginning to see that uniqueness, that something special that has kept us going. So it's something that we can't put aside. We got to see it through, whatever it is."

The group has moved from an originally risky position of promoter of traditional music in a nontraditional setting—mass media—to its current role of definer of a new style in those media.

> *David:* Our first album [on] Slash Records. . . they didn't know what to do with it. They figured we had something going, but they didn't know what to do with it. They put it out, people accepted it. So now they have more respect for us, so it's just like a step up. And we produce some good music. They are behind us. They want us to do well. We want to do well. . . .
>
> We haven't compromised in any way. We've always done what we felt or want to do. And whether it's different or not, I mean that's just it, that's the way it is. We've gotten flack from people here and there, but we've just done what we want to do, and luckily we've gotten where we're at and we'll just take it as far as we can go, that's all.

Examples of Musical Style

The song "Anselma" represents the group's experiment within the last five years of performing authentic *norteño* music along with musical sets of rock and roll. As David Hidalgo pointed out in the interview, the incorporation of the accordion inspired the group to integrate *norteño* musical concepts into some of its rock-based music. An example of this fusion is the song "Let's Say Goodnight" (analyzed below).

The fact that "Anselma," from the *And a Time to Dance* album, won a Grammy Award in 1984 attests to the popularity of the *norteño* and Tex-Mex styles among Mexican Americans throughout the Southwest (and now throughout the United States and Europe). Its inclusion in the album also provides an example of syncretic musical taste, for the other tracks on the record are assorted genres including vintage rock and roll (Ritchie Valens's "C'mon Let's Go"); rockabilly ("How Much Can I Do?"); a border song sung in typical *corrido* style ("Ay te dejo en San Antonio"); current, hard-driving, original rock and roll ("Walking Song," "Why Do You Do?"); and a rock and roll–*norteño* hybrid ("Let's Say Goodnight").

"Anselma," written by Mexicans César Suedan and Guadalupe Trigo, incorporates the style of Tex-Mex music known as *conjunto tejano,* which uses the Hohner accordion, *bajo sexto,* electric bass, and drums. The song employs a common chorus through all three cycles of the verse, bridged by accordion interludes that are replicas of the instrumental introduction (which is also the first statement of the vocal melody).

"Anselma"

Cuando te cases con el
  otro iré a tu boda
Cuando pregunten en seguida
  me opondré,
Y si pregunta el jura que
  porqué me opongo,
Yo le diré que porque tu eres
  mi querer.

If you marry the other man,
  I'll be at your wedding
And if someone should ask me
  I'll say I disapprove
When the judge asks why

I'll say it is because you're
  my true love.

Y si se enoja el que irá ser
  tu esposo,
Saco mi cuete y me pongo a
  disparar
Al fin y al cabo yo no le
  temo a la muerte
Y voy al bote porque soy la
  autoridad.

Now, if your fiancé
  should get angry
I'll take out my gun and
  start shooting up the place
It doesn't matter because I'm
  not afraid of dying
I'll probably go to jail, but
  I don't care because I'm
  the boss.

Chorus:

¡Ay! Anselma, Anselma,
  Anselma
Chaparra de mis pesares,

O, dejas que te visite
O, te mando a los gendarmes?

Oh, Anselma, Anselma, Anselma

My little sweetheart of pain
  and sorrow
Please let me see you
Or do I have to send out the
  police?

Y si te niegas a matrimoniar conmigo	If you refuse to marry me
Les quito el rancho y propiedad de tu papá	I'll take away your father's ranch and property
Les pongo puestos y hasta les quemo la casa	I'll even go as far as to burn your house down
Porque por algo soy aquí la autoridad.	You see, for some reason people listen to me.
Yo ordeno, y mando en todo este municipio	I order and command around this land
Yo te lo digo por si quieres escapar	I'm letting you know in case you're thinking of escaping
Allá en el otro él que manda es mi. tío Elijio	I'm not worried because my uncle runs the next town
No más le digo y te tiene que agarrar.	I'll just let him know and he'll bring you back to me.

Chorus

As the musical transcription of "Anselma" demonstrates, each chorus is preceded by seven measures of accordion embellishment or fill. The accordion part notated on the transcription primarily focuses on the instrument's melodic contour, which it plays in unison with the tenor saxophone, although the accordion player also uses harmonic interpolation and improvisation to support those lead and background melodies. One device not standard in *conjunto* style that Los Lobos incorporate into their version of "Anselma" is the common break at the end of each eight-bar phrase within all the instrumental statements of the main melody, or head. The one and a half beats of abrupt silence add surprise and humor. Because of the break, the unusually fast tempo can maintain its momentum (see example 12).

The saxophone style (Steve Berlin joined in 1983) is another deviation from traditional *conjunto* style. The saxophone plays primarily in unison or in harmony with the accordion, as in the instrumental introduction, verse bridge reiterations of the main melody, and various ensemble riffs (measures 1–8, 24, and 36). Also, the bass player, Lozano, interpolates the basic polka rhythm fluidly, drawing on his experience with other musical genres (R&B, rock and roll, Mexican syncopated forms, and salsa).

Los Lobos' vocal style varies somewhat from typical *conjunto* singing style. In "Anselma" César sings the primary melody while David sings the second part a third above in falsetto, sounding much like a woman's voice, common in *norteño* music.

Example 12

Example 12 (cont.)

Example 12 (cont.)

Example 12 (cont.)

pon - go_a dis - pa - rar   Al fin (y)al ca - bo yo no le

G

simile . . .

simile . . .

simile . . .

te - mo la muer - te   Y voy al   bo - te por - que

D

simile . . .

simile . . .

simile . . .

Accordian Embellishment

soy la au-tor- ri - dad.

G

simile . . .

simile . . .

simile . . .

Example 12 (cont.)

Another example of Los Lobos' musical style is "Let's Say Goodnight," the opening track of the *And a Time to Dance* LP, composed by David Hidalgo and Louie Pérez. Structured according to the sixteen-bar blues harmonic pattern, the arrangement consists of a thematic instrumental section, or head, occupying the sixteen measure I-IV-V progression followed by two sung verses, accordion and saxophone solos, a third verse, and closing with a repetition of the opening theme.

"Let's Say Goodnight" superimposes on a basic rock and roll instrumental texture (electric guitar, electric bass, trap set, and saxophone) the Hohner *conjunto* accordion, commonly used in *norteño* and Tex-Mex styles. In light of the accordion's typical role in traditional formats, including that of Los Lobos, such incorporation constitutes innovative adaptation, both stylistically and functionally. Of particular interest is the orchestration of the opening sixteen measure theme, played in unison by the accordion and lead guitar and embellished with synchronized saxophone riffs. Rhythmic unison breaks bridge the pauses in the main theme executed by the accordion and guitar (see example 13).

The text of the song bears no relation to *norteño* text style; it draws instead on the English rock and roll tradition, alluding in the first verse to a Beatles' tune. There are eight-line stanzas, each conforming to the sixteen-bar blues progression. Of thematic interest is the simple, seemingly hopeless problem expressed in stanza 1 and the changing tone in stanza 2, which conveys a philosophical explanation. Stanza 3 then completes the text with an optimistic perspective on the troubled relationship. Although cynicism pervades the metaphoric style of the verses, its intended humor creates a gradual, organic development. Thematically, the song text offers coherence and idealistic consumation.

"Let's Say Goodnight"

If I say yes,
I'm sure you'll say no
If I say stop
I know you'll say go.
What seems to be
The problem here is you and me,
'Cause we just can't agree
So let's just say goodnight and go home.

You're always right,
And I have never been wrong.
The way we are,
It's getting harder to hang on.

Example 13

Example 13 (cont.)

But who's to blame,
When two things are never the same,
It's not people that change,
It's maybe living from day to day.

What can I say,
The Lord just made us this way.
What can I do?
You know what I've been through.
It's just this world,
It makes it hard for a guy and a girl,
But we could give it a whirl,
So let's just say goodnight and go home.

A third sample of Los Lobos' repertoire is the Hidalgo and Perez composition "How Will the Wolf Survive?" Structurally, the song is based on a country rock beat performed at a moderate tempo. Instrumentation is reduced to a simple, typical format: two electric guitars, electric bass, and drums. The song was also released as a music video in 1985 and received substantial television screenings on various music video programs and MTV, the cable network that screens and markets such videos.

Unlike the typical lyrics of the previous two examples, this text is innovative, in that it makes direct reference to the name Los Lobos (which means "the wolves") and to the issue of Mexican immigration to the United States and the condition of the undocumented worker. In the video these themes are manifested through various forms of visual imagery. A young man stares through a chain link fence toward a young woman whom he finally meets in a Los Angeles restaurant after different scenes depict him wandering through the city. David Hidalgo, a member of the group, plays an American owner/cook of the restaurant, which adds a satirical element. The young man and woman finally flee the small, urban restaurant and return to the rural, open country of the border region. Thus, through the dialectical verses and the symbolic imagery of the metaphoric question about the Wolf's survival, Los Lobos ask for an answer regarding the future of both themselves and their people.

"How Will the Wolf Survive?"

Through the chill of winter
Running across the frozen lake
Hunters hard on his trail
All the odds are against him
With a family to provide for
The one thing he must keep alive
Will the Wolf survive?

Drifting by the roadside
Lines etched on an aging face
Wants to make some honest pay
Losing to the range war
He's got two strong legs to guide him
Two strong arms keep him alive
Will the Wolf survive?

Standing in the pouring rain
All alone in a world that's changed
Running scared, now forced to hide
In a land where he once stood with pride
But he'll find his way
By the morning light.

Sounds across the nation
Coming from young hearts and minds
Battered drums and old guitars
Singing songs of passion

It's the truth that they are lookin' for
Something they must keep alive
Will the Wolf survive?
Will the Wolf survive?

The third verse has a different musical structure from the others and serves somewhat as a bridge, the harmonic progression changing and the rhythm stretching out under the lyrics. Embellishing this rather minimalist section are subtle percussive patterns and effects played on an assortment of wood block and roto tom drums (simulating rain drops) by drummer Pérez. A serene, almost mystic ambience supports the textual metaphor.

Notes

1. The *guajira* is a Cuban musical genre often associated with country life. The style is characterized by a blend of Spanish and African influences. One of its dominant traits is the strict application of Spanish poetic verse structure.

2. The cha cha chá is a Cuban popular music and dance form that gained international popularity during the 1950s. It has continued to be a popular dance rhythm throughout Latin America and the Hispanic United States. The term is often shortened to cha cha.

3. *Huapango* is a music and dance genre from the Huastec region of southeastern Mexico. The style eventually became incorporated into Mexican popular music and is still a popular folk form. Well-known *huapangos* are "Malagueña Salerosa" and "Cu-cu-ru-cu-cu Paloma."

4. *Guaguanó* is one of the most popular forms of the Afro-Cuban rumba. Developed in the Matanzas province of Cuba, it is characterized by drumming, poetically structured vocals, and highly intricate dancing. The *guaguancó* became one of the rumba forms adapted to Cuban arrangements for popular music and dance.

5. Timbales are Cuban metal drums originating with the *charanga* ensemble. The pattern played on the sides of the drums is called *cáscara*.

6. The *guajeo* is an interlocking pattern traditionally performed on piano, violin, or *tres* (a Cuban guitarlike instrument) that adheres to the basic *clave* and various syncopations of the specific rhythms being employed.

7. The *charanga* is a Cuban ensemble developed during the 1930s and the 1940s characterized by instrumentation including flute, violins, timbales, piano, and *tumbadoras* (congas). Styles especially popularized by *charanga* ensembles included the *danzón*, bolero, and cha cha chá.

8. A *montuno* is a solo section for instrumentalists that begins after the principal verse and chorus sections in many Afro-Cuban genres. The term *son montuno* implies a specific Afro-Cuban rhythm.

9. *Son conjunto* is the term for the typical Afro-Cuban ensemble developed by the Cuban musician Arsenio Rodríguez in the 1930s. Instrumentation of the *son conjunto* included *tres* and/or piano, bongos, *tumbadoras* (congas), bass, trumpets, and vocals. The singers were frequently divided into two groups: a lead singer, called the *sonero/a,* and a chorus, called *coristas.*

10. The *tres* is a Cuban guitar type specifically used in the Cuban *son* style and instrumentation.

11. In this instance, *tumbao* refers to the basic bass and conga pattern.

12. *Pan Bimbo* was a marketing term used by the Wonderbread Company that referred to their commercial white bread in the United States and Mexico.

13. *Coyote* is the colloquial term for people who negotiate illegal border crossings, especially between Mexico and the United States.

14. These are phrases from the Spanish versions of Catholic prayers—the Hail Mary, the Our Father, and the Apostles' Creed.

15. Different kinds of *pan dulce mexicano* (Mexican sweet bread).

16. "Zorro" was a popular television series during the early 1960s, based on the legendary Latin Robin Hood.

17. *Cholos* are young men, generally adolescents and frequently members of gangs, car clubs, or other social organizations. They are distinguishable by their mode of dress (white t-shirts, khakis, and Pendleton shirts), tatoos, and manner of speech. Quite often, the *cholo* style is adopted by young men as an outward expression and not necessarily in association with the negative aspects of the style and role.

18. *Menudo* is Mexican soup made with tripe, hominy, and red chili and seasoned with onion, oregano, cilantro, and lemon.

19. The *jarana* is a small type of guitar used in the *jarocho* musical genre from Veracruz, Mexico.

20. The *requinto* is a smaller version of the Spanish guitar, tuned up a fourth. It is a standard instrument of the trio format especially popular in Mexico and the rest of Latin America during the 1940s and 1950s.

21. The *bajo sexto* is a type of guitar that includes bass strings and is used in *norteño*-styled *conjunto* music originally from northern Mexico and south Texas.

22. The *guitarrón* and *vihuela* are both variants of the Spanish guitar and distinctive of Mexico. The *guitarrón* is a folk bass instrument used in the mariachi. The *vihuela* is also used in the mariachi; it is a five-string, higher pitched guitar type dynamically used in a rhythmic/harmonic role.

23. The *charango* is a small double-stringed instrument constructed with the shell of an armadillo. It is a traditional instrument of the Andean region in South America, particularly Bolivia.

Part III
Reflections

Chapter 6

Change, Conflict, and Childhoods

Social anthropology is not, and should not aim to be, a "science" in the natural science sense. If anything it is a form of art. Social anthropologists should not see themselves as seekers after objective truth; their purpose is to gain insight into other people's behavior or, for that matter, into their own. "Insight" may seem a very vague concept but it is one which we admire in other contexts; it is a quality of deep understanding which, as critics, we attribute to those whom we regard as *great* artists, dramatists, novelists, composers; it is the difference between fully understanding the nuances of a language and simply knowing the dictionary glosses of the individual words.

—SIR EDMUND LEACH (1982:52)

In her book *Patterns of Culture* (1934), Ruth Benedict examines the method and thought involved in deciphering the patterns that create a particular culture. What are the patterns that can be perceived from the musical lives of the fifteen people profiled in the previous chapter? And what are some of the methods that might be used to detect those patterns?

The ethnographic profiles, coupled with the brief musical analyses, reflect a cross-section of styles. They also provide substantial data that can be applied to selected theoretical frameworks for a cultural analysis. Questions about the processes of maintenance, change, and adaption arise as a consequence of this ethnography. How have these three processes become articulated as products of sociopolitical history and artistic expression, two essential elements in any living culture?

I have focused on three basic analytic frameworks that I believe will shed some light on the patterns of social behavior, traditions, and philosophies of these fifteen people, who represent a cross-section of the Mexican-American community in Los Angeles. These three theoretical frameworks are built on three concepts: enculturation, the formation of style, and inter-cultural conflict.

Enculturation

Johannes Wilbert (1976a:20) describes enculturation as "a process in which informal and nonformal modes of teaching alternate in frequency and in intensity throughout the learner's life." The theory of enculturation is the methodological backbone of the nine case studies presented here, especially given that the music arises from the processes of maintenance, change, and adaptation as expressed through behavior, tradition, and worldview. The musicians and their music can be studied through this comprehensive notion of enculturation.

According to Wilbert's analytic model, the goals of enculturation are accomplished within a process dimension that entails the skill training, socialization, and moral education of the individual. Skill training involves the teaching of manual and mental skills. Socialization entails the transmission of knowledge "required by the individual to become integrated into his society by adapting to his fellowpersons and by acquiring his position through achieving status and role" (22). Moral education is interpreted as the teaching of the concept of correct behavior.

This threefold objective of enculturation is visualized through the plane of a time dimension, encompassing three stages of a person's life cycle: infancy, childhood, and adulthood. "The delineation of the life stages varies from one society to another but their basic categorization is universal. Their definition ought to follow native norms" (23).

The dimension of space in Wilbert's model circumscribes the total ambience of enculturation: environment, society, and culture.

A study of enculturation thus must ask the following complex question: during each of the stages of infancy, childhood, and adulthood, "how are skill-training, socialization, and moral education effected in a particular environment, society, and culture" (23)?

Through the process of enculturation, the development of particular musical styles can be juxtaposed with particular attitudes in relation to musical preference. The musicians presented here created styles that are a product of their continuing enculturation. Learning, adaptation, and change are aspects of cultural maintenance during the life cycle. The nine case studies represent different historical periods and political stages during the last forty-five years in Los Angeles. By comparing these findings, the outlines of a particular musical subculture emerge, characterized by both musical and philosophical concepts. I believe that such an analysis will help us understand the interfacing processes more clearly.

Wilbert's empirical questions can be applied to the present study's data. As a case in point, Lalo Guerrero has a musical life cycle that spans his infancy, childhood, and adulthood. The latter stage can be further parceled into substages, as Wilbert suggests (1976a).

Guerrero's early enculturation was dominated by his mother's fondness and talent for musical expression, specifically, Mexican musical expression. She provided Guerrero with his principal resource for early skill training in voice, guitar, and language. Guerrero's mother positively reinforced their ethnic identity, although the socialization process outside the home contributed in a negative way to her son's enculturation. Guerrero experienced and learned, both formally and informally, in a matrix of environments: his household, his barrio, his school (with its Anglo culture), and eventually his musical enterprise. His society consisted of intersecting and often conflicting personalities: his family, his teachers, and eventually his musical colleagues. Early on, Guerrero was aware of his ethnicity and its aesthetics, including those of symbolic expression and religion. Fidelity to Mexican culture became a natural vehicle for cultural maintenance and thus for learning. His bicultural experience was dualistic; his two cultures developed separately. A conflict between his two languages was imposed on him: only English was permitted in elementary school; Spanish was preferred at home. Lalo wanted to sing U.S. popular music, but he felt that his racially typical physical features prevented this. These conflicts, which represent his inability to penetrate the mainstream, therefore reinforced Guerrero's decision to develop his ethnic art form ("ethnic" in terms of U.S. mainstream art forms) as an entertainer in the United States.

Andy Russell and his music provide a somewhat different example of enculturation. Whereas Guerrero was born in Tucson, Arizona, and moved to Los Angeles in the late 1930s, Russell was a native of East Los Angeles. Ironically, Guerrero's musical career evolved in the same area of the city where Russell's early enculturation took place, but the latter left Los Angeles to pursue an international career.

Although raised with a positive image of Mexican music and culture, Russell was determined to perform mainstream, popular music in the United States. His negative feelings about the pachuco cult of the 1940s and the term *Chicano* demonstrate how he chose to distance himself from the early expressions of Chicano culture. Guerrero, conversely, actually wrote songs using the *Caló* dialect popular among the pachucos and referred to himself as a Chicano (which had also been reinforced by his mother's aphorism "*Soy pura Chicanita*"). Russell's father worked in the Hollywood studios—a mainstream symbol—and his son attended Roosevelt High School in Boyle Heights, an ethnically integrated, middle-class neighborhood. Russell became highly successful in Mexico and Latin America as a consequence of his popularity as a mainstream U.S. celebrity. Guerrero, on the other hand, ventured to Mexico City as a young adult and returned discouraged to his bicultural world in Los Angeles after only one year. Another mainstream world had eluded him.

Another contrast in the musical enculturation of Guerrero and Russell was how they learned songs. Guerrero's mother taught him traditional Mexican *rancheras* and *corridos,* whereas neither of Russell's parents was a musician. For Russell, Mexican music became more inaccessible because he spoke only simple Spanish as a child and preferred that his mother respond to him in English.

Eddie Cano, raised in Chávez Ravine and Lincoln Heights, was relatively close in age to both Guerrero and Russell. Cano's musical enculturation provides another contrast. During his childhood Cano received formal training on piano. Guerrero never received such formal instruction, and Russell did not begin his formal music education until high school. Cano's family reinforced his formal training; they listened to and practiced both classical art forms and folk traditions. Cano's father enjoyed opera, and his uncle and grandfather were professional musicians. One of Cano's most vivid early memories was that of his uncles and family friends performing traditional Mexican music on the porch of his grandfather's house on Sundays. Other significant experiences included daily piano practice and informal recitals for his grandfather, and later, playing in high school and military instrumental ensembles.

In terms of socialization, Cano, like Guerrero and Russell, was exposed to both negative and positive factors. Confronted by sailors stationed near his house, he experienced firsthand the fruits of the pachuco riots of 1943. As an adult Cano also came in contact with the realities of ethnic discrimination and racial prejudice. On the positive side, he learned from jazz artist Charles Mingus that color has no place in music.

Cano pursued his private, formal musical education at the Los Angeles Music Conservatory, earning a credential while serving in the army. As his adult musical life progressed, he encountered a variety of musical opportunities. His formal musical training, coupled with the natural talent that developed during his childhood and early adult years, enabled him to work in diverse musical environments.

In the realm of culture, Cano has a positive attitude toward *Mexicanismo* from both his informal, household training and his formal, school training. His family maintained the Spanish language and listened to Mexican music. His early positive impression of mariachi music was reinforced when his music theory teacher, demonstrating considerable insight, instructed the class to transcribe complex *son* musical structures.

The younger informants—Poncho Sánchez, Irma Rangel, Teresa Covarrubias, Los Lobos, and Los Illegals—show an even greater diversity of enculturative patterns. Within that group various directions and musical styles are represented against a backdrop of different learning experiences in Mexican-American life and tradition. Cultural dynamics emerge as the principal reason for the diverse musical styles, which range from rural

Mexican *rancheras* to urban punk rock. Although the enculturation of these young artists follows a common pattern, their musical styles are different.

Poncho Sánchez's musical enculturation began during infancy in a Texas border town. Although his family relocated to Los Angeles County when Sánchez was only four years old, as a young child he had been exposed to the intense bicultural environment of the border region, where Spanish is spoken fluently among a distinct Tejano population. Relocating to a Los Angeles barrio provided stability and cultural continuity, but Sánchez's musical philosophy was shaped by his new environment—an inner-city subculture adjacent to the macroculture, spatially integrated yet culturally segregated. His access to the Mexican/Chicano population influenced his musical development without discouraging his musical preference for Afro-Cuban music and Latin jazz.

During his childhood in Norwalk, Sánchez's sisters gave him an appreciation for Cuban mambos and cha chas; later, during his high school years, Sánchez became fascinated with the R&B sound of James Brown. Poncho had no formal training, yet his sisters, the radio, and records informally provided his skill training, first on guitar, then on the trap set, and finally on the conga drums.

Sánchez's socialization and moral education were compatible with his musical development. During his interview he related how he had struggled with English when he arrived in Los Angeles, and he fondly reminisced about his parents' custom of going dancing every Sunday, their only day off work. He constantly emphasized the importance of his family, both during his formative years and today as a husband and parent.

Sánchez's adult musical enculturation involved a rapid transition in his life cycle. Because of his natural talent and self-training, he was able to perfect his craft by learning from professional artists like Cal Tjader and Mongo Santamaría, whom he had emulated since childhood. His spatial enculturation within his environment, society, and culture continues to expand on the local and international levels.

As a young female vocalist, Irma Rangel represents another dimension of the contemporary Mexican-American musical scene in Los Angeles. As a vocalist she has emulated the traditional Mexican music from her family environment. At the same time, she is a product of second-generation acculturation and adaptation to other musical influences.

During the interview, Rangel referred to the influence of the Mexican artists that her parents listened to. When, as a young girl, she had sung to the record jacket photographs of those Mexican female singers, she absorbed images, sounds, and stylistic nuances of their music. Her family demonstrated that this music was a significant cultural and social form of emotional expression through their enjoyment of it. In addition to the emotional aspect, however, the music was infused with other themes: expressions of Mexican patriotism; subtle or overt political sentiment, especially in the traditional *corridos* of the 1910 Mexican Revolution; and the metaphoric, textually symbolic genres from various regions in Mexico.

Rangel's musical skill training during childhood and adolescence consisted of informal learning. She began to imitate what she heard. As a teenager, she attempted to become involved with the mainstream popular theater productions at her high school, but that opportunity did not satisfy her artistic curiosity. She therefore sought other outlets in Mexican/Chicano classes and projects. She was attracted to R&B music as well as Latin and Mexican musical styles and began to search for such groups to perform with.

Irma's family moved to Sante Fe Springs, a southeast suburb, where her socialization spanned a diverse and integrated spectrum. The change from the exclusively Mexican population in East Los Angeles, where she was born, to the integrated environment of Anglo-Americans and Mexican Americans in Santa Fe Springs exposed Irma to intercultural dynamics at an early age. Eventually, in Santa Fe Springs, she became involved with the Chicano *cholo* cult and lowriding and developed a preference for particular styles of music, primarily oldies and R&B. Later, especially during her college years, Irma devoted her creative energies to the study of Mexican and American indigenous cultures (cultural history, indigenous and folk dance from Mexico, and Mexican and other Latin American musical genres).

Rangel's moral attitude stressed the importance of becoming a symbolic expression of and model for Latino people. The singer's concern for achievement in performance, the recording industry, teaching, and raising a family reflected her idealistic and multifaceted worldview.

Although singer/composer Teresa Covarrubias was born and raised in East Los Angeles, she grew up in the context of third-generation acculturation and assimilation. English was the principal language spoken in the Covarrubias household—unlike the situation for Pancho Sánchez—and her parents, both born in the United States, listened to big band swing music. She began to appreciate Mexican music during adolescence.

Much of her earliest musical experiences came from hearing the styles her older siblings listened to—rock—rather than the popular music of her peer group—top forty, R&B, and disco. During high school she became fascinated with what she called "underground" music, such as British new wave.

Covarrubias's socialization and moral education took place primarily within the environment, society, and culture of her family household, her neighborhood, and the various schools she attended. Eventually, during late adolescence, she became acquainted with the Hollywood and westside clubs that catered to punk rock and new wave audiences. That socialization process transcended the music to include more general cultural and environmental elements. The rock cult movement had its own political thought and used symbolic codes in dress and language.

Covarrubias's curiosity, however, was not piqued merely by the bizarre yet sparkling thrill of this musical culture that allowed both expression and public recognition. She began to write prose and short stories in high school, and for a number of years afterward she read extensively. She also sang in the high school glee club. On joining The Brat she applied her skills to writing lyrics and collaborated with the other musicians in composing songs. Teresa's musical skill training thus included musical and nonmusical experiences and formal and nonformal education.

Elements of Covarrubias's moral education often influence her lyrics, both through political symbolism and through her personal experiences with questions of morality. In addition to expressing the political concerns given voice in "The Wolf" (analyzed in chap. 5), the young artist composed a song titled "Catholic School" about the social games adolescent males and females play. Nonetheless, she considered the experience of attending Catholic schools to be a positive factor in her personal development.

Through nineteen years as professional musicians, the members of Los Lobos have maintained traditional Mexican folk music, changed or assimilated various rock genres, and adapted traits or stylistic nuances of Mexican music to their hybrid rock and roll. This dexterity of style adaptation is confirmed by their individual life experiences.

Louie Pérez's parents were born in the United States and moved to East Los Angeles, where Louie was born. His early memories included that of his father as a soldier and his mother as a seamstress. English was the dominant language in the home, and Pérez learned Spanish in order to communicate with his grandmother, who lived with the family for a time.

Pérez's early enculturation was molded by the music his sister listened to on radio and records. When his mother bought him a guitar, he learned to play, teaching himself by listening to records. His serious interest in Mexican and Latin American music began when he joined Los Lobos and the group adopted a folk style. The group used their parents' record collections as the prime research resource.

César Rosas was born in Mexico and came to Los Angeles as a young child, where he lived in various East Los Angeles barrios. Unlike the Pérez family, Rosas's family communicated exclusively in Spanish. He was first influenced by the music his parents liked, Mexican popular and folk genres. His mother listened to mariachis, *rancheras,* and trio music, as well as country and western music. His older sister was a fan of current radio hits, especially the music of Ray Charles. The first time Rosas saw a record was when his sister brought home Ray Charles's "Hit the Road, Jack." That steered him in a new musical direction.

In 1962, at the age of eight, Rosas became interested in playing popular, media-based music. He was prompted to learn guitar after seeing an Elvis Presley movie. Soon after, The Beatles arrived on the American musical scene. His musical enculturation thus evolved from his family environment to a diversity of mainstream media.

Another important aspect of Rosas's musical enculturation was performing in top-forty R&B bands in the eastside circuit (described in chap. 3). Working within that enterprise network became César's livelihood, and the music he performed was therefore not completely based on aesthetics. Saturated with the environment, society, and culture of the business, he eventually began to pursue other expressions during a period of high level Chicano consciousness. Los Lobos became part of that pursuit.

David Hidalgo, like Rosas, heard traditional Mexican music as well as a panorama of musical sounds and styles at home. His parents, born in the United States, listened to Louie Prima, The Ink Spots, Louis Jordan, and Joe Liggins. Through radio, Hidalgo was influenced by The Beatles, The Rolling Stones, and Motown artists.

Conrad Lozano, the fourth member of Los Lobos, described his musical enculturation as an integrative, organic process.

Los Angles is an urban cosmopolis on which much media attention is focused. Yet a pocket of subculture existed within it where the musical enculturation of Los Lobos took place. For years, after their decision to perform Mexican and other Latin American folk music, the group performed primarily for the Mexican/Chicano population, at fiestas, restaurants, schools, public and private functions, and universities. Young, middle-aged, and older people enjoyed the group's talent and enterprise. The musicians' growth coincided with their efforts to maintain and adapt to both musical culture and a culture-specific audience.

Los Lobos, in effect, reversed the standard process and began to enculturate their audience, making the socialization process reciprocal. Observing the effect of their music on the audience, the group's desire to develop its ideas intensified. Many whites began to support the group's music, especially college professors, students, and professionals.

Los Lobos' innovative musical style is the product of the members' varied learning experiences. While maintaining particular musical genres, they have adapted numerous cross-cultural musical concepts and instrumentation. Although not the sole product of enculturation, the resulting musical style has reached a diverse, international audience. Los Lobos communicate the developed expression of a specific environment, society, and culture, and the public at large has learned another worldview that originated as local knowledge in a nuclear subculture.

As the name Los Illegals suggests, the crisis of the illegal alien has become a dominant focus in the group members' lives. Each musician in the band is dedicated to teaching a listening public. The way they merge a musical and a social message was not as common in the 1980s as it was during the 1960s, much less in the heart of East Los Angeles by a group recording on a major label.

Jesse Velo heard a great deal of Mexican music as a young child and listened to popular top-forty music during his adolescence. He continued to perform in the eastside circuit while attending college, until he met Willie Herrón. Velo experienced negative attitudes toward Mexican culture throughout his formal education, especially in terms of political indoctrination and cultural voids (e.g., Mexican history). Velo expressed pride in his rebellious spirit, which he attributed in part to his grandmother, who taught him about the ideology of the Mexican Revolution, often through traditional songs of the period, such as "La Adelita." He also witnessed the deportation of his father, an illegal immigrant from Chihuahua. Along with these experiences were school classes in English and the U.S. mainstream popular music, mostly R&B and top forty, although about 15 percent of the radio play he heard was on Spanish-language stations.

In sum, Velo's enculturation took place in two cultures. He was formally and informally educated politically and socially in a bipolar framework. He does not, however, regret the experience and its inherent contradictions; he uses his sociopolitical, university-trained imagination to create such songs as "We Don't Need a Tan."

Another interesting facet of Velo's musical enculturation was his affinity for black R&B artists.

Like Jesse, Sandra Hahn was raised in a family household of lower socioeconomic status. Her father had no legal residence, and her mother was a resident but not a citizen. The "illegal" way of life, therefore, was certainly part of her training, socialization, and moral education. During her childhood, communication in a second language (English) was a struggle, which led her to withdraw from formal education at a very early age. Another negative factor in her upbringing was traditional male dominance. During adolescence and early adulthood she again rebelled through symbolic behavior, the *chola* subculture, her beautician business, professional fashion design, and eventually, her creative and collective musical enterprises.

Hahn's musical enculturation encompassed a diversity of sounds in her home. Her father emphasized the importance of Mexican mariachi music, and her mother introduced her to Mexican-American and Latin American music, in addition to swing and jazz. Sandra's father also had an intense appreciation for classical music; he made her listen to classical music on the radio so that she would learn that genre. Later, Hahn listened to top-forty music, especially oldies, with her high school and *chola* friends. At seventeen she bought an old piano and then a small synthesizer and began training herself informally.

Hahn's parents avoided discussing Mexican historical or political issues. When undocumented relatives stayed in the house temporarily, much secrecy was associated with their presence. Part of her socialization was thus imbued with secrecy and puzzlement. On the other hand, her parents did reinforce the integrity of her biculturalism. One of their principal concerns was that their children receive a quality formal education.

Bill Reyes's musical enculturation differed from that of the other members of Los Illegals in that he had more formal training. He studied with a private percussion teacher between the ages of seven and twelve. In high school he was helped a great deal by the music director. Reyes joined a band that played in the Santana Latin-rock style, where he learned the basics of Latin percussion through an informal mode of skill training. Following that experience he performed with assorted bands representative of the eastside circuit.

In a musical group composed almost exclusively of second-generation Chicanos, Reyes is the only third-generation member. His musical enculturation is part of his earliest memories. His father, an elementary school principal in Pico Rivera, had been raised within a cosmopolitan range of musical styles. Reyes's parents exposed their young son to the music of Duke Ellington and Frank Sinatra. One of Reyes's first encounters with Mexican music was hearing a mariachi at the school where his father taught. Other musical styles such as top forty, big band, and jazz were also part of his socialization through his own musical training and performance, his peers, his family's social network, and popular radio play.

Reyes's experiences differ subtly from those of the other members of the group in terms of environment and socialization. His negative experiences within the Mexican/Chicano socioeconomic and political milieu did not parallel the overt feelings of displacement and conflict described by the other musicians. Although he reflects a different social class both economically and linguistically, Reyes did not accept the notion that those factors accounted for the contrasting patterns of enculturation. Instead, he claimed that his parents' emphasis on quality education was the difference. Of course, Reyes's degree of acculturation and cultural assimilation also differed from that of his peers in Los Illegals.

Like Jesse Velo, Willie Herrón is outspoken and articulate. Most of Herrón's artistic life has been in the visual arts—painting, sketching, and murals. Over the last ten years he has established himself as one of the most provocative Chicano artists in the country. His association with Los Illegals, which he initiated, began when he decided that many of his artistic concepts could be converted into music. He perceives sounds in the same way that he sees colors—visually. Having no formal training in music, as a young teenager he began to learn by rote, experimenting on the electric organ.

Although Herrón still does not use formal musical practice, his compositional style is fluid and harmonically and rhythmically complex. His lyrics are the focus of his musical goals. Much of his energy and creativity derives from his artistic enculturation, which reflects particular characteristics in skill training, socialization, and moral education. A set of ethnic, political, and artistic dynamics pervades the spatial dimension of his environment, society, and culture.

As an adolescent in the 1960s, Herrón performed in young, local British-influenced Chicano bands. Although he had been raised at home with the cha cha, mambo, and modern salsa, he did not incorporate those sounds into his repertoire at that time, nor did the bands with which he was affiliated play either Latin or top-forty. Because Los Illegals incorporated both British and Latin genres, Herrón considered their music a synthesis of the two modal experiences.

Some of Herrón's most lucid comments during the interview were about social issues—family strife, gang violence, murder, police brutality, the working-class environment, rapid aging, childhood confusion, undocumented immigration, and how he was used as a decoy in those contexts. In addition to Herrón's artistic talent, his environment and socialization produced "a tendency to lean towards the arts at a really, really early age, because that was the thing that became real natural to me." He also said he "had this real strong drive for visual and mental and material success, because I didn't want to continue [in that situation]." Herrón's reality had become unnatural to him, and part of his enculturation caused him to defy a particular mode of life. He commented, "I think the arts sort of led me into everything and anything that had to do with being artistic. It was acting. It was fashion. It was music. It was painting. It was all of that stuff. And a lot of the music at that time . . . was so diverse."

Herrón listened to a great deal of traditional Latin American music, polkas, European imports, rock and roll, and soul. His sister had introduced him to the Motown wave during the 1960s through her record collecting, whereas his exposure to the British styles was via radio. Through the rhythm, vocal nuances, and the harmonic quality of R&B, Herrón expressed the "urgency and passion" that James Brown provided for him. Herrón "related to . . . that *grito* he had." Brown was Herrón's primary initiation into the R&B sound. Herrón also mentioned the influence of the music his family listened to, including traditional Mexican forms. Reinforcing the Mexican traditions, including the family's *panadería* (bakery) business, was religion, manifested in the form of collective prayers. Throughout Herrón's life, his prolific output has demonstrated a diverse, almost jagged, yet organic and rational framework that he has constructed within his environment.

The Formation of Style

Although *style* can be defined pragmatically, the term can imply numerous ideas, theories, and interpretations. Although difficult to describe, several have attempted to express the nature and components of style (Pascall 1980; Schapiro 1953; Kroeber 1963; Sachs 1946; Nettl 1964; Herzog 1928; Hood 1971; Schneider 1960). In identifying musical style it is necessary to distinguish the aspect of music being considered. The terms *manner, mode of expression,* or *type of presentation* imply particular generalities that may apply to the concept of style. The interpretation of these terms, however, may also vary according to the specific context.

Did Mexican-American musicians in Los Angeles during the postwar era exhibit particular musical styles? In South Texas, the *conjunto, orquesta,* and Tex-Mex regional styles can be identified. Los Angeles, however, presents a different case of stylistic development. In an earlier work (Loza 1982a) I discuss the development of musical style, concluding that comparative analysis thus becomes an important factor for consideration. In Texas, a specific "style" has emerged. Los Lobos represent this referent process of interpreting music via Mexico and its regional styles; it is, in effect, the creation of another style . . . but is it an East Los Angeles style? The social process experienced there is quite distinct, as exemplified through David Torres, Héctor Aguíñiga, and Poncho Sánchez (three of the five case studies in the paper).

In Texas styles seem to emerge and develop with fewer restrictions. In Los Angeles, as pointed out by drummer Joe Heredia (the subject of another of the case studies), the styles are too many; in effect, they are scattered, whether they be Mexican music, commercial top forty, or progressive forms. In Heredia's opinion such a diffusion of different styles makes it much more difficult to generate a particular style in East L.A. than in Texas.

However, certain statements in these interviews did allude to some characteristics of Chicano musicians in Los Angeles—for example, Poncho Sánchez's reference to the Santana syndrome, which generated much imitation through a "sound" that seemed "familiar," a syndrome also reflected in groups such as El Chicano, Azteca, Malo, and Tierra, which were groups that always interpreted songs in both English and Spanish, exhibiting a consistent, profound influence from both Latin music and rhythm and blues. David Torres mentioned the Salas Brothers' use of parallel thirds in vocal style, which in effect was almost an imitation of the stylistically typical harmonization for mariachi trumpets. Conrad Lozano (the fifth case study) spoke of the effect of rhythm and blues and rock on the vocal phrasing and instrumentation of Los Lobos' interpretations of traditional Mexican musical forms, whether they be *jarocho, ranchera,* bolero, *huapango,* or other genres.

Folklorist Alicia González advised me at the time that perhaps the essential factor of the five case studies that I chose to examine was the unique musical environment of Los Angeles as compared to other areas of the Chicano Southwest and the musical affinity or aesthetic that has developed among these young Chicano musicians. This musical aesthetic is a product that has expanded after exposure to many forms manifested by different factors that are discussed in the five interviews: peer pressure, displacement, reaffirmation, reinforcement, and ideals. The most important development was that these musicians found a particular musical style and were then able to appreciate music in a more general sense, including the process of "reverting" to traditional musical forms in some cases. As demonstrated through the interviews, the musical styles expressed by these five musicians involved a diversity of directions. The reaffirmation or reinforcement of the traditional styles represented for these individuals something that they had not appreciated at an earlier stage of their musical development. González also raised the issue of nationalism in terms of "a nationalist period" and spoke of comparative parallels: post–World War I Germany and the American Indian (Loza 1982a:20–21).

Particular forms to which Chicano rock and R&B musicians have adapted represent stylistic tendencies and preferences, that is, the music of the eastside bands. However, a distinct genre has not actually emanated from Los Angeles. Although Los Lobos, Los Illegals, and Califas all exhibit a group style, they do not represent a particular genre, instrumentation, or repertoire representative of Los Angeles.

In terms of musical components, however, there are certain commonalities in the musical style of Chicano musicians in Los Angeles. Vocal and instrumental tone and inflection, improvisational motives, harmonic progressions, rhythmic references and preferences, training in technique, and vocal/instrumental voicing all exhibit some specific commonalities that frequently cross-identify the styles of various Chicano musicians; that is, they apply to the venue of tone and inflection, as in the case of singer Li'l Ray Jimenez and his nephew, Mike Jimenez. Both possess a wide range and have a lyrical "cry" quality in the higher register, especially at the ends of phrases in ballads. Improvisationally, a commonality often exists in terms of melodic solo passages imitative of Mexican or other Latin American styles. Harmonic progression in English ballads (or "oldies") is often similar to Mexican bolero standards from the 1940s to 1960s. Rhythmic concepts are extensively conceived through the hybridization of Caribbean, Mexican, and U.S.-based genre structures, and Latin American percussion instruments are often standard ensemble components. Instrumental and vocal technique is often highly developed or virtuosic although not formally trained. Voicing nuances in harmonic structure are frequently indicative of enculturated Mexican stylistic practice, for example, the Salas Brothers' transference of the mariachi and *ranchera* use of parallel thirds, vocally and instrumentally.

Intercultural Conflict

Mexican music has existed in Los Angeles through the last few centuries, but with the constant influx of both non-Mexicans and Mexicans into the rapidly growing metropolis, a cosmopolitan complex emerged—and Mexican Americans, like any other ethnic group, assimilated in varying degrees to the American way of life. Whereas other groups assimilated more fluidly, Mexicans faced a unique circumstance. They were in a land that at one time had been part of Mexico and were still associated with "being Mexican," regardless of the degree of assimilation. They retained their names and many Mexican traditions and, what is perhaps most significant, lived in geographic proximity to Mexico. When confronted with the constant arrival of Mexican people from Mexico, Chicanos (or Mexican Americans) remain conscious of their ethnicity, traditions, and the political problems of their culture and community.

América Paredes considers the conflict between the two dominant groups, the Anglo-Americans and the Chicanos, to be the most important feature of Chicano folklore in Texas. He refers to this social phenomenon of confrontation as "intercultural conflict" (Paredes 1976). The border conflict factor appears to have been the salient theme of the ballads of Mexicans in Texas. Los Angeles does not represent a border experience, however, and the emerging conflict has evolved from a different, yet similar multifaceted process.

Music provides perhaps one of the clearest illustrations of this confrontation, or intercultural conflict. Although Chicanos expand their musical preference and vocabulary through adaptation to certain musical styles representative of the American mainstream, they also experience a cultural loss. Meanings change symbolically and linguistically because of a partial lack of culture maintenance that occurs not necessarily through a denial of these traditions but because of sociological factors.

América Paredes has applied the concept of intercultural conflict to the Texas-Mexican border experience as expressed through music—specifically, through traditional folk types, for example, *corridos, danzas mexicanas,* romances, and *huapangos.* (Paredes [1976] describes sixty-six folk songs of the lower Texas-Mexican border.) In relation to the *"orquesta-conjunto* nexus" of south Texas, Peña (1985b:30) has posited two hypotheses on the relationship between the two musics:

> First, I propose that at the historical level the two musics unfolded within a framework of emerging class difference and conflict among Texas-Mexicans, and that as such they have signified an intrinsic class dialectic working itself out within Texas-Mexican society. My second hypothesis is linked to the first, but builds on a more "synchronic" base, as it were. That is, it posits orquesta and conjunto as symbolic projections of a Texas-Mexican social structure that was solid enough to survive both the disruptive effects of interethnic contact with American society and the fragmentation introduced by class differences. To put it another way, from a synchronic ("structural") perspective the two styles should be considered dual expressions of a unitary musico-symbolic whole that emerged out of the conflict between an ethnic tejano culture and a dominant, often hostile Anglo-American social order.

In another work, Peña (1982a:284–85) expresses the specifics of this conflictual duality.

> Clearly, changes in the social structure were being transformed into changes in the musical (and dance) structures. The move toward assimilation by some segments of Chicano society was countered by a corresponding move by the proletariat to strengthen its cultural position. And the music-and-dance innovations symbolically articulated this move.
>
> On another front, both American and Mexican musics have exerted powerful influences on conjunto. This influence, however, has been felt more strongly by the orquestas, which have tended to reflect Mexican, American, and the more conservative conjunto styles in turn. Orquesta expresses the cultural duality (cf. Marks 1974) of Chicano society; it functions as a kind of symbolic style-switching, somewhat analogous to Blom and Gumperz's concept of metaphorical switching (1972), allowing Chicanos access to both Mexican and American socio-musical systems. The outspoken orquesta leader Little Joe has perceptively interpreted this dual access as demonstrating the "flexibility" of Chicanos.
>
> In sum, then, the symbolic structure(s) of conjunto and orquesta

reflect the state of flux in which Chicano society is maintained, owing to the push and pull across the ethnic boundary (Barth 1969) or the play of what Jansen (1965) calls the esoteric-exoteric factor. This factor may be described as the element which maintains the differences in the sense of ethnicity and of class that the various segments of Chicano society ascribe to themselves and others. And that esoteric-exoteric factor itself operates on the principles of cultural confrontation and accommodation (cf. Barth 1969; Bateson 1972), or what Paredes (1976) has described more specifically as the intercultural conflict between Chicanos and Anglos. It is against this backdrop that conjunto and orquesta have played out their dialectic.

Whether such a dialectic exists in Los Angeles Mexican/Chicano musical expression is debatable. Certainly, Lalo Guerrero represents Peña's conceptualizations of duality and Little Joe's perception of a "flexibility" among Chicanos. Guerrero's "No Way José" is no more an expression of intercultural conflict than is "Canción mexicana," the latter predating the former by forty-five years. Also characteristic of such conflict are Los Illegals's "El Lay," The Brat's "The Wolf," Los Lobos' "How Will the Wolf Survive?" Ruben Guevara's "C/S," and, through a nontextual form of symbolic meaning, Thee Midniters' "Whittier Boulevard."

One major difference, however, can still be attributed to the lack of any particular, regional musical style comparable to the stylistic development examined by Peña in South Texas, which is based on the emergence of two distinct yet related ensemble genres and their repertoire. One viable argument for this hypothesis might be based on the styles of the East Los Angeles bands of the 1960s previously surveyed. Although the styles practiced by these bands were not internal, regional innovations, they were certainly perceptively stylistic adaptations, largely to R&B and rock.

Mexican/Chicano musicians in Los Angeles have assimilated, changed, and perhaps introduced a variety of musical styles that originated in both Mexico and the United States. The existence of such a clarified dialectic as that posited by Peña in relation to the *conjunto-orquesta* relationship, however, is difficult to detect in Los Angeles. A comparison of variables of musical practice in relation to meaning and history may be helpful in this regard.

Regardless of how viably the concept of intercultural conflict may be applied to postwar Mexican/Chicano musical life of Los Angeles, conflict is not the overriding element in this cultural study. Other theoretical frameworks must be incorporated into the analysis of the musical culture of Los Angeles. One alternative to Peña's dialectic analysis of intercultural conflict is the application of a framework called "networks of marginality": organized, formal or nonformal responses to the existence of social conflict.

Vélez-Ibáñez (1983:17) has observed that "there is a substantive theoretical, empirical, and political literature in opposition to the use of 'marginality' as a heuristic, theoretical, or descriptive idea." He cites Perlman (1975) as the "most persuasive in this regard by showing that the notion of marginality consists of a series of myths used to describe persons in 'squatments' (Leeds 1969) who are economically exploited and politically repressed" (1983:17). According to Perlman, such myths are empirically false and analytically misleading. Nonetheless, in his study of Ciudad Netzahualcoyotl, an urban sub-metropolis of four million people adjacent to Mexico City, Vélez-Ibáñez uses the term *marginality* to structure an ethnography of the economic and political dimensions of the city's population.

Perlman (1975) argues that such societies are not politically and economically marginal but instead exploited, repressed, and actively marginalized. Vélez-Ibáñez opts to use the term *marginal,* however, pointing out that characteristics associated with marginal behaviors cannot be regarded as peculiar or specific to the population he studied in Ciudad Netzahualcoyotl, which he views as "economically and politically excluded from the economic and political benefits of the nation-state and its economic system" (1983:18).

Although the Mexican/Chicano population in Los Angeles represents a demographic and migration history different from that of Ciudad Netzahualcoyotl, certain similarities can be ascribed to these urban concentrations of Mexican settlement and relocation. Important to this particular study is the application of Vélez-Ibáñez's theoretical perspective in relation to networks of marginality and their evolution as "rituals of marginality."

Social ties or networks are often based on exchanges generated through reciprocal favors within kinship, friendship, fictive kinship (Vélez-Ibáñez 1983:20), community interdependence, and ethnicity. Several examples from the case studies presented here illustrate such patterns in the enterprises of various Mexican/Chicano musicians and businesspeople in Los Angeles over the past forty years. John Ovalle, for example, referred to the marketing practices of local record distributors in Los Angeles's East Side. Catering to the Chicano record-buying public, Ovalle established a chain of small eastside record stores to which he distributed merchandise, in his case on a bicultural setting, selling both Spanish and English recordings.

Lalo Guerrero described at length the closely integrated network of nightclubs and restaurants that catered to the Mexican public in Los Angeles during the 1940s and 1950s. That network provided the framework for numerous musical livelihoods among Chicano, Mexican, and other Latin American professional musicians. Business negotiations were usually handled by the musicians themselves or their agents, most frequently members of the same ethnic network. Joe Herrera, an agent for many eastside entertainers, also represented major musical acts from Mexico that performed as special attractions in Los Angeles (Loza 1983b).

An interesting example of network expansion is the musical chronology of Los Lobos. Having begun their recording career through a locally produced LP and in the performance network of East Los Angeles and the Chicano Southwest, the group rose to international status after ten years in that ethnically isolated musical culture. That network of exchange, experimentation, enculturation, and response, however, enabled Los Lobos to attract a major recording contract during a period when the journalistic community and local artists had begun to turn to East Los Angeles for fresh musical concepts.

Certainly one of the best examples of musical networking among Chicano musicians was the eastside top-forty band and club circuit of the late 1960s through the late 1970s—a decade characterized by "battles of the bands" and the interaction of musical and business competition in a variety of performance contexts. Such was the cultural environment and socio-musical ambience that contributed to the evolution of networks into metaphoric dimensions. The concept of "meaning" applied here revolves around a particular cult or mysticism that pervaded the eastside band network and in essence became a "ritual of marginality." In Mexico City the same ritual was being enacted by dozens of mariachis at the Garibaldi plaza. In East Los Angeles the mariachi ritual simply took on the voice and costume of a different environment, society, and culture.

Leach (1979) posits that ritual does not necessarily refer to symbolic representations or behaviors that occur exclusively in "sacred" contexts. Rather, he asserts that ritual expresses a pattern of symbols revealing the system of "socially approved 'proper' relations between individuals and groups" (15). Vélez-Ibáñez (1983:23) adds that "ritual expressions of social relations are especially rich where populations are in asymmetrical relationships of dominance and subservience, or where relationships are established between sectors in which resources are in the hands of some but not in the hands of others." For Vélez-Ibáñez, "the expression 'rituals of marginality' refers to the manifestation of seemingly fixed patterns of social relations based on scarcity and inequality between individuals, groups, and organizations. The specific manner in which such rituals are organized depends upon culture, context, and historical period" (1983:23). In his study of Ciudad Netzahualcoyotl, Vélez-Ibáñez observed such rituals between formal and informal sectors. "These rituals are largely noninstitutionalized mechanisms such as patron-client relations, brokerage, friendships of convenience, and informal arrangements by which persons receive intermittent 'favors'" (1983:23).

Rituals of marginality thus patterned appear to permeate the musical life (or Wilbert's space dimensions of environment, society, and culture) of the Mexican/Chicano musicians in Los Angeles. A case in point is the mariachi.

Based on his extensive study of the mariachi culture of Los Angeles, Pearlman concludes that it is a network "largely of and for immigrants and their descendants, a transplanted people's music" (1983:12). Pearlman also notes that performing contexts differ subtly from the traditional contexts in Mexico. He thus classifies the organizational context of mariachi performance in Los Angeles into three loosely divided categories "related to the degree of cohesiveness or performance of the group" (1983:12). The first category encompasses the transient groups, similar to many mariachi contexts in Mexico. Such groups work *"al talón,"* meaning that they play in one or more cantinas in a given evening and depend completely on patronage donations, tips, or set fees charged to the clientele. The second category consists of the *planta*-based mariachi, characterized by a performance context comprising "bands of fixed or relatively fixed membership performing on a regular basis at one or more locations, with their primary source of income being money paid by the location itself" (1983:12). The third category is those mariachis that play at Los Angeles restaurants—for example, Los Camperos at La Fonda and Los Galleros at El Rey.

The range of performance contexts appears to correspond to the networks of mariachi musicians and their clientele. The *al talón* style is regularly encountered among mariachis who play at numerous small restaurants and cantinas in areas with high-density Mexican populations. *Planta*-based mariachis can be found in major hotels, amusement parks, and in Mexican restaurants and bars catering to a predominantly Latino clientele. The less numerous but more commercialized single restaurant–based mariachis perform for a diverse clientele, ranging from the general Mexican population and its second- and third-generation descendants to a large number of non-Mexicans and tourists.

In a landmark essay examining the problem of culture among the people of Mexican descent in the United States, Gómez-Quiñones (1977:9) notes the factors of diversity characteristic of that population in terms of commonality, ethnicity, class, history, and domination. He describes this regional variety as follows:

In the United States north of the Rio Bravo, the space is vast and varied and the Mexican population diverse. Historically, regional variety is related to the regional economy, to the rate, length and type of settlement, the culture of local Indian groups, the relation with local Indian groups, rate, and manner of displacement by Anglo North Americans. The local regional differences are, in addition, a result of differing regional Anglo economic-political, cultural, social, demographic complexes, and of culture brought over by succeeding generations of Mexicanos to the communities at different times as general patterns of migratory preference shifted. Within each of the regional diversities, differences are determined by occupation of the person and his family, racial features, individual and family sense of history, identity and culture, length of residence, education, use of Spanish, type of English, acculturation, degree of participation in Anglo society, urban or rural residence, and individual experience of exploitation and discrimination.

Gómez-Quiñones explains that such exploitation is rejected by people contesting dominant cultural institutions and that "assimilation deforms but never does it bring about integration or acceptance of the discriminated population by the dominant group . . . those who accept the mystique are doomed to be marginal" (1977:8). Cultural resistance, "the rejection of cultural domination, is the negation of assimilation. This may take two routes: tradition for its own sake, or a synthesis of tradition and creation. . . . Political dissent, class conflict, and cultural resistance reinforce each other" (1977:8). Gómez-Quiñones further claims that culture must be joined to the politics of liberation for it to be an act of resistance. At this juncture cultural creation supersedes "tradition" (1977:8).

One example of this cultural transgression is the case study of Teresa Covarrubias. There is no preference given to traditional form in the contemporary textual and musical construct of "The Wolf"; instead, priority is given, through metaphorical expression of crisis, to "class and cultural resistance [by assuming] political form which is all encompassing" (Gómez-Quiñones 1977:8).

Chapter 7

Reflections of a Homeboy

. . . and so I decided to say an Act of Contrition.

—STEVE LOZA

You can't create an inspiration . . . you have to receive it. The trick is to receive it while you're creating.

Late one afternoon in the fall of 1987 I was walking on the campus of the University of Notre Dame. I heard some astonishing drum cadences, and I was immediately turned on by the intense and well-executed rhythms being rehearsed by the percussion section of Notre Dame's marching band (obviously rehearsing for the Alabama game two days later). I was flooded with fond memories of my high school marching days, yet I also almost immediately recognized the rhythm itself: it was "Tequila." And sure enough, the bell lyres came in with the melody of The Champs' classic. The spirit of East L.A. was living in South Bend, Indiana.

The experience wasn't a bit surprising to me. And I felt as if I were a part of something rather beautiful. It struck me that Mexican-American/Chicano/Latino popular music interpretation, if one must label it, had become part of American lore in the United States. The kids in the band didn't care where the music came from. They just dug playing it . . . and they played it well.

We've all seen what happened with the film *La Bamba* and Los Lobos' subsequent ascension to the number one spot on the national charts with the title track. In fact, I recently heard that the record had also been number one in Australia and that Los Lobos were touring with the Irish rock band U2, in recent years one of the most popular groups in the Western world. "La Bamba" has traveled the world over at least a thousand times since it was composed by a folk musician in Veracruz, Mexico, sometime in the last two hundred years. Ritchie Valens reinterpreted it almost thirty years before Los Lobos' homage to him, and both versions were major national hits.

A legacy thus lives, and not just in popular music. Linda Ronstadt, a

Mexican American, recorded her Grammy Award–winning album of Mexican music with members of the mariachis Vargas de Tecalitlán, Los Camperos, Los Galleros, and Sol de México. In 1991 Ronstadt recorded a second album of Mexican styled music with Mariachi Los Camperos de Nati Cano and Vargas de Tecalitlán. Andy Russell continued to entertain nostalgic swing audiences in the 1980s by occasionally singing in front of a big band. Poncho Sánchez continues to record a new album every year and has recently performed throughout Europe, in the major jazz clubs of New York and the East Coast, in the Orient, and in parts of Latin America. Irma Rangel recently hosted an oldies show on Los Angeles radio station KRLA and continues to sing a diversity of musical styles. In 1986 Eddie Cano acted as president of the Hispanic Musicians Association in Los Angeles, the first group of its kind. I recently worked as musical director on a revue of the music of Lalo Guerrero with a contingent of Los Angeles–based musicians, dancers, and producers. I also coproduced with Rudy Salas and the UCLA Center for the Performing Arts a concert billed as "Chicano Pop Legends Revue," which featured the eastside bands Tierra, El Chicano, and Thee Midniters in Royce Hall on 8 December 1990.

Rubén Guevara has called this movement an "Eastside Renaissance." It may be more than a marginal, temporary movement. I think the Mexican— and for that matter, the Latin—is on the verge of sparking a general renaissance in American society. Almost every other ethnic group in America has had its turn. But this could be a different kind of "turn." Nachos, for example, are much like pizza in America, part of the American vocabulary and part of the American appetite. Pizza is Italian and nachos are Mexican, but both are elements of folklore in the United States. Perhaps Frank Sinatra and Los Lobos can be compared to pizza and nachos.

The turn thus becomes a thread in the fabric of American society, whether it is a Stephen Foster, a Scott Joplin, a Louis Armstrong, a Bing Crosby, a Frank Sinatra, or a Linda Ronstadt. Marginality inevitably becomes the epitome of the mainstream. This notion is not just theory; history consistently supports such patterns of culture. Indeed, such a turn has in fact been manifested through many interrelated processes, including change, integration, and idealism. Through the ethnological evaluation of the nine case studies, I have assessed the testimony of artists and their experience with different modes of enculturation, conflict, and musical style.

One important area of music is the recording industry, itself a byproduct of change. Some years ago, for example, a new category—Mexican American—was added to the Grammy Awards competition (the other two Latin categories include Latin Pop and Tropical). Los Lobos won the award the first year (1984) and were followed in subsequent years by Sheena Easton and José Miguel, Vikki Carr, Flaco Jiménez, Los Tigres del

Norte, Linda Ronstadt, and again, Los Lobos (1990). Mexican-American and Mexican artists are eligible for consideration, for the category encompasses Mexican-influenced styles representing both sides of the border.

An extremely important development in the record industry is the marketability of such categories in the mainstream, as illustrated by the international popularity of Los Lobos. An interesting parallel is that of Miami Sound Machine, a predominantly Cuban-American group featuring singer Gloria Estefan that has achieved international stardom in the mainstream pop music market. This is not necessarily a new phenomenon. Carlos Santana achieved success in the music industry twenty-five years ago with his Latin rock innovations. But there is one significant difference. Los Lobos and certain others are literally adapting Mexican musical styles to the American concept of rock and roll—and doing it successfully in terms of musicality and marketability.

This leads me to my other topic: integration. By becoming part of mainstream, commercial radio lore, Los Lobos have penetrated the subconscious of the American mind and public. In other words, a young, contemporary rock fan listens to the bilingual, bicultural repertoire of Los Lobos without the burden of negative images of ethnicity or isolation. Taking the notion of "integration" a step further, I suggest that groups such as Los Lobos have extended the traditional definition of America in the United States to include the more encompassing, borderless, Latin American concept of the word "America." A Mexican song interpreted by Los Lobos in the *jarocho* style symbolizes this borderless, bicultural concept of America.

It is interesting to juxtapose the present scenario, exemplified by the success of Los Lobos, to the situation of Lalo Guerrero some years ago. Caught between the industrial mainstreams of commercial music in Mexico and the United States, Guerrero had to market his recordings on local Los Angeles labels that catered specifically to the Mexican American. Los Lobos distributed their first LP, *Just Another Band from East L.A.*, in the same fashion. The hybrid, bizarre, postdisco rock scene of the 1980s, however, enabled them to make the transition to the commercial recording industry. Through much the same process, Carlos Santana emerged in the late 1960s, another period of musical flux and innovation.

In contrast to these comparisons is the 1960–1980 Eastside Sound, a movement that produced such bands as El Chicano and Tierra. These popular bands of East Los Angeles imitated R&B stylists of the period while experimenting with Spanish verse or Latin musical styles, although to a different extent as have such groups as Los Lobos, Santana, and Miami Sound Machine. Ironically, a sound that was more mainstream in quality was less mainstream in marketability. Again, marginality inevitably becomes the very epitome of the mainstream. Los Lobos play what many critics have called "good quality American rock and roll," and the young San Francisco–based Carlos Santana was an avid exponent of blues before his Latin-rock innovations. Miami Sound Machine, on the other hand, made a major transition from a totally Spanish repertoire to a mixed, dual-market enterprise. Although not as spectacular in international impact, the eastside groups Tierra and El Chicano did manage to break the ice during their brief stay at the top of the charts in the 1970s and early 1980s.

What inevitably emerges from all this experimentation and the industrial complex are various forms of musical style. Whereas Santana incorporated conga drums and timbales as essential elements of Latin rock, Los Lobos introduced the northern Mexican, South Texan accordion to their style. Thanks to the innovation of Los Lobos, the accordion may become a common element in rock bands.

Certain stylistic techniques do not easily enter the mainstream; such is the case of Los Illegals. Their modes of experimentation involved direct social satire and considerable use of Spanish. Although the latter device may have been innovative, and therefore perhaps marketable during the punk rock and new wave eras, the lyrics were heavily laden with social metaphor within a complex musical structure. It was not meant to be party music. Whereas Los Illegals' expression was direct, Los Lobos' metaphoric material was textually more indirect. Compare the titles "El Lay" and "How Will the Wolf Survive?" Los Lobos, however, were musically more radical; they infused the accordion into their hybrid rock style, while Los Illegals created a heavy punk/new wave texture. Another aspect of their relative mainstream success is that, although punk made a market impact in England, where it was born, its influence in the United States gradually gave way to the glitzier new wave style. Los Illegals may have fallen victim to this trend. As vogues changed from punk to new wave to rebirth 1950s rock and roll, Los Illegals found themselves in a marketing quandary.

On another front, the attitude of Poncho Sánchez represents, in his own words, that of a "purist." He is one of the leading stylists among musicians who play in the Afro-Cuban and Latin jazz traditions. Although not based on Mexican genres, his music still symbolizes a form that has been highly popular among Mexican people and has also been generated by them. Historically, the case of Eddie Cano certainly supports such a hypothesis, as do many Mexican-American musicians involved in Latin, tropical, salsa, and Afro-Cuban styles. A market for this musical style has existed in Los Angeles for years. The label for which Sanchez records, Concord Picante, was also the label for his mentor, Cal Tjader, and continues to record Tito Puente, a four-time Grammy Award recipient.

Irma Rangel represents perhaps the most complete composite of what is and is not a "purist approach" among the nine case studies presented here.

Firmly rooted in traditional Mexican styles, but also possessing a repertoire of R&B, pop, and tropical music (both salsa and *cumbia*), Rangel symbolizes openness, a sense of adventure, and flexibility. In fact, the women profiled in this book communicated something to me beyond a preoccupation with musical style. Irma Rangel, Teresa Covarrubias, and Sandra Hahn all tended to associate musical style with patterns of life. Rangel spoke of the record covers of Mexican women singers; Hahn recalled the "heavenly music" she heard on the classical radio station; Covarrubias highlighted her experimentation with poetry. These women were not discussing the mechanics of their music, perhaps because women have not traditionally been encouraged, especially during childhood, to train themselves as musicians, either formally or nonformally. Their attitudes, as a reflection of their enculturation as women, are essential components of the cultural matrix.

In addition to gender, other elements in this cultural matrix that should be assessed are class, ethnicity, and age.[1] Ethnicity, of course, is the principal motif that holds together this ethnography. Through all nine case studies and the chronicle of musical life presented in chapter 3, various philosophical perspectives have been discussed and individual experiences described to render a composite personality—the Mexican-American musician in Los Angeles. Moreover, I have suggested that this composite personality is the product of a cultural movement—enmeshed in the constructs and ideals of aesthetics and politics. These ideals, in turn, have been generated through such processes as structural and ethnic assimilation, acculturation, conflict, marginalization, and integration.

Among the five 1988 Grammy Award nominees for Best Record of the Year were three performers of Latin background: Los Lobos, Linda Ronstadt (nominated with Emmy Lou Harris and Dolly Parton), and Suzanne Vega. The other two nominees were Paul Simon and the group U2. Ethnicity as a factor in U.S. popular music has been a constant for many years, but seems to be gradually expanding, for these five represent vast diversity. Paul Simon represents a long-standing institution in U.S. popular music, and his album *Graceland,* which won the award, thrust South Africa and its music into popular consciousness, whereas U2, an Irish rock group, had, as they say, "caught the world by its heels." Ronstadt has crossed from country-rock to Big Band to country to mariachi. Suzanne Vega, of Puerto Rican heritage, has emerged as a symbol of new, fresh material, yet also as the reincarnation of Joni Mitchell. Perhaps America is, to some extent, overlooking the image and the stereotype.

These Grammy nominations also demonstrate that artists entering the mainstream are not now classified according to ethnicity. Los Lobos' hit "La Bamba" has been recognized because of its mainstream viability. Stylistically, it is rock and roll, vintage Ritchie Valens. Linguistically, it becomes both foreign and native. In terms of marketability, the mainstream film *La Bamba,* which features the song, has re-created the song's commercial success. Ethnically, nothing really seems to matter—at least not the existence of social problems—in producing and marketing such a film and recording.

With respect to class, Los Lobos have changed their economic position through their success. Artists nominated in the Best Record category have usually become quite successful financially, owing to the "hype" and the market. Los Lobos are not in the same financial situation that they were in when I took them to Tijuana some years ago, nor should they be. I can remember Conrad Lozano telling me on the way back to L.A., "We're just poor."

No longer "just poor," Los Lobos achieved major success in the commercial mainstream of pop music. So what does this mean in terms of the ideas and theoretical notions that I have formulated here? Has their financial success changed the group's importance as a reflection of marginal society? I think not, and I would simply posit another notion—that the cultural matrix is one that evolved according to changing trends and ideals in society. Los Lobos' economic class structure has changed, but their social class structure has not. Literally hordes of Hispanics have watched the group's ascension in the music industry as a symbol not only of integration but also of economic class mobility. It is also possible that this has been the view of corporate members of the music industry searching for new marketing trends and mobility.

And what about age—an element of both unity and diversity in the cultural matrix. Along with the notion of an Eastside Renaissance is the popularity of such older Mexican-American musicians as Lalo Guerrero, Eddie Cano (until his death), and Nati Cano, themselves members of an ongoing musical momentum and continuum. Simultaneously, both innovation and tradition are personified in the many younger Los Angeles natives such as Poncho Sánchez, Irma Rangel, Teresa Covarrubias, and Los Lobos. Just as Jorge Negrete and other voices of the past live on in the minds and hearts of many, so does the present in the form of Carlos Santana, Stevie Wonder, Ray Charles, and U2—all examples of innovation, tradition, and integration.

Unity and diversity lie at the core of integration. Perhaps integration is really what is occurring, not only in America, north and south but in the world at large. It is taking time, but it is also taking shape.

In speaking of polarities and borders, integration and ideals, I can think of one notion that might also be considered part of our cultural matrix: hope. Add faith and love to the cultural matrix, and I think we might start actually believing in human nature.

The sunlight plays upon my windowpane
I wake up to a world that's still the same
My father said to be strong
And that a good man could never do wrong
In a dream I had last night in America

> Los Lobos, "One Time, One Night in America"

Note

1. This cultural matrix model was suggested to me as a tool for analysis by Carlos Vélez-Ibáñez.

Bibliography

Aceves, Joseph B. 1978. "Competence by Blood: Ethnological Fieldwork in the Ancestral Village." Paper presented at the Annual Meeting of the American Anthropological Association, Los Angeles, California.

Acuña, Rodolfo. 1984. *A Community under Siege: A Chronicle of Chicanos East of the Los Angeles River, 1945–1975*. Chicano Studies Research Center Publications Monograph no. 11. Berkeley and Los Angeles: University of California Press.

———. 1972. *Occupied America: The Chicano's Struggle toward Liberation*. San Francisco: Canfield.

Alarcón, Alicia. 1988. "Histórica presentación de la Orquesta Sinfónica Nacional de México en el sur de California." *La Opinión,* May 28.

Alvarez, Rodolfo. 1982. "The Psycho-Historical and Socioeconomic Development of the Chicano Community in the United States." In *Chicano: The Evolution of a People,* edited by Renato Rosaldo, Robert S. Calvert, and Gustav L. Seligmann, 28–46. Malabar, Fla.: Krieger.

Alwardt, Jo Ann. 1982. "Vikki Carr." *Goldmine* 69 (Feb.): 18–19.

Avila, Guillermo. 1983. "Santana." *Avance* 2:17–19.

Ayala, Ernie. 1974. "Richard Leos, L.A.'s Leading Latin Jazz D.J." *Latin Quarter* 1:19–21.

Bakaler, Jay, Brigette Bernstein, Jennifer Hall, and Kami Kellams. 1985. "Latino New Wave Music: An Ethnological Study of an Acculturated Music Form." Unpublished manuscript.

"The Ballad of an Unsung Hero." 1983. PBS video broadcast. San Diego: Cinewest.

Bancroft, Hubert Howe. 1884–90. *The History of California.* 7 vols. San Francisco: History Book.

Bandini, Don Arturo. 1958. *Navidad: A Christmas Day with the Early Californians.* San Francisco: California Historical Society.

Baron, Robert. 1977. "Syncretism and Ideology: Latin New York Salsa Musicians." *Western Folklore* 1 (3): 209–25.

Barth, Fredrik. 1969. *Ethnic Groups and Boundaries.* Boston: Little, Brown.

Barrera, Mario. 1979. *Race and Class in the Southwest: A Theory of Racial Inequality.* Notre Dame, Ind.: University of Notre Dame Press.

Bateson, Gregory. 1972. "Culture Contact and Schismo Genesis." In *Steps to an Ecology of Mind.* San Francisco: Chandler.

Baur, John E. "José De La Rosa, Early Ventura's Centenarian Printer." *Ventura County Historical Quarterly* 19.4 (Summer): 14–25.

Beals, Ralph Leon, and Norman D. Humphrey. 1957. *No Frontiers to Learning: The Mexican Student in the United States*. Minneapolis: University of Minnesota Press.

Benedict, Ruth. 1934. *Patterns of Culture*. Boston: Houghton Mifflin.

Blacking, John. 1974. *How Musical Is Man?* Seattle: University of Washington Press.

————. 1970. "Tonal Organization in the Music of Two Venda Initiation Schools." *Ethnomusicology* 14 (1): 1–56.

Blom, Jan-Petter, and John J. Gumperz. 1972. "Social Meaning in Linguistic Code-Switching in Norway." In *Directions in Sociolinguistics,* ed. John Gomperz and Dell Hymes. New York: Holt, Rinehart, and Winston.

Bryant, Edwin. 1936. *What I Saw in California*. Santa Ana: Fine Arts.

————. 1883. "Echoes in the City of Angels." *Century Magazine* 5:196.

Burciaga, José Antonio. 1987. "Linda Ronstadt: My Mexican Soul." *Vista (Los Angeles Herald Examiner)* 2 (10): 6–8.

Camarillo, Albert. 1979. *Chicanos in a Changing Society*. Cambridge: Harvard University Press.

Campa, Arthur. 1979. *Hispanic Culture in the Southwest*. Norman: University of Oklahoma Press.

Cleland, Robert G. 1944. *California in Our Time*. New York: Alfred Knopf.

Cooper, Marc. 1990. "The Rise of *La Opinión*." *L.A. Style,* March.

————. 1984. *Early Los Angeles*. Santa Barbara: Bellerophon.

Cortes, Carlos E. 1983. "'The Greaser's Revenge to 'Boulevard Nights': The Mass Media Curriculum on Chicanos." In *History, Culture and Society: Chicano Studies in the 1980s,* 125–40. National Association for Chicano Studies. Ypsilanti, Mich.: Bilingual Press.

————. 1970. "CHICOP: A Response of Local Chicano History." *Aztlán,* 1 (2): 1–14.

Cromelin, Richard. 1981. "A Twist—East L.A. Bands Visit Roxy." *Los Angeles Times,* March 14.

Dale, Harrison C. 1941. *The Ashley-Smith Explorations and the Discovery of a Central Route to the Pacific*. Glendale: Arthur C. Clark.

Da Silva, Owen F. 1941. *Mission Music of California*. Los Angeles: Warren F. Lewis.

Davis, William Heath. 1929. *Seventy-Five Years in California*. San Francisco: John Howell.

Dawson, Jim, and Bob Keane. 1981a. Liner notes. *The Best of Ritchie Valens*. (Del Fi Records 1958, 1959.) Santa Monica, Calif.: Rhino Records.

————. 1981b. "Ritchie Valens: His Life Story." LP anthology booklet and notes. (Los Angeles: Del Fi.) Santa Monica, Calif.: Rhino Records.

Deglar, Carl N. 1971. *Neither Black nor White: Slavery and Race Relations in Brazil and the United States*. New York: Macmillan.

Diamond, Darcy. 1984a. "Se Habla Español? Executives on the Turntable." *L.A. Weekly,* March 2–8.

————. 1984b. "East L.A.: 'The Sound and the Fury.'" *L.A. Weekly*, March 2–8.

————. N.d. "East L.A." *New Vinyl Times*.

————. 1981. "Putting East L.A. New Wave on a Label." *Sound*, February 27.

Escalante, Virginia. 1983. "Sanchez Takes Flight on Own Wings." *Los Angeles Times* ("Calendar"), October 4.

————. 1981. "With Cal Tjader: The Conga Madness of Poncho Sanchez." *Los Angeles Times*, March 12.

Everett, Todd. 1989. "In Any Language, Vikki Carr Impresses: Singer, Ronstadt team up for Mexican Arts Series Benefit." *Los Angeles Herald Examiner* ("Style"), May 8.

Ferguson, Donald N. 1973. *Music as Metaphor*. Westport, Conn.: Greenwood.

Fernández, Celestino. 1983. "Newspaper Coverage of Undocumented Mexican Immigration during the 1970s: A Qualitative Analysis of Pictures and Headings," In *History, Culture, and Society: Chicano Studies in the 1980s*, 177–98. National Association for Chicano Studies. Ypsilanti, Mich.: Bilingual Press.

Flans, Robyn. 1990. "Joey Heredia: Modern Latin Drummer." *Modern Drummer*, July.

Fogelquist, Mark Stephen. 1975. "Rhythm and Form in the Contemporary Son Jalisciense." Master's thesis, University of California, Los Angeles.

Foster, George M. 1975. *Contemporary Latin American Culture: An Anthropological Sourcebook*. Berkeley and Los Angeles: University of California.

Friedman, Robert. 1977. Liner notes. *Caliente = Hot: Puerto Rican and Cuban Musical Expression in New York*. New York: New World Records.

García y Griego, Larry. 1973. "Los Primeros Pasos del Norte: Mexican Migration to the United States." Bachelor's thesis, Princeton University.

García, Richard A. 1983. "The Mexican-American Mind: A Product of the 1930s." In *History, Culture and Society: Chicano Studies in the 1980s*, 67–94. National Association for Chicano Studies. Ypsilanti, Mich.: Bilingual Press.

Garrido, Juan S. 1974. *Historia de la música popular en México: 1896–1973*. Mexico: Editorial Extemporaneos.

Geertz, Clifford. 1983. *Local Knowledge: Further Essays in Interpretive Anthropology*. New York: Basic.

————. 1973. *The Interpretation of Cultures*. New York: Basic.

Gehman, Pleasant. 1981. "The Brat: The Eastside Beat." *L.A. Weekly*, February 20–26.

Gelgand, Donald E., and Russell D. Lee. 1973. *Ethnic Conflicts and Power: A Cross-National Perspective*. New York: Wiley.

Geyer, Anne. 1984. "Un espectáculo fantástico." *Los Angeles Times* ("Calendar"), November 25.

Gilmore, Mikal. 1985. "Los Lobos: Dance to the Howl of the Urban Wolves." *Los Angeles Herald Examiner* ("Weekend Magazine"), February 22.

Gladstone, Mark. 1978. "Conga's Heavy Beat Steals Show at Long Beach Jazz Festival." *Long Beach Independent Press Telegram*, September 4.

Gómez-Quiñones, Juan. 1982. "Plan de San Diego Reviewed." In *Chicano: The Evolution of a People*, edited by Renato Rosaldo, Robert A. Calvert, and Gustav L. Seligmann, 119–23. Malabar, Fla.: Robert E. Krieger.

————. 1977. "On Culture." *Revista Chicano-Riqueña* 5(2): 29–47.

————. 1971. "Toward a Perspective on Chicano History." *Aztlán* 2:1–51.

González-Roth, Gloria. 1981. "Willie Garcia: Exclusive Interview." *Q-VO* 10:10–11.

Gordon, Milton M. 1978. *Human Nature, Class, and Ethnicity*. New York: Oxford University Press.

————. 1964. *Assimilation in American Life*. New York: Oxford University Press.

Gradante, William. 1982. "'El Hijo del Pueblo': José Alfredo Jiménez and the Mexican *Canción Ranchera*." *Latin American Music Review* 3 (1): 36–59.

Griswold del Castillo, Richard. 1983. "Chicano Family History—Methodology and Theory: A Survey of Contemporary Research Directions." In *History, Culture and Society: Chicano Studies in the 1980s*, 67–94. National Association for Chicano Studies. Ypsilanti, Mich.: Bilingual Press.

————. 1979. *The Los Angeles Barrio, 1850–1890: A Social History*. Berkeley and Los Angeles: University of California Press.

Guevara, Rubén. 1990. "La Bambá and Beyond." *L.A. Style*, March.

————. 1988. "El Chicano." Liner notes. *Viva El Chicano*. Universal City, Calif.: MCA Records.

————. 1985. "The View from the Sixth Street Bridge: The History of Chicano Rock." In *The First Rock & Roll Confidential Report*, edited by David Marsh and the editors of *Rock & Roll Confidential*, 113–26. New York: Pantheon.

Guinn, James M. 1901. *Historical and Biographical Record of Los Angeles and Vicinity*. Chicago: Chapman.

Guyette, Susan. 1983. *Community Based Research*. Los Angeles: American Indian Studies Center, University of California.

Hague, Eleanor. 1922. *Early Spanish-Californian Folk-Songs*. New York: Fischer.

————. 1917. *Spanish-American Folk-Songs*. Lancaster, Penn.: American Folklore Society.

Harris, Marvin. 1968. *The Rise of Anthropological Theory*. New York: Harper and Row.

Hayes, Benjamin. 1929. *Pioneer Notes*. Edited by Marjorie Tisdale Wolcott. Los Angeles: Marjorie Tisdale Wolcott.

Heckman, Don. 1990. "A Discordant Note in Mariachi Style." *Los Angeles Times* ("Calendar"), June 23.

————. 1989. "Ronstadt and Carr: Gifted and Glossy." *Los Angeles Times* ("Calendar"), May 8.

Heisley, Michael. 1988. "Sources for the Study of Mexican Music in California." In *California's Musical Wealth: Sources for the Study of Music in California*, edited by Stephen M. Fry, 55–78 (papers presented at the 1985 Joint Conference of the Northern and Southern California Chapters of the Music Library Association). Southern California Chapter, Music Library Association.

————. 1985. "Lummis and Mexican American Folklore." In *Charles M. Lummis: The Centennial Exhibition*, edited by Daniela P. Moneta, 60–67. Los Angeles: Southwest Museum.

Henríquez, C. Nelson. 1988. "Linda Ronstadt: Un corazón que late al ritmo de la mejor tradición mexicana." *Mundo Artístico* 7 (22): 8–9.

Hernández, Al Carlos. 1983a. "Joe King Carrasco." *Avance* 2:20–21.

———. 1983b. "Nostalgia Isn't What It Used To Be: The Chicano Oldies Experience." *Avance* 1 (2): 8–9.

Hernández, Guillermo. N.d. "The Chicano Experience." Liner notes. *Texas Mexican Border Music*, vol. 14. El Cerrito, Calif.: Folklyric Records. 9021.

———. 1978. *Cancionero de la Raza: Songs of the Chicano Experience*. Berkeley: El Fuego de Aztlán.

Hernández, Marita. 1983. "Generation in Search of Its Legacy." *Los Angeles Times*, August 14. Reprinted in *Southern California's Latino Community*.

Hernández, Virginia, and Diane Preciado. 1985. "Success in the Latino Music Market of Los Angeles." Unpublished paper.

Herrera-Sobek, Maria. 1979. *The Bracero Experience: Elitelore Versus Folklore*. Los Angeles: Latin American Center, University of California.

Herskovits, M. J. 1945. "Problem, Method and Theory in Afroamerican Studies." Reprinted in *The New World Negro*, 55–58. Bloomington: University of Indiana Press.

———. 1938. *Acculturation: The Study of Culture Contact*. New York: Augustin.

Herzog, George. 1928. "The Yuman Musical Style." *Journal of American Folklore* 41:183–231.

Heth, Charlotte. 1982. "Can Ethnohistory Help the Ethnomusicologist?" *American Indian Culture and Research Journal* 6 (1): 63–78.

Hilburn, Robert. 1984. "Los Lobos Bring Joy with Spirit, Substance." *Los Angeles Times* ("Calendar"), November 19.

Hochman, Steve. 1990. "A Vibrant Mariachi Fest." *Los Angeles Times* ("Calendar"), June 26.

Hood, Mantle. 1971. *The Ethnomusicologist*. New York: McGraw-Hill.

Humphrey, Norman D. 1941. "Mexican Repatriation from Michigan: Public Assistance in Historical Perspective." *Social Service Review* 15 (Sept.): 497–513.

Hunt, Dennis. 1982. "Rudy Salas: Crusader for the Latino Bands." *Los Angeles Times*, October 2.

Janson, William. 1965. "The Esoteric-Exoteric Factor in Folklore." In *The Study of Folklore*, edited by Alan Dundes. Englewood Cliffs, N.J.: Prentice-Hall.

"Jazz Valley's Musical Feast." 1983. *Fresno Bee* ("Tempo,") September 6.

Juárez, Rolando A. 1976. "What the Tape Recorder Has Created: A Broadly Based Exploration into Contemporary Oral History Practice." *Aztlán*, 7 (1): 99–118.

Kanellos, Nicolás. 1987. *Mexican American Theater: Legacy and Reality*. Pittsburgh: Latin American Literary Review.

Kelsey, Harry. 1977. "A New Look at the Founding of Old Los Angeles." *California Historical Quarterly* 55 (4): 326–39.

Kirsch, Jonathan. 1978. "Chicano Power." *The Decade of the Chicano: California's Emerging Third World Majority*, special issue of *New West*, September 11.

Knoedelseder, William, Jr. 1989. "Burst of New Music: Young Latins Find a Voice in U.S. Pop." *Los Angeles Times*, August 4.

Kroeber, A. L. 1963. *Style and Civilizations*. Berkeley and Los Angeles: University of California Press.

Lankevich, George J. 1981. *Ethnic America, 1978–1980*. London: Oceana.

Leach, Edmund. 1982. *Social Anthropology*. New York, Oxford: Oxford University Press.

———. 1979. *Political Systems of Highland Burma*. 2d ed. Boston: Beacon Press.

Leeds, Anthony. 1969. "The Significant Variables Determining the Characteristics of Squatter Settlements." *America Latina* 12:44–86.

Liberman, Frank, & Associates. N.d. "Vikki Carr: Biography." Los Angeles: Frank Liberman & Associates.

Limón, José. 1983a. "The Rise, Fall, and 'Revival' of the Mexican-American Corrido: A Review Essay." *Studies in Latin American Popular Culture* 2:202–7.

———. 1983b. "Texas Mexican Popular Music and Dancing: Some Notes on History and Symbolic Process." *Latin American Music Review* 4 (2): 229–46.

Lipsitz, George. 1990. *Time Passages: Collective Memory and American Popular Culture*. Minneapolis: University of Minnesota Press.

———. 1986. "Cruising around the Historical Bloc—Postmodernism and Popular Music in East Los Angeles." *Culture Critique* 5:157–77.

Lomnitz, Larissa Adler. 1977. *Networks and Marginality: Life in a Mexican Shantytown*. New York: Academic.

López, José Y. 1975. "Chico Sesma: A Man and his Music." *Latin Quarter* 1 (4): 10–15.

Lopez, Ronald W., and Darryl D. Enos. 1973. "Spanish Language Only Television in Los Angeles County." *Aztlán* 4 (2): 283–313.

Los Angeles County Latino Community Profile. 1988. Claremont, Calif.: Tomás Rivera Center.

Loza, Steven J. 1985. "The Musical Life of the Mexican/Chicano People in Los Angeles: A Study in Maintenance, Change, and Adaptation. Ph.D. diss., University of California, Los Angeles.

———. 1983a. "The Battle of the Bands in East L.A." *Caminos*, November.

———. 1983b. "The Great Mexican Legends in Music." *Caminos*, November.

———. 1983c. "El Rey del Timbal." Interview with Tito Puente. *Caminos*, November.

———. 1983d. "Los Illegals: Internal Exile." Record review. *Caminos*, November.

———. 1982a. "Acculturative Patterns in Music within the Chicano Community of Los Angeles." Paper presented at Southern California Chapter Conference, National Society for Ethnomusicology, March.

———. 1982b. "A Model for Sound Analysis: Motion and Structures." Graduate seminar paper, University of California, Los Angeles, Department of Music.

———. 1982c. "Origins, Form, and Development of the Son Jarocho: Veracruz, Mexico." *Aztlán* 13 (1 and 2): 257–74.

———. 1980. "Tierra Together." *La Gente* (ASUCLA [Associated Students of the University of California, Los Angeles]), October.

Luhman, Reid, and Stuart Gilman. 1980. *Race and Ethnic Relations: The Social and Political Experience of Minority Groups*. Belmont, Calif.: Wadsworth.

Lummis, Charles F. 1923. *Spanish Songs of Old California*. New York: Schirmer.

Macías, Alberto. 1982. "Rock y Ondas." *La Opinión*, February 3.

MacMinn, George R. 1941. *The Theater of the Golden Era in California*. Caldwell, Idaho: Caxton.

Madrid-Barela, Arturo. 1982. "In Search of the Authentic Pachuco: An Interpretive Essay." In *Chicano: The Evolution of a People,* edited by Renato Rosaldo, Robert A. Calvert, and Gustav Seligmann, 202–19. Malabar, Fla.: Robert E. Krieger.

———. 1976. "Pochos, the Different Mexicans: An Interpretive Essay, Part I." *Aztlán* 7 (1): 51–64

Mandel, Howard. 1977. "Devadip Carlos Santana: Ethnic Evolution." *Downbeat,* April 21.

Marks, Morton. 1974. "Uncovering Ritual Stuctures in Afro-American Music." In *Religious Movements in Contemporary America,* ed. Irving Zaretsky and Mark Leon. Princeton: Princeton University Press.

Marsh, David. 1985. "Rock & Roll's Latin Tinge." In *The First Rock & Roll Confidential Report,* 110–12. New York: Pantheon.

———. 1984. "Rock and Roll's Latin Tinge: The Proof Is in the Salsa." *The Boston Phoenix,* January 17.

Martínez, Oscar J. 1978. "Chicano Oral History: Status and Prospects." *Aztlán* 9 (1): 119–31.

Mason, William. 1984. "Indian-Mexican Cultural Exchange in the Los Angeles Area, 1781–1834." *Aztlán* 15 (1): 123–44.

McWilliams, Carey. 1968. *North from Mexico: The Spanish-Speaking People of the United States.* New York: Greenwood.

Medina, Luis. "California Salsa." *Avance* 1 (2): 27–28.

Meier, Matt S. 1984. *Bibliography of Mexican American History.* Westport, Conn.: Greenwood.

Mendheim, Beverly. 1987. *Ritchie Valens: The First Latino Rocker.* Tempe, Ariz: Bilingual Press.

Mendoza, Vicente T. 1961. *La canción mexicana: ensayo de clasificación y antología.* Mexico City: Instituto de Investigaciones Estéticas, Universidad Nacional Autónoma de México.

Moneta, Daniela P., ed. 1985. *Chas. F. Lummis—The Centennial Exhibition Commemorating His Tramp across the Continent.* Los Angeles: Southwest Museum.

Moore, Joan W. (with Harry Pachón). 1976. *Mexican Americans.* Englewood Cliffs, N.J.: Prentice-Hall.

Morthland, John. 1984. "Los Lobos Con Safos." *The Village Voice,* Feb. 28 .

Muñoz, Sergio. 1980. "Cultura Chicana: Los Angeles." *La Opinión* (Suplemento Cultural), July 13.

Murray, William. 1978. "Zoot Suit: The Triumph of El Pachuco." *New West,* September 11.

Nettl, Bruno. 1964. *Theory and Method in Ethnomusicology.* New York: Macmillan.

Nketia, J. H. Kwabema. 1981. "The Juncture of the Social and the Musical: The Methodology of Cultural Analysis." *The World of Music* 23 (2): 22–35.

Orth, Maureen. 1978. "The Soaring Spirit of Chicano Arts." *New West,* September 11.

Pachón, Harry P., and Joan W. Moore. 1981. "Mexican-Americans." In *America as a Multicultural Society,* edited by Milton M. Gordon, 111–24. Vol. 454 of the

Annals of the American Academy of Political and Social Science. Philadelphia: American Academy of Political and Social Science.

Padilla, Amado M., ed. 1980. *Acculturation: Theory, Models, and Some New Findings.* American Association for the Advancement of Sciences Selected Symposium no. 39. Boulder: AAAS.

Paredes, Américo. 1976. *A Texas-Mexican Cancionero: Folksongs of the Lower Border.* Urbana: University of Illinois Press.

————. 1968. "Folk Medicine and the Intercultural Jest." In *Spanish Speaking People in the United States,* edited by June Helm, 104–19. Seattle: University of Washington Press.

————. 1958. *With His Pistol in His Hand: A Border Ballad and Its Hero.* Austin: University of Texas Press.

Paredes, Américo, and Ellen J. Stekert, eds. 1971. *The Urban Experience and Folk Tradition.* Austin: University of Texas Press.

Pascall, R. J. 1980. "Style." In *The New Grove Dictionary of Music and Musicians,* edited by Stanley Sadie. London: Macmillan.

Peacock, James L. 1968. *Rites of Modernization: Symbolic and Social Aspects of Indonesian Proletarian Drama.* Chicago: University of Chicago Press.

Pearlman, Steven Ray. 1988. "Mariachi Music in Los Angeles." Ph.D. diss., University of California, Los Angeles.

————. 1984. "Standardization and Innovation in Mariachi Music Performance in Los Angeles." *Pacific Review of Ethnomusicology* 1:1–12.

————. 1983. "Mariachi Music in Los Angeles." *Caminos,* November.

Peña, Manuel. 1989. "Notes toward an Interpretive History of California-Mexican Music." In *From the Inside Out: Perspectives on Mexican and Mexican American Folk Art,* edited by Karana Hattersly-Drayton, Joyce M. Bishop, and Tomás Ybarra-Frausto, 64–75. San Francisco: The Mexican Museum.

————. 1985a. *The Texas-Mexican Conjunto: History of a Working-Class Music.* Austin: University of Texas Press.

————. 1985b. "From Ranchero to Jaitón: Ethnicity and Class in Texas-Mexican Music (Two Styles in the Form of a Pair)." *Ethnomusicology* 29 (1): 29–55.

————. 1982a. "The Emergence of Conjunto Music, 1935–1955." In *And Other Neighborly Names: Social Process and Cultural Image in Texas Folklore,* edited by Richard Bauman and Roger Abrahams, 280–99. Austin: University of Texas Press.

————. 1982b. "Folksong and Social Change: Two Corridos as Interpretive Sources." *Aztlán* 13 (1 and 2): 13–42.

————. 1980. "Ritual Structure in a Chicano Dance." *Latin American Music Review* 1 (1): 47–73.

Perlman, Janice. 1975. "Rio Favelas and the Myth of Marginality." *Politics and Society* 5:131–60.

Phelps, William D. 1871. *Fore and Aft.* Boston: Nichols and Hall.

Plascencia, Luis F. B. 1983. "Low Riding in the Southwest: Cultural Symbols in the Mexican Community." In *History, Culture, and Society: Chicano Studies in the 1980s,* 141–76. National Association for Chicano Studies. Ypsilanti, Mich.: Bilingual Press.

Puig, Claudia. 1989. "L.A. Latinos and a New Harmony: Benefit Concerts to Help Mexican-American Youths Learn Leadership Roles." *Los Angeles Times* ("Calendar"), August 1.

Puterbaugh, Parke. 1987. Liner notes. *The History of Rock Instrumentals*. Santa Monica, Calif.: Rhino Records.

Quiñones, Andrew J. 1981. "Exclusive Interview: Tierra." *Q-VO* 3 (3): 7–9, 67.

Rael, Juan B. 1951. "More Light on the Origin of Los Pastores." *New Mexico Folklore Record* 6:1–6.

Reveles, Julian. 1989. "Make Mine Mariachi." *Vista (Los Angeles Herald Examiner)* 4 (33): 6–9.

Reyes, David, and Tom Waldman. 1982. "Thee Midniters." *Goldmine*, Feb. 28.

Reyna, José. 1982. "Notes on Tejano Music." *Aztlán* 13 (1 and 2): 13–42.

Richman, Irving Berdine. 1911. *California under Spain and Mexico: 1535–1847*. Boston: Houghton Mifflin.

Ríos-Bustamante, Antonio, and Pedro Castillo. 1986. *An Illustrated History of Mexican Los Angeles, 1781–1985*. Los Angeles: UCLA Chicano Studies Research Center.

"Ritchie Valens to Get Walk of Fame Star." 1989. *Los Angeles Times* ("Metro Digest"), Aug. 17.

Rizo, José. 1980. "Carlos Santana." *Q-VO* 2 (7): 16–17.

———. 1989. "Roland Vasquez." *Jazziz*, Oct./Nov.

———. 1981. "Tierra's First National Tour—A Dynamic Success." *Firme* 1 (5): 20–21, 62–63.

Robe, Stanley. 1954. *Coloquios de pastores from Jalisco, Mexico*. Berkeley and Los Angeles: University of California Press.

Roberts, John Storm. 1979. *The Latin Tinge: The Influence of Latin American Music in the United States*. New York: Oxford University Press.

Robinson, Alfred. 1891. *Life in California*. San Francisco: William Doxey.

Rodríguez, Luis. 1980a. "Eastside Story, Part II." *L.A. Weekly*, August 15–21.

———. 1980b. "The History of the 'Eastside Sound.'" *L.A. Weekly*, August 1–7.

———. 1980c. "Eastside Sound." *Q-VO* 2 (7): 27–29, 69, 76–78.

Romo, Ricardo. 1983a. "The Urbanization of Southwestern Chicanos in the Early Twentieth Century." In *Chicano: The Evolution of a People*, edited by Renato Rosaldo, Robert A. Calvert, and Gustav L. Seligmann, 146–59. Malabar, Fla.: Robert E. Krieger.

———. 1983b. *East Los Angeles: History of a Barrio*. Austin: University of Texas Press.

Sachs, Curt. 1946. *The Commonwealth of Art*. New York: W.W. Norton.

"Salesian Rock 'n Roll Shows '75" (program booklet). 1975. Produced and directed by Bill Taggart, February 9, 16, 23; March 2, 16. Salesian High School, Los Angeles.

Sandow, Gregory. 1988. "¡Ay, que Linda!: Ronstadt Sings Songs She Grew Up With." *Los Angeles Herald Examiner* ("Style"), February 20.

———. 1988. "Los Lobos Parties Down: Music Had the Fans Dancing." *Los Angeles Herald Examiner* ("Style"), November 21.

Schapiro, Meyer. 1953. "Style." In *Anthropology Today,* edited by A. L. Kroeber. Chicago: University of Chicago Press.

Schneider, Marius. 1960. "Primitive Music." In *Ancient and Oriental Music,* edited by Egon Wellesz. Vol. 1 of *The New Oxford History of Music.* 2d ed. London: Oxford University Press.

Schwartz, Bob. 1988. "Music of Mexico: Mariachis in Search of U.S. Respect." *Los Angeles Times,* March 1.

Sheehy, Daniel Edward. 1979. "The Son Jarocho: The History, Style, and Repertory of a Changing Musical Tradition." Ph.D. diss., University of California, Los Angeles.

———. 1975. "Speech Deviations as One of the Determinants of Style in the Son Jarocho of Veracruz, Mexico." Master's thesis, University of California, Los Angeles.

Sheviya, Eytan ben. 1983. "Salsa—Taste The Music." *L.A. Weekly,* June 24–30.

Singer, Roberta. 1983. "Innovation and Symbolic Process among Contemporary Latin Musicians in New York City." *Latin American Music Review* 1 (1): 1–12.

Snowdon, Don. 1984. "The Sound of East L.A., 1964." *Los Angeles Times* ("Calendar"), October 28.

———. 1984. "Zyanya: Tuned to New Latino Rock." *Los Angeles Times* ("Calendar"), February 5.

Sonnichsen, Philip. 1984. "Los Primeros Duetos Femininas: The First Women Duets (1930–1955)." Liner notes. *Texas-Mexican Border Music,* vol. 17. El Cerrito: Folklyric Records. 9035.

———. 1977a. "Lalo Guerrero: Pioneer in Mexican American Music." *La Luz,* May.

———. 1977b. *"Los madrugadores:* Early Spanish Radio in California." *La Luz,* June.

———. N.d. "Texas Mexican Border Music: Corridos, Part 1 & 2." Booklet. *Texas-Mexican Border Music,* vols. 2 & 3. El Cerrito: Folklyric Records.

Sordinas, Augustus. 1978. "Ethnography: In Need of Native Ethnographers." Paper presented at the 77th Annual Meeting of the American Anthropological Association, 18 November 1978, Los Angeles, California.

Sotomayor, Frank. 1983. "Latinos: Diverse Group Tied by Ethnicity." *Los Angeles Times,* July 25. Reprinted in *Southern California's Latino Community.*

Southern California's Latino Community: A Series of Articles Reprinted from the "Los Angeles Times." 1983. Los Angeles: *Los Angeles Times.*

Spradley, James P. 1979. *The Ethnographic Interview.* New York: Holt, Rinehart and Winston.

Spradley, James P., and David W. McCurdy. 1972. *The Cultural Experience: Ethnography in a Complex Society.* Chicago: Science Research Associates.

Spottswood, Richard K. 1990. *Ethnic Music on Records: A Discography of Ethnic Recordings Produced in the United States, 1893–1942.* Urbana: University of Illinois Press.

Steiner, Stanley. 1970. *La Raza: The Mexican Americans.* New York: Harper and Row.

Stevenson, Robert M. 1988a. "Local Music History Research in Los Angeles Area Libraries: Part I." *Inter-American Music Review* 10 (1): 19–38.

———. 1988b. "Music in Southern California: A Tale of Two Cities. (Los Angeles: The First Biennium and Beyond)." *Inter-American Music Review* 10 (1): 39–111.

———. 1986. "Los Angeles." In *The New Grove Dictionary of American Music,* ed. H. Wiley Hitchcock and Eric Sadie, 107–15. London: Macmillan.

———. 1968. *Music in Aztec and Inca Territory.* Berkeley and Los Angeles: University California Press.

———. 1952. *Music in Mexico.* New York: Thomas Y. Crowell.

Swan, Howard. 1952. *Music in the Southwest, 1825–1950.* San Marino, Calif.: Huntington.

Tavera-King, Ben. 1978. "¡Ajua! Música Chicana Takes Off." *Nuestro,* February.

Treutlein, Theodore E. 1973. "Los Angeles, California: The Question of the City's Original Spanish Name." *Southern California Quarterly* 55 (1): 1–7.

Turner, Victor. 1974. *Dramas, Fields, and Metaphors.* Ithaca: Cornell University Press.

———. 1969. *The Ritual Process: Structure and Anti-Structure.* Chicago: Aldine.

Underhill, Ruth Murray. 1938. *Singing for Power: The Song Magic of the Papago Indians of Southern Arizona.* Berkeley and Los Angeles: University of California Press.

United States Immigration and Naturalization Service. 1986 *Annual Report.* Washington: GPO.

Valdez, Luis, and Stan Steiner, eds. 1972. *Aztlán: An Anthology of Mexican American Literature.* New York: Random House.

Valle, Victor. 1989. "Benefit for National Hispanic Institute a Coming of Age." *Los Angeles Times* ("Calendar"), August 4.

———. 1988a. "The Changing Sounds of Mariachi Music." *Los Angeles Times* ("Calendar"), March 1.

———. 1988b. "All-Spanish Los Lobos LP Due in Fall." *Los Angeles Times* ("Calendar"), July 29.

———. 1987. "Los Lobos: The Wolf Survives." *Los Angeles Times* ("Calendar"), January 25.

———. 1987. "Ronstadt Sings Her Mexican Heritage in 'Canciones.'" *Los Angeles Times* ("Calendar"), December 25.

Van de Voorde, Andy. 1983. "Ruben and the Hits: The Rebirth of the East L.A. Sound." *New Vinyl Times,* December 7–13.

Vélez-Ibáñez, Carlos G. 1983. *Rituals of Marginality: Politics, Process, and Culture Change in Central Urban Mexico, 1969–1974.* Berkeley and Los Angeles: University of California Press.

———. 1975. "An Evening in Ciudad Reyes: A Processual Approach to Mexican Politics." *The New Scholar* 5 (1): 5–17.

Wagner, Nathaniel N., and Marsh J. Haug. 1971. *Chicanos: Social and Psychological Perspectives.* St. Louis: C.V. Mosby.

Waller, Don. 1981. "Ritchie Valens Lives!" *L.A. Weekly,* October 23–29.

Walsh, Michael. 1988. "Shake Your Body: The 'Black-Bean Invasion' Arrives: from Salsa to Hip-hop, Latino Sounds Go Pop." *Time*, July 11.

Weaver, Robert C. 1982. "The Impact of Ethnicity upon Urban America." In *Ethnic Relations in America*, edited by Lance Liebman, 66–100. Englewood Cliffs, N.J.: Prentice-Hall.

Wilbert, Johannes. 1976a. "Introduction." In *Enculturation in Latin America: An Anthology*, edited by Johannes Wilbert, 1–27. Los Angeles: UCLA Latin American Center, University of California.

———. 1976b. "To Become a Maker of Canoes: An Essay in Warao Enculturation." In *Enculturation in Latin America: An Anthology*, edited by Johannes Wilbert, 308–58. Los Angeles: UCLA Latin American Center, University of California.

Discography

The following discography lists the recordings cited in the nine case studies in addition to a selection of LPs reflecting the musical life of the Mexican/Chicano people in Los Angeles since 1945, focusing especially on the music of East Los Angeles. All vinyl discs listed below are 12-inch, 33 ⅓ rpm recordings. Also listed are tape cassettes and compact discs.

Acuña, Manuel. *Canciones de Manuel S. Acuña.* Círculo Social Amigos Nacozarenses CSAN 61075.
Los Angelinos: The Eastside Renaissance. Zyanya, 1983; distributed by Rhino.
La Bamba: Original Motion Picture Soundtrack. 1987. Slash/Warner Brothers 9–25605–1.
Cano, Eddie. *Broadway Right Now.* Reprise R-6124.
Cano, Eddie. *Deep In a Drum.* 1958. RCA Victor LPM-1645.
Cano, Eddie. *His Piano and His Rhythm.* 1962. RCA Victor LPM/LSP-2636.
Los Camperos de Nati Cano. *El super mariachi los Camperos.* 1972. Discos Latin International DLIS 2003.
El Chicano. *El Chicano V.* 1974. MCA.
El Chicano. *Let Me Dance With You.* 1984. Columbia 7464–04997–1.
El Chicano. *Revolución.* 1971. MCA (Kap) KS-3640.
The Chicano Experience. 1975. Vol. 14 of *Texas-Mexican Border Music.* Folklyric 9021.
Corridos, Part 1: 1930–1934. 1975. Vol. 2 of *Texas-Mexican Border Music.* Folklyric 9004.
Corridos, Part 2: 1929–1936. 1975. Vol. 3 of *Texas-Mexican Border Music.* Folklyric 9005.
Eastside Connection. Rampart RPT-SS-7610.
East Side Story (vols. 1–12). Trojan LP-2012.
East Side Revue: 40 Hits by East Los Angeles' Most Popular Groups. 1966[1969]. Rampart; distributed by American Pie as LP 3303.
Golden Treasures, vol.1: West Coast East Side Revue. 1966. Rampart 3303.
Golden Treasures, vol.2: West Coast East Side Revue. 1969. Rampart 3305.
Guerrero, Lalo. *Las Ardillitas de Lalo Guerrero.* Discos Odeón; distributed by Alhambra as OMS-73186.
The History of Latino Rock, vol.1: 1956–1965: The Eastside Sound. 1983. Zyanya; distributed by Rhino.

The History of Rock Instrumentals, vol.2. 1987. Rhino RNC-70138.

Los Illegals. *Internal Exile.* 1983. A&M 7502–14925–1.

Los Lobos. *And a Time to Dance.* 1984. Slash; distributed by Warner Brothers as 7599–23963–1.

Los Lobos. *By the Light of the Moon.* 1987. Slash/Warner Brothers.

Los Lobos. *How Will the Wolf Survive?* 1985 Slash; distributed by Warner Brothers as 7599–25177–1.

Los Lobos. *Just Another Band From East L.A.* 1978. New Vista.

Los Lobos. *Kiko.* 1992. Slash/Warner Brothers.

Los Lobos. *The Neighborhood.* 1990. Slash/Warner Brothers.

Los Lobos. *La Pistola y El Corazón.* 1988. Slash/Warner Brothers.

Los Madrugadores. *Los Madrugadores.* 1985. Vol. 18 of *Texas-Mexican Border Music.* Folklyric 9036.

Martínez, Johnny "Chano." *¡Salsa Revolution!* 1974. Sonotropic, Producción Musimex, ST-7001.

Pagán, Ralfi. *With Love.* Fania; distributed by Mark West as SLP 397.

Reyes, Lucha. *Canciones Mexicanas en La Voz Inolvidable de Lucha Reyes.* RCA Victor MKL-1120, Disco Popular.

Rodríguez. *Tell an Amigo.* 1986. Sea Breeze SB-2030.

Ronstadt, Linda. *Canciones de mi Padre.* 1987. Elektra/Asylum (Warner Communications).

Ronstadt, Linda. *Más Canciones.* 1992. Elektra/Asylum (Warner Communications).

Russell, Andy. *Ayer, Hoy, y Siempre.* 1982. Kim K-725.

Sánchez, Poncho. *Bien Sabroso.* 1984. Concord (Picante) CJP-239.

Sánchez, Poncho. *Chile Con Soul.* 1990. Concord (Picante) CJP-406-C.

Sánchez, Poncho. *Live at Kimball's East.* 1991. Concord (Picante) CJP-472-C.

Sánchez, Poncho. *Papa Gato.* 1987. Concord (Picante) CJP-310.

Sánchez, Poncho. *Sonando.* 1983. Concord (Picante) CJP-201.

Sánchez, Poncho. *Straight Ahead.* 1980. Discovery; distributed by Trend as DA-813.

Strachwitz, Howard. *Texas-Mexican Border Music, vol. 1: An Introduction, 1930–1960.* 1973. Folklyric.

Thee Midniters. *Best of Thee Midniters.* 1983. Zyanya; distributed by Rhino as RNLP 063.

Thee Midniters. *Giants.* Distributed by Marketing West as 1002-C.

Thee Midniters. *Thee Midniters.* Distributed by Marketing West as 1001-C.

Thee Midniters. *Thee Midniters Bring You Love Special Delivery.* Whittier; distributed by Marketing West as WS-5000.

Thee Midniters. *Unlimited.* Distributed by Marketing West as 1003-C.

Tierra. *Bad City Boys.* Boardwalk 7912–33255–1.

Tierra. *City Nights.* 1980. Boardwalk 7912–36995–1.

Tierra. *Stranded.* 1975. Salsoul (Mericana) SSP-5500

Tierra. *Tierra.* 1973. 20th Century T-412.

Valens, Ritchie. *The Best of Ritchie Valens.* 1958, 1959. Del-Fi; distributed by Rhino as RNDF 200.

Valens, Ritchie. *The History of Ritchie Valens.* Rhino RNBC 2798.

Valens, Ritchie. *Ritchie.* Del-Fi; distributed by Rhino as RNLP 70232.

Valens, Ritchie. *Ritchie Valens.* MGM GAS-117.

Valens, Ritchie. *Ritchie Valens.* Del-Fi; distributed by Rhino as RNLP 70231.

Valens, Ritchie. *Ritchie Valens in Concert at Pacoima Jr. High.* Del-Fi; distributed by Rhino as RNLP 70233.

El Chicano. *Viva! El Chicano: Their Very Best.* 1988. MCA.

El Chicano. *Viva El Tirado.* Kapp MCA-548.

Yaqui. *Yaqui.* 1973. Playboy PB-127.

Zootsuit: Music from the Original Motion Picture. MCA 5267 (MCA 2757).

Index

Sánchez, Miguel, 75
Sánchez, Poncho, 109, 117, 121, 122, 126, 155, 157, 193, 196–201, 262–64, 270, 280, 282, 284
Sánchez, Víctor, 33
Sandoval, Blanca, 117
Sandoval, David, 233
Sandoval, Joe, 107, 239,
Santa Cruz, Petrita, 64
Santa Fe Springs (L.A. sur-burb), 202, 264
Santa Monica Public Library, 120
Santa Susana Mountains, 3
Santamaría, Mongo, 193, 199, 201, 263
Santana, 102, 140, 226, 228, 270, 281, 282
Santana, Carlos, 96, 116, 117, 121, 140, 154, 281, 282, 284
Santancra, Sonora, 74, 75, 85
Santuario de Guadalupe, 63
Sarabia, Juanito, 66
Saracho, Garrett, 120, 126
Saucedo, Víctor, 119, 121
Sauret, Emile, 14
Savaillos, Benny, 99
Schifrin, Lalo, 116
Schireson Brothers, 79
Scorzo, Dolores, 104
Scorzo, Harry, 104
"Se acabó el WPA," 22, 25
Sea Breeze (record com-pany), 116
Seaver Center for Western History Research, 13
"Secret Society," 212
Segovia, Andrés, 56, 141
"Serenata," 63
Serra, Fray Junipero, 4
Serra, Mincho, 75
Serrano, Bertica, 59
Sesma, Chico, 71, 74, 84, 85, 122, 196
Sesma, Lionel. *See* Sesma, Chico
Setzer, Brian, 234
Sex Pistols, 188

Shalomar, 140
Shearing, George, 85, 154
Sheehy, Daniel, 90, 122
Sheila E. *See* Escobedo, Sheila
Shh-Boom, 108
Shining Star, 107
Shirelles, 202
Shoshone, 3
Shrine Auditorium, 59, 67
"Siempre en Domingo," 164
Silva, Armando, 64
Silver Dollar Cafe, 47
Silvester, 140
Simon, Paul, 283
Simplemente mujer, 87, 115
Sinatra, Frank, 56, 102, 143, 145, 156, 268, 280
Sinfónica del Barrio, 119, 120
Sinfónica Nacional de México, 150
Sisters, The, 102, 135
Sistine Chapel, 62
Six-Pac, The, 103
Skelton, Red, 58
Sky, 108
Skylite, 104
Slapsi Maxi's, 154
Slash Records, 115, 242
Slauson Brothers, The, 102, 135
Sleepy Lagoon case, 37
"Slow Down," 100
Sly, Slick, and Wicked, 107
Smith, Alfonso, 126
Smith, Jedediah, 4
Smith, Rosalía, 63
Smothers Brothers, 223
Soft Cell, 140
"Solamente una vez," 69
"Solid Gold," 105
Solid Senders, The, 80
Solís, Javier, 104, 159, 202
Son conjunto, 210
Son jalisciense, 87, 90, 166, 224
Son(es), 56, 68, 73, 157, 166, 167, 178, 180, 193, 210, 262
Sonnichsen, Philip, 33
"Sonny," 136
Sonny and the Sunlighters, 198

"Sonora querido," 34
Sonoratown (nickname for L.A.), 16, 17
Sophistafunk, 107
Sosa, Leopoldo, 89
Soto, Enrique, 117
Soto, Joaquín, 91
"Soul Train," 105
"Sound of Music," 155
South El Monte (L.A. sub-urb), 90
South Pacific, 86
South Pasadena (L.A. sub-urb), 150
Southern California Coun-cil of Mexican American Relations, 43
Southwest Museum, 17, 19
Spanish Songs of Old Califor-nia, 17
Specialty Records, 80, 81, 134
Stalin, Joseph, 65
Stan Kenton Orchestra, 142, 144, 145
Standells, 100
Starwood, 187
Steven's, 109
Stevenson, Robert, 4, 119, 122
Stewart, Rod, 140
Stockton, Commodore, 8
Stone Ponies, 92
Stranded, 104
"Streetscapers of East Los Angeles," 50
"Stubborn Kind of Fel-low," 100
Student Nonviolent Co-ordinating Committee (SNCC), 43
Students for a Democratic Society (SDS), 43
Style: adaptation, 265; forma-tion of, 259, 270, 280
Stylistics, The, 140
Sudden Urge, 108
Suedan, César, 243
"Sueño," 63
Sugar Daddy's, 109
"Suicidio de Juan Reyna," 30
Sulam, Vanessa, 117

A Note on the Author

STEVEN LOZA is an assistant professor of ethnomusicology at the University of California, Los Angeles, where he is also director of both the Mexican Arts Series and the Latin American music ensemble UCLATINO. Loza's academic achievements include Fulbright and Ford Foundation fellowships and numerous publications in both the scholarly and popular press on the topics of Mexican and Latin American music; in addition, he has extensive experience as a professional musician playing in and around the Los Angeles scene.

Books in the Series Music in American Life

Early American Music Engraving and Printing: A History of Music Publishing in America from 1787 to 1825 with Commentary on Earlier and Later Practices
Richard J. Wolfe

Sing a Sad Song: The Life of Hank Williams
Roger M. Williams

Long Steel Rail: The Railroad in American Folksong
Norm Cohen

Resources of American Music History: A Directory of Source Materials from Colonial Times to World War II
D. W. Krummel, Jean Geil, Doris J. Dyen, and Deane L. Root

Tenement Songs: The Popular Music of the Jewish Immigrants
Mark Slobin

Ozark Folksongs
Vance Randolph; edited and abridged by Norm Cohen

Oscar Sonneck and American Music
Edited by William Lichtenwanger

Bluegrass Breakdown: The Making of the Old Southern Sound
Robert Cantwell

Bluegrass: A History
Neil V. Rosenberg

Music at the White House: A History of the American Spirit
Elise K. Kirk

Red River Blues: The Blues Tradition in the Southeast
Bruce Bastin

Good Friends and Bad Enemies: Robert Winslow Gordon and the Study of American Folksong
Debora Kodish

Fiddlin' Georgia Crazy: Fiddlin' John Carson, His Real World, and the World of His Songs
Gene Wiggins

America's Music: From the Pilgrims to the Present, Revised Third Edition
Gilbert Chase

Secular Music in Colonial Annapolis: The Tuesday Club, 1745–56
John Barry Talley

Bibliographical Handbook of American Music
D. W. Krummel

Goin' to Kansas City
Nathan W. Pearson, Jr.

"Susanna," "Jeanie," and "The Old Folks at Home": The Songs of
Stephen C. Foster from His Time to Ours
Second Edition
William W. Austin

Songprints: The Musical Experience of Five Shoshone Women
Judith Vander

"Happy in the Service of the Lord": Afro-American Gospel Quartets in Memphis
Kip Lornell

Paul Hindemith in the United States
Luther Noss

"My Song Is My Weapon": People's Songs, American Communism, and the
Politics of Culture
Robbie Lieberman

Chosen Voices: The Story of the American Cantorate
Mark Slobin

Theodore Thomas: America's Conductor and Builder of Orchestras, 1835–1905
Ezra Schabas

"The Whorehouse Bells Were Ringing" and
Other Songs Cowboys Sing
Guy Logsdon

Crazeology: The Autobiography of a Chicago Jazzman
Bud Freeman, as Told to Robert Wolf

Discoursing Sweet Music: Brass Bands and Community Life in
Turn-of-the-Century Pennsylvania
Kenneth Kreitner

Mormonism and Music: A History
Michael Hicks

Voices of the Jazz Age: Profiles of Eight Vintage Jazzmen
Chip Deffaa

Pickin' on Peachtree: A History of Country Music in Atlanta, Georgia
Wayne W. Daniel

Bitter Music: Collected Journals, Essays, Introductions, and Librettos
Harry Partch; edited by Thomas McGeary

Ethnic Music on Records: A Discography of Ethnic Recordings
Produced in the United States, 1893 to 1942
Richard K. Spottswood

Downhome Blues Lyrics: An Anthology from the Post-World War II Era
Jeff Todd Titon

Ellington: The Early Years
Mark Tucker

Chicago Soul
Robert Pruter

That Half-Barbaric Twang: The Banjo in American Popular Culture
Karen Linn

Hot Man: The Life of Art Hodes
Art Hodes and Chadwick Hansen

The Erotic Muse: American Bawdy Songs
Second Edition
Ed Cray

The Creation of Jazz: Music, Race, and Culture in Urban America
Burton W. Peretti

Barrio Rhythm: Mexican American Music in Los Angeles
Steven Loza